D0742652

SIR WALTER SCOTT

SIR WALTER SCOTT

From a sketch by Sir Edwin Landseer in the National Portrait Gallery

SIR WALTER SCOTT

823.73
B851

BY

JOHN BUCHAN

WITHDRAWN

KENNIKAT PRESS, INC./PORT WASHINGTON, N. Y.

151137

LIBRARY ST. MARY'S COLLEGE

8/o.57 mu 6-29.83 (replace.)

First Published in 1932
Reissued in 1967 by Kennikat Press

Library of Congress Catalog Card No: 67-27580

Manufactured in the United States of America

To

TWO FRIENDS

LOVERS OF SIR WALTER

STANLEY BALDWIN

AND

GEORGE MACAULAY TREVELYAN

PREFACE

THE centenary of the death of Sir Walter Scott is my
excuse for the re-cutting of some of the lines of Lockhart's imperishable memorial, and for an attempt at a
valuation of the man and his work after the lapse of a
hundred years. It is a book which I was bound one
day or other to write, for I have had the fortune to be
born and bred under the shadow of that great tradition.
The following abbreviations have been used :—

A. Constable   *Archibald Constable and His Literary Correspondents.* 3 vols. Edinburgh, 1873.

Ballantyne Humbug   *The Ballantyne - Humbug Handled in a
Letter to Sir Adam Ferguson.* Edin-
burgh, 1839.

Cockburn, Mem.   *Memorials of His Time,* by Henry, Lord
Cockburn. Edinburgh, 1856.

Dom. Manners   *The Domestic Manners and Private Life of
Sir Walter Scott,* by James Hogg. Glas-
gow, 1834.

Fam. Letters   *Familiar Letters of Sir Walter Scott.* 2 vols.
Edinburgh, 1894.

Gillies   *Recollections of Sir Walter Scott, Bart.,* by
R. P. Gillies. London, 1837.

Journal   *The Journal of Sir Walter Scott.* 2 vols.
Edinburgh, 1891.

Lang   *The Life and Letters of John Gibson Lockhart,*
by Andrew Lang. 2 vols. London, 1897.

Lockhart   *Memoirs of the Life of Sir Walter Scott,
Bart.,* by John Gibson Lockhart. 7 vols.
Edinburgh, 1837–8.

Misc. Prose Works   *The Miscellaneous Prose Works of Sir
Walter Scott, Bart.* 28 vols. Edinburgh,
1843–6.

P. L. B.   *The Private Letter-Books of Sir Walter Scott.*
London, 1930.

Refutation	*Refutation of the Misstatements and Calumnies Contained in Mr Lockhart's Life of Sir Walter Scott.* Edinburgh, 1838.
Reply	*A Reply to Mr Lockhart's Pamphlet,* by the authors of the *Refutation.* Edinburgh, 1839.
S. Q.	*The Sir Walter Scott Quarterly.* Edinburgh, 1827–8.
Sederunt Book	*The Sederunt Book of James Ballantyne and Company's Trust.* 3 vols. in National Library of Scotland.
Skene	*Memories of Sir Walter Scott,* by James Skene. London, 1909.

I have given authority for most of my references, since Scott's own writings and the books about him are bulky works, and the reader may be glad of finger-posts.

J. B.

ELSFIELD MANOR, OXON.
December 1931

CONTENTS

SIR WALTER SCOTT

CHAPTER I

ANTECEDENTS

I

In the autumn of the year 1771 an Edinburgh citizen, returning after many years' absence, would have noted certain changes in his native city. If, on the morning after his arrival at the White Horse Inn in the Canongate, he had ascended to the high places of the Castle hill, and looked north and east, he would have missed one familiar landmark. The Nor' Loch, his haunt on youthful holidays and the odorous grave of city refuse, had been drained, and its bed was now grass and shingle. Across the hollow which once had held its waters a huge mound of earth had been thrown, giving access to the distant fields. Farther east, another crossing was in process of making, a bridge to carry a broad highway. Before he had left home the Canongate had burst its bonds into New Street and St John Street, and he noted that the city had spilled itself farther southward beyond the South Bridge of the Cowgate into new streets and squares. But now the moat of the Nor' Loch was spanned, and on its farther shore building had begun according to the plans of the ingenious Mr Craig. He had heard much of these plans that morning in Lucky Boyd's hostelry— of how a new Register House, with the Adam brothers as architects, and paid for out of the forfeited Jacobite estates, was designed to rise at the end of the new bridge. And the spectator, according as he was a lover of old things or an amateur of novelties, would have sighed or approved. The little city, strung from the Castle to

Holyroodhouse along her rib of hill, where more history
had been made than in any place of like size save Athens,
Rome and Jerusalem—which, according to the weather
and the observer's standpoint, looked like a flag flung
against the sky or a ship riding by the shore—was
enlarging her bounds and entering upon a new career.

Another sight of some significance was to be had in
the same year at the same season. From every corner
of the north droves of black cattle were converging on
Falkirk moor for the great autumn Tryst. It was the
clearing-house of the Highlands, as Stagshawbank on
the Tyne was the clearing-house of Scotland. The drover
from Glen Affric, herding his kyloes among the autumn
bracken, could see from his bivouac a cloud of dark
smoke on the banks of the Carron river, and hear by day
and night the clang of hammers. This was the Carron
Ironworks, now eleven years old, and a canal was being
made from Grangemouth-on-Forth to carry their products to the world. There, within sight of the Highland
Line, a quarter of a century after a Jacobite army had
campaigned on that very ground, the coal and iron of
the Scottish midlands were being used in a promising
industry. Cannon were being made for many nations,
and the Carron pipes and sugar-boilers and fire-grates
were soon to be famous throughout the land. The
Highland drover, already perplexed by the intrusion of
Lowland sheep on his hills and the cutting of his native
woods by English companies, saw in the flame and
smoke of the ironworks a final proof that his ancient
world was crumbling.

There was a third portent, the most pregnant of all,
which our returned exile, if he were a man of some
education, had a chance of noting. He had heard with
pleasure during his absence a rumour of good literature
coming from the north. The London critics had spoken
well of Mr David Hume's works in history and philosophy,
of Mr Robertson's excursions in the former domain, of
Mr Ferguson's treatise on civil society, and of the poetry
of Mr Beattie of Aberdeen, while visitors had reported
the surpassing eloquence of Mr Hugh Blair of the High

Kirk of St Giles'. Our traveller, when he had access to
these famous men, found that Edinburgh had indeed
become a home of brilliant talk and genial company—
Edinburgh with her endless taverns where entertainment was cheap, since the Forth at the door gave her
oysters, and sound claret was to be had at eighteen
shillings a dozen. Around the tavern board or the dinner-
table he found the illuminati good Scotsmen, speaking
the tongue he fondly remembered, and perpetuating the
tales and humours of his youth. But their public performance surprised him, for it was a sedulous aping of
London. They strove without much success to acquire
an English accent, and Mr Adam Smith was envied
because Balliol had trimmed the roughness of his Fife
tongue. They cultivated a thing called rhetoric, which
was supposed to be a canonical use of language freed
from local vulgarities, and in the shabby old college
Mr Hugh Blair lectured on that dismal science with much
acceptance. In their writings they laboriously assisted
each other to correct the solecisms of the northern idiom,
and a year or two later, when David Hume lay on his
death-bed, it was the jest of a caustic Lord of Session
that the philosopher confessed not his sins but his
Scotticisms.

So our restored exile may have regarded the scene
with mingled feelings. His countrymen beyond doubt
had their heads at last above water, but the land they
were making for was not the kindly soil he had known.

II

Let us look a little closer at the Scotland of 1771.

The Union of Parliaments in 1707 had been a blessing
beyond doubt, but for a quarter of a century it had been
a blessing well disguised. The land and the people were
grievously poor, and north of Forth the Highlands had
to face the decadence of their ancient social and economic
structure, and in the space of a man's lifetime adjust
themselves to the change from a mediæval to a modern
world. The failure of Jacobitism flung Scotland back

upon herself and forced her to work out her own salvation. But that bitter task did not increase her love for her southern neighbour. She was conscious of being poverty-stricken and backward, a mere northern appanage which England had once seen fit to conciliate, and, the Union accomplished, could now neglect. A friendly visitor like Pennant might find something to patronize and praise, but the common traveller's tale was only of a bleak land, vile weather, bad inns, bad roads, dirty farms and shabby stone towns. Even Lady Louisa Stuart, with Scots blood in her veins, had little good to say of it; to cross the Border into Cumberland was for her to return to civilization and decency.

Nor was Scotland's sense of inferiority likely to be soothed by the attitude of her neighbours. In truth she had given England small cause to love her. The seventeenth century, with its invasion of England by a Scots army, the bartering of their king by that army for arrears of pay, and the attempt to impose the Presbyterian discipline upon all Britain, had left an ugly memory. In the early eighteenth century Scotland had been a storm-centre from which came most of the threats to English peace. Scotsmen in droves had journeyed south, and had won fame and fortune in many callings —at the Bar, in medicine, in commerce, in letters; but their very success increased the unpopularity of their race. There was no one to mediate between the two peoples. The Scotsman Bute was the most hated of politicians, Wedderburn's conscience was elastic even for a Georgian lawyer, while, in letters, sleek creatures like Mallet and an ill-tempered genius like Smollett only widened the breach. Mansfield might have done something, but the great Chief-Justice had lost every Caledonian trait, including most of his accent. Scotsmen were blamed alike for their rudeness and their servility, their clannishness and their passion to get on in the world, their pence-saving prudence and their high-flying politics. The dislike of Scotland, shown in the venom of Churchill and *The North Briton*, the gibes of Dr Johnson, and the decorous belittlement of Horace

Walpole, was a universal feeling in the south. It was returned in kind, and David Hume was for ever crying out against " the factious barbarians of London."

In such a case, disliked abroad and deeply embarrassed at home, Scotland was compelled to look for succour to her own efforts. The victories overseas won under Chatham's rule, and the recruitment of the Highlands in the British army gave her an interest in the nascent Empire, but in British politics she had no part to play. Her domestic affairs were for the most part beneath the concern of Westminster. Of resident Scotsmen the Fife laird, Oswald of Dunnikier, alone made any considerable show in Parliament. Her system of representation had no popular basis, and was to the last degree fantastic and corrupt, and the members elected under it were in the main dutiful servants of the party in power. The liberalism which has since been so marked a characteristic of the nation flickered only in George Dempster, the member for the Forfar burghs, who had the hardihood on one occasion to act as teller with John Wilkes. British politics had for the time ceased to interest a people, whose mind was bent on more urgent matters.

Nor was there any compensating vigour of life in that church, which had once been the chief voice of Scotland. Patronage had been restored in 1712, and the Erastian principle was firmly established. The dominant party, the Moderates, made religion a thing of social decency and private virtues, and their sober, if shallow, creed was undoubtedly a stabilizing factor in a difficult time. But if the extravagance of the earlier Kirk had gone, so too had its power and vision. The High-flyers, the other party, were equally void of inspiration, and disputed chiefly on questions of church government. For a spark of the old fire we must look to the numerous sects, who sustained some of the doctrinal vigour of Calvinism. But sufficient remained of the bequest from the seventeenth century to perpetuate in many quarters spiritual pride and an intolerant formalism. The ministers satirized by Burns in his " Holy Fair " were representative types, but little overdrawn, of the then church in

Scotland—a church from which most that was vital in the national life was deeply estranged.

The two main pre-occupations of the country in and around the year 1771 were to make a better living and to cut a braver figure in the world. In both she was beginning to succeed. Glasgow in the west and Leith in the east had become notable ports, and to the former came more than half of the tobacco imported into Britain. Coal and iron were being mined on a large scale ; linen and woollen manufactures were thriving ; Scottish agriculture had begun the long upward stride which was soon to make it a model for the globe ; new banks had come into being, and the Bank of Scotland had multiplied its capital by six, while its shares were quoted on the London Exchange at 100 per cent. premium. As for fame, Edinburgh had become a hot-bed of talent, the merit of which the south was quick to acknowledge. " I stand at the Cross of Edinburgh," said an admiring visitor, " and can in a few minutes take fifty men of genius by the hand." London might sneer at her, but the metropolis was forced to buy the books of her scholars—Hume and Ferguson and Robertson in history, Hume and Reid in philosophy, Adam Smith in political economy, Blair and Lord Kames in aesthetics. These men were no *émigrés* like Mansfield and Wedderburn, Smollett and Thomson, Allan Ramsay the painter and Adam the architect, but her own domiciled sons who owed nothing to alien patronage, and of them she was inordinately proud. She saw her wealth and repute increasing, and felt that at last she could talk on equal terms with her critics. Scotland had recovered her confidence.

But in the process she was shutting the door upon her past. There were two strains in her history—the aristocratic and Cavalier ; the Covenanting and democratic ; and both were so overlaid by novelties that they were in danger of being choked and forgotten. The first, having suffered downfall with Jacobitism, survived only as a dim sentiment, the inspiration of songs when the claret went round, a thing of brocades and lace and

twilit windows. The second had lost itself in formalism
or eccentricity, and its stubborn democratic tradition
was half forgotten. There was a danger lest the land,
setting out confidently on new paths, might condemn
as provincial and antiquated what was the very core
and essence of her being. She was in the van of the new
enlightenment: was her progress to be that of the rocket
which shoots from earth into high places and then falls,
or like the slow growth of a tree, deep-rooted by ancient
waters ?

In 1771 Scotland stood at the parting of the ways.
That she chose rightly was due to two children who were
then alive on her soil. One was a boy of twelve, the son
of a small farmer in Ayrshire, who was picking up an
education on a moorland croft. The other was an infant
in an old house in the College Wynd in Edinburgh, who
on the 15th of August of that year had been born to a
respectable middle-aged lawyer, a certain Mr Walter
Scott.

III

The Border, where Scotland touched the soil of her
ancient adversary, had always cherished in its extremest
form the national idiom in mind and manners. It had
been the cockpit where most of the lesser battles of her
independence had been fought ; for generations it had
been emptied from vessel to vessel ; its sons had been
the keepers of the gate and had spoken effectively
therein with their enemies. The result was the survival
of the fittest, a people conscious of a stalwart ancestry
and a long tradition of adventure and self-reliance. In
the Middle Ages the king's law had had but a feeble hold
upon all the country from Berwick in the east to Dumfries in the west, and from the Cheviots northward to
the Moorfoots. There the hand had to keep the head,
and the spear was not left to rust in the thatch. The
life bred a hardy and vigilant race, good friends and
pestilent foes, tenacious of their honour and their scanty
belongings. " They delight in their own," wrote Bar-
tholomew the Englishman in the thirteenth century,

" and they love not peace." But the traveller chronicled other qualities. They were a mirthful and humorous folk, as " light of heart " as they were " fierce on their enemies." They were skilled musicians, too, and, said Bishop Lesley in the sixteenth century, " lovers of eloquence and poetry."

The Borderer differed in certain ways from the rest of his countrymen. He lived in an enclave of his own, for, though on the main track of marching armies, he was a little remote from the centres of national life. His eyes did not turn north to the capital, but south to the English frontier, where danger lay, and around him to his urgent local concerns. He lived under a clan system, different from that of the Highlands, but hardly less compelling. This absorption in special interests kept the Borderer, gentle and simple, from sharing largely in those national movements which had their origin in the Scottish midlands and the eastern littoral. The wars of religion, for example, affected him little. The Border bred few noted Covenant enthusiasts, as it sent few men to Montrose's standard. It was damp tinder for the fires of either reaction or revolution.

Yet the centuries of guerrilla fighting had produced something more than hardihood and independence. The Border was the home of harpers and violers, and from it came some of the loveliest of northern airs, and most of the greatest ballads in any literature. It had always had a tradition of a rude minstrelsy, for during the peace of the winter season, at the Yule and Hogmanay revels, at the burgh fairs, at sheep clippings and " kirns " and at the shieling doors in the long summer twilights, wandering minstrels would sing of old days, of the fairies in the greenwood and the kelpies in the loch, and of some deed of prowess the rumour of which had drifted across the hills. Out of this tradition, perhaps some time in the sixteenth century, the great ballads were made by singers whose names have been lost— maybe the dead poets chronicled in Dunbar's "Lament of the Makars." The innominate balladists left behind them poetry which often reached the highest levels of art, and which at the same time woke an immediate response in those for whom it was composed. So the Borderer, however scanty his learning, fell heir to a body of great literature, passed by word of mouth from father to son—a literature bare as the grey bent of his hills, rarely mirthful, telling mostly of tragic loves and tragic hates, but inculcating, as fiercely as the Sagas, the noble austerities of courage and duty.

At the beginning of the seventeenth century the old life of the Border came to an end, since the Governments of both nations combined to coerce its turbulence. As with the Highlands after 1745, there followed a decline of population, since the livelihood of many had gone. In Liddesdale the single clan of Elliot numbered some 1500 souls in the sixteenth century, while in the eighteenth that figure represented the total population of the valley. Since the riding days were over, and most of the hill land was poor and uncultivable, the glens became sheep-walks, and one shepherd could serve a wide area. Till the mid-eighteenth century the Border was as poor as the rest of Scotland. But it shared in the revival of Scottish agriculture, and by the year 1771 there had been a vast deal of draining done in the valley bottoms ; stone dykes seamed the uplands ; the more progressive lairds were planting not only in their demesnes but far up the hillsides, so that many slopes were feathered with young firs ; a better system had taken the place of the old shiftless Scots tillage ; the prices were good for both sheep and cattle, and rural life was everywhere thriving. It was different with the little towns. They had never been of great importance except when they nestled beneath the shadow of an abbey or a castle, but under many difficulties they had striven for centuries to preserve their close burghal life. Once they had been smuggling centres, but after 1707 this activity ceased. Their more enterprising sons flocked into north England. Jedburgh, which had had 6000 citizens before the Union, had now scarcely 2000, and Adam Smith speaking apparently of the burghs, told a correspondent that " the Scotch on the Borders were to this day in extreme poverty."

Of the nature of rural Border society at this time we have ample evidence. A village had its assorted craftsmen, which made it independent of the towns, its wauk-mill and its corn-mill, its schoolmaster and its minister. The bonnet-laird farmed his own land ; on the great estates there were tenants cultivating large acreages, and the lairds, since they were themselves prosperous, were as a rule good masters. The Border yeoman was a great lover of sport, an inheritance from his active forbears, and came nearer to the English type of hunting farmer than to the ordinary Scots tacksman. In the upland glens the shepherds made a community by themselves —a strong and responsible race, men of the " lang stride and the clear eye," accustomed to take many risks in their calling, for the most part literate and for the most part pious, but living close to tradition and the elder world of faery. The youth of Leyden and Hogg gives a picture of their lives. If superstition was always at their elbow, the spirit of critical independence was also there. They were under no blind bondage either to creed or custom. The householder would stop his reading of the Bible at family prayers with the remark : " If it hadna been the Lord's will, that verse had been better left out." They lived in a semi-patriarchal society, where the laird was king, but they dealt with him as free men. He was greater and richer than they, but of the same blood, for a Scott or a Kerr, whose hirsel lay at the back of beyond, could count far-away kin with Buccleuch or Lothian. The clan system still survived in a wholesome and universal pride of race. Most Borderers rightly held themselves to be gently born.

The greater Border houses were a late growth. In the distant days of Scottish history, when the political game was played by Comyns and Bruces, Douglases and Stewarts, Lindsays and Hamiltons, there is little mention of Kerr or Scott. The Border chiefs till the Union of the Crowns were only heads of turbulent septs who come into the national story in the tail of some great

Warden of the Marches. But at the beginning of the
seventeenth century these chiefs were ennobled, and
Buccleuch and Roxburgh and Lothian took their place
as landed magnates.

By 1771 the Scotts of Buccleuch had become one of
the most powerful families in Britain. Coming originally
from upper Tweeddale and Lanarkshire, we find them
settled on Teviot and Ettrick at the end of the thirteenth
century. They had the byname of the " rough clan,"
they were formidable reivers and at times effective
March Wardens, and they maintained always a stubborn
patriotism not too common among Scots grandees. The
Sir Walter Scott of Buccleuch, who rescued Kinmont
Willie of the ballad from Carlisle castle, became Lord
Scott of Buccleuch in 1606, and his only son was the
first earl. The daughter of the second earl, Anne,
Countess of Buccleuch in her own right, and the heiress of
vast lands in Lothian and on the Border, married James,
Duke of Monmouth, and, after his execution, was permitted to retain his English estates. Henceforth the
" rough clan " ranked among the major nobility of the
land. They were as fortunate as the Hapsburgs in their
marriages, which brought them estates from the ducal
houses of Argyll and Montagu, and ultimately both the
estates and titles of the dukedom of Queensberry.

From the family of Buccleuch there was an early
offshoot, called first of Sinton and then of Harden, whose
tower still stands in a dark nook of Borthwick water.
The Scotts of Harden were scarcely less noted in the
Border wars than the parent house, and they produced
such figures of ballad and folk story as Auld Wat of
Harden, who in 1567 married Mary Scott, the " Flower
of Yarrow," and his son William, who espoused the
daughter of Sir Gideon Murray of Elibank, the " Muckle
Mou'd Meg " of a tale which is probably apocryphal.
The third son of this William of Harden became laird of
Raeburn, and his wife was a MacDougal of Makerstoun,
of a family which has some claim to be the oldest in
Scotland. This Walter Scott was a Whig and a Quaker,
but his sons walked in other paths, for his eldest fell in

a duel, and the second, Walter, was known on Teviotside as Beardie, from the great beard which he allowed to grow in token of his regret for the banished Stuarts. Beardie, after narrowly escaping the gallows on account of his politics, married a kinswoman of the Campbells of Blythswood, and in his old age had some repute for learning. His second son took to sheep-farming, and leased the farm of Sandy Knowe from the Scotts of Harden, after staking all his fortune on the purchase of a hunter, which he fortunately sold for double the price he gave. He prospered, and made a great name on the Border as a judge of stock. His wife was a Haliburton of Newmains, who brought to the family the right of burial in Dryburgh Abbey. The sheep-farmer's eldest son, Walter, forsook the family pursuits and, first of his race, settled in a town and adopted a learned profession, for he became a Writer to the Signet in Edinburgh, the highest stage in Scotland of the solicitor's calling. His wife was Anne Rutherford, the eldest daughter of the professor of medicine in the University, and with her came into the blood two other ancient strains. For the Rutherfords had been longer settled on the Border than the Scotts, and her mother was a Swinton of that ilk, one of the most sounding names in early Scottish history, and a descendant of Ben Jonson's friend, the poet Earl of Stirling.

So much for the details of pedigree. The child born in August, 1771, to Anne Rutherford and Walter Scott at the head of the College Wynd, had a more varied ancestry than falls to the lot of most men. No doubt the ancestry of all of us is oddly mixed, but in his case the record was known. He was linked collaterally through the Buccleuchs with the greater *noblesse*. He had behind him the most historic of the Border stocks in Scott and Murray and Rutherford and Swinton. He had Celtic blood from MacDougal and Campbell. Of the many painted shields on the ceiling of the hall at Abbotsford which enshrine his pedigree, only three lack a verified heraldic cognizance. Among his forbears were saints and sinners, scholars and sportsmen and men-at-arms, barons and sheep-farmers, divines and doctors of medicine, Whigs and Jacobites, Cavaliers and Quakers. Above all he had that kindest bequest of the good fairies at his cradle, a tradition, bone of his bone, of ancient pastoral, of a free life lived among clear waters and green hills as in the innocency of the world.

Chapter II

BOYHOOD AND YOUTH
(1771–1792)

I

1771 THE College Wynd was a mountain path from the ravine of the Cowgate to the ridge where stood the sixteenth-century College. It had been called in old days the Wynd of the Blessed Virgin-in-the-Fields, and the tall gabled house at the head of it was built on the site of the very Kirk-o'-Field where Darnley had met his death in the unhallowed February night of 1567. The house stood in the corner of a small court, the flats were reached by a foul common stair, and the narrow windows looked out upon wynds where refuse rotted in heaps, and pigs roamed as in a farmyard, and well-born children played barefoot in the gutters. Nowhere was there space or light, and the tenements, though their fireplaces might bear historic scutcheons, were habitations of filth and nursing grounds of disease. Eight children had been born to Mr Walter Scott, and six had died in infancy, so a little after the young Walter's birth he moved his household to one of the pleasant houses in the new George Square, near the Meadows, where the eye looked out on trim gardens and the air blew sweet from the Pentlands and the Firth.

A clear picture of the elder Scott has come down to us. His portrait shows him " uncommonly handsome," as his son boasted, but with an air of puzzled gentleness and melancholy which scarcely accords with the robust Border stock from which he sprang. It is possible that there was some delicacy of body which he transmitted to his family, for he had not the longevity of his race,

dying at sixty-eight after two years of broken health. 1771
His industry and his love of dry legal details qualified
him well for his profession, and he began with high
prospects, for his father bought him a good partnership,
he could count on the patronage of a clan of litigious
sheep-farmers and lairds, and the Jacobite forfeitures had
filled Edinburgh with legal business. But he was perhaps
better suited to the upper than the lower branch of his
craft. His son thought that he would have made a fine
special pleader, had the Scots Bar known such a thing,
and he was deeply learned in feudal tenures. For the
business side he had little aptitude. He was ingenuous
and simple, accepting men at their own high valuation ;
he refused to take advantage of their follies and neces-
sities, and no Dandie Dinmont with his consent ever
went to law with a Jock o' Dawston Cleugh ; his quixotic
zeal for his clients' welfare led to his being out of pocket
over the work he did for them ; his scruples were always
at war with his interests. Such a man may acquire a
large practice, but it will not be a lucrative one. He
could on occasion be a genial host, but his usual habits
were ascetic ; in a toping age he drank little wine, and,
if someone at his board praised the richness of the soup,
he would dilute his own portion with water. He had no
hobbies, and his notion of relaxation was sombre ; he
told his son, when presented with his notes of the Scots
Law class copied out and bound, that they would provide
pleasant reading for his leisure hours ! The main interest
of his life was theology, and in the seclusion of his study
he was more often engaged with Knox and Spottiswoode
than with Stair and Erskine. His religion was Calvinism,
high and dry, not a dogma only but a stern discipline of
life. The Sabbath days were filled with long diets of
worship, the Sabbath evenings with the reading of lengthy
sermons and the catechizing of a sleepy household. On
that day he would neither speak nor think of secular
affairs.

This pale gentleman in the black knee-breeches and
snowy ruffles, with his kind, anxious face and formal
manners, was a strange father for such a son. In the

1771 eyes of the one to " crucify the body," as the phrase
went, to " mortify the flesh," was the first duty of a
Christian, and life was a melancholy vale with no place
for cordials ; to the other the living, breathing world
around him seemed a gift of God ordained for the enjoyment of His creatures. Some tastes the two had in
common. The elder Scott had a profound clannishness,
for he kept a record of the remotest collaterals, and
diligently attended their funerals as a tribal rite. He
had odd moments of romance, as when he flung from
his window in George Square the cup out of which his
wife had rashly given tea to the traitor Murray of
Broughton. He had even a dim interest in stage plays,
and private theatricals were permitted in his dining-
room. But for the rest Calvinist and humanist had no
common ground. There was also the secular conflict
between age and youth, since the father had little
tolerance for the whimsies of young blood, and measured
success by standards which the son contemned. For the
elder was in all things genteel, as Edinburgh understood
the thing. Conscious of good blood in his veins, he was
profoundly respectful to those who had it in an ampler
measure, and not above an innocent condescension to
those who lacked it. The Calvinism of eighteenth-
century Edinburgh carried with it a worship of respec-
tability. It was respectable to be a busy lawyer ; it
was not respectable to scribble verses, and tramp the
roads, and hobnob with all and sundry. Between
Walter and his father there was affection, and for the
elder's integrity and kindness the younger had a deep
regard. But there was no intimacy, and for long only
an imperfect comprehension.

The mother, Anne Rutherford, was " short of stature "
says Lockhart, " and by no means comely." Her plain
features were those of her father, the professor of
medicine, whose portrait hangs on the walls of the
Edinburgh College of Physicians. But it was a face of
infinite sagacity, shrewdness, friendliness and humour.
She had been bred in the old school of deportment, and
to her dying day sat upright in her chair without touching

its back. She was an anxious parent with her uncertain 1771
brood, and a notable mistress of a household. Unlike
her husband's, her tastes had a wide range, for her head
was stored with ballads and proverbs and tales. She
was one of those women who are worthy of a long life,
for she had the kind of mind which can profit and make
the world profit by the processes of time, and she made
a bridge between the generations. She lived to the verge
of eighty, and saw Waterloo fought and Wellington enter
Paris, and in her youth she had talked with a man who
remembered the battle of Dunbar and Cromwell's entry
into Edinburgh. Scott owed much to her, for she was
able to recreate for him the immediate past—that
period so dim to most of us, and it was she who first
introduced him to the enchanted world of poetry. His
boyish ailments established a special intimacy between
them, and he was always her favourite child. She had
that homely tenderness which the Scots call "innerli-
ness," and when her son was the laird of Abbotsford
and one of the most famous of living men, he was still to
her "Wattie, my lamb." Her life was happy, for she
rejoiced in his success, and she preserved her vigour of
mind and body unimpaired, so that at eighty she was
telling stories to her grandchildren at tea in her little
house. "She was a strict economist," Scott wrote to
Lady Louisa Stuart, "which she said enabled her to be
liberal; out of her little income of about £300 a year she
bestowed at least a third in well-chosen charities, and
with the rest lived like a gentlewoman, and even with
hospitality more general than seemed to suit her age;
yet I could never prevail upon her to accept of any
assistance."[1] A Baskerville Bible which she had given
him he treasured to the last year of his life and
bequeathed as an heirloom to his descendants; and
when, after his death, his executors opened his desk,
they found, arranged so that he might see them when
at work, the boxes which had stood on her dressing-table,
and the silver taper-stand which he had bought for her
with his first fees.

[1] Lockhart, IV. 339.

1771   Walter Scott had always a great love for mementoes. In the same desk were six locks of fair hair, relics of his six brothers and sisters who had died in infancy. There seems to have been talent in all the surviving children, mingled with something febrile and ill-balanced, derived perhaps from their father. All died in middle life, and only one left descendants. The eldest, Robert, was something of a tyrant to the young Walter, but won his love through their common passion for poetry. He entered the Navy, fought under Rodney, quarrelled with his superiors, joined the East India Company's service, and died of malaria at forty-one. John became a soldier, lost his health and died in Edinburgh in his mother's house at forty-seven. Thomas, two years younger than Walter and his favourite brother, succeeded to his father's law business, speculated and failed, and died in Canada as a regimental paymaster in his fiftieth year. Daniel the youngest, the family scapegrace, was in his grave before he was thirty. The one daughter, Anne, a year Walter's junior, was a nervous, ailing girl, the sport of every kind of accident, who died at the same age as Daniel, having passed her life " in an ideal world which she had framed for herself by the force of imagination."

The early childhood of Walter Scott was not spent in the family circle. He was a robust infant, and having survived the perils of a first nurse who was suffering from consumption, might have grown to a physical stalwartness like that of his Border forbears. But, at the age of eighteen months he fell ill of a teething fever, and on the fourth day it was discovered that he had lost the use of his right leg, through some form of infantile paralysis. Physicians and surgeons could do nothing, and, on the advice of his grandfather, Dr Rutherford, it was decided to try what country air could do and to send him to his other grandfather at his farm of Sandy Knowe. So it fell out that the first memories of this city child were of country folk and the green spaces of Tweeddale.

The leg did not improve, but the Border winds dispelled the malaise of Edinburgh, and gave him abounding

health and spirits. The world opened to him as a wide
wind-blown country, with a prospect of twenty miles
past the triple peaks of Eildon to the line of Cheviot, the
homely fragrance and bustle of a moorland farm, the
old keep of Smailholm as a background, and a motley
of figures out of an earlier age. His tenacious memory
preserved those first impressions. He remembered his
grandfather, though he died when the boy was three, a
magnificent old man, who apart from the lameness and
the high peak of the head, looked much as he looked
himself in after life. He remembered being wrapped in
the new-flayed skin of a sheep—a device out of some
hoar-ancient medical lore, and an old gentleman, who
was his grandfather's second cousin, Sir George Mac-
Dougal of Makerstoun, " with a small cocked hat deeply
laced, an embroidered scarlet waistcoat, and a light-
coloured coat, with milk-white locks tied in a military
fashion," kneeling on the parlour floor and dragging his
watch along the carpet to induce him to crawl. He was
sweet-tempered and very talkative, so that the aged
parish minister on his visits declared that " one may as
well speak in the mouth of a cannon as where that child
is." The ewe-milkers carried him up to the crags above
the house, and he learned to know every sheep by head-
mark. Once he was forgotten there during a thunder-
storm and was found clapping his hands at the lightning
and crying " Bonny, bonny ! " His sworn henchman was
Sandy Ormistoun, the cow-baillie, on whose shoulder he
peregrinated the farm. Neighbours dropped in, and the
child's quick ears heard the news of the American War
and Jacobite tales from a man who had seen the Carlisle
executions. On the winter evenings his grandmother
sat beside the fire at her spinning-wheel, and his grandfather opposite in his elbow-chair, while he lay on the
floor and heard his Aunt Janet read, or his grandmother
tell of the Border merry men and their wild ways out of
a memory in which they were a living tradition. In his
aunt's reading the Bible was varied with one or two
books from a pile on the window-seat—an odd volume of
Josephus, that portentous author whom few Scottish

1774-75 children in older days escaped, and Allan Ramsay's *Tea-Table Miscellany*. From the latter he learned by heart the ballad of " Hardicanute," which he shouted about the house.

In his fourth year there came an interlude, for it was resolved, as a remedy for his lameness, to exchange raw sheepskins for the waters of Bath. Miss Janet took charge of him and they went by sea to London, where he saw the Tower and Westminster Abbey. At Bath they were joined by his uncle Captain Robert Scott, home on leave from India. There they stayed for the better part of a year ; the baths did no good to his lameness, but his general health was now excellent, and at a dame's school he learned to read. His chief recollection was of meeting John Home, author of *Douglas*, now a very old man, and of seeing his first play in the company of his uncle Robert. " The play was *As You Like It*, and the witchery of the whole scene is alive in my mind at this moment," he wrote more than thirty years later. " I made, I believe, noise more than enough, and re-member being so much scandalized by the quarrel between Orlando and his brother in the first scene that I screamed out ' An't they brothers ? ' "

From Bath, with a pronounced English accent, he returned for a few weeks to his family in George Square, where, after four years among indulgent elders, he was to learn the possibility of fraternal bickering. Of the boy at this stage we have a glimpse in a letter of a kins-woman of his mother's, Mrs Cockburn, the author of the modern version of " The Flowers of the Forest," who had been Alison Rutherford of Fairnilee :—

I last night supped at Mr Walter Scott's. He has the most extraordinary genius of a boy I ever saw. He was reading a poem to his mother when I went in. I made him read on ; it was the description of a shipwreck. His passion rose with the storm. " There's the mast gone," says he. " Crash it goes ! They will all perish ! " After his agitation he turns to me. " That is too melancholy," says he. " I had better read you something more amusing." I proposed a little chat and asked his opinion of Milton and other books he was reading, which he gave me wonderfully. One of his observations was,

" How strange it is that Adam, just new come into the world, should know everything—that must be the poet's fancy," says he. But when he was told that he was created perfect by God, he instantly yielded. When taken to bed last night, he told his aunt he liked that lady. " What lady ? " says she. " Why, Mrs Cockburn, for I think she is a virtuoso, like myself." " Dear Walter," says Aunt Jenny, " what is a virtuoso ? " " Don't you know ? Why, it's one that wishes and will know everything." Now, sir, you will think this a very silly story. Pray, what age do you suppose that boy to be ? Name it now, before I tell you. Why, twelve or fourteen. No such thing ; he is not quite six years old. He has a lame leg, for which he was a year at Bath, and has acquired the perfect English accent, which he has not lost since he came, and he reads like a Garrick. You will allow this an uncommon exotic.

The solitary stage of his childhood was not yet closed, for presently he went back to Sandy Knowe for the better part of two years. There he continued to listen to his grandmother's tales and Aunt Janet's reading, but he was now able on his own account to adventure in books.[1] He got his first pony, a tiny Shetland mare called Marion ; he was less with the ewe-milkers now, and more with the cow-baillie and the shepherds ; the world extended for him, and he became aware of the lovely environs, the woods of Merton and the shining reaches of Tweed. He was sent to Prestonpans for sea-bathing, and there discussed the war in America with an ancient ensign, and prophesied with only too much truth that trouble awaited Burgoyne. The ensign's name was Dalgetty. At Prestonpans, too, he met his father's friend George Constable, the antiquary, who remembered the 'Forty-five and talked to him of Shakespeare's characters, and who was to appear one day in the character of Jonathan Oldbuck.

When he was between seven and eight he returned to George Square, and Sandy Knowe became only a place for summer holidays. The virtuoso had now to go through a short space of disillusionment and discipline.

[1] " I cannot at the moment tell how or when I learned to read, but it was by fits and snatches, as one aunt or another in the old rumble-tumble farmhouse could give me a lift, and I am sure it increased my love and habit of reading more than the austerities of a school could have done." Scott to Lockhart, 3rd March 1826.

1778–79 " I felt the change," he wrote, " from being a single indulged brat, to becoming a member of a large family, very severely ; for under the gentle government of my kind grandmother, who was meekness itself, and of my aunt, who, although of a higher temper, was exceedingly attached to me, I had acquired a degree of license which could not be permitted in a large family. I had sense enough, however, to bend my temper to my new circumstances, but such was the agony that I had internally experienced, that I have guarded against nothing more in the education of my own family, than against their acquiring habits of self-willed caprice and domination." His formal education had scarcely begun, and he had to start at the beginning in a private school in Bristo Port, and, when this experiment failed, under a tutor, a young probationer called Fraser, who taught him the Latin rudiments.

It was a hard transition stage for the " poetic child," but the wind was tempered to him by his mother's sympathy. With her he read Homer in Pope's translation, and from her he acquired his undying passion for Shakespeare. He never forgot the rapture of reading the plays by the fire in her dressing-room, until the sound of the family rising from supper warned him that it was time to creep back to bed. He was inclined to be priggish, and objected to playing with the boys in the Square on the ground of their ignorance, but this foible was soon hammered out of him by hard-fisted brothers. To the elder Walter Scott he must have seemed only a loquacious child who was lamentably backward in sound learning, but his mother and his mother's friends saw to it that the discipline necessary to fit him for normal life did not destroy his world of dreams. These friends were notable women. There was Mrs Cockburn, whom I have quoted, and who carried a merry heart through a long life of sorrows ; there were his aunts, Janet (afterwards Mrs Russel of Ashestiel) and Christian Rutherford ; there was old Lady Balcarres with her family of brilliant girls ; above all there was Mrs Anne Murray Keith, who on his behalf did for an elder Edinburgh what his grand-

mother had done for the old life of the Border. She 1779
spoke the courtly Holyrood Scots, and illumined for him
a world which had passed and which he was one day to
refashion.

With his eighth year the first stage of childhood closed.
The nuts, in Martial's phrase, had now to be left behind—

> Jam tristis nucibus puer relictis
> Clamoso revocatur a magistro !

It had been a stage of supreme importance, for it saw
the making of the man Walter Scott. As the sapling
was then bent, so the tree was to grow. On a memory,
which was wax to receive and granite to retain, had been
impressed affections and interests which were to dominate
his life. A certain kind of landscape had captured his
heart—the green pastoral simplicity of Tweedside—and
it remained his abiding passion. Scott's love was never
for the wilder scenes in the Border country, such as
Gameshope and Loch Skene ; it was for the pastoral
fringes, for " Leaderhaughs and Yarrow," for the Tweeddale champaign, where the moorland sank into meadows
and gardens marched with the heather. This taste, born
of those early years at Sandy Knowe, was the parent of
Abbotsford. He won, too, an insight—the unconscious
but penetrating insight of a child—into a society which
was fast disappearing, the society from which the ballads
had sprung. A whole lost world had been reborn in his
brain, and the learning of after years was only to supplement the far more potent imaginative construction of
childhood. The past had become a reality for him, since
he had himself seen and touched its flying wing. Henceforth, in the words of de l'Isle Adam, " il gardait au
cœur les richesses stériles d'un grand nombre de rois
oubliés."

II

In October 1779, at the age of eight, he entered Mr
Luke Fraser's second class in the ancient High School
of Edinburgh. He was younger than most of his class-

mates and but ill grounded in his Latin rudiments, and, since Mr Fraser was no more than a grammarian, he at first made little progress. But three years later, when he attained to the class of the headmaster, Dr Adam,[1] his ambition awoke, and Latin literature became for him a living interest. He read in class Cæsar, Livy and Sallust, Terence, Horace and Virgil, and Dr Adam pronounced that, while many were better scholars in the language, Walter Scott had few equals in probing to the author's meaning. His verse translations from the Roman poets were approved—translations somewhat in the manner of Pope's *Homer*—and he began to write verses on his own account, in which the chief influence seems to have been the Scottish Paraphrases. He had also a private tutor during these years, a certain James Mitchell, who ultimately became minister at Montrose, where Scott visited him at a critical hour of his life.[2] Mr Mitchell was a stiff Calvinist and sabbatarian, and from arguments with him the boy imbibed a good deal of divinity and church history. " I, with a head on fire for chivalry," he wrote, " was a Cavalier ; my friend was a Roundhead ; I was a Tory and he was a Whig. I hated Presbyterians, and admired Montrose with his victorious Highlanders ; he liked the Presbyterian Ulysses, the dark and politic Argyle, so that we never wanted subjects of dispute, but our disputes were always amicable."

The real education of these years was not in the High School, not even in Dr Adam's class, but in the playground and the Edinburgh streets, and in the boy's private adventures among books. The story of his escapades may be read in Lockhart. He was desperately pugnacious, and, since his lameness put him at a disadvantage, was permitted to fight his battles, as he said, " *in banco*," both combatants being strapped to a deal board. He scrambled over the Salisbury Crags, and ascended the " kittle nine stanes " on the Castle Rock. In winter he

---

[1] " He was born to teach Latin, some Greek, and all virtue." Cockburn, *Mem.*, 5.
[2] See p. 53.

helped to " man the Cowgate Port " in the snowball 1783
fights, and he was a leader in the bickers with the street
boys, where stones were the chief missiles, and broken
heads were the common fortune of war. He was a
leader in other things, for he was the saga-man of his
class, a spinner of tales, a maker of phrases, a dreamer of
dreams, who was often carried away by his fancies. Had
Scott never put pen to paper, he would still have told
himself stories. He was also busy with his own private
reading, in which occasionally he found a like-minded
friend to share during a holiday afternoon among the hills.
Presently he had devoured Shakespeare, and any other
plays that came his way ; he fell in love with, but soon
tired of, Ossian ; he read Tasso and Ariosto in translations ; Spenser he knew by heart, and, since his memory
retained whatever impressed his mind, could repeat an
immense number of stanzas. From his mother and his
mother's friends he collected old ballads, and out of
penny chap-books laid the foundations of a library. We
have one glimpse from a fellow-pupil of the dreaming
boy :—" In walking he used always to keep his eyes
turned downward as if thinking, but with a pleasing
expression of countenance, as if enjoying his thoughts."
Scott left the High School in the spring of 1783, and,
since he was not due to enter college before the autumn,
he was sent for six months to his Aunt Janet, who had
now moved from Sandy Knowe to Kelso. There he was
to spend many of his later holidays, and we may fairly
regard the Kelso period as a formative stage in his
education. The little house stood in a large garden,
which was decorated with mazes, labyrinth and bowers
according to the fashion of the period, and in front of
which rolled the " glittering and resolute streams of
Tweed." It was his first real introduction to the spell of
that noble river, for at Sandy Knowe Tweed had been too
far away for a child's feet. He attended the Kelso school,
where his Latin improved, and he sat on the same bench as
the son of a local tradesman, a certain James Ballantyne,
whose life was to be curiously linked with his. At Kelso
he discovered Percy's *Reliques*, which he first read under

1783-86 a great plane-tree in the garden, and thereafter recited to all who would listen. There, too, his æsthetic sense received a new stimulus.

> To this period—he wrote—I can trace the awakening of that delightful feeling for the beauties of natural objects which has never since deserted me. The neighbourhood of Kelso, the most beautiful, if not the most romantic village in Scotland, is eminently calculated to awaken these ideas. It presents objects not only grand in themselves, but venerable from their associations. . . . The romantic feelings which I have described as predominating in my mind, naturally rested upon and associated themselves with these grand features of the landscape around me, and the historical incidents, or traditional legends connected with many of them, gave to my admiration a sort of intense impression of reverence, which at times made my heart feel too big for its bosom. From this time the love of natural beauty, more especially when combined with ancient ruins, or remains of our fathers' piety or splendour, became with me an insatiable passion.

He was confirmed in that preference which he had half-consciously acquired at Sandy Knowe—for a pastoral land interpenetrated with the poetry of man's endeavour. In his love of nature he was always the humanist, never the metaphysician.

In the autumn of 1783 Scott laid aside the round black hat, the gaudy waistcoat, and the brown corduroy breeches of the High School boy, and matriculated at the town's college of Edinburgh. It was the old college, an ancient shabby place of small courts and dingy class-rooms, where world-famous professors lectured to lads of thirteen and fourteen. He attended the Latin or Humanity class, where he forgot most of what he had learned at school, for that class seems to have been what Lord Cockburn found it ten years later, " the constant scene of unchecked idleness and disrespectful mirth." He attended the first Greek class under Dalzell, but, since he had to begin by learning the alphabet, and discovered that all his fellow-students started at a higher level, he tried to carry off his incompetence by announcing his contempt for the language and comparing Homer unfavourably with Ariosto. Yet the gentle enthusiasm of the professor might well have won his respect, for he shared 1783–86 most of the boy's prejudices. Dalzell used to maintain that Presbytery had killed classical scholarship in Scotland, and Sydney Smith once heard him murmur to himself : " If it had not been for that confounded Solemn League and Covenant, we would have made as good longs and shorts as England." [1] Scott was a pupil also in the logic class, and studied mathematics with a private tutor. Four years later, when he was a law student, he sat under Lord Woodhouselee in history and Dugald Stewart in moral philosophy ; but Stewart was not to him, as he was to many of his contemporaries, an inspiring revelation. Likewise he took lessons in drawing and painting, in which he did not conspicuously progress, and in music, where he did not progress at all. Like Burns, he had much music in his soul, and little in his voice.

During these years his attendance at college was intermittent, for his health was weak, since he had outgrown his strength. In his convalescence he was again at Kelso, this time at the villa which his uncle, Captain Robert Scott, had acquired on Tweed a little below the town. Meantime the voracious reading went on. If he neglected the Latin classics he was dabbling in Buchanan and Matthew Paris and the monkish chronicles, and if Greece was a sealed book to him he was beginning to explore the literatures of Italy and France.

In May 1786 when he was not yet fifteen, he signed indentures for five years as his father's apprentice. The elder Scott had decided that his son should follow the profession of the law, but had not yet determined which branch it should be. The church seems to have been considered, but, though it offered good prospects, it was not pressed, for it was clear that the boy had no vocation in that quarter.[2] So the young Walter found himself set to a desk for many hours every day, immured in the dreariest of labours. He was not an idle apprentice, for he had always a remarkable capacity for solid, plodding toil. " The drudgery of the office," he confesses, " I disliked, and the confinement I altogether detested ; but

---

[1] Cockburn, *Mem.*, 21. [2] Lang, I. 406.

1787 I loved my father, and I felt the natural pride and pleasure of rendering myself useful to him. I was ambitious also ; and among my companions in labour the only way to gratify ambition was to labour hard and well." The tasks had one alleviation. The copying of legal documents was paid for at the rate of threepence per folio, and by these means he could acquire pocket-money for books and the theatre. Once he wrote one hundred and twenty folio pages (probably about ten thousand words) without a single interval for food or rest. This was an invaluable training for his later feats of scribing, and it gave him a good running hand. Till the end of his life he continued to finish off a page with a flourish of the pen, and at Abbotsford used to be heard to mutter, " There goes the old shop again." The work brought him closer to his father, who, if he did little to mould his mind, taught him habits of care and application. He won an insight into the eternal disparities of father and son, and he learned to make allowances for the rigid, buttoned-up old gentleman whom he had come to comprehend as well as to love. The portrait of Saunders Fairford in *Redgauntlet* is a tribute, at once shrewd and affectionate, to the taskmaster of the young apprentice.

When he was sixteen, he burst a blood-vessel in his bowels, and had to lie for weeks on his back in a room with open windows, his only resources chess, military history and the poets. But after that he seemed to outgrow his early delicacy. He shot up into a tall, broad-shouldered lad, very deep in the chest, and with arms like a blacksmith's. His lameness did not embitter him, as it embittered Byron ; there were heroes in his pantheon, like Boltfoot and John the Lamiter, who had had the same handicap. He could walk thirty miles in a day, and ride as long as a horse could carry him. A year or two later he defended himself with his stick against three assailants for an hour by the Tron clock, like Corporal Raddlebanes in *Old Mortality*. When he was come to full strength James Hogg considered him the strongest man of his acquaintance, and Ettrick

Forest did not breed weaklings.[1] Among other feats he 1787–89
could with one hand lift a smith's anvil by the horn.[2]
His spirit matched his body. Said a naval officer :
" Though you may think him a poor lamiter, he's the
first to begin a row, and the last to end it."

The diversions of his middle teens were many. In
those days boys went to college at twelve, and at fifteen
they were guests at grown-up dinner-parties. A gentleman, however young, was expected to drink his share of
wine, and to carry it well, and till this skill was attained
there were apt to be disastrous experiments. Edinburgh
society was not the best school of health, and Scott lived
to censure the extravagances of his youth ; but it is very
certain that he never repented of them. In March, 1827,
he wrote :

> There is a touch of the old spirit in me yet that bids me brave
> the tempest—the spirit that in spite of manifold infirmities
> made me a roaring boy in my youth, a desperate climber, a
> bold rider, a deep drinker, and a stout player at singlestick.[3]

There were debating societies, where young men talked
the sun down. There were celebrities to be gazed at with
reverence and addressed with circumspection—John
Home, whom he had met in Bath, the blind poet Black-
lock, Robert Burns whom he saw as a schoolboy in
Sibbald's circulating library, and much later at the house
of Adam Ferguson—which meeting he has described in
one of his best pieces of prose.[4] There was his circle
of friends—chief among them John Irving, the young
Adam Ferguson, and William Clerk, son of that Sir
John Clerk of Eldin who forecast the tactics to which
Rodney owed his victories—with whom he roamed the
hills on summer holidays. And sometimes romance
fluttered the pages even of his legal folios. In the first
autumn of his apprenticeship he visited Alexander
Stewart of Invernahyle, who had been out in both the
'Fifteen and the 'Forty-five, and he had that vision of
the champaign of the lower Tay which he describes in

---

[1] *Dom. Manners*, 128.   [2] *Journal*, I. 114.
[3] *Journal*, I. 379.   [4] Lockhart, I. 136-8.

1789–92 the introduction to *The Fair Maid of Perth*. Another year he was sent north on business, to enforce execution against some refractory Maclarens, tenants of Stewart of Appin. With an escort of a sergeant and six men from Stirling Castle, each with loaded arms, the romantic lawyer's clerk most fittingly made his first entry into the Trossachs.

At seventeen his future was determined. He was to follow the higher branch of the legal calling, and he began his law classes at the college. The two elder brothers had chosen the Army and the Navy, and, apart from his lameness, it was inevitable that he should pursue the third of the normal callings of a gentleman. The three years which followed were a period of serious preparation. Scott, who never claimed a virtue which he did not abundantly possess, wrote : " Let me do justice to the only years of my life in which I applied to learning with stern, steady, and undeviating industry." He and William Clerk worked together, examining themselves daily in points of law, and every morning in summer Scott would walk the two miles to the west end of Princes Street to beat up his friend. The two passed their final trials on July 11th, 1792, and assumed the gown of the advocate.[1] After the ceremony they mingled with the crowd in the Parliament Hall, and Scott, mimicking the voice of a Highland girl at a hiring fair, complained to his companion ; " We've stood here an hour by the Tron, hinny, and deil a ane has speired our price." But a friendly solicitor gave him his first guinea before the courts rose.

In the law classes Scott met his old school friends and many others—Irving and Ferguson, George Cranstoun, Francis Jeffrey, George Abercromby, Edmonstone of Newton, Murray of Ochtertyre, and Murray of Simprin —a brilliant coterie, not a few of whom rose to the Scottish Bench. He had now left his boyhood behind him, for in those days men matured early, and he

---

[1] Scott's thesis for admission, " Disputatio Juridica de Cadaveribus Damnatorum, *Just. Dig.*, lib. XLVIII. tit. xxiv.," is a very creditable piece of legal Latin. It was dedicated to Lord Braxfield. See W. K. Dickson, " Sir Walter Scott and the Parliament House," *Juridical Review*, March 1930.

plunged heartily into the delights of a very social city. 1792
He learned to drink square, and, though he had a head
like a rock, he used to complain in later life that these
bouts were the source of some of his stomach troubles.
He indulged in herculean walking trips, sometimes not
returning home till the next morning, so that his father
was moved to complain that he was "born for nae
better than a gangrel scrape-gut." He belonged to
many clubs ; the Literary Society, where his antiquarian
learning won him the name of Duns Scotus ; a body
called The Club, which met in Carrubber's Close ; a
Teviotdale Club, where he renewed acquaintance with
his Kelso friend, James Ballantyne : and finally in 1791,
the famous Speculative Society, the nursery of so much
literary and legal talent. He abandoned his former
carelessness in dress, and became a point-device young
man, able to talk to women without shyness. Meantime
on every holiday he was off to his beloved Border, to
Kelso, to Jedburgh, to the Northumbrian side of the
Cheviots, whence he wrote rollicking epistles to his
friends. We have a glimpse of him at home in George
Square, where Jeffrey found him in a small den in the
basement surrounded by dingy books, cabinets of curios,
and rusty armour. He was a good boon-companion and
a delightful comrade for the road, but he left on his
friends also an impression of whinstone good sense. We
find him at eighteen intervening to reconcile a foolish
boy with his family, and when quarrels broke out over
the wine he was the chief peacemaker.

Scott passed into manhood with a remarkable assort-
ment of knowledge, for from the age of five his mind
had never been idle. He was a sound lawyer, especially
well versed in feudal niceties. Philosophy he had never
touched ; nor theology, except what he had picked up
from his Calvinistic tutor. In history he was widely and
curiously read, and his memory for detail enabled him
to retain every fragment of out-of-the-way learning
which had colour and drama. He had browsed over the
whole field of English literature, and was a mine of
Shakespearean lore. He had enough French, German,

1792 Spanish and Italian to read the works in these languages which appealed to him ; French he spoke after a fashion, but, as one of the attendants of the exiled Charles X said, it was the French of the good Sire de Joinville. He was still in the acquisitive rather than the critical stage of mental development, and his taste in poetry was for things like the lisping iambics of Mickle's " Cumnor Hall." [1]

He was always of the opinion that a knowledge of Latin and Greek was the basis of every sound education. " Though some people," he once wrote to his son Charles, " may have scrambled into distinction without it, it is always with the greatest difficulty, like climbing over a wall instead of giving your ticket at the door." Greek, as we have seen, he had none ; the chief of the later Homeridæ scarcely knew Homer's alphabet. It was a lack, no doubt, for some acquaintance with the Greek masterpieces, some tincture of the Greek spirit, might have trimmed that prolixity which was to be his besetting sin. But of Latin he had a full measure. He was, indeed, never a good " pure scholar," as the phrase goes, and could not detect a false quantity ; but few men of his day, not professed scholars, had a wider acquaintance with Latin literature. He quotes constantly from Virgil and Horace, but that was the fashion of the age ; more notable is the minute knowledge which he shows of Juvenal and Ovid, while he also can aptly cite Lucan, Catullus, Plautus, Terence, Livy and Tacitus.[2]

It is the fashion to repeat that it was Scott's weak leg alone that made him a writer, that otherwise he would have followed the profession of arms ; and he himself once told Southey, speaking of his eldest son's wish to enter the army, " I have no call to combat a choice which would have been my own had lameness permitted." He might have been a soldier, even a great soldier, but he would most certainly have been also a writer ; for the instinct to express his thoughts and moods in words was in the fibre of his being. In January,

---

[1] Preface to *Kenilworth*.
[2] See Vernon Rendall's " Scott and the Latin classics," in *S. Q.*, 129-138.

1826, in the hour of disaster, he wrote to Lockhart, " I 1792
never knew the day that I would have given up literature
for ten times my present income." All his education
was contributory to this purpose, for never had a creative
writer a more happy apprenticeship. " What a life mine
has been ! " he wrote in later years, " half-educated,
almost wholly neglected or left to myself, stuffing my
head with most nonsensical trash." Yet it was the
education most consonant with his genius, most exquisitely fitted for the achievements of his life. Thomas
Moore tells of a conversation he once had with him. " I
said how well calculated the way in which Scott had
been brought up was to make a writer of poetry and
romance, as it combined all that knowledge of rural life
and rural legend which is to be gained by living among
the peasantry and joining in their sport, with all the
advantages which an aristocratic education gives. I
said that the want of this manly training showed itself
in my poetry, which would, perhaps, have had a far more
vigorous character if it had not been for the sort of
boudoir education I had received." Scott had the kind
of childhood and youth which fits a man to follow what
Aristotle calls the " main march of the human affections."
He had mingled intimately with every class and condition
of men ; he had enough education to broaden his outlook
but not enough to dim it ; he was familiar alike with
city and moorland, with the sown and the desert, and
he escaped the pedantry of both the class-room and the
drawing-room ; above all he had the good fortune to
stand at the meeting-place of two worlds, and to have
it in him to be their chief interpreter.

Chapter III

EARLY MANHOOD

(1792–1799)

1792–95 A SCOTS advocate in his first years at the Bar has commonly a superfluity of leisure. He walks the floor of the Parliament House waiting to be hired, and shares in what used to be one of the most friendly and jovial of societies. That floor, looked down upon by the grave periwigged judges of the past, has always been a breeding-ground of good stories, and in this gentle art Walter Scott shone among his contemporaries. He was a famous mimic, especially of such farcical judicial figures as Lord Eskgrove, with his low muttering voice and projected chin, who would in sentencing a prisoner to death console him thus : " Whatever your relig-ious persua-shon may be, there are plenty of rever-end gentle-men who will be most happy for to show you the way to yeternal life." Scott was noted for taking the tales of other men and sharpening their point—putting, as he said, " a cocked hat on their heads and a cane into their hands."

But his legal career was not wholly occupied with the pleasantries of the Outer House. In 1795 he was appointed one of the curators of the Advocates' Library, an office reserved for the more literary members of the faculty. A certain amount of work reached him from his father's office, chiefly the endless legal *paperasserie* known as " informations," with which the administra-tion of law was cumbered. He defended poor prisoners without a fee, and on circuit at Jedburgh had as clients local poachers and sheepstealers. One case took him for the first time into Galloway, and gave him the landscape

44

for *Guy Mannering.* The minister of Girthon was
accused of " toying with a sweetie-wife " at a penny-
wedding and of singing doubtful songs, and Scott
defended him before the General Assembly, drawing a
nice distinction between *ebrius* and *ebriosus,* between
being occasionally drunk and being a habitual drunkard.
He lost his case, but his argument greatly edified his
brethren of the Covenant Close.

It was a life which enlarged his knowledge of the
human comedy and took him into odd by-paths. If he
won few guineas by it he was paid often in a better coin,
as in the case of a housebreaker at Jedburgh who remunerated him with two pieces of advice—never to
keep a watch-dog out of doors but to tie up a noisy
terrier within, and to trust not to clever new locks but
to the old heavy kind with the rude keys. As he once
told Lord Meadowbank,

> Yelping terrier, rusty key,
> Was Walter Scott's best Jeddart fee.

Cockburn has a tale of a dinner given by an old drunken
Selkirk attorney to Scott, Cranstoun and Will Erskine,
when Scott as a toper nearly triumphed over the host.
" As they were mounting their horses to ride home, the
entertainer let the other two go without speaking to
them, but he embraced Scott, assuring him that he
would rise high. ' And I'll tell ye what, Maister Walter
—that lad Cranstoun may get to the tap of the bar if
he can; but tak' ma word for't—it's no' be by drinking.' "[1]

He learned more from his practice than the humours
of humanity, for Scots law was one of the main
educative influences in his life. Its complexity and
exactness formed a valuable corrective to a riotous
imagination. It was the one form of science which he
ever cultivated. Moreover, when he became a novelist,
it was to give immense point and gusto to his Scots
conversations. In an older Scotland the language of the
law, like the language of the Bible, interpenetrated the
speech of every class. A smattering of it was considered

---

[1] *Mem.,* 456.

proof of gravity and practical good sense. Consequently it was often misused, and this farcical side adds perpetual salt to his dialogues. His years at the Bar not only enabled him to draw characters like Pleydell and the elder Fairford, but also to give to some of his minor figures their most idiomatic humours—as witness the speech of Bailie Macwheeble, and mine host Mackitchinson, and Andrew Fairservice, and Bartoline Saddletree.

For the rest, as he wrote of Alan Fairford, he " laughed and made others laugh ; drank claret at Bayle's, Fortune's and Walker's, and ate oysters in the Covenant Close," while on his desk " the new novel most in repute lay snugly intrenched beneath Stair's Institutes or an open volume of Decisions," and his table was littered with every kind of document " but briefs and banknotes." He was fortunate in his friends, some of whom we have already met. Will Clerk, his boyhood ally, remained an intimate, though he was a Whig in politics, and had no share in Scott's literary and sporting interests. As the years of his youth passed an inner circle grew up for him in his immense acquaintanceship. Chief of that circle was William Erskine, the son of an Episcopalian clergyman in Perthshire, who became to Scott both an exacting literary censor and a second conscience. Erskine was a small, frail man, no lover of sport, awkward on horseback, a being of quick sensibilities and delicate nerves—a strange contrast to his big-boned, bluff, adventurous friend. The two men were complementary : Erskine rested upon Scott's sanity and vigour, and Scott looked to Erskine's finer perceptions to correct his own ebullience in letters and life. No two friends were ever closer together, or more complete partakers of each other's intimate thoughts.

Then there was Thomas Thomson, the son of an Ayrshire minister ; he became one of the most learned of Scottish antiquaries and was to Scott at once a boon-companion and an esteemed fellow-worker in the quarries of the past. Of all his friends, perhaps, Thomson was the one whom Scott most esteemed as a table companion. " I pray you of all loves," so ran his usual invitation form, " to dine with me to-morrow at half-past five." There was George Cranstoun, afterwards Lord Corehouse, who belonged to a family which Lord Dudley told Mrs Dugald Stewart—herself a member of it—was reputed to consist of " the cleverest but the oddest people in the world." Cranstoun was shy, proud, notably able, an excellent critic and a storehouse of good sense. There was James Skene of Rubislaw, who was especially a brother sportsman. There were young women, too, in the circle, who played a part in Scott's education—Erskine's sister, Mary Anne ; Cranstoun's sister, Jane Anne, who became Countess Purgstall ; the young Lady Harden, the wife of the head of his sept, who lent him German books and corrected his Scotticisms, the " first woman of real fashion," he used to say, " that took me up."

These were the years of the Revolution in France, but to Scott it was no blissful dawn, as it appeared to the young Wordsworth, but a carnival of disorder distasteful to the lawyer, and a menace to his country hateful to the patriot. He was always wholly insensitive to the appeal of abstract ideas. As we shall see, he developed a strong interest in the technique of government and the practical workings of society, and few novelists have had such a masculine grasp of its economic framework. But the political ideas which were beginning to work like yeast in many of the younger minds in Scotland, problems like the ultimate purpose of human society, and the relation between the power of the state and the rights of the individual, left him cold. His mind was in a high degree concrete and practical ; he might take arms against a proven abuse but not against a dubious theory, and his devotion to the past made him abhor all that was speculative and rootless. He had none of his countrymen's love of metaphysics, which was generally linked to the Calvinism of their training. Scott had early put behind him Calvinism and all that it implied, whether exemplified in his father or his tutor. He had escaped that fate which befell so many Scottish children and which was to befall Stevenson, a " Covenanting childhood." Though he was the great-grandson of the

1797 minister of Yarrow, the traditional Scottish theology did
not affect him; he neither fell under its burden nor
reacted against it; he simply gave it the go-by. The
new seeds of thought sown by the French Revolution
found a prepared soil in minds accustomed to the toils of
religious speculation, minds which were compelled to
work out for themselves a reasoned philosophy of life.
Scott never felt the compulsion. In practice he regarded
all men as his brothers, but he would have nothing to do
with whimsies about the Brotherhood of Man. He was
a Tory, not on the philosophical grounds of Burke and
Bolingbroke, but because as a poet he loved the old ways,
and as a practical man would conserve them, however
logically indefensible, so long as they seemed to serve
their purpose. So he joined heartily in breaking the
heads of Irish students who sang rebel songs in the
theatre, and, when the volunteering movement began,
wrote to Kelso for " a strong gelding such as would suit
a stalwart dragoon," to purchase which he was prepared
to sell his collection of Scottish coins.

Scott's experience as a volunteer was of value, for
it gave him a means of working off his high spirits,
and enabled one who was man of action as well as man
of letters to satisfy at a critical stage both demands of
his nature. In 1794 his brother Thomas was enrolled as
a grenadier in an Edinburgh regiment, but Scott's own
lameness prevented him joining the infantry. In 1797,
however, he had his chance when a cavalry corps, the
Royal Edinburgh Volunteer Light Dragoons, was embodied and he became its quartermaster. Stevenson
has told us that his dream was always to be " the leader
of a great horde of irregular cavalry," and that on his
sick bed he saw himself " turning in the saddle to look
back at my whole command (some five thousand strong)
following me at a hand gallop up the road out of the
burning valley by moonlight." Such fancies were at the
back of Scott's head as he manœuvred on Portobello
sands, or took part in the policing of an occasional meal
riot. Once in Paris the Tsar of Russia, observing his
uniform, asked in what battles he had been engaged,

and was told " in some slight actions, such as the battle 1792–99
of the Cross Causeway and the affair of Moredoun Mill."
He was an exemplary volunteer, playing the game
according to its extreme rigour, his heart making martial
music within him, and thereby preparing himself for
the galloping speed of his verses; and his humour and
ardour were the inspiration of his corps. Lord Cockburn,
the Whig, has a pleasant note on a performance with
which he did not wholly sympathize :—

> It was not a duty with him, or a necessity, or a pastime,
> but an absolute passion, indulgence in which gratified his
> feudal taste for war, and his jovial sociableness. He drilled,
> and drank, and made songs, with a hearty conscientious
> earnestness which inspired or shamed everybody within the
> attraction. I do not know if it is usual, but his troop used to
> practise, individually, with the sabre at a turnip, which was
> stuck on the top of a staff, to represent a Frenchman, in front
> of the line. Every other trooper, when he set forward in his
> turn, was far less concerned about the success of his aim at
> the turnip, than about how he was to tumble. But Walter
> pricked forward gallantly, saying to himself : " Cut them
> down, the villains, cut them down ! " and made his blow,
> which from his lameness was often an awkward one, cordially,
> muttering curses all the while at the detested enemy.[1]

He spent his holidays in exploring Scotland, not
a common occupation in those days of comfortless
travelling. He visited a dozen country houses from
Angus to Lennox—Glamis, Meigle, Craighall, Newton,
Tullibody, Cambusmore, Keir, Blairdrummond—which,
being situated near the half-moon of the Highland
Line, gave him some knowledge of the northern borderland. But it was to his own Border that he devoted
most of his leisure. He had already explored the main
valleys of Tweed and Teviot, and both sides of the
central Cheviots, and now he began to push farther into
the wild hill country that bounded the Debatable Land.
In the autumn of 1792, along with Robert Shortreed,
the Sheriff-substitute of Roxburghshire, he made his
first incursion into Liddesdale, and thereafter for seven
successive years the raid was annually repeated. In

[1] *Mem.*, 195-6.

1792–99 those days there were no roads for a wheeled carriage in Liddesdale, and therefore no tolls, and on the first journey the only expense which the travellers incurred was the feed of corn for their horses at Riccarton Mill. They slept in cot-houses or farms or manses as their road led them, and enjoyed an Homeric hospitality. Scott, as a young advocate, at first inspired some awe, till the herds and store-farmers discovered that " he was just a chield like ourselves." A chield he was, for he could drink and jest, hunt and fish, walk and ride with any Dandie Dinmont. " Drunk or sober," Shortreed reported, " he was aye the gentleman." Family worship would suddenly be broken up by the arrival of a keg of smuggled brandy from the Solway shore, whisky punch was drunk out of milk-pails, and breakfast would consist of porter and devilled ducks. Those days in sun and rain on the Liddesdale bent and nights by the peat-fire were filled with more than roystering. Scott was getting deeper into the ancient Border life and enlarging his knowledge of mankind and himself : " makin' himsell a' the time," said his companion. He was collecting ' gabions ' too, like Border war horns and steel bonnets, and—more important—the songs and tunes and tales of a vanishing world.

His literary education followed the fashionable groove. Henry Mackenzie, the author of *The Man of Feeling*, read a paper to the Edinburgh Royal Society in April 1788 which started in the capital a craze for German literature. Scott in 1792 joined a class to study the subject, and a few years later was stirred to enthusiasm by hearing Mrs Barbauld read a translation of Bürger's "Lenore." Miss Jane Anne Cranstoun, his friend's sister, and the young Lady Harden encouraged his interest and corrected his German. It was the peak moment of Gothick extravagance, for in 1794 Mrs Radcliffe published her *Mysteries of Udolpho*, and a certain odd, undersized youth of twenty-one, Matthew Lewis by name, next year issued a tale, *Ambrosio or The Monk*, which took the town by storm. Scott fell deeply under the glamour of this pasteboard romance.

" I wish to Heaven," he declared to a friend, " I could
get a skull and two cross-bones." In October 1796 he
published in a slim quarto his own verse translations of
" Lenore " and " Der Wilde Jäger," which were perhaps
not much worse than the originals, and revealed some
talent for fluent verse. Three months before a poet
worth a thousand Bürgers had died in Dumfries, but
Scott had forgotten all about Burns, of whom he had
been thrilled to get a casual glimpse as a boy. He was
passing through the inevitable stage in a literary education, when the foreign seems marvellous because it is
strange, and the domestic humdrum because it is
familiar. He was soon to return by way of Liddesdale
and the ballads to his own kindly earth.

Meanwhile, in addition to his advocate's work and
ballad-hunting and soldiering, he was living the life of
an ordinary young man, and met other women besides
lettered ladies. He had become a personable being, and
appeared thus to one female observer. " His eyes were
clear, open and well set, with a changeful radiance, to
which teeth of the most perfect regularity and whiteness
lent their assistance, while the noble expanse and elevation of his brow gave to the whole aspect a dignity far
above the charm of mere features. His smile was always
delightful, and I can easily fancy the peculiar inter-
mixture of tenderness and gravity, with playful innocent
hilarity and humour in the expression, as being well
calculated to fix a fair lady's eye. His figure, excepting
the blemish in one limb, must in those days have been
eminently handsome—tall, much above the usual stature,
cast in the very mould of a youthful Hercules ; the head
set on with singular grace, the throat and chest after the
truest model of the antique, the hands delicately finished,
the whole outline that of extraordinary vigour without
as yet a touch of clumsiness."[1] The portrait is perhaps
too highly coloured ; Scott himself always declared that
he had the largest pair of hands north of Tweed, and he
was not for nothing a descendant of Muckle Mou'd Meg.
His figure was what is called in Scotland " buirdly " ;

[1] Lockhart, I. 162.

he had a noble peaked head thatched with light brown hair, grey-blue eyes, a deep voice, and a pleasant Border burr. The lower part of his face, with its long upper lip and heavy jowl, gave him a slightly lumpish air—till he smiled, when the whole countenance became whimsical and kindly. There was obvious power in him, but of the ruder kind, and it needed a discerning eye to penetrate to the poetry below the bluffness. What was not in doubt was the friendliness. " I said to myself," Joanna Baillie wrote after her first sight of him, " if I had been in a crowd and at a loss to do, I should have fixed upon his face among a thousand, as the sure index of bene-volence and the shrewdness that would and could help me in any strait."

Such a young man could not escape the common fate. Scott belonged to the familiar northern type to which sex is not the sole mainspring of being. He preferred the society of men to that of women; he had no disposition to casual amours; in this domain of life he had an almost virginal fastidiousness.[1] The love affairs of such a man are apt to begin with a fairy tale and to conclude with a marriage of convenience. Happily he did not miss the first, for he had a taste of the old Romeo and Juliet romance, that ecstatic, child-like idealization of one woman which belongs especially to a poetic youth. Before he was quite out of his teens he offered the shelter of his umbrella to a girl one wet Sunday in Greyfriars churchyard, and had a glimpse of a face which was to be a *profile de rêve* to him for many a day. She was only fifteen, the daughter of Sir John Stuart-Belsches of Fettercairn, and his wife, Lady Jane, who was a daughter of the Earl of Leven and Melville. She was not only well-born but a considerable heiress, and her portrait shows composed features, large blue eyes, dark brown ringlets and a complexion of cream and roses. The two had probably met before, for their parents were acquaintances. The elder Scott, in an excess of conscientiousness, thought it his duty to inform Sir John of the young people's growing friendship, but

[1] Lockhart, I. 161-2.

no bar was put in its way, and the Lady of the Green
Mantle became a toast among Scott's friends. He tells
us that he had three years of dreaming, and two of
wakening ; some time during the year 1795 he declared
himself, and by the end of that year he began to doubt
whether he had won the lady's hand. The story is like
the baseless fabric of a dream, but it would appear that
his hopes revived again in 1796, and that, during a tour
in the north in April and May of that year, he visited
Fettercairn and returned south in better spirits. But
some time in the early autumn he got his dismissal.
Miss Williamina, though Scott suspected her mother's
influence, had given her heart elsewhere, and in January
1797 she married the banker, Sir William Forbes of
Pitsligo, who had been a college friend of Scott and a
fellow-volunteer.[1]

Scott had perhaps been a timid and hesitating lover,
for he was shy of women, and had marvellously idealized
this woman. Some of his friends dreaded the consequences for one whom they knew to be full of banked
fires. " I now shudder at the violence of his most
irritable and ungovernable mind." But Scott was no
sigher in the shades. In Lockhart's phrase he " digested "
his agony. His philosophy was that of Quentin Durward :
" Melancholy, even love-melancholy, is not so deeply
seated, at least in minds of a manly and elastic character,
as the soft enthusiasts who suffer under it are fond of
believing. It yields to unexpected and striking impressions, to changes of plans . . . and to the busy hum
of mankind." Nevertheless the shaft went deep, and
though the sting passed away the memory remained till
his dying day. The first lines he wrote with any of the
freshness of reality owed their inspiration to the lost
lady, those beginning, " The violet is her greenwood
bower " ; and in the last decade of his life he either
composed or copied other verses on the same topic.[2]
The wraith of Green Mantle glimmers in Margaret of

---

[1] Lord Sands in *Sir Walter Scott's Congé* (3rd edition, 1931) has collected
many details of the affair, and corrected some of Lockhart's mistakes.
[2] Lockhart, I. 244: but see Adam Scott's *Sir Walter Scott's First Love*, 157.

1797 Branksome in *The Lay of the Last Minstrel*, in her namesake in *Redgauntlet*, in Matilda in *Rokeby*, maybe, too, in Diana Vernon, when she stoops from her saddle on the midnight moor with a kiss as light as the touch of a bird's wing. He had cut Williamina's name on the turf at the castle gate of St Andrews as a young lover, and thirty-four years after sat on an adjacent gravestone and wondered why the name " should still agitate my heart." Three months later he met Lady Jane in Edinburgh ; she was then well over seventy, and her daughter had been dead for seventeen years. The meeting was like opening a sepulchre.

> I fairly softened myself, like an old fool, with recalling stories, till I was fit for nothing but shedding tears and repeating verses for the whole night. This is sad work. The very grave gives up its dead, and time rolls back thirty years to add to my perplexities.[1]

The emotion must have been deep which could leave such traces. He put it behind him, as he put all things of whose futility he was convinced, but it survived in the secret places of his soul. It is wrong, I think, to argue that Scott was never seriously in love with Williamina, that it was a mere boyish fancy, and that what attracted him was her birth and the long-descended world in which she moved. These things no doubt played a part in his idealization of the girl, but the enduring power of the idealization lay in the fact that she came to represent for him the first ardour of his youth and all youth's dear and unsubstantial visions. No one can read his letters at the time without concluding that this was that rare thing, a deep and enduring love. Rare, I mean, among the fleeting, volcanic passions of the poets, who wear their hearts on their sleeves and protest to the world that the pang of an hour is an eternal sorrow. Scott's passion was a profounder emotion than any which the lives of Burns or Shelley or Byron can show. He never saw Williamina again, and he did not wish to ; there was no bitterness in his memory of her, but there was regret—

---

[1] *Journal*, II. 62.

regret perhaps less for a thing of flesh and blood than 1797 for the " glory and the freshness of a dream." Somewhere at the back of his mind the thought of her dwelt, and on the eve of any great misfortune she came to him in sleep. It is a strange tale, but one which carries the key to most of his life, for we shall not understand Scott unless we realize how much he lived in a secret world of his own, an inner world of dream and memory, from which he brought great treasures, but which now and then to his undoing invaded the world of facts.

His heart, he has told us, was soon " handsomely pierced " and this time the wooer had his feet on solid earth. In July 1797 he set out with his brother John and Adam Ferguson on a visit to the English lakes, and at the little Cumberland watering-place of Gilsland met a young lady of just over twenty-one, with a slight graceful figure, a suspicion of a foreign accent, a clear olive complexion, jet black hair, and large brown eyes. He was afterwards to draw her portrait in Julia Mannering. She was witty, sprightly, and full of hard Latin good sense. Her name was Charlotte Margaret Carpenter ; her father had been Jean Charpentier, a royalist refugee from Lyons and a Huguenot ; her guardian (some have without reason suspected a closer relationship) was Lord Downshire : and her only brother, thanks to the Downshire interest, was doing well in the East India service. Scott went to a ball in his Light Horse regimentals, fell in love, promptly offered marriage, and was accepted subject to Lord Downshire's consent, which arrived early in October. The elder Scott, now paralysed and dying, made no objection, and on Christmas Eve 1797, the young couple were married in St Mary's Church, Carlisle.

Scott was in wild spirits during his engagement, and raved about the lady to his friends, but it seems certain that his heart was not greatly affected. He liked the idea of marriage as a step in that progress in life to which one side of him (his father's side) was vowed. He wanted a cheerful companion for the road, and he believed that he had found one. Twelve years afterwards he wrote to Lady Abercorn :

> Mrs Scott's match and mine was of our own making, and proceeded from the most sincere affection on both sides, which has rather increased than diminished during twelve years' marriage. But it was something short of love in all its forms, which I suspect people only feel once in all their lives ; folk who have been nearly drowned in bathing rarely venturing a second time out of their depth.[1]

The brisk Julia Mannering was not Diana Vernon, and never entered into his secret world. But she made him an admirable wife, and no quarrel clouded their thirty years of matrimony. She loved show—" I am glad you don't give up the cavalry, as I love anything that is stylish " ; gaiety—in Edinburgh they went to the play nearly every night, and consistently entertained up to and beyond their means ; money, perhaps, for what it brought. She had no interest in the things of the mind, and doubted whether thoughtful people could ever be happy. She was not a good manager, in spite of her French blood. But she was loyal, wholly free from jealousy, courageous, and her son once wrote to her " I admire above all things your laughing philosophy." When the fierce light of popularity blazed on him, she was not shrivelled, as Mrs Grant of Laggan feared she might be. She had no part in her husband's inner world of dreams, but she helped him abundantly to enjoy the externals of life.

The young people took up house in the New Town of Edinburgh, first in rooms in George Street, then in South Castle Street, and finally in the house, No 39 North Castle Street, which was to be their home till 1826. Scott was making about £150 a year at the Bar, his wife had a few hundreds, and he had an allowance from his father, so he was able in 1798 to take a country cottage at Lasswade on the Esk, half a dozen miles from Edinburgh. There he was close to his friends, the Clerks at Pennycuik, the Fraser Tytlers at Woodhouselee, Henry Mackenzie at Auchendinny, not to speak of

[1] *Fam. Letters*, I. 167.

grandees like the Duke of Buccleuch and Lord Melville, 1799
whose acquaintance his Light Horse service had brought
him. The Lasswade cottage was a little place by the
roadside, with a view, a garden, and one big living-
room. It was to be for Scott the Sabine farm where he
first held serious converse with the Muses.

Will Erskine had been in London, where he had met
Matt Lewis, who in that day of small things passed for
a literary arbiter. Lewis was projecting a miscellany,
and, when Erskine showed him Scott's Bürger translations, welcomed him as a contributor. Presently Lewis
came to Edinburgh and summoned Scott to dine with
him at his hotel. The young advocate approached the
presence with awe, and was kindly received, and the
upshot was that his translation of Goethe's *Götz von
Berlichingen*, through Lewis's offices, was issued by a
London bookseller, one Bell, in February 1799—the
first publication to which Scott put his name. It is a
performance of much the same merit, or lack of merit,
as the earlier " Lenore." But meantime the poet, with
Lewis's miscellany in mind, was busy on better tasks.
He wrote the ballads of " Glenfinlas," " The Gray
Brother," and " The Eve of St John "—prentice work,
full of dubious echoes and conventional artifice, yet with,
as a foundation, the stuff of folk legend from which he
was soon to draw richer ore.

The year 1799 was eventful. In the spring the Scotts
went to London, where, under the guidance of Lewis,
they had their first taste of literary society. In April
death mercifully delivered his father from his afflictions.
In the winter he met again James Ballantyne, now
publishing a newspaper in Kelso, and gave him some of
his verses to print : the result so pleased him that he
proposed to Ballantyne a small volume of old Border
ballads. Then came the death of the Sheriff-deputy of
Selkirkshire, Andrew Plummer of Middlestead, and
through the Melville and Buccleuch influence Scott was
appointed to succeed him.

So at twenty-eight we may regard him as being settled
in life. From his Bar earnings, his wife's allowance, his

1799 father's estate, and his sheriffship, he had now nearly
£1000 a year—which in the Scotland of that age may be
regarded as the equivalent of £3000 to-day.[1] He was
happily married, with the beginnings of a family, and
possessed a large circle of attached friends. He had
found in literature an engrossing hobby, though he had
no intention of making it his chief calling. That must
remain the law, but, having made little success of
advocacy, he was now a little weary of its drudgery, and
looked rather to legal appointments. " My profession
and I," he wrote, " came to stand nearly upon the
footing which honest Slender consoled himself on having
established with Mistress Anne Page : ' There was not
great love between us at the beginning, and it pleased
heaven to decrease it on further acquaintance.' "[2] He
held his father's view that the making of books was not
enough to fill the life of an active man ; that, as he put
it, literature was a good staff but a bad crutch. The
drums and trumpets of life still sounded for him, and he
had one ear always at their service, though the other
might be rapt by the flutes of his secret world. His
ambitions at this stage can be summed up in the letter
of his friend Charles Kerr of Abbotrule.

> With your strong sense and hourly ripening knowledge, that
> you must rise to the top of the tree in the Parliament House
> in due season I hold as certain as that Murray died Lord
> Mansfield. But don't let many an Ovid, or rather many a
> Burns (which is better) be lost in you. I rather think men of
> business have produced as good poetry in their by-hours as
> the professed regulars ; and I don't see any sufficient reason
> why a Lord President Scott should not be a famous poet (in
> the vacation time), when we have seen a President Montesquieu
> step so nobly beyond the trammels in the *Esprit des Loix*.[3]

[1] Jeffrey at the same age, after nine anxious years at the Bar, was only
earning £240.

[2] Introd. to *Lay of the Last Minstrel*, 1830.   [3] Lockhart, I. 315.

CHAPTER IV

LASSWADE AND ASHESTIEL

(1799–1810)

I

SCOTT had now "taken sasine" of the Border, for he 1799–1803
was the local justiciar of a shire which held the upper
waters of its most famous rivers—the beautiful stretch
of Tweed where it breaks from the hills, the vale of
Yarrow with its dens and lochs and wan shallows amid
grey-green bent, the long trench of Ettrick running into
the heart of lonely moorlands. Here lay his principal
occupation, and he had now an excuse for constant
visits. But for five years his homes were still Lasswade
and Edinburgh, and he continued his precarious practice
at the Bar, varied with his duties as quartermaster of
the Light Horse. He had the friends of his youth about
him, his young wife made a gracious hostess, and the
Lothian cottage was the rendezvous of a distinguished
coterie. His work as a collecter of ballads brought him
into touch not only with Scottish contemporaries like
Skene and John Leyden and James Hogg, but with the
great English bibliophile, Richard Heber, who came to
Edinburgh in the winter of 1800 ; with Thomas Campbell the poet ; with George Ellis, diplomat, connoisseur,
contributor to the *Anti-Jacobin* and compiler of
Specimens of Ancient English Poetry ; with the crabbed
antiquary, Joseph Ritson, Bishop Percy's acidulous
critic, who visited Lasswade ; with Wordsworth and
his sister, who stayed with him on their Scottish tour
in 1803. He went to London in the spring of that year,
where he met Mackintosh and Samuel Rogers, and
studied the manuscripts in the Duke of Roxburgh's

library ; and visited Oxford, where he breakfasted in Brasenose with Reginald Heber and suggested to the latter the best lines in his Newdigate poem. He paid many visits to Scottish country-houses, like Harden and Bowhill, Bothwell and Hamilton Palace, where he made friends with Harriet, Lady Dalkeith, the daughter of Tommy Townshend ; with Frances, the young Lady Douglas, a sister of Lord Dalkeith and the stepdaughter of Charles Townshend ; and above all, with Lord Bute's daughter, Lady Louisa Stuart, who was to be to the end one of his closest allies. Scott had always in Lady Louisa's phrase " an old-fashioned partiality for a gentlewoman," which was something more than what Hogg described as his " only foible . . . a too strong leaning to the old aristocracy of the country." During these years, too, he was trying his prentice hand at letters—contributions to the newly founded *Edinburgh Review*, an edition of the metrical romance of *Sir Tristram* which he believed to be the work of Thomas the Rhymer, and above all that collecting and editing of folk ballads which took shape in the *Minstrelsy of the Scottish Border*.

It is uncommon for a great creative writer to develop out of an antiquary and an editor. But it was Scott's happy fate to find at the outset of his career precisely the task which was needed for the nurture of his genius. His memory was full of bad models, Augustan jingles, faked Gothick *diablerie* and rococo sentiment, and from them he was delivered by the *Minstrelsy* and restored to the ancient simplicities of earth. He came late to the business, for he was now twenty-eight. Wordsworth, a year his senior, and Coleridge a year his junior, had already published their epoch-making *Lyrical Ballads*. At twenty-eight Byron and Shelley had written most of their best verse, and long before that age Keats had completed his immortal bequest, while Scott had nothing to show but a few indifferent lyrics and " Germanised brats " of artificial ballads. The impulse which led to the *Minstrelsy* was historical and patriotic rather than poetic. He wished to save the relics of a fast-vanishing

world, and with them to preserve an authentic part of 1799-1803
his country's tradition. In his own words :

> By such efforts, feeble as they are, I may contribute some-
> thing to the history of my native country ; the peculiar
> features of whose manners and character are daily melting and
> dissolving into those of her sister and ally. And, trivial as
> may appear such an offering to the Manes of a kingdom, once
> proud and independent, I hang it upon her altar with a mixture
> of feelings which I shall not attempt to describe.[1]

In his wanderings about the Border Scott had for
years been collecting ballads, before it occurred to him
that James Ballantyne at Kelso, with his neat fount of
type, might make a little volume out of them. His
office as Sheriff brought him close to the heart of the
most storied part of the countryside, and his collection
grew apace. Much depended upon local assistants and
he was fortunate in finding several of the best. The
ballads were not in books, and rarely even in broadsheets ;
they lingered in corners of memory among the country
folk, with odd corruptions and misunderstandings, and
could only be elicited by tact and patience.

The first of his colleagues was John Leyden, one of
those prodigies of learning and zeal in learning which
have often appeared among the Scottish peasantry. A
shepherd's son from the Roxburghshire hills, he had no
regular schooling, but, " hydroptic with a sacred thirst,"
he fought his way to Edinburgh University, and at the
age of nineteen, says Lockhart, confounded the professors by his portentous attainments in most depart-
ments of knowledge. Big-boned, garrulous, violent, with
great bodily strength and unflagging ardour, poetic, sentimental and proud as Lucifer, he was a curious blend
of the polymath and the Border reiver. " His first
appearance," Scott wrote, " was somewhat appalling to
persons of low animal spirits." [2] He was proficient in
many tongues, but declined to learn genteel English, on
the ground, as he said, that it would spoil his Scots.
Richard Heber found him in Archibald Constable's little
bookshop in the High Street, and introduced him to

---

[1] *Minstrelsy*, Introd. cxxxi.   [2] *Edinburgh Annual Register*, 1811.

Scott, to whom he became an invaluable lieutenant. Leyden was a scholar, which Scott was not, and his austere conscience about texts had a salutary influence upon his colleague. Moreover he saw the project on ampler lines and would have none of Ballantyne's one-volume idea. " Dash it, does Mr Scott mean another thin thing like *Goetz of Berlichingen?* I have more than that in my head myself ; we shall turn out three or four such volumes at least." He found instructive parallels in other literatures, he delved among the broadsheets, and he tramped the Border on the quest for versions.

In 1803 Leyden went out as an assistant-surgeon to India, " a distant and a deadly shore " from which he was not to return. But in the meantime Scott had discovered other helpers. Penetrating into Yarrow from the inn at Clovenfords, he had found lodging at the farm of Blackhouse on the Douglas burn. The farmer was a young man called William Laidlaw, who entered eagerly into Scott's quest, and called in to help him a certain James Hogg, once a shepherd of his father's, but now herding at Ettrick House. This Hogg came of interesting stock, for there had been witches on the paternal side, and his maternal grandfather, Will o' Phawhope, was the last man on the Border who had spoken with the fairies. It was a promising source for balladry, and the ballads were duly forthcoming—some verses of " The Outlaw Murray," and the whole of the sixty-five stanzas of " Auld Maitland," taken down from his mother's recitation. In the summer of 1802 Laidlaw guided Scott by the Loch o' the Lowes over the hills to Ettrick, and the latter had his first meeting with Hogg. " Jamie the Poeter " was sent for to join the visitors at Ramsaycleuch, and Scott beheld a young man of his own age, burly, brawny, blue-eyed and red-headed, who was in no way abashed by the presence of the Sheriff. They had an evening of conviviality and anecdotage, and the next day Scott and Laidlaw visited Hogg's mother. She proved to be a formidable old woman, who criticized with vigour and point the first volume of the *Minstrelsy* which had just appeared. " There was never ane o' my

sangs prentit till ye prentit them yoursel', and ye have 1799–1803
spoilt them awthegither. They were made for singin'
and no' for readin', but ye have broken the charm now,
an' they'll never be sung mair." But she was clear as
to the *provenance* of her songs, notably " Auld Maitland,"
about which Scott and Leyden had been suspicious. " My
brother and me learned it and many mae frae auld
Andrew Moor, and he learned it frae auld Baby Mettlin,
who was housekeeper to the first laird o' Tushielaw.
She was said to have been anither than a gude ane. . . ."[1]

So came together two men who were destined to
many years of acquaintanceship and—intermittently—
of friendship. Hogg on one side was the essential
peasant, with all a peasant's hard shrewdness and suspicion, but without the good-breeding which is common
in that class on the Border. He was as uncouth a figure
as Leyden, but lacked Leyden's innate gentility. He
took more for granted than most men, and as a rule
managed to carry it off. Unlike Burns he was almost
wholly uneducated, and his self-tuition never gave him
any real mental discipline. He was clever enough to
see that he must adopt character parts and play with a
heavy " make up," and the result was the Shepherd of
the *Noctes Ambrosianæ* and the " Boar of the Forest."
He was without delicate perceptions or the finer kind of
pride ; yet he was a warm-hearted, engaging being, with
a magnificent zest for life. By presuming much he
attained to a good deal. As has been well said, " the
stony social wall against which Burns so often and so
bloodily battered his proud head simply did not exist
for his brother of Ettrick ; and what the one preached
defiantly in song and speech the other innocently
practised."[2] Of his talent there is no question. If, in
Scott's words a " vile sixpenny planet " presided at his
birth, so also did the dancing star under which Beatrice
was born. He was, as he himself claimed, the poet of

[1] There are two versions of the meeting in Ettrick—Hogg's in *Dom. Manners*,
and Laidlaw's in the " Abbotsford Notanda " appended to R. Chambers'
Life of Scott (1871).
[2] Carswell, *Sir Walter : A Four-part Study in Biography*, 175—the most
acute study of Hogg which I have seen.

1802-3 Fairyland, a remote diaphanous fairyland where few can dispute his title ; he had gifts of popular song and produced the best in that line since Burns ; he had the true ballad sense, and could recapture the spirit of the Middle Ages with its shivering jollity and scoffing credulity. For the purpose of the *Minstrelsy* no man could have been better fitted.

The first two volumes, printed by James Ballantyne at Kelso, and bearing the London imprint of Cadell and Davies, were published in 1802. The second edition and the third volume, which appeared a year later, were issued by Longman, Hurst and Co. It met with an immediate success, and was reprinted several times during the following decade. The introduction and notes, which a contemporary reviewer declared to hold material for a hundred romances, reveal how deeply Scott had read himself into the literature and life of the Border. The preliminary essay, though much of it would now be regarded as unhistorical, gives a brilliant panorama of Border history and a sympathetic study of the origins of the ballad. This editorial work was an admirable training for the poet, and still more for the prose writer.

The *Minstrelsy* is a milestone both in Scott's life and in the story of Scottish letters. Motherwell, who looked upon it with a critical eye, estimated that it gave to the world not less than forty-three pieces never before accessible—among them that marvel of the half-world of dreams, " The Wife of Usher's Well " and some of the best riding ballads like " Johnny Armstrong's Goodnight " and " Jamie Telfer." Without Scott these things might have survived, but only in shapeless fragments. Moreover, he has given us versions of many others, prepared by one who was himself a poet, and these versions remain to-day the standard text. Scott was modest about the performance. " I have contrived," he wrote to a friend, " to turn a very slender portion of literary talent to account by a poetical record of the antiquities of the Border." That was his purpose rather than a scholarly edition of different texts, and he therefore not unnaturally included in the volumes modern 1802–3 imitations, based on authentic legends, by himself and Leyden.

His handling of his material has been often criticized. With Leyden's eye on him, he was more careful with his texts than Bishop Percy had been, and his work passed the scrutiny of the austere Ritson. But he had neither the scholar's conscience nor the scholar's apparatus of a modern editor like Professor Child of Harvard. The question of ballad origins is one of the most intricate of literary problems, and it is easy to be over-dogmatic. The wandering violers of genius, who, as I believe, sometime in the sixteenth century made the greatest of the ballads, left no manuscripts, and the folk memory plays odd tricks, now adapting lines to secure a local point, now boldly amending that of which the first meaning has been lost. Scott was reasonably conscientious, but his primary aim was to achieve a standard text—a literary not a scientific purpose ; and he avowedly made up a text out of a variety of copies. Such has been the method of popular editors since literature began. But it seems clear that he never attempted to palm off a piece of his own manufacture as an old ballad, and that, with rare exceptions, he confined his emendations to making sense out of nonsense. Now and then, as in " Jamie Telfer " where he had no text to work from, he interpolated a good deal, very much to the ballad's advantage, and in " Kinmont Willie," where he had only a few half-forgotten lines, he produced what is substantially a work of his own. For the rest he was a skilful, and, up to his lights, a faithful editor of authentic ancient material.[1]

The task played a major part in the direction of his genius. Constant familiarity with the noble bareness of the ballads did much to purify his taste, and to weaken—

[1] The subject has been exhaustively discussed by Mr T. F. Henderson in his edition of the *Minstrelsy* (1892) and by Child in his great collection of ballads (1882-1898). The case against Scott's conscientiousness will be found in Colonel Elliot's *Further Essays on Border Ballads* (1910), which is answered—to my mind conclusively—by Andrew Lang's *Sir W. Scott and the Border Minstrelsy* (1910).

1802-3 unfortunately it did not wholly destroy—the dominance
of the bad models of his youth. It was an education in
directness, in economy of speech at moments of high
drama, in the simplicities of great passion. Wordsworth
writes the story of Helen of Kirkconnell, and achieves
this masterpiece of the falsetto :—

> Proud Gordon, maddened by the thoughts
> That through his brain were travelling,
> Rushed forth, and at the heart of Bruce
> He launched a deadly javelin !
> Fair Ellen saw it as it came,
> And, starting up to meet the same,
> Did with her body cover
> The youth, her chosen lover.

The ballad in the *Minstrelsy* runs :

> I wish I were where Helen lies !
> Night and day on me she cries ;
> And I am weary of the skies,
> For her sake that died for me.

The penultimate line is Scott's own ; not much trace
here of Bürger or Matt Lewis. Take again, this verse
from " Sir Patrick Spens "—

> They hadna sail'd a league, a league,
>   A league but barely three,
> When the lift grew dark, and the wind blew loud,
>   And gurly grew the sea.

The last couplet is almost certainly Scott's. And there
is no doubt at all about his authorship of these stanzas
from " Kinmont Willie."

> He has ta'en the table wi' his hand,
> He garr'd the red wine spring on hie—
> " Now Christ's curse on my head," he said,
> " But avenged on Lord Scrope I'll be !
>
> " O is my basnet a widow's curch ?
>   Or my lance a wand of the willow tree ?
> Or my arm a lady's lily hand
>   That an English lord should lightly me ? "

The versifier has become a poet.

II

The lord-lieutenant of Selkirkshire was a finicking old 1804 gentleman who had once been a lord of the Bedchamber, and was very particular about the fashion of his neck-cloths. To his orderly soul it seemed wrong that the Sheriff should have no dwelling in the Forest, where he was bound by statute to reside for part of the year, but should live in the environs of Edinburgh and behave more like a cavalry officer than a Crown official. He conveyed his views to Scott, and, after protest, Scott submitted. In the spring of 1804 he was looking for a house on the Border. Harden was suggested, but Borthwick water was a bad centre for county business, and he finally decided to take a lease of Ashestiel, the property of a cousin on his mother's side, who was then in India. It was a busy and eventful year for Scott. He had to pack off his scapegrace brother Daniel to the West Indies, and, as a trustee, wind up his uncle Robert Scott's estate. Rosebank near Kelso was left to him, which he sold profitably, and with his share of the residue he found himself richer by some £6000. In the late summer he left Lasswade (the Gandercleugh of the novels) and moved to Ashestiel—a fortunate young man, said the world, with an income of well over £1000, a son of three years and daughters of five and one, perfect bodily health, a comfortable little niche at the Bar, and a rising literary reputation.

The house, half-farm, half-manor, and very ancient in parts, stood on a steep bank which a strip of meadow-land separated from Tweed. There was a little farm attached, with fields of old pasture ; the garden was a beautiful old-world place with green terraces and tall holly hedges. It was reasonably convenient for Edinburgh and the county town ; but it was also a sanctuary, for Tweed beneath it was unbridged and the only road was by a difficult ford, while it fulfilled the traditional desideratum of a Scots dwelling, being seven miles from kirk and market. The place was in the most haunted part of the Border. There the Tweed valley is as yet

1804 a mountain glen, for the river has some miles to go before it breaks from the hills at Yair into the champaign of the lower strath. Behind it to the south lies a dark field of heathery mountains, still clad at that period on the lower slopes with the wildwood of the old Ettrick Forest. An easy pass leads to Yarrow, with Ettrick beyond it and Esk and Ewes, while to the north lie Gala water and the vale of Leader. Minchmoor, across which Montrose fled after Philiphaugh, hangs like a cloud in the west ; the road upstream passes the tower of Elibank, the home of Scott's ancestress Muckle Mou'd Meg, and leads by the little Peeblesshire burghs to the pastoral loveliness of Manor and Holms, the haunts of Merlin Sylvestris, and the wild moorland where Tweed has its springs. There were pleasant or curious neighbours at hand—the Pringles at Yair, the Laidlaws (" Laird Nippy ") at the Peel, the Plummers at Sunderland Hall with its excellent library, and, across the Yarrow bounds, the Buccleuchs at Bowhill, Willie Laidlaw at Blackhouse, and Scott's new friend Mungo Park at the cottage of Foulshiels. Legend and ballad were linked to every field and burn, and the landscape most exquisitely conformed to its human associations, for that corner of Tweedside seems to me especially in tune with Border romance. It is at once wild and habitable, the savagery of nature is tempered by a quality of gracious pastoral, and Tweed, with its pools and runs and gleaming shallows, has not lost its mountain magic.

But Scott could not buy Ashestiel, and he would not be content for long with a hired dwelling. He wanted a home of his own, which he could beautify at his pleasure and leave to his son. He began to cast about for a permanent habitation, and his eyes fell on the little estate of Broadmeadows, just across the hills at the point where Yarrow leaves its bare upper valley for the wooded gorge overhung by Newark's " birchen bower." The place would be presently in the market, and the proceeds of the sale of Rosebank might be used to purchase it. It is hard not to regret that this project failed. Broadmeadows stood on a narrow shelf above

the stream, and no ambition could have made of it 1805
anything but a modest country house ; moreover Scott
would not have been able to spend money on buying
land, for he would have been surrounded, not by bonnet
lairds very ready to sell, but by the inviolable domain
of Buccleuch. Perhaps it was not really the kind of
thing of which he dreamed : his taste was always more
for the broader champaign country which he had learned
to love at Sandy Knowe and Kelso. At any rate, as
we shall see, his uncle Robert's legacy was used for a
very different purpose.

In his new home Scott found a refuge where he could
turn from the common interests of his bustling life to
the serious cultivation of the Muses. Which of the Nine
was to be his chosen deity was not yet clear. But from
his work on the ballads one thing remained over with
which he proposed to try his fortune. He moved into
Ashestiel in the early autumn, and about the same time
sent to the printers a poem of his own, which had proved
to be too long for inclusion in the *Minstrelsy*. He and
his family spent New Year's Day, 1805, on Tweedside,
journeying thither in a snowstorm, preceded by " a
detachment of brandy and mince-pies " in case they
were beleaguered by the weather. In the following week
the *Lay of the Last Minstrel* was given to the world.

It had been long simmering in his brain. Some years
before young Lady Dalkeith at Bowhill had asked him
to write a ballad on the subject of a mysterious goblin,
called Gilpin Horner, whose doings were a legend on the
Border. At Lasswade in 1802 he began his attempt to
carry out the command, and, having a year or two before
heard Sir John Stoddart recite Coleridge's unpublished
" Christabel " and being haunted by its rhythm,[1] he
adopted in the opening stanzas the same manner. Erskine,
to whom he read them, did not care for them, but they
stuck in his memory and presently he changed his
opinion and encouraged his friend to continue. That
autumn Scott finished the first canto, while he was laid

[1] See E. H. Coleridge's edition of *Christabel* (1907), 44-45, where the
subject is fully discussed.

1805 up in Musselburgh lodgings owing to a kick from a trooper's horse. Next year he had several cantos to read to George Ellis under an oak in Windsor Forest, and in the autumn the Wordsworths heard four of the six during their visit to Lasswade " partly read and partly recited in an enthusiastic style of chant," and were delighted by " the novelty of the manner, the clear picturesque descriptions, and the easy flowing energy of much of the verse." Scott had soon abandoned the "Christabel" music, and adopted the rapid octosyllables which were to be the staple of his narrative verse.

His purpose was consciously that of the Minstrel. In the first place he had written the poem at the command of the wife of one who would one day be the head of his clan, and this duty was never forgotten ; compliments and allusions to the family of Buccleuch star the poem, and the felicitous use of the old harper is a piece of pure feudal loyalty. It is dedicated to Lord Dalkeith, and the beautiful close is at once a tribute to a great lady, and the confession of a dream then filling his mind (he was considering the purchase of Broadmeadows) of a lettered life to be spent in the sacred places of chivalry.

> . . . But still
> When summer smiled on sweet Bowhill,
> And July's eve, with balmy breath,
> Wav'd the bluebells on Newark heath ;
> When throstles sung in Hareheadshaw,
> And corn was green on Carterhaugh,
> And flourish'd broad Blackandro's oak,
> The aged Harper's soul awoke.
> Then would he sing achievements high,
> And circumstance of chivalry,
> Till the rapt traveller would stay,
> Forgetful of the closing day ;
> And noble youths, the strain to hear,
> Forsook the hunting of the deer ;
> And Yarrow, as he roll'd along,
> Bore burden to the Minstrel's song.

Again, faithful to the creed which he expressed in his review of Southey's translation of " Amadis of Gaul," he held that a metrical romance should be episodic, a

rhapsody—linked together more tightly indeed than the 1805
old rhapsodies, since it was meant to be read and not
heard, but loose enough to permit the inclusion of wide
variations of matter and manner. He also claimed the
minstrel's historical licence. The events of the *Lay* must
have taken place about 1560—not seventy years, but
several centuries, after Michael Scott's death; not in
the age of faith, when people made their prayer to St
Mary of the Cross, but in the first stress of the Reformation, when the Church was toppling and three years
earlier St Mary's chapel had been burned.

The *Lay*, Scott told Wordsworth, " has the merit of
being written with heart and good will, and for no other
reason than to discharge my mind of the ideas which
from infancy have rushed upon it." That is its primary
charm—it is the first and freshest of Scott's poems, the
one most directly sprung from the memories of his youth.
That is why, too, it is so hard to criticize for one who has
had a similar upbringing and has inherited the same
loyalties. Consideration of Scott as a poet must be
reserved for a later chapter. Here we are rather concerned with the *Lay* as an event in its author's career.
He was modestly convinced that it would have some
success, since it was the ballad manner enlarged and
adapted to a modern audience, and the ballad manner
had already its vogue : he thought that its horseman's
verse and atmosphere of high romance might be new
things to a public a little weary of the decorous strains
of the Augustans. It appeared at a fortunate time, for
Cowper was the only popular poet, and he was not
romantic : Wordsworth and Coleridge were not even
names to the ordinary reader : Burns was inaccessible
to most, and the Popian style had suffered a sad decline.
Upon a world weary of the old measures Scott burst
with a new melody, and to those once captured by the
false glamour of Mrs Radcliffe and Matt Lewis, and
already sated, he brought authentic magic and enduring
romance. The blemishes of the *Lay* are there for a child
to note. The main plot is faulty and much of the
workmanship is hasty and imperfect. There are relapses

1805 into sham Gothick, and Augustan banality, and insipid sweetness. But it is full of noble things, fuller perhaps than any other of Scott's poems—the version of " Dies Iræ," the ballad of " Rosabelle," the ride of William of Deloraine, the muster of the moss-troopers ; there are moments of grim ballad simplicity which he rarely achieved again : and out of resounding place names and family names he got the true Homeric speed and mystery.

With the *Lay* Scott became famous, no longer a connoisseur esteemed by the elect, but the most popular poet of the day. Fox and Pitt alike praised it, the latter making the shrewd comment that some of the effects were what he expected in painting, but had not thought capable of being given by poetry. Edition followed edition at handsome prices to an extent unparalleled in the record of British poetry. The critics were kind, and Jeffrey in the *Edinburgh Review* was notably civil, though he did not satisfy Scott's friends like Ellis and John Hookham Frere. He complained, oddly enough, that the poem lacked incident, and he also considered the style parochial. " Mr Scott," he wrote (and it is one of the inspired follies in the history of criticism)," must either sacrifice his Border prejudices, or offend his readers in other parts of the Empire." Scott had £169, 6s. in royalties from the first edition, and, when a second was called for, sold the copyright to Longmans for £500, receiving also £100 to buy a horse.

III

About the beginning of the century there was a stirring among the dry bones of the book-trade throughout the land. It was part of a universal movement which had been going on for the last decade, owing to a wider diffusion of ideas and a consequent impulse toward self-education ; Napoleon in his youth, observing it as he observed all things, had toyed with the notion of becoming a bookseller. In 1805 Edinburgh, already the centre of a vigorous idiomatic culture, was also becoming

1802

celebrated for its activity in printing and publishing. People were reading more, buying more books, cultivating a taste for magazines—a natural result of the tension of spirit produced by a great war.

This revival, so far as Scotland was concerned, was largely due to a good-looking, full-faced lad, Archibald Constable by name, who seventeen years before, at the age of fourteen, had come from the East Neuk of Fife to be an apprentice in Peter Hill's bookshop in the High Street. He saw the decrepit state of Edinburgh bookselling, and set himself to reform it. At twenty he married the daughter of a prosperous printer and used her dowry to start business next year on his own account. He was inspired by a passionate love of books and all things connected with them, and he had that rare combination, the connoisseurship of the bibliophile and a sound literary judgment. Above all he was an excellent man of business, with an acute perception of the popular taste and its likely developments, and with the courage to back his fancy. Presently the youth grew into a handsome, portly being with an impressive manner, popular for his generosity and good-fellowship, and generally respected for his business talents and patent success. His foible was less pride, for he had that diplomatic skill which demands at least a pretence of modesty, than overweening ambition. He was resolved to create a famous business and to be the Mæcenas of his age; to build up a landed family, too, for he had the traditional Scots passion for acres, and the estate of Balniel in his native shire was to be its foundation.

He had the wit to see that the new readers he wished to cultivate were mostly liberal in politics, so his firm acquired a Whig atmosphere. There was a young English clergyman in Edinburgh, Mr Sydney Smith, who had a plan for an enlightened journal of opinion. In 1802 Constable took up the scheme, greatly enlarged it, and started the *Edinburgh Review* with the parson as editor. Sydney Smith was soon succeeded by Francis Jeffrey, the most brilliant of the young illuminates of the Scots Bar, and the review sprang at once into a wide

1805 popularity, with the editor and Brougham and Horner
as its chief contributors. Scott was also included, for the
Edinburgh's politics at the start were not extreme. The
review, in the publisher's eyes, was less an enterprise
embarked upon for its own sake than an advertisement
on a grand scale for the house of Constable. He was
now, in the year 1805, by far the most commanding
figure in the Scottish book world, and already a name
of repute among London publishers. He had been
associated with Longmans in the publication of the *Lay*,
and had his eye on the Border Sheriff, three years his
senior, who, like himself, seemed both to know what the
public wanted and to be a pioneer in new paths.

Scott was not as yet bound to any publisher, but he
had his favourite printer, James Ballantyne, the friend
of his Kelso schooldays. Ballantyne had none of Constable's magnificence. He was short, stout, bearded and
pompous, a great *bon vivant*, a merry companion, a
preposterous, endearing creature, with one eyebrow
drooping and the other cocked to heaven. He was faithful,
affectionate, and scrupulously honest, and so far he had
been as unsuccessful as other good-natured men. In
Kelso he was doing nothing in his attorney's practice,
and not very much as the editor of the local paper. But
as a printer he had genuine gifts, and, as we have seen,
the *Minstrelsy* had been entrusted to him. Scott did
more for his friend. He had always a peculiar tenderness
for an old crony ; it seemed to him that Ballantyne's
talents as a printer demanded a wider sphere, so he
encouraged him to migrate to Edinburgh. In the
capital he might get a good deal of miscellaneous work
—perhaps the printing of some new journal, or a Scottish
Annual Register, and he might also have a share in the
production of law process-papers. Ballantyne jumped
at the idea, borrowed some hundreds from Scott for the
move, and by the end of 1802 was established with his
two presses in a dingy little shop at Abbeyhill in the
precincts of Holyroodhouse, where the third volume of
the *Minstrelsy* was printed.

At first things went well. Scott procured orders for

the new venture, including the printing of the *Lay*, and 1805
Ballantyne transferred himself to more commodious
premises in the Canongate. But with the enlargement of
his business came the need for further capital, for neither
of the pair seems to have understood that more money
must be risked before bigger profits could be won. The
success of the *Lay* embarrassed the printer and he applied
to Scott for another loan. The request came at a moment
when Scott had suddenly marched into literary fame,
and saw before him a career very different from that of
an advocate in small practice. He had come to sit very
loose to that calling, and was beginning to envisage the
future in a new light. Ashestiel was increasing his love
for the life of a country gentleman, he had an assured
income of something over £1000 a year, and the prospect
of soon obtaining a well-paid post as one of the Clerks of
the Supreme Court. This would give him the necessary
crutch, and literature would add a welcome staff.[1] But
why should he confine literature to the work of his own
pen ? He had in his mind poems which he meant to
write, histories too, and a vast amount of editing. But
might he not also have a share in the commercial side,
for he had always an eager interest in affairs, and loved
the atmosphere of them as much as Dr Johnson when he
became Mr Thrale's executor. He had enough of his
father in him to respect those engaged in the practical
work of the world. James Ballantyne's business seemed
to offer the chance of a lifetime. Here was one who
understood printing and had already made a name for
his work ; he himself would feed the press with his own
productions and those of his friends : the liabilities
seemed trifling, the profits a certainty. So he gave up
all thought of the purchase of Broadmeadows, and in
the early months of 1805 used his uncle Robert's legacy
to buy a third share in Ballantyne's firm. The arrangement was kept profoundly confidential, only Erskine
being in the secret.

On this matter much arrant nonsense has been written.
It has been condemned as somehow discreditable and

---

[1] Introd. to *Lay*, 1830.

1805 dishonest, incompatible with Scott's position as a judge
and a prospective Court official. A barrister, it has been
urged, should not be a partner in a secret commercial
enterprise. I can see no warrant for the view. Before
the modern development of joint-stock companies one
of the commonest ways of investing spare capital was
by lending money to some enterprise and receiving in
lieu of interest a certain share in the profits. It was no
more the custom to blazon such investments abroad than
it is the custom to-day for a man to broadcast his share
holdings. There was nothing to be ashamed of in investing money in the printing trade. Books were the fashion,
fine printing was becoming the hobby of all cultivated
men, and what hobby more suitable for a man of Scott's
tastes and position than this association with an old
friend in a craft to which his interest was deeply pledged ?
Had Scott remained a lawyer and nothing else, I cannot
see how his association with the Ballantyne business
could be criticized.

Criticism arises because he was a writer, and because
he and his partner were the men they were. The step he
took in 1805 was not dishonourable, but it was rash and
ill-advised. Scott himself had a sound instinct for
business, when he had the time to give his mind to it ;
but he could not, owing to the conditions of his life, pay
much attention to the printing house in the Canongate.
The mere fact that the matter was kept secret excluded
it from the atmosphere of common sense. It became a
part of that inner world of his to which he was prone
to retire, a magical device for earning easy money, and
his usual robust intelligence was never brought into play.
Nor was Ballantyne the man to supplement his partner's
defects. He was enthusiastic, excitable, a muddler in
finance, incapable of presenting at any time an accurate
statement of his assets and liabilities. Neither he nor
Scott, as I have said, realized that the more a business
extends the more capital it needs, since incomings have
a way of lagging behind outgoings. He had no capital,
except two printing presses cumbered with debts, and
as his orders increased he must have recourse to his

partner, and to the banks. Uncle Robert's legacy was 1805 bound to be only the first of the contributions from Ashestiel.

The venture was peculiarly dangerous for a man of letters. Scott wanted grist for the Ballantyne mill, and therefore he was fertile in proposals to publishers for tasks to be undertaken by him and executed in the Canongate. This was to involve him in much laborious hack-work, which was scarcely worthy of his genius. Moreover—and this is the one point on which a moral criticism is perhaps justified—it obscured his judgment of commercial values, and, though he did not realize it, put more than one publisher in a false position. If Scott recommended a book, and Ballantyne printed it, Scott had no liability and he had a share of the printing profits, but the publishers were unable, through their ignorance of the partnership, to discount the bias in his judgment. Lockhart has written on this point with fairness and reason :—

It is an old saying, that wherever there is a secret there must be something wrong ; and dearly did he pay the penalty for the mystery in which he had chosen to involve this transaction. It was his rule, from the beginning, that whatever he wrote or edited must be printed at that press ; and had he catered for it only as author and sole editor, all had been well ; but had the booksellers known his direct pecuniary interest in keeping up and extending the operation of these types, they would have taken into account his lively imagination and sanguine temperament, as well as his taste and judgment, and considered, far more deliberately than they often did, his multifarious recommendations of new literary schemes, coupled though these were with some dim undertaking that, if the Ballantyne press were employed, his own literary skill would be at his friend's disposal for the general superintendence of the undertaking. On the other hand, Scott's suggestions were, in many cases, perhaps in the majority of them, conveyed through Ballantyne, whose habitual deference to his opinion induced him to advocate them with enthusiastic zeal ; and the printer, who had thus pledged his personal authority for the merits of the proposed scheme, must have felt himself committed to the booksellers, and could hardly refuse with decency to take a certain share of the pecuniary risk, by allowing the time and method of his own payment to be regulated according to the employer's convenience. Hence, by degrees, was woven a web of entanglement from which neither Ballantyne nor his adviser had any means of escape. . . .[1]

For the next nine years Scott led the life of a miscellaneous writer at its busiest. He must feed the Canongate mill which was to bring him fortune, and he must find scope for his eager interest in books and the life of the past and a use for the store of varied knowledge which he had been accumulating since boyhood. Many of his tasks must be dreary collar-work, but that did not deter one who in his father's office had learned to toil at uncongenial labours ; most must be obscure and anonymous, but that rather pleased him. Some of the best had preferred anonymity—Swift, for example, whose works he thought of editing, and who had scarcely acknowledged one of his books, and his old friend Henry Mackenzie. He had no special desire for literary fame, and he had no delusions about his own talents. A Border laird was his ideal rather than a distinguished man of letters, but a Border laird must have an agreeable hobby to fill his time and money to support his dignity.

His mind turned first to those editions of the English classics which no gentleman's library could be without. Literature was not yet an article of popular consumption —he himself was to assist in making it that—and the booksellers' chief hope lay in the cabinets of lettered squires and the stately libraries of the great, which must have a quota of books to furnish the spaces between the family portraits. These books must be edited, and the name of the author of the *Lay* would well become a title-page. Poetry, as he told Ellis a year or two later, was a scourging crop which should not be overdone, but editing was to be likened to a " good crop of turnips and peas, extremely useful for those whose circumstances do not admit of their giving their farm a summer fallow."

His first scheme, suggested to Constable, which mercifully came to nothing, was for a complete edition of the British poets, ancient and modern, in at least a hundred tomes. There was also a proposal to Longmans for a

[1] II. 42.

corpus of the English chroniclers. Finally Mr Miller of 1808
Albemarle Street commissioned an edition of Dryden in
eighteen volumes at fifty guineas a volume. Scott
plunged with zest into the task, read widely, visited the
English libraries, employed a staff of amanuenses and
copyists. He would have nothing to do with an expur-
gated text, which was Ellis's suggestion. " I will not
castrate John Dryden. I would as soon castrate my own
father, as I believe Jupiter did of yore. . . . It is not
passages of ludicrous indelicacy that corrupt the manners
of the people—it is the sonnets which a prurient genius
. . . sings *virginibus puerisque*—it is the sentimental slang,
half lewd, half methodistic, that debauches the understanding."[1] The subject was after his own heart, for he
had an instinctive comprehension of the seventeenth
century, and Dryden with his robust intelligence and
magnificent ardour was the kind of poet he was well able
to understand. Dryden was not a poet's poet, any more
than his editor ; as Wordsworth complained, " his is
not a poetical genius." The edition was published in
April 1808, and was well received, Hallam reviewing it
sympathetically in the *Edinburgh*. Indeed it is an
excellent piece of work, which Mr Saintsbury has called
one of the best edited books in the language. Scott
proved himself an accurate, laborious and sagacious com-
mentator, and his life of Dryden is at once good biography
and good criticism. There is an excellent passage on the
respective values of the rapier and the bludgeon in satire,
some acute comments on Dryden's religious beliefs, and
on his character—" his indelicacy was like the forced
impudence of a bashful man " ; Dryden's prose is
judiciously praised and his intellectual limits (with which
the editor sympathized) shrewdly defined :—

> He is often contented to leave the path of argument which
> must have conducted him to the fountain of truth, and to
> resort with indolence or indifference to the leaky cisterns
> which had been hewn out by former critics.[2]

Never is the editor's style more spirited than when
discussing Dryden's literary earnings.

[1] Lockhart, II. 77.   [2] *Misc. Prose Works*, I. 407.

1809-14   The next main venture in editing, the *Swift* which
took six years to complete, was less fortunate. The price
indeed was nearly doubled—£1500 from Constable ; but,
though the Dean of St Patrick's was one of Scott's
favourite authors, he did not start, as in the case of
Dryden, with a sound knowledge of the times, and he
had not the interest in the intrigues of Whig and Tory
that he had in Commonwealth and Restoration and
Revolution. Moreover, to understand the intricacies of
Swift's character required a sharper psychological insight
than Scott possessed, and to assess the virtues of his
style a more fastidious ear for prose rhythms. Yet the
preliminary memoir is well worth reading, for it is full
of strong good sense, and sheds much light on Scott's
own philosophy of life and letters. In particular there
is a passage on the art of fiction, which is one of the few
occasions when Scott theorizes on the literary form in
which he was to win his chief successes.[1] I quote two
other extracts which illuminate Scott's own code. Take
this on inverted snobbery :—

> The whim of publicly sending the prime minister into the
> House of Commons to call out the first secretary of state, only
> to let him know that he would not dine with him if he dined
> late ; the insisting that a duke should make him the first visit
> merely because he was a duke—these, and other capricious
> exertions of despotic authority over the usual customs of
> society, are unworthy of Swift's good sense and penetration.
> In a free country, the barriers of etiquette between the ranks
> of society are but frail and low, the regular gate is open, and
> the tax of admittance a trifle ; and he who, out of mere wanton-
> ness, overleaps the fence, may be justly supposed not to have
> attained a philosophical indifference to the circumstance of
> being born in the excluded district.[2]

And this, which may be taken as the editor's own rule
of life :—

> From the life of Swift, therefore, may be derived the
> important lesson, that, as no misfortunes should induce genius
> to despair, no rank or fame, however elevated, should encourage
> its possessor to presumption.[3]

---

[1] *Misc. Prose Works,* II. 437-440.   [2] *Ibid.,* II. 119.   [3] *Ibid.,* II. 2.

On the upper shelves of old libraries we may still find handsome quartos and octavos, the fruits of the Ballantyne press, which contain Scott's other editorial labours, for the *Dryden* and the *Swift* were only the larger fish in a great shoal. There was Sir Ralph Sadleir's *State Papers* in three volumes, and Somers's *Tracts* in thirteen, the *Memoirs* of Sir Henry Slingsby and of Captain Hodgson, of Captain Carleton and of Robert Cary, Earl of Monmouth, besides lesser antiquarian *curiosa*. These things delighted Scott as an historian, and they provided work for James Ballantyne, but they did not pay the publishers. There was even a vast edition of the British novelists, projected by young Mr Murray, which fortunately had to be postponed. It was all a colossal labour, undertaken partly from enthusiasm, partly for gain, and largely out of kindness, for it gave Scott a chance of doing a good turn to less fortunate writers than himself. " I like well," Constable once complained, "Scott's ain bairns, but Heaven preserve me from those of his following ! " " It was enough to tear me to pieces," Scott once told Lockhart, " but there was a wonderful exhilaration about it all ; my blood was kept at fever-pitch—I felt as if I could have grappled with anything and everything ; then, there was hardly one of my schemes that did not afford me the means of serving some poor devil of a brother author. There were always huge piles of material to be arranged, sifted, or indexed—volumes of extracts to be transcribed—journeys to be made hither and thither, for ascertaining the little facts and dates—in short, I could commonly keep half a dozen of the ragged regiment of Parnassus in tolerable ease." Like coal-wagons linked to an engine, Lockhart suggested. Scott laughed—" Yes, but there was a cursed lot of dung carts too."[1]

Nor were books all. There was a steady flow of contributions to the *Edinburgh* on topics as diverse as Spenser and cookery books, Ossian and Colonel Thornton's Sporting Tour. Presently Scott began to find this

[1] Lockhart, II. 173-4.

1808 connexion trying to his temper. Jeffrey, the editor, reviewed his work in a strain of high condescension, not free from acidity, and the politics of the review seemed to be becoming not Whiggish merely, but Jacobin. The number which contained the criticism of *Marmion* contained a paper on current politics which made the shrewd Mr Murray calculate that the alliance could not last, since " Walter Scott has feelings both as a gentleman and a Tory which these people have wounded." An article on the Spanish situation, which we should describe to-day as " defeatist," was the last straw, and Scott withdrew his subscription.[1] In October 1808 Mr Murray arrived at Ashestiel with a proposal for a rival to the *Edinburgh*, a Tory review to be called the *Quarterly*, with behind it the old staff of the *Anti-Jacobin*, men like Canning and Hookham Frere, and with Heber, Ellis and Southey as contributors. Scott was offered and refused the editorship, which went to William Gifford, but he gladly promised his support, and thereby began a long connexion with the new review, under both Gifford and Lockhart. Some of his best essays appeared in its pages, for Scott, like other men of letters, had to have some outlet for episodic work, *causeries* which were often the expansion of his table talk. He was always a kindly and courteous critic, and held himself aloof from the bludgeoning treatment of the " Cockney school " and the new Jacobinical poets, for he had in literature a true spirit of freemasonry.

But the alliance with the *Quarterly* was to bring him unhappily into the rancours of the political world. Scott escaped the maleficent extension of these rancours into literature, and never fell into the " facetious and rejoicing ignorance " of the swashbucklers on both sides. For, let it be remembered that the one was as bad as the other, and that the venom of the *Quarterly* towards Keats was paralleled by the savagery of the *Edinburgh* towards Wordsworth and Coleridge. The brisk com-

---

[1] Scott and Lockhart believed the article to have been written by Brougham ; but the author was Jeffrey himself. Cockburn, *Life of Jeffrey*, I. 191.

placency of Jeffrey, which made Wordsworth's toe itch
for his hinder parts,[1] was bound sooner or later to
revolt a man of Scott's fundamental reverence and
deep historic sense. But in his alliance with the *Edinburgh's* opponents he did more than profess a different
philosophy of life ; he aligned himself definitely as a
political partisan and acquired a party colour, which
was, not altogether happily, to affect his career. Political
views he had always had, but hitherto they had been
confined to two simple loyalties—an affection for Britain,
which made him a furious opponent of all that crippled
her arms in the greatest war that she had ever fought,
and a still deeper and more abiding affection for Scotland.
To the illuminati of the *Edinburgh*, as to the illuminati
in every age, such simple emotions were scarcely intelligible—they might be condescendingly approved, but
could never be shared. Lockhart has a tale of Scott
walking back with Jeffrey from a discussion on some
proposed Scottish legal change, when the latter tried to
treat the matter as a joke. " No, no," Scott cried, " 'tis
no laughing matter. Little by little, whatever your
wishes may be, you will destroy and undermine, until
nothing of what makes Scotland shall remain." And
he turned away to hide his tears.[2]

But now he had gone further, and had enlisted under
the Tory flag, and, being a born fighter, was certain to
lay lustily about him. A party affiliation is doubtless
a good thing for the ordinary citizen, but it is less good
for one who, not being a politician, acquires from his
temperament the politician's restless combativeness. It
would have been well for his future peace if he had taken
Lord Dalkeith's advice :—" Talk not, think not, of
Politics. Go to the hills and converse with the Spirit of
the Fell, or any spirit but the Spirit of Party, which is
the fellest fiend that ever disturbed harmony and social
pleasure." [3]

Throughout all his editorial and journalistic labours
the " regiment of horse " was still exercising in his

---

[1] *P. L. B.*, 65.   [2] Lockhart, II. 110.   [3] *Fam. Letters*, I. 33.

1808 head. He was still in his dreams leading his troops by moonlight out of the burning valley. He wanted money to help his brother Thomas, and Constable offered a thousand guineas for a poem before he had seen a line of it. The new work, unlike the *Lay*, had not its origin in the Border lore of his youth, for it was a concocted tale of chivalry, with an elaborate plot, culminating in the great national tragedy of Flodden. Its inspiration was the martial fervour which ran in Scott's veins, the ardent patriotism with which the spectacle of the great events on the Continent filled his mind. He put into it also the friendships which had come to fill his life, and the introductory epistles to the cantos are a happy diary of his Border wanderings and the sights and sounds of Ashestiel. He enjoyed every moment of the writing of it, and to the end of his life he used to recall happily places associated with its composition. The speed of the verse is due to the fact that passages like the description of Flodden were conceived while with his regiment on Portobello sands, or galloping among the hills between Tweed and Yarrow. He made no parade of a high poetic purpose. As it approached its close he wrote to Lady Louisa Stuart :—" Marmion is at this instant gasping upon Flodden Field, and there I have been obliged to leave him for these few days in the death pangs. I hope I shall find time enough this morning to knock him on the head with two or three thumping stanzas."

A poem, thus conceived in delight, was bound to please. *Marmion* was published in February 1808 and proceeded to race through editions. The critics were divided. Wordsworth thought that Scott had achieved his end, but added : " That it is not the end which I should wish you to propose to yourself, you will be well aware, from what you know of my notions of composition, both as to manner and matter." Jeffrey in the *Edinburgh*, curiously enough, chose to regard it as insufficiently Scottish in spirit, and having " throughout neglected Scottish feelings and Scottish character." The rest of the review was a solemn warning that the romance

of chivalry was a bogus fashion which could not last. 1810
" Fine ladies and gentlemen now talk of donjons, keeps,
tabards, scutcheons, caps of maintenance, portcullises,
wimples, and I know not what beside ; just as they did
in the days of Dr Darwin's popularity of gnomes, sylphs,
oxygen, gossamer, polygynia, and polyandria. That
fashion, however, passed rapidly away, and Mr Scott
should take care that a different sort of pedantry does
not produce the same effects."

Jeffrey was attacking the genus without considering
closely the particular example, for it is hard to find
pedantry in *Marmion*. Halting lines, rhetoric which
misses its mark, machinery that creaks—of these there
is plenty. The plot is roughly that of *Ivanhoe*, a commonplace of romance. But the virtue lies not in it, but in
the speed of the journeys, the fire of the battle scenes,
the many faithful and beautiful pictures of nature, the
noble and disciplined eloquence of the lines on Nelson
and Fox and Pitt. It was the tonic which the nation
needed in a dark time to strengthen its heart, and
if the critics were lukewarm the common reader was
enchanted.

Next year Scott visited the Highlands, for he had long
had it in mind to produce a northern pendant to the
Lay and *Marmion*. More scrupulous than most poets,
he rode the course from the mouth of Loch Vennachar
to Stirling Castle to make certain that his hero could do
it in three hours. At Buchanan he recited bits of his
new poem to Lady Douglas and Lady Louisa Stuart, and
in May 1810 it was given to the world under a title
reminiscent of Arthurian legend, *The Lady of the Lake*.
No one of Scott's poems was more eagerly awaited or
more ardently received. It made the Trossachs a classic
country, to which the curious flocked in post-chaises. It
brought the Highlands, of which Scott knew next to
nothing, inside the comprehension of the Lowlands and
of England. So great was its verisimilitude that Border
farmers argued hotly about the details of the stag-hunt,
and so enthralling its interest that Adam Ferguson,
serving under Wellington in the Peninsula with the

1810 "Black Cuffs," obtained extra rations because of his reading of the poem aloud, and on one occasion read the battle scene to keep his company steady while under fire. Such tributes are not paid to a pedantic muse.

The book marks the height of Scott's popularity as a poet, for 20,000 copies were sold in a few months. For once the critics were unanimous in their verdict, and Jeffrey in the *Edinburgh* was as cordial as Ellis in the *Quarterly*. The success was so extraordinary, Scott himself wrote, "as to induce me for a moment to conclude that I had at last fixed a nail in the proverbially inconstant wheel of Fortune." Re-read to-day, the poem has not lost its freshness. There are perhaps too many Gothick echoes, to which a Celtic subject always made Scott prone, and there is much slipshod verse. But it begins magically; everywhere there are lovely glimpses of scene and weather; the stag-hunt, the dispatch of the fiery cross, the battle, the final "recognition" have still power to thrill hearts that have not forgotten their youth; and the intercalated lyrics, like Blanche's song, and the "Coronach," and "Soldier, rest, thy warfare o'er," foreshadowed what the novels were to reveal, a Shakespearean gift of producing little snatches of music which fit into their place with an exquisite and effortless aptness.

IV

The Ashestiel years are the pleasantest to contemplate in Scott's life. If they were not the time of greatest achievement, and if they were not altogether unbroken by anxieties, they had the wide horizons and the fresh colours which come only once in a man's career.

He was fortunate to begin with to find a permanent post which relieved him of anxiety about the future. Mr George Home of Wedderburn had been a Clerk of Session for more than thirty years and was very willing to retire, on condition that he was allowed to retain his emoluments during his life. Scott was nominated his successor, and his appointment was ratified by the Whig

government which came into office on Pitt's death. So
after the spring recess in 1806 he took up his duties,
sitting below the judges for from four to six hours daily
during nearly six months of the year. His fellow Clerks
were intimate friends, and the work kept him in close
touch with the Bar and Bench, and gave him a wonderful
viewpoint from which to study that large section of
humanity which goes to law. It was—or would be,
when Mr Home was gathered to his fathers—an ideal
crutch for a man of letters.

His office not only provided a ritual for his days, but
bound him to the life of the capital, and prevented him
rusticating on the Border. He continued his volunteer
service, and, while in Cumberland in the autumn of
1805, was summoned north by a mistaken rumour that
a French invasion was imminent, and rode a hundred
miles in twenty-four hours to join the muster at Dalkeith.
He paid various visits to London, staying either with his
friends the Doumergues in Piccadilly or with Morritt in
Portland Place. In London he was now something of a
figure, met most of the great people in literature and
politics, was presented at the little Court at Blackheath
to Caroline, Princess of Wales, whom he found em-
barrassingly flirtatious, and even dined at Holland
House. He made many trips up and down Scotland,
including a visit to the Western Isles in 1810, where he
projected a poem which took shape later as *The Lord of
the Isles*, and acquired a new store of Highland legends.
Once, after the publication of *The Lady of the Lake*, he
dreamed of a bolder journey, of " taking a peep at Lord
Wellington and his merry men in Portugal "; for his
imagination had been fired by the adventure of a civilian
friend, who had been mixed up with the retreat to Torres
Vedras, had stumbled on a Scottish regiment, and had
served with it as a volunteer sharpshooter at Busaco.
For such an experience Scott would have given a year's
income. But he had to content himself with writing
patriotic prose and militant verse, and with drinking
Lord Wellington's health at the dinners of the Friday
Club.

For more than six months of the year he was at
Ashestiel and to Ashestiel came many friends. It was
not a large house, but any roof that sheltered Scott was
elastic in its hospitality. Thither came his Edinburgh
legal colleagues, intimates like Skene and Erskine and
Morritt, publishers like young Mr Murray, fellow book-
men like Southey and Heber, and a great clan of country
neighbours. No man was more popular than Scott in
the Forest with gentle and simple alike, and Laird Nippy
next door at the Peel, an austere and parsimonious
Presbyterian, became a regular attendant of a Sunday
at the Sheriff's readings from the English prayer-book.
Scott carried his guests far and wide over the Border—
to Melrose and Dryburgh, to course hares on the steep
green hills above St Mary's Loch, and to the clippings
and kirns of Yarrow and Ettrick. As a host he had
every virtue, and there is ample evidence that at his
own table he was a famous story-teller, full of drollery
and wild fun. His recitations of poetry, too, were
memorable, but, though his head was full of books, his
talk was not often of literature. " He always maintained the same estimate of it," says Morritt, " as
subordinate and auxiliary to the purposes of life, and
rather talked of men and events than of books and
criticism." Even Hogg, who liked the sound of his
own voice and was a severe judge of after-dinner tales,
admits that he never heard him tell the same story
twice.

Scott was now a man in early middle life, strong in
body, unshaken in health, keeping down his inclination
to heaviness by hard exercise, with an overflowing zest
for both work and play. At Lasswade he had been in the
habit of writing and reading late into the night, but,
with his new accumulation of work, he realized that he
must revise his ways, since the midnight oil gave him
headaches. So at Ashestiel he rose at five, lit his own
fire, if a fire were needed, and was at his desk in breeches
and shooting jacket by six o'clock. There, with a dog
at his feet, he worked till between nine and ten, when
he breakfasted with his family. By then he had, in his

own phrase, " broken the neck of the day's work," and 1804–12
after another couple of hours he was free. He was
usually in the saddle by one o'clock. On a wet day he
would work longer, so as to provide a reserve which he
could draw upon when an expedition was planned which
meant starting after breakfast. He answered every
letter the day it arrived, and he kept his papers and
books in perfect order, so that no time was wasted. On
Sunday he read prayers in the parlour to his household
and such neighbours as cared to attend ; the horses
were never taken out on that day, but, if fine, he and
the family would picnic out of doors, and, if it rained,
he would tell them Bible stories.

There were now four children, Sophia, born in 1799,
Walter (whom the family called " Gilnockie "), born in
1801, Anne, born in the beginning of 1803, and Charles,
who was born the day before the Christmas of 1805.
Scott was a great lover of the plain human child, such
as were his own, for the young Scotts had none of the
precocious brilliance of Marjorie Fleming.[1] As soon
as they could move about they became his companions,
and were allowed to run in and out of his study as they
pleased. He disliked the idea of boarding-schools, so
the girls had a governess, while the boys went to the
High School in Edinburgh, and at Ashestiel were tutored
by their father, who yawned prodigiously over the Latin
grammar. He taught them old songs and tales, played
with them, rode and walked with them, and let them sit
up to supper as a reward of virtue—that close companion-
ship which is the greatest formative force in childhood.
Above all he taught them his own cheerful stoicism.

There was one thing, however, on which he fixed his heart
hardly less than the ancient Persians of the Cyropædia ; like
them, next to love of truth, he held love of horsemanship for
the prime point of education. As soon as his eldest girl could
sit a pony, she was made the regular attendant of his mountain
rides ; and they all, as they attained sufficient strength, had
the like advancement. He taught them to think nothing of

---

[1] See Dr John Brown's *Horæ Subsecivæ*, 3rd Series, 199, etc.

tumbles, and habituated them to his own reckless delight in perilous fords and flooded streams ; and they all imbibed in great perfection his passion for horses—as well, I may venture to add, as his deep reverence for the more important article of that Persian training. "Without courage," he said, "there cannot be truth, and without truth there can be no other virtue." [1]

In that household there was little talk of modern books and none at all of the father's work. Apart from the fact that he did not regard his own poetry as of supreme merit, Scott had the good sense to see that an atmosphere of domestic admiration is bad for both admired and admirer. James Ballantyne once asked Sophia what she thought of *The Lady of the Lake*, and her answer was, " Oh, I have not read it. Papa says there's nothing so bad for young people as reading bad poetry." Young Walter was dubbed the Lady of the Lake at the High School, and, not having heard of the work, assumed that he had been called a girl, and engaged in violent fisticuffs. But the supreme instance of that indifference to their father's poetic fame which the father so notably shared is Lockhart's tale of how the same boy was once cross-examined by one of Scott's colleagues in the Court as to why people made so much fuss about his father. The child pondered for a little and then answered gravely : " It's commonly *him* that sees the hare sitting."

Next to the children in the family circle came the dogs, the first of the retinue which attended Scott all his days. There were a couple of greyhounds, Douglas and Percy, who leaped in and out of the open study window, and were noted performers on the hill. Especially there was Camp, the bull-terrier, to whom Scott always spoke as he would to a man, a wise old fellow as compared to the lighthearted grews. Camp began to fail in 1808, and could no longer accompany his master's pony, but waited on the hearth-rug to greet his homecoming. The old dog died in Edinburgh in the beginning of the following year and was buried in the little garden

1 Lockhart, II. 191.

behind the house in Castle Street, while the whole family stood in tears round the grave.

At Ashestiel, too, Scott laid the foundation of the clan of serving-men who played so large a part in his life. One day in the Selkirk sheriff-court a poacher called Tom Purdie came up for trial, and escaped on some formality. Scott liked his looks, and took him into his employ as shepherd, and presently Tom became the "laird's man," factotum, guardian and affectionate tyrant—a familiar Scots relationship. He was the most faithful of henchmen, and his manner was a kind of genial ferocity. Years later, when Tom was fifty-seven, Scott drew what seems to be his portrait in *Redgauntlet*: "His brow was not much furrowed, and his jet-black hair was only grizzled, not whitened, by the advance of age. . . . Though rather undersized, he had very broad shoulders, was square made, thin-flanked, and apparently combined in his frame muscular strength and activity. . . . A hard and harsh countenance, eyes far sunk under projecting eyebrows which were grizzled like his hair, a wide mouth furnished from ear to ear with a range of unimpaired teeth of uncommon whiteness, and of a size and breadth which might have become the jaws of an ogre." Then there was Tom Purdie's brother-in-law, Peter Mathieson, the coachman, who was a safer charioteer in the rough fords of Tweed than his master. Nor must the portly butler be omitted, John Macbeth, who regarded with disfavour those guests who kept Scott up into the small hours over rummers of toddy.

There was a little farm at Ashestiel on which Scott tried his amateur's hand at sheep. When he first took the place, as he wrote to Ellis, "long sheep and short sheep, and tups, and gimmers, and hogs, and dinmonts made a perfect sheepfold of my understanding." To begin with he had a notion of getting James Hogg to superintend the business, which would have led to disaster, for Hogg, though he wrote a book on the diseases of sheep, was a muddler in practice. Mrs Scott had a chicken-run, which was devastated by a formidable local breed of wild-cat. His own main interest was

1804–12 forestry, and at Ashestiel, though the land was only leased, he began those experiments in planting which were later to clothe the Abbotsford braes. Scott was never intended for a farmer, for, as he told Joanna Baillie, it gave him no pleasure to see his turnips better than his neighbour's, and he preferred his shearers to be happy rather than efficient. All his employees were sportsmen—" my hind shall kill a salmon, and my plough-boy find a hare sitting with any man in the Forest "—and he would not have had it otherwise.

Sport, indeed, was, apart from letters, the serious business of Ashestiel. Scott liked to be ten hours a day in the open air, shooting, fishing, coursing and riding, a " rattle-skulled half-lawyer, half-sportsman," as he called himself. In fishing he was no great performer in the orthodox parts, but he loved to " burn the water " of an autumn night, when the salmon were " turning up their sides like swine." On such occasions he was as much in the river as out of it, and indeed he seems to have had an extraordinary talent for falling into fords and pools and bogs and emerging unharmed. He was constantly wet, and rarely troubled to change, thereby sowing the seeds of his later rheumatism. He was noted for the boldness of his riding in a countryside of bold riders. It was a common prophecy that some day he would be brought home with his feet foremost. He rode horses which no one else could mount, and he was also an assiduous horse-master, loving the ritual of their management. " Mr Scott, that's the maddest deil o' a beast," Hogg cried on one occasion. " Can ye no' gar him tak' a wee mair time ? He's just out o' ae lair intil another wi' ye." [1]

In those happy days, quartering the Border hills, mixing freely with all classes, sitting as judge in the little sheriff-court,[2] or in his seat below the Edinburgh Bench watching that panorama of the law which is a reflex of the panorama of life, Scott was amassing stores

---

[1] *Dom. Manners*, 65-6.
[2] Scott made an excellent Sheriff, and his decisions may be studied in Chisholm's *Sir Walter Scott as a Judge* (1918).

of knowledge which needed for their outlet something
greater than romantic lays. The novelist was in the
making. What was taken in by the eye was ruminated
upon in the long sessions of thought which fall to those
who tramp the moors or watch by the riverside. The
creative imagination was beginning its work. " While
Tom marks out a dyke or a drain as I directed him, my
fancy may be running its ain riggs in another world."

CHAPTER V

FAREWELL TO POESY

(1810–1814)

I

1810 IN the envoy to *The Lady of the Lake*, when the Minstrel bids farewell to his harp, there are these lines :—

> Much have I owed thy strains on life's long way,
>   Through secret woes the world has never known,
> When on the weary night dawn'd wearier day
>   And bitterer was the grief devour'd alone.
> That I o'erlive such woes, Enchantress ! is thine own.

The reference is, of course, to his old love affair with Williamina Stuart, but there may be other things included, for Scott had many thorns in his bed of life. One was his kindred. For as he advanced in the world his brothers declined.

Thomas, who had inherited the family business and had been his brother's chief client, so mismanaged his affairs that he became insolvent. He had been appointed the Edinburgh " doer " for the Abercorn estate, and Scott, since he had been one of his guarantors, was compelled to take a hand in clearing up the mess, for which settlement, as we have seen, Constable's advance on *Marmion* fell in opportunely. Thomas, pending an arrangement with his creditors, was compelled to withdraw to the sanctuary of the Isle of Man, where Scott tried to persuade him to cultivate letters and to become one of the *Quarterly's* contributors. Thomas, however, preferred to dabble in soldiering, took a hand in raising the new Manx Fusiliers, and ultimately became paymaster of the 70th Regiment. Presently his brotherly

kindness involved Scott in an unpleasant affair. When 1810
Thomas's finances grew embarrassed, a subordinate post
in the Court became vacant to which Scott had the
right of presentation. He promoted a veteran official,
but gave his brother the smaller office thus vacated,
worth about £250 a year. The duties were the merest
routine, and could be performed, as they had often been
in the past, by deputy, so Thomas in the Isle of Man
could still be the nominal holder and draw the salary.
But, when the appointment was made, a Commission
of Judicature was at work, pruning some of the dead
wood from the tree of Scots law, and it was certain that
Thomas's little sinecure would be one of the first to
disappear. Sure enough the Commission recommended
it for abolition, and assessed the compensation to the
holder at £130 per annum. This was a loss to the refugee
Thomas, which Scott did his best to make up to him,
but worse was to follow. The bill, embodying the
Commission's findings, came before the House of Lords
in 1810, and two Whig peers, Lord Lauderdale and Lord
Holland, attacked the proposed compensation as a
flagrant Tory job, arguing that Thomas had been appointed
when the end of the office was foreseen, and that the
Isle of Man was not the best place for performing the
work of an Edinburgh Court official. The bill duly
passed, but Scott was furious at the insult. The thing
had been a job, no doubt, but such jobs were sanctioned
by long custom, and he believed that, in refusing to
appoint his brother to the better paid post, he had
behaved with quixotic scrupulousness. Lauderdale was
a crazy Jacobin, but Holland should have known better,
and he markedly cut the latter nobleman at a dinner of
the Friday Club.

The case of his youngest brother was a far deeper
vexation. Daniel Scott, having taken to evil courses,
was shipped off to the West Indies. But Jamaica proved
no cure, he went downhill in mind and body, and during a
negro rebellion on the plantation where he was employed
he did not show the family courage. He returned home
with this stigma on his name, was taken into his mother's

house, and soon died. Scott would not see him ; he called him his " relative," not his brother ; he declined to go to his funeral or wear mourning for him. In those high-flying days he could forgive most faults, but not cowardice, and he felt that by the unhappy Dan the family scutcheon had been indelibly stained. It was almost the only case where Scott's abundant charity failed him. The years were to bring him to a humaner mind, and in *The Fair Maid of Perth* he attempted in his account of Conachar the justification of a temporary coward, an expiation, he told Lockhart, to the *manes* of poor Dan. " I have now learned to have more tolerance and compassion than I had in those days."

But the sore which never ceased to gall the steed was the long-drawn bickering with his publishers, and all that it involved. We have seen his quarrel with Constable over the *Edinburgh*, but there was more than politics in the disagreement. Constable was well enough in his way—he was a shrewd man with some pretensions to manners, but he had a partner whom Scott could not abide. This was one Alexander Gibson Hunter, an Angus laird who had a good head for figures and a rough tongue, and who seemed to Scott to reduce every question to a matter of pounds and pence. Hunter was undoubtedly impetuous and plain-spoken, and had the insensitiveness of a gross eater and drinker ; but his letters reveal him as a man of education and judgment. and something very far from the mere parsimonious tradesman.[1] When Scott showed a tendency to dally with John Murray, Hunter demanded, not unnaturally, that he should first finish his *Swift*, for which Constable had paid so monstrous a price.[2] The consequence was a complete estrangement. The oak, in Constable's phrase, considered that it could now support itself. Scott was determined to cut the comb of a firm which had wounded his feelings and talked to him like a huckster. He was not content to be his own printer, but with the assistance

---

[1] See his letters in *A. Constable*, I.
[2] Under the contract the book should have been ready for publication by Christmas 1810 ; it was not published till 1814.

o² John Murray and his London friends he would be his
own publisher.

Now James Ballantyne had a younger brother, John
by name, who had begun life in his father's shop, had
spent some time in business in London, had returned to
the Kelso counter where he had not prospered, and was
now chief clerk in the Canongate printing-house. John
was a small vivacious creature, as lean as his brother
was plump, with the large melting eyes and the nervous
hilarity of the consumptive. He was a wag and a mimic,
could sing an excellent song—the " Cobbler of Kelso "
was his masterpiece—loved all forms of sport, and had
a taste for raffish dandyism. He had not much education, but he was full of ideas, usually bad ones; and a
smattering of banking knowledge which he had picked
up, made him pose as the complete financier. It would
be hard to imagine a more dangerous business ally,
but Scott, in his fit of pique, resolved to set up the
two brothers in a publishing business that should
rival Constable's. In July 1809 the firm of John
Ballantyne and Co., publishers, opened in Hanover
Street. Scott contributed one half of the capital and
advanced the money for the fourth, which was John's
portion.

The venture is hard to defend on any ground of
common sense. It was undertaken in a not very justifiable
fit of temper. Constable had not behaved ill; indeed
to the end of his life his behaviour to Scott was consistently generous and loyal. He was not responsible
for the views of his *Edinburgh* contributors, and, even
if he had been, the offence was amply avenged by the
setting up of the new *Quarterly*. No doubt his partner
was tactless, but Hunter's bad temper had some justification, and his warning to Scott against making his name
too cheap was timely and wise. The truth is that Scott
had no real affection for Constable, though he respected
his abilities. The " Emperor " was not the kind of man
who appealed to him. He did not regard him as an equal
in birth and education, moving on the same plane as
Erskine and Clerk and Morritt. Nor could he patronize

LIBRARY ST. MARY'S COLLEGE

1809 him as he patronized James the plump and John the lean, for whom he had the pet names of " Aldiboronti-phoscophornio " and " Rigdumfunnidos." He could work comfortably with only two types of man—his indubitable equals and those upon whom he could condescend. Constable he did not regard as an equal, and Constable would not allow himself to be patronized. Scott loved " characters," and the Ballantynes were such, which Constable emphatically was not ; he was the ambitious, four-square, normal, middle-class merchant, whose value in his calmer moments Scott willingly recognized. But now he was not calm. " Convince my understanding," he once wrote, " and I am perfectly docile ; stir my passions by coldness or affronts and the devil would not drive me from my purpose." He believed that he had had coldness from Constable and affronts from Hunter.

On the business side the enterprise was a wild folly. The printing concern had been more or less limited in its liability. James Ballantyne might be compelled now and then to await the booksellers' convenience in the settlement of an account, but the printing-house worked for orders and knew within reasonable limits its commitments. But this safeguard disappeared once it became also a publishing house. It had now to undertake liabilities to authors, to paper-makers and binders, and to its own printing-house, and it had to meet them from the public sale of its productions. No more firm orders for the presses from the publishers, for it was its own publisher. In the case of unsuccessful books it would be left with a load of stock. A consistently successful list would involve the frequent raising of fresh capital, since the profits, being belated in their realization, would not suffice ; an unsuccessful list would load it with debt. Scott embarked in it the greater part of his recent literary earnings, but as the firm extended its operations, however successful these might be, more capital would be needed. If it had many failures there would be liabilities and no profits to meet them, and that meant recourse to Scott himself, and to the crazy system of bills and counter bills then in vogue among the 1810 Scottish banks.

But, as a matter of plain fact the firm could not succeed, because no one of the partners understood the craft of publishing. James Ballantyne was first and last a printer; he had a printer's taste in types and some literary judgment, but no understanding of finance; John was a will-o'-the-wisp, light-headed and irresponsible, whose chief talent lay in the dubious game of obtaining credit. Neither had any notion of the rudiments of sound trading. Scott could not oversee the details, but he believed that he had an instinct for what the public wanted—true enough, but he needed Constable's good sense to make that instinct marketable. He was apt to assume that because his own writings interested the multitude, all that interested himself would also infallibly attract other people. Moreover he had his ragged regiment of Parnassus to provide for. So he planted upon the new firm a history of the Culdees which no one could read, and an edition of Beaumont and Fletcher by an impecunious and distraught German, of whom Constable had very properly fought shy.

The new firm started with a good connexion among the London booksellers, and especially with John Murray. It published *The Lady of the Lake*, a profitable venture. But before the end of 1810 the business was becoming embarrassed, and the two yearly volumes of the new *Edinburgh Annual Register* were beyond the capacity of the public to absorb. John Ballantyne was an adept at the vicious practice by which two firms, whose *personnel* and assets were the same, could obtain credit by backing each other's bills. But there were limits to this device, and Scott's life was constantly harassed by demands for a few hundreds here and a few hundreds there to tide over an awkward moment. He found himself becoming the milch-cow of a firm from which he could never obtain a balance-sheet or a plain statement of profit and loss. But his affection for the partners prevented his irritation resulting in any practical reform. John's melting eye and James's snuffy optimism always induced him to postpone the day of account-taking.

Yet he was profoundly uneasy, and the dread of what might be the true state of the Hanover Street ledgers came between him and his comfort. The legal side of his work too, promised difficulties, for he foresaw and disliked certain imminent judicial innovations. By November 1810 the exhilaration caused by the success of *The Lady of the Lake* had died away and he was seriously contemplating a complete change of life. He toyed with the notion of becoming a high Indian official. To his brother Thomas he wrote : " I have no objection to tell you in confidence that, were Dundas (Lord Melville) to go out as Governor-General to India and were he willing to take me with him in a good situation, I would not hesitate to pitch the Court of Session and the booksellers to the Devil, and try my fortune in another climate." He was not yet forty, still young enough to pull up his roots, and he may have dreamed of a taste of that life of action for which he had always hankered, and the possibility of returning in a few years with a fortune which would enable him to live as he desired for the rest of his days.

But in the summer of the following year Lord Melville died, and the Indian project had, perforce, to be forgotten. Scott was a careful business man, as the keeping of his own private accounts shows, but he had a curious shrinking from cross-examining his partners, partly perhaps because he had provided nearly all the capital and regarded them as his dependents and retainers. Towards retainers he could not behave otherwise than royally. And yet he was virtually the sole partner and the sole capitalist in both the printing and the publishing businesses ; James and John were men of straw, and disaster would fall wholly on his shoulders. Strange that such a man with such a sword hanging over him did not attempt to envisage the truth. The firm paid away in dividends every penny it earned and was consequently without adequate capital and without reserves. Profits, often delusive profits, were drawn out and spent

as soon as they accrued. " The large sums received," 1811
James Ballantyne confessed, " never formed an addition
to stock. In fact they were all expended by the partners,
who, being then young and sanguine men, not unwillingly adopted my brother John's sanguine results."

Meantime Scott must earn money and do more than
toil at his edition of *Swift*. In 1811 he published *The
Vision of Don Roderick*, an exercise in the Spenserian
stanza, the profits of which went to the relief of the
sufferers from Masséna's campaign in Portugal. He had
another poem in his head on an English subject, which
he believed would please. Already in 1810 he had
written a few prose chapters in a new vein—an attempt
at a novel, but James Ballantyne had received them
tepidly and they had been laid aside. But during the
course of the year 1811 he began to see more light in
his future. A superannuation scheme had been introduced into the Scottish Courts, which meant that the
emoluments of his Clerkship of Session would soon be
his own, and that from the first day of 1812 he would
have an official salary of £1300 a year. All his own
fortune and past earnings were in the Ballantyne firm,
but with his sheriffdom and his wife's income he could
now count on a certain £2000 a year—a very substantial
revenue in those days for a country gentleman. Moreover, even if there were no printing or publishing profits,
he could reckon on making at least a thousand a year by
his pen. The skies cleared for him, his spirits rose, and
he could turn his mind to what had long been a darling
scheme. The lease of Ashestiel was nearly up ; he would
purchase a small lairdship and build himself a house.

His thoughts turned to the wider part of the Tweed
valley, the opening of that champaign country which
had always been his dream. On the road between
Melrose and Selkirk, overlooking Tweed a little above
where it receives the Gala, was the site of the last clan
battle in Border history, that fought in 1526 between
the Kerrs and the Scotts. The spot, too, was in the
heart of the world of fairy legend. There was a little
farm there of about a hundred acres, called Cartley Hole,

1812 belonging to Dr Douglas, the minister of Galashiels. The
buildings were poor, and the land consisted of a bit of
marshy haugh, some rough hill pastures, and a solitary
plantation of ragged firs. It looked out upon low moorish
uplands and was without obvious picturesqueness, except
for the noble streams of Tweed at its door. But it was
a place which could be " made," and Scott had always
in him much of the pioneer. He paid an astonishing
price for it, no less than £4000, and to meet the
purchase he borrowed £2000 from his elder brother John,
and £2000 from the Ballantyne firm on the security of a
poem of which he had not yet written a line. This last
was a fateful step. For the first time he put Pegasus
between the shafts, and counted upon literature to meet
the normal expenses of his life.

His ambition was modest. He wanted no more than
a country cottage to comply with his obligations as
Sheriff, where he could spend the vacations, potter about
with a little forestry, and entertain an occasional friend ;
a second Ashestiel, but his very own. He wrote to
Joanna Baillie : " My present intention is to have only
two spare bedrooms, with dressing-rooms, each of which
will have at a pinch a couch bed ; but I cannot relinquish
my Border principle of accommodating all the cousins
and *duniwastles*, who will rather sleep on chairs, and on
the floor, and in the hay-loft, than be absent when folks
are gathered together ; and truly I think Ashestiel was
very like the tent of Paribanou, in the Arabian Nights,
that suited alike all numbers of company equally ; ten
people fill it at any time, and I remember its lodging
thirty-two without any complaint." [1]

An architect was engaged, masons were set to work,
and in London Scott's friend Daniel Terry, the actor,
busied himself in buying " auld knicknackets " for the
new cottage. It was to be called Abbotsford, since there
was a ford in Tweed below it, and the land had once
belonged to Melrose Abbey. One day in the end of May
1812, Scott left Ashestiel, with many a long look behind
him, and took up his quarters in what had been the

[1] Lockhart, II. 361.

farmhouse of Cartley Hole amid the din and dust of the 1812 new building. A letter to Lady Alvanley describes the " flitting " :

> The neighbours have been much delighted with the procession of my furniture, in which old swords, bows, targets and lances made a very conspicuous show. A family of turkeys was accommodated within the helmet of some *preux chevalier* of ancient Border fame ; and the very cows, for aught I know, were bearing banners and muskets. I assure your ladyship that this caravan, attended by a dozen of ragged rosy peasant children, carrying fishing-rods and spears, and leading poneys, greyhounds and spaniels, would, as it crossed the Tweed, have furnished no bad subject for the pencil, and really reminded me of one of the gypsy groups of Callot upon their march.[1]

II

The new home, thus light-heartedly entered, was not at first to be a domain of peace. The summer of 1812 was a busy season. Scott spent every week-end and all the vacations at Abbotsford, where he was out most of the day superintending his new plantations of oaks and Spanish chestnuts, and stringing verses which he wrote down when he got to his desk. That desk stood in a corner of the single living-room of the old farm, which had to serve for drawing-room, dining-room, school-room and study. " As for the house and the poem, there are twelve masons hammering at the one, and one poor noddle at the other." The poem was *Rokeby,* which he had begun at Ashestiel, a romance of Cavalier and Roundhead which, being laid in an English scene, would, he hoped, attract a wider public than the Scots pieces. He devoted especial care to its composition, for his financial future seemed to depend upon its success. He had written to his friend Morritt, the squire of Rokeby, for books and information. " Pray help me in this—by truth, or fiction, or tradition—I care not which, if it be picturesque." He destroyed his draft of the first canto, because he felt that he had corrected all the spirit out of it. In the autumn he and his wife visited

[1] Lockhart, III. 3.

1812 Teesdale to revive his memories, and he took immense pains with the local details He made notes of the flowers in the Brignall quarries, and, when Morritt protested against such scrupulosity, made the remarkable answer :—

> That in nature herself no two scenes were exactly alike, and that whoever copied truly what was before his eyes, would possess the same variety in his description, and exhibit apparently an imagination as boundless as the range of nature in the scenes he recorded ; whereas, whoever trusted to imagination, would find his own mind circumscribed and contracted to a few favourite images, and the repetition of these would sooner or later produce that very monotony and barrenness which had always haunted descriptive poetry in the hands of any but the patient worshippers of truth. Besides which, local names and peculiarities make a fictitious story look so much better in the face.[1]

These novel solicitudes show how much Scott felt to be at stake in the new poem.

But the success, æsthetic and commercial, of *Rokeby*, which was published in the last days of 1812, was not " answerable to the honesty and simplicity of the design." The story limped ; the elaborate landscape did not delight and convince as the less studied Border and Highland scenes had delighted ; the poet seemed to have left his $\phi\upsilon\sigma\iota\zeta o o\varsigma$ $a\hat{\imath}a$ behind him. Morritt thought it the best of the poems, but the world did not endorse his view. Scott himself called it a " pseudo-romance of pseudo-chivalry," and we need not cavil at the description. Yet it had many fine things, some of them new and unexpected. Its lyrics " Brignall Banks " and " Allen-a-dale " and " A weary lot is thine, fair maid," were the best he had yet written, and to the discerning it was clear that a man who could create a character like Bertram — whom Swinburne pronounced " a figure alive to the very finger tips "—had all the novelist's gifts. Lockhart has said with justice that the substance of *Rokeby* would have made a great prose romance. But as a poem it was a comparative failure. There were profits indeed, and the Ballantyne

---

[1] Lockhart, III. 15.

firm was recouped for its advance, but the profits were 1813 not on the old scale. Others had stolen the seed and were growing the flower, and the public ear was getting a little dulled to his octosyllables. During the composition of *Rokeby* Scott had amused himself by scribbling another poem, *The Bridal of Triermain*, which was published anonymously in March 1813, as a piece of mystification. He wanted it to be attributed to Erskine, but only George Ellis in the *Quarterly* was deceived, and presently it was issued under Scott's name. It is a curious production, a blend of Tom Moore and himself in his minor vein, but it contains eight of his most haunting lines :—

> Bewcastle now must keep the hold,
> Speir-Adam's steeds must bide in stall,
> Of Hartley-burn the bowmen bold
> Must only shoot from battled wall ;
>
> And Liddesdale may buckle spur,
> And Teviot now may belt the brand,
> Taras and Ewes keep nightly stir,
> And Eskdale foray Cumberland.

The year 1813 therefore opened in disappointment, and the shadows darkened as the summer advanced. It was plain to Scott that his vogue as a poet was declining. Moore in the *Twopenny Post-Bag* had made fun of *Rokeby*, and suggested that Scott was working his way south through the various gentlemen's seats, preparing a metrical guide to the best houses. If people could talk thus, his verse must have lost its glamour. Moreover, a new star had appeared in the firmament. Byron in 1812 published the first two cantos of *Childe Harold*, which took the town by storm. Three years before, at Buchanan, Scott had read *English Bards and Scotch Reviewers*, and the phrase " Apollo's venal son " had rankled. " It is funny enough," he wrote to Southey, " to see a whelp of a young Lord Byron abusing me, of whose circumstances he knows nothing, for endeavouring to scratch out a living with my pen. God help the bear if, having little else to eat, he must not even suck his

1813 own paws. I can assure the noble imp of fame that it is not my fault that I was not born to a park and £5000 a year." But *Childe Harold* profoundly impressed one who never allowed a private grievance to warp his literary judgment. He wrote to Joanna Baillie urging her to read it, though he disliked its misanthropy and questioned its morals. Presently John Murray reported a conversation with the author, who had quoted and endorsed some friendly remarks of the Prince Regent on Scott, and the latter took the occasion to open a correspondence with his former assailant. He praised the new poem, and explained the circumstances under which *Marmion* had been published and on which Byron had based his charge of venality. Scott heeded ordinary criticism not at all, but he did not like to be misunderstood by those whom he admired. Byron replied in the friendliest spirit, and recapitulated all the pleasant things which the Prince Regent had said. It was the beginning of a correspondence which did equal credit to both. But the mere fact that he now numbered Byron among his friends sharpened the realization that here was a rival against whom he could not stand. How could a middle-aged Scottish lawyer compete with the romantically-minded against a young and handsome lordling, who had about him the glamour of a wild life and a broken heart ? How could the homely glens of his own land vie with the glittering cities of the South and the magic of the ancient East ? Scott beheld a large part of his occupation gone.

Yet he had never had greater need to earn money, for in 1813 the affairs of the Ballantyne firm were moving straight to disaster. That year saw the last throes of the struggle with Napoleon, as well as a fantastic war with the United States. In Britain prices soared, the people were starving and mutinous, bankruptcies filled the Gazette, and even firms of ancient stability were tottering. In such yeasty waters the Ballantyne cockle-shell could not hope to live. Morritt and others had backed its bills, but credit was now at an end. Wherever Scott went, at Abbotsford, at Drumlanrig, at Rokeby, he was pursued by the wailful choir of the brethren.

At last his even temper cracked, and in May he forced 1813
himself to a resolution which he should have taken long
before. The publishing business, which was the more
speculative one, must be wound up. But how was this to
be done without that bankruptcy which Edinburgh gossip
had long anticipated ? Bankruptcy could not be thought
of, for it would reveal the Sheriff of the Forest, the Clerk
of Court, and the world-famous poet as the chief partner
in a wild-cat concern, and would involve the forced sale
of valuable copyrights. The sole hope lay in some
brother publisher who would take the reconstruction in
hand, and that publisher could only be Constable. The
obnoxious Hunter was now dead, and Constable had got
as partners a well-mannered Writer to the Signet, Mr
Cathcart, and Cathcart's brother-in-law, a discreet young
man named Robert Cadell. Scott swallowed his pride,
and approached the friend with whom four years before
he had quarrelled.

Constable was willing to help—on his own terms. The
first question was how to surmount the immediate
trouble. He would not take over the disastrous *Annual
Register*, which had been losing a steady thousand a
year, but he would buy a quarter share in the *Rokeby*
copyright, and some of the Ballantyne stock, thereby
helping the firm to the extent of £2000. He promised
also to make a careful examination of the whole position.
His report came in August and it was not cheerful. The
two concerns, taken together, might be just solvent,
assets and liabilities balancing at about £15,000, but in
an immediate winding up the assets would be difficult
to realize.[1] Four thousand pounds must be got at once,
and he himself was not in a position to provide the sum.
Scott must either raise the money or part with his share
in the copyrights. After an anxious week help was
forthcoming from the young Duke of Buccleuch, who
guaranteed Scott's overdraft for £4000. Then in October
came the victories of Leipzig and Vittoria, business
revived in Britain, credit became easier, and the Ballantyne firm was saved. The publishing business was kept

---

[1] *A. Constable*, III. 27-29.

alive only till its stock could be realized, and John
Ballantyne migrated to the more suitable activities of
an auctioneer. Scott at one moment decided to cut his
connexion with the printing business also (which would
have involved its winding up), but was prevented by his
care for James Ballantyne's interests and his disinclination
to lose the considerable sum he had already invested in it.

The misfortune was that, though distracted by worries,
he did not fully realize the gravity of the crisis through
which he had passed. That at the worst moment he
should have continued to lend money to impecunious
friends may be set down to his credit, but he was also
commissioning Terry in London to buy him old armour,
and he had begun to negotiate for the ground which
ran back behind Abbotsford to Cauldshiels loch. Land
hunger had laid its spell on him. The British victories
on the Continent had sent his spirits soaring, and once
again the future seemed rosy. He was quit for the
moment of the Ballantyne incubus, and would find a
way to live at Abbotsford like a gentleman. There were
many shots in the locker—principally a new poem of
the Highlands which he had begun, to be called *The
Lord of the Isles*. Surely the great Bruce would make as
strong an appeal to the world as any Greek bandit or
turbaned Mussulman.

Yet at the back of his head he knew that his vogue
had gone. He had caught a favouring breeze of popular
favour, but the wind now blew from another quarter.
In August, while the Ballantyne difficulty was at its
worst, he had received a letter from the Lord Chamber-
lain, offering him the Poet Laureateship in succession
to Pye. He was disinclined to accept it for a variety
of reasons, the chief of which, perhaps, was that he did
not wish to incur the charge, which Tom Moore had
already made, of being a kind of poetic usher to the
great world. The Duke of Buccleuch, when consulted,
took the same view. The post was slightly ridiculous.
" The poet laureate would stick to you and your productions like a piece of court-plaster. Your muse has
hitherto been independent—don't put her in harness.

We know how lightly she trots along when left to her 1813
natural paces, but do not try driving." The offer was
declined, on the ground of his unsuitability for the work,
and for the better reason that he already held two
official posts. Through Croker and others he pushed the
claims of Southey, to whom a small regular income
would be a godsend, and Southey was duly appointed.[1]
Meantime, while the masons hammered on the new
Abbotsford roof, Scott busied himself with *The Lord of
the Isles*, but in his heart he had already bidden farewell
to poesy as the staple of his life.

III

We shall err if we take Scott's poetic self-depreciation
too literally. As a poet he always stood in his own light,
and that humorous, deprecating figure has ever since
come between the light and the critics. In some degree
it was a mannerism, springing from the modesty which
was his prime characteristic ; he disliked flattery and
was shy even of praise, and he averted both by an aggres-
sive humility. In so far as it was serious, it was based
upon two deeply held convictions. The first was that
poetry, indeed literature in any form, was not the highest
of human callings. His true heroes belonged to a different
sphere, the sphere of action. This was no snobbish
contempt of letters as beneath the dignity of coat-
armour ; it was the man not the gentleman who spoke :
it was a protest against the exaggerated repute of the
spinner of words in contrast with those whose homelier
virtues " spun the great wheel of earth about." He was
more interested in life than in art, in character than in
intellect. He confessed that he never felt abashed or
awed except in the presence of one man—the Duke of
Wellington. "The immortality of poetry," he wrote to
Miss Seward in 1808, " is not so firm a point of my creed
as the immortality of the soul." [2] The second was that
his own verse simply did not attain what he regarded

---

[1] He invested the salary in a life policy for £3000. See his letter to Scott,
P. L. B., 79.
[2] *Fam. Letters*, I. 126.

1813 as the loftiest poetic excellence. Shakespeare was his
supreme love, and at the end of his life he declared that
he was not worthy to tie Shakespeare's brogues. With
Byron he considered himself on an equality, since they
ran for the same stakes ; but he held himself inferior to
many contemporaries in what moved him most—the
poetry of simple passion, and the poetry of reflection.
Burns and himself, he thought, should not be " named
in the same day." He profoundly admired Wordsworth ; he wrote in all sincerity to Southey—" I am
not such an ass as not to know that you are my better
in poetry " : his own favourite pieces in all literature
were Johnson's " London " and " The Vanity of Human
Wisdom " ;[1] his love for the grave meditative vein even
led him to the surprising judgment that in 1810 Joanna
Baillie was " the highest genius of our country." [2]

These preferences must be kept in mind in judging
Scott's tales in verse. He was producing something in
which he delighted, which he believed to be of use to his
country, but which he did not himself regard as the
highest kind of poetry. He would have agreed with Lord
Dudley when he wrote : " I have all along harboured
in my mind certain heretical doubts and misgivings as
to Walter Scott's style of writing, and am apt to suspect
that, as my late lord of Rochester (speaking of no
less a person than Cowley) did somewhat profanely
remark, ' it is not of God, and therefore cannot stand.' " [3]
He was a minstrel on the ancient pattern, and it was his
business to capture popular favour and give the world
what it wanted. If popular favour turned from him,
he must stand back or try something new. To such a
prosaic wooer the Muses do not give their secret hearts.

It is a platitude, taking all his work into account, to
say that Scott was a far greater poet than his poetry
reveals. But his specific achievement was remarkable
enough. He invented a new form, from which the
novelty has long ago departed ; and this very familiarity

---

[1] The last lines Scott sent to the press were a quotation from the latter.
[2] Lockhart, II. 307.
[3] *Letters to " Ivy " from the First Earl of Dudley*, 200.

with him has bred in many quarters a friendly contempt. 1813
He is a writer, says a foreign critic, " whom all grown-up
people have read, and no grown-up people read."[1] But
if we come to him with fresh minds, we shall not under-
rate his quality. He essayed a new type of poetic
narrative, a kind of miniature epic. He discovered a
measure which was apt for both rapid movement and
detailed description. In a very simple rhythm he
introduced variations which prevent monotony and
permit of vigorous emphasis, and yet in no way break
the flow. He adapted the old ballad form so as to fit it
for a long and often complex narrative. Scott's octosyllables embrace, if carefully studied, surprising varieties
of manner, and they are far more artful than they appear ;
he has told us that he often wrote his verses two or three
times over. They can gallop and they can jig, they can
move placidly in some piece of argument, and now and
then they can sing themselves into a lyrical exaltation.

The dangers and defects of such a medium are obvious,
and, now that the novelty has worn off, it is these defects
which the critic chiefly sees. We have all fallen under
his spell in childhood, but age is apt to react against
what ravishes youth. Too often the lines run with an
unpleasing facility, so that he resembles the early Roman
satirist, of whom Horace said that he could write six
hundred lines "stans pede in uno." Too often the fluency
is monotonous and dulls the ear. Too often he seems to
gird his loins and leap unashamedly into a pit of Gothick
extravagance. Too often he falls into a polite jargon,
and calls tartan the " bosom's chequered shroud," and
revels in falsetto Augustan epithets, and writes bathos
in the Shenstone style :—

> Then first alarmed, his sire and train
> Tried every art, but tried in vain.
> The soul, too soft its ills to bear,
> Had left our mortal hemisphere,
> And sought in better world the meed
> To blameless life by Heaven decreed.

---

[1] Georg Brandes, *Main Currents in Nineteenth-Century Literature* (Eng.
Trans.), IV. 102.

1813 Sometimes he can be at his worst and best in consecutive
lines—

> Till gallant Cessford's heart-blood dear
> Reeked on dark Elliot's Border spear.

The pieces are first of all to be judged as poetic narra-
tions, which is their strict artistic type—that is to say,
on the credibility and interest of the characters, the
skill of the telling, and the emotion of the high dramatic
moments. Judged in this sphere, they show a progressive
advance. The *Lay* and *Marmion* are faulty in construction, though the latter rises to a fine tragic conclusion. *The Lady of the Lake* is pure airy romance, getting
its effects as swiftly and surely as a fairy tale, and
possessing a background which straightway captures the
fancy. In it the dispatch of the fiery cross, the combat
between Fitz James and Roderick Dhu, and the closing
scene in Stirling Castle are models of story-telling, as
lucid as any prose and yet with the exaltation of poetry.
That piece, also, contains an example of argument in
verse, where, without the waste of one word and without
dropping from the poetic level, an economic situation is
admirably expounded—Roderick's account in Canto V
of the origin of Highland reiving. *Rokeby* is an attempt
on a bigger scale, with an excellent but too intricate
plot, which checks the speed. It is, as I have said, the
precursor of the prose novels. But it contains character-
drawing of a subtler kind than the others, and in Bertram
a Byronic figure far more convincing than any of Byron's
own. But I am inclined to think that it is in the poem
which was published after his farewell to poetry, *The
Lord of the Isles*, that Scott reveals his highest narrative
powers. The verse is fresher and simpler, with more
play and sinew in it, and the scene in Canto II when the
Abbot, like another Balaam, tries to curse and is forced
to bless, touches the austere magnificence of the Sagas.
Bannockburn, too, seems to me Scott's best battle-piece,
with the death of Argentine and the beautiful " falling
close."

This narrative skill, this power of presenting human

action, especially heroic action, so as at once to convince 1813
and delight, is a poetic merit of a high order. In English
poetry, save for Chaucer, and Burns in " Tam o' Shanter,"
Scott has in this respect no serious rival. He has other
strictly poetic qualities. For one thing he invented a
new kind of description, a light, glittering summary of
relevant features which rarely impedes the flow of the tale.
Take the picture of St Mary's loch in the introduction
to Canto II of *Marmion*, or that of Loch Katrine in
Canto I of *The Lady of the Lake*. The secret of success
lies in the effortless choice of significant and memorable
details ; he fails when, as in *Rokeby*, he peeps and
botanizes. Again, no poet has ever produced so easily
the impression of sustained movement, and, at moments,
of headlong speed. A journey, a ride against time, a
muster, all are set to swift music. Take the *Lay*—

> Already on dark Ruberslaw
> The Douglas holds his weapon-schaw :
> The lances, waving in his train,
> Clothe the dun heath like autumn grain ;
> And on the Liddle's northern strand,
> To bar retreat to Cumberland,
> Lord Maxwell ranks his merrymen good
> Beneath the eagle and the rood.

Take a dozen passages in *Marmion*—Marmion's reply
to James beginning

> But Nottingham has archers good
> And Yorkshire men are stern of mood ;

or Clare's charge to De Wilton, or the quarrel with Angus
at Tantallon, or the whole tale of Flodden. Take the
superb opening of *The Lady of the Lake*, and the breathless excitement of the scene when the whistle of Roderick
calls up the Highland ambush. One secret of the speed
is the use of proper names—the thunderous, cumulative
topography, which gives at one and the same time an
impression of a spacious background, and of a hurrying
to and fro within it. The place-names mark the course
like the posts in a stadium.

This is one of the matters in which Scott is akin to

1813 Homer.   Another is the sudden drop into a humorous
simplicity which Jeffrey disliked, and thought " offensive
to every reader of delicacy."   It is part of Scott's gift,
which we shall find everywhere in the novels, of linking
his heroics with mother earth.   Let me cite as examples
William of Deloraine's

> Letter nor line know I never a one
> Wer't my neck-verse at Hairibee—

or Wat Tinlin's :

> They crossed the Liddle at curfew hour
> And burned my little lonely tower ;
> The fiend receive their souls therefor !
> It had not been burned this year or more—

or the comments of the Borderers on Marmion's train :
or old Angus's

> Thanks to Saint Bothan, son of mine,
> Save Gawain, ne'er could pen a line—

or the sports in the castle-hall of Stirling.   Such homeliness is of the essence of true romance, but it was alien
to the bloodless thing which before Scott had passed for
romantic.[1]

The magic, inseparable from poetry, is not to be found
in any curious verbal felicities, or in the occasional
excursions into *diablerie*.   In the long poems Scott is
consistently unhappy in his use of the supernatural.   It
dwells rather in the total effect of the gleaming landscapes
and the brightly coloured pageants, and, most of all, in
his power of rounding off an episode or a description
with a ringing note, which sets the blood running.   He
can do this in narration, and he can do it in argument
and reflection.   The best instance of the latter, perhaps,
is outside the main poems, in the verses in his usual
metre which Waverley wrote on receiving the news of
his captain's commission.   A piece of respectable but

---

[1] A good example of this Homeric gift is the description in *The Pirate* of the
Udaller going down to fish, with his guests following. "They followed his
stately steps to the shore *as the herd of deer follows the leading stag,* with all
manner of respectful observances."

uninspired description, an exercise on the grand piano, 1813 ends with a clarion note—

> So on the idle dreams of youth
> Breaks the loud trumpet-call of truth,
> Bids each fair vision pass away,
> Like landscape on the lake that lay,
> As fair, as flitting, and as frail
> As that which fled the autumn gale—
> For ever dead to fancy's eye
> Be each gay form that glided by,
> While dreams of love and lady's charms
> Give place to honour and to arms.

Another and a rarer magic reveals itself now and then in the long poems—in the interspersed lyrics ; and it is in such pieces, especially in those scattered through the novels, that Scott attains his real poetic stature. He has been called with justice the greatest of our lyric poets between Burns and Shelley,[1] greater than Coleridge or Wordsworth because more truly a singer. His inspiration here came from the vernacular songs and ballads, and was the chief boon which his work on the *Minstrelsy* gave him. It put tunes in his head far subtler than the conventional things which he officially admired ; and these tunes remained, singing themselves to him at work and play, so that, when in the novels he needed a snatch of verse, they rushed upon him unbidden, and flowed from his pen as easily as dialogue. Hence his lyrical genius shows a steady growth so long as his powers endured. By their very nature the octosyllables of the narrative poems could not be muted to the silences of great poetry, those " ditties of no tone " which are piped only to the spirit ; but in his greater lyrics Scott penetrated to the final mystery of the poet.

He is in the first place a master of the pure lyric, the song for music. It takes many forms, but has always two characteristics : it may be different in style from the surrounding narrative, but it is exactly appropriate to its mood ; and it carries its own music with it—there

---

[1] O. Elton, *A Survey of Eng. Literature*, 1780-1830, I. 310.

is no need to set it formally to a tune. Its emotion is usually the emotion of external things, the hunt, the combat, the battle, the bridal, as much fitting subjects for lyric as the subtler passions. It may be a marching song, like " Blue Bonnets over the Border " in the *Minstrelsy*, or " Donald Caird," or " Allen-a-dale " or " Bonnie Dundee " ; or a lullaby like " Soldier, rest, thy warfare o'er " ; or a lover's farewell like " The heath this night must be my bed," and " A weary lot is thine, fair maid " ; or a fairy tale, like " Alice Brand," and the strange snatch about the " stag of ten " in *The Lady of the Lake ;* or the eternal love-plaint like " Brignall Banks." Such pieces are different in kind from the rest of his poetry. His lyric talent here has no redundancies or false notes ; he achieves his effect, often a subtle and delicate effect, with extreme precision.

But there is a second type of lyric or lyrical ballad, mostly to be found in the novels, which mounts still higher, which at its best, indeed, is beyond analysis, producing that sense of something inexplicable and overwhelming which is the token of genius. Its subjects are the mysteries of life, not its gallant bustle, and the supreme mystery of death. It deals with enchantments and the things which " tease us out of thought," with the pale light of another world, with the crooked shadows from the outer darkness which steal over the brightness of youth and love. The ballad of Elspeth of the Craig-burnfoot in *The Antiquary* is such a piece—it is romance seen through dying eyes. The " Coronach " in *The Lady of the Lake* is another, a lament which has the poignant sorrow of a wandering wind. Sometimes the atmosphere of them is translunary, not of this earth. Sometimes they are sober reflections upon the transience of mortal things, and the minstrel becomes the prophet. They are Scott's final credentials as a poet, even as a great poet, for they have the *desiderium* of great poetry. Such is the snatch in *Guy Mannering*, which has Shakespeare's high oracular spell—

> Twist ye, twine ye ! even so,
> Mingle shades of joy and woe.

Such is Lucy Ashton's song in *The Bride of Lammermoor*— 1813

> Look not thou on beauty's charming,
> Sit thou still when kings are arming,
> Taste not when the wine-cup glistens,
> Speak not when the people listens.
> Stop thine ear against the singer
> From the red gold keep thy finger,—
> Vacant heart, and hand and eye,
> Easy live and quiet die.

Such is that haunting fragment in *The Pirate*, beginning

> And you shall deal the funeral dole ;
>   Ay, deal it, mother mine,
> To weary body and to heavy soul,
>   The white bread and the wine.

And, greater still, there is " Proud Maisie," Madge Wildfire's dying song. These things are sung mostly by the distraught ; they appear in the narrative to enhance a mood ; not like the solid carpentry of the larger poems, but like some sudden breath of inspiration from an inner shrine. They are Scott's way of linking the prosaic earth with the things that were never on sea or land, the ultimate matter of poetry.[1]

IV

Very early in his literary career Scott's mind had turned to the writing of romances in prose. He began one on Thomas the Rhymer and another on the Civil War. In 1805, when he was settled at Ashestiel and busy on his *Dryden*, he projected a tale of the Highlands in the 'Forty-five to be called " Waverley : 'Tis Fifty Years Since." Seven chapters were completed, and shown to Erskine, who pronounced them dull. The success of *The Lady of the Lake* turned his thoughts again to the Highlands and Prince Charlie, which Surtees had long been pressing on him as a fitting subject. A few more chapters were written and the whole was submitted to

---

[1] It is possible that Scott wrote other verses which he never claimed: A good case can be made out for his authorship of " The Highland Exile's Boat Song." See *The Lone Shieling* (1925).

1813 James Ballantyne, who shook his head at their prosiness, though he counselled perseverance. Scott was discouraged and put the thing aside. He had already in 1807 finished Joseph Strutt's romance of *Queen-Hoo Hall* for Mr Murray, and neither the fragment nor its continuation had been successful. But the plan had always been at the back of his head, though it was overlaid by more urgent duties. The manuscript of the Jacobite novel had been mislaid in the " flitting " from Ashestiel, and did not lie in a corner of his desk to spur his memory. But in 1813, in the autumn when the salmon run well in Tweed, a guest at Abbotsford proposed to go fishing. Scott ascended to the garret to find his tackle, and in a corner of an old escritoire he came upon the lost chapters. It was a moment when he had escaped from his worst financial anxieties, but to live at Abbotsford as he desired to live he must earn money by his pen, and he had already the clear conviction that his meridian as a poet was past. He carried the manuscript downstairs to see what could be made of it, and thereby entered into his true kingdom.[1]

For his poems had never been more than the skimming of a mighty cauldron. They had been tales told under the shackles of metre and rhyme, a form inadequate to the immense volume of his resources. " Whole buried towns support the dancer's heel." To do justice to the wealth of memories and knowledge which he had been storing up all his life, he needed an ampler method and a more generous convention. Few men have ever approached the task of fiction more superbly endowed than this lawyer-squire of forty-three. He was widely read in several literatures, and so deeply learned in many histories that he could look upon a past age almost with the eye of a contemporary. His life had brought him into touch with most aspects of men's work ; he knew something of law, something of business, something of politics, something of agriculture ;

---

[1] The story of the finding of the MS. is told by Scott in a letter to Morritt (Lockhart, III. 126) and in his General Introduction to the novels. There seems to me to be no reason to regard it as part of the later mystification.

he had mixed with many societies, from the brethren of 1813
the Covenant Close to the politicians of Whitehall, from
the lairds of the Forest to the lords and ladies of St
James's. Every man he met he treated like a kinsman,
and there was no cranny of human experience which did
not attract his lively interest. Moreover he knew most
of them from the inside, for by virtue of his ready
sympathy and quick imagination he could penetrate
their secrets. He valued his dignity so highly, he used
to say, that he never stood upon it. He could understand the dark places of the human spirit, but especially
he understood its normal sphere and the ordinary
conduct of life. It could not be said of him, as it was
said of Timon of Athens, that he never knew the middle of
humanity but only the extremities. He had that kindly
affection for the commonplace which belongs to a large
enjoying temperament—the mood of Rupert Brooke
when he wrote that he could " watch a dirty, middle-aged
tradesman in a railway carriage for hours, and love every
dirty, greasy, sulky wrinkle in his weak chin and every
button on his spotted, unclean waistcoat." The very
characteristics which cramped him as a poet were
shining assets for the novelist, since he did not dramatize
himself and see the world in terms of his own moods, but
looked out upon it shrewdly, calmly and steadfastly.
He was no raw boy, compelled to spin imaginative stuff
out of his inner consciousness, but mature in mind and
character, one who had himself struggled and suffered,
and rubbed against the sharp corners of life. Yet, in
his devouring relish for the human pageant, he had still
the ardour of a boy.

Above all he knew his native land, the prose and the
poetry of it, as no Scotsman had ever known it before.
He thrilled to its ancient heroics, and every nook was
peopled for him with familiar ghosts. He understood
the tragedy of its stark poverty, and the comedy of its
new-won prosperity. It was all a book in which he had
read deep ; the cities with their provosts and bailies,
the lawyers of the Parliament House and the High Street
closes, the doctors in the colleges, the brisk merchants

1813 who were building a new Scotland, the porters and
caddies and the riff-raff in the gutter; the burgh towns
—was he not the presiding judge of one?—with their
snuffy burgesses and poaching vagabonds; the countryside in all its ways—lairds and tacksmen, ale-wives and
tinkers, ministers and dominies, the bandsters and
shearers in harvest-time, the drovers on the green roads,
the shepherds in the far shielings. He had the impulse
and the material which go to the making of great epics;
it remained to be seen whether he had the shaping power.

Chapter VI

THE EARLY NOVELS
(1814–1817)

I

When Scott returned to Edinburgh in January, 1814, after the Christmas vacation, he had completed most of the first volume of the new novel, and John Ballantyne copied the manuscript for the press. The Ballantynes printed it, and Constable undertook the publication on the basis of an equal division of profits between himself and the author. It was announced to appear in March, but its completion was delayed by papers that Scott undertook to write for the supplement to the *Encyclopædia Britannica*, the copyright of which Constable had recently acquired. On the 4th of June he began the second volume, and the book was finished by the end of that month, while he was spending six hours in Court for five days of the week. Lockhart has given us a glimpse of the strenuous toil of those June twilights. He had been dining with some young advocates in a house in George Street, which commanded a back view of Scott's house in North Castle Street.

When my companion's worthy father and uncle, after seeing two or three bottles go round, left the juveniles to themselves, the weather being hot, we adjourned to a library which had one large window looking northward. After conversing here for an hour or more, I observed that a shade had come over the aspect of my friend, who happened to be placed immediately opposite to myself, and said something that intimated a fear of his being unwell. "No," said he, "I shall be well enough presently, if you will only let me sit where you are, and take my chair ; for there is a confounded hand in sight of me here, which has often bothered me before, and now it won't let me

1814 fill my glass with a good will." I rose to change places with him accordingly, and he pointed out to me this hand which, like the writing on Belshazzar's wall, distracted his hour of hilarity. "Since we sat down," he said, "I have been watching it—it fascinates my eye—it never stops—page after page is finished and thrown on that heap of MS., and still it goes on unwearied—and so it will be till candles are brought in, and God knows how long after that. It is the same every night— I can't stand the sight of it when I am not at my books."— "Some stupid, dogged, engrossing clerk, probably," exclaimed myself or some other giddy youth in our society. "No, boys," said our host, "I well know what hand it is—'tis Walter Scott's."[1]

Waverley ; or 'Tis Sixty Years Since appeared on July 7th in three shabby little volumes, the price one guinea. No author's name stood on the title-page, and so began the tangled tale of Scott's anonymity. His reasons for it were given explicitly in two letters written that month to Morritt. "I am something in the condition of Joseph Surface, who was embarrassed by getting himself too good a reputation ; for many things may please people well enough anonymously, which, if they have me in the title-page, would just give me that sort of ill name which precedes hanging—and that would be in many respects inconvenient if I thought of again trying a *grande opus*." And a fortnight later : "I shall *not* own Waverley ; my chief reason is that it would prevent me of the pleasure of writing again. . . . In truth, I am not sure it would be considered quite decorous of me, as a Clerk of Session, to write novels. Judges being monks, Clerks are a sort of lay brethren, from whom some solemnity of walk and conduct may be expected.[2] So, whatever I may do of this kind, I shall whistle it down the wind to pray a fortune. . . . I do not see how my silence can be considered as imposing on the public. . . . In point of emolument, everybody knows that I sacrifice much money by withholding my name ; and

---

[1] III. 128-9.
[2] Lord Hailes, when he contributed to Henry Mackenzie's *Mirror*, insisted on anonymity, because "his situation in life, in a narrow country, and in one not remarkable for liberality of sentiment, makes it improper that his name or description should be seen in a periodical publication."

what should I gain by it that any human being has a right to consider as an unfair advantage ? In fact, only the freedom of writing trifles with less personal responsibility, and perhaps more frequently than I otherwise might do."

These are solid and intelligible grounds. The novel was not the form of literature in the best repute, and a Clerk of Court, who had hopes of the Bench, and whose name had so far only been associated with the responsible rôles of poet, critic and antiquary, might well seek an incognito when he appeared in the character of popular entertainer. Moreover, the warning of Constable's former partner, Hunter, against cheapening his name had sunk deep into Scott's mind. He had already a large mass of published work to his credit, and his circumstances made it necessary that he should steadily add to it ; it would be fatal if he stood before the world as a bookseller's hack. With his shrewd eye for economic facts, he realized that a market might be glutted by an author's name, though the demand for that author's work might be unsated. We see this motive in some doggerel lines to John Ballantyne :—

> No, John, I will not own the book—
> I won't, you picaroon.
> When next I try St Grubby's brook,
> The " A. of Wa—" shall bait the hook—
> And flat-fish bite as soon
> As if before them they had got
> The worn-out wriggler Walter Scott.

He did not want the name of a worn-out wriggler. It was not that he feared a new venture, and desired to test the flood before he committed himself to it ; Scott was never afraid of experiment, and had always refused to bind himself to one line ; but he was wisely anxious not to mortgage his future. Nor did he doubt the merits of his new work ; he was as certain of them as against dubious friends, as Bunyan in a similar case had been about the *Pilgrim's Progress*.

There was another motive, a love of the game of mystification for its own sake. It amused him enor-

1814 mously to see sapient critics hallooing on a false scent, and he was quite ready to encourage their vagaries.[1] At first the secret was confined to Erskine, Morritt and the Ballantynes, but as the novels increased some twenty people shared the knowledge of the authorship. Scott stood resolutely to his denial, and thereby involved himself in a good deal of tortuous prevarication, and some downright falsehoods, justified only on the legal plea that he was not bound to incriminate himself.[2] Presently the world came to regard it as Scott's amiable fad, and it may fairly be said that no student of contemporary literature was for one moment misled. The mass of corroborative evidence was too great, and his best critic, J. L. Adolphus, quotes appositely from *Twelfth Night*—

> An apple cleft in two is not more twin
> Than these two creatures.[3]

While Edinburgh was beginning to hum with gossip about the new novel, Scott disappeared from its streets on what was perhaps the happiest holiday of his life. He was in high spirits ; his new venture promised to be a success, he was relieved for the present of financial cares, and his beloved Abbotsford was growing under his hand ; he was setting out on a voyage of exploration to parts of his native land which had hitherto been only names to him ; he had congenial company, including Erskine, and he had the holiday feeling which follows a long spell of strenuous work. He sailed on July 29th from Leith in the Lighthouse yacht, under the guidance of Mr Stevenson, the Surveyor of the Lights, who was Robert Louis Stevenson's grandfather. There is no better proof of Scott's inveterate passion for the pen than that, after long weeks of scribing, he should have kept in five little paper books a full journal of his trip. As a " tour to the Highlands " it is a curious contrast to the books of Johnson and Boswell—the stately introspective

---

[1] His brother Thomas was suspected as the author of *Waverley*, and we find Scott writing to him in Canada, urging him to take advantage of the rumour and produce a novel of his own. Lockhart, III. 301.
[2] See *P. L. B.*, 108, etc.   [3] *Letters to Richard Heber*, 47.

record of the Londoner who carried his vehement 1814
idiosyncrasies intact through a barbarous and unfamiliar
land, the not less introspective gossip of the Londoner's
henchman; for it is the work of a keen observer who
was more interested in things than in his reactions to
them, and who brought to his observation a great store
of sympathy and knowledge. And yet no journal could
be more self-revealing. In Lockhart's words, " we have
before us, according to the scene and occasion, the poet,
the antiquary, the magistrate, the planter and the
agriculturist; but everywhere the warm yet sagacious
philanthropist—everywhere the courtesy, based on the
unselfishness, of the thoroughbred gentleman."

At first he was in familiar scenes. He visited the
ruined abbey of Arbroath, which awoke memories of
Williamina Stuart, in whose company he had first seen
it. He had his one and only bout of sea-sickness, though
the rest of the company suffered much. In the Orkneys
and Shetlands he studied the antiquities and the habits
of the people, and had the felicity to meet a genuine
witch, who, like Æolus, sold favourable winds to sailors;
he explored the wild coast around Cape Wrath; in the
outer Hebrides he followed the track of Prince Charlie's
wanderings; in Skye he saw Macleod's fairy flag, heard
Macrimmon's Lament played by a Macrimmon, and
was solemnized by the majesty of Loch Coruisk; he
made a difficult landing on the reef which was afterwards to carry the lighthouse of Skerryvore, and, amid
the tombs of Iona, reflected that the last Scottish king
said to have been buried there owed all his fame to
Shakespeare. "A few weeks' labour of an obscure
player has done more for the memory of Macbeth than
all the gifts, wealth and monuments of this cemetery of
princes have been able to secure to the rest of its in-
habitants."

The voyage gave him the landscape he needed for the
forthcoming *Lord of the Isles*, and the knowledge of
island life which afterwards bore fruit in *The Pirate*. It
gave him more—an insight into certain aspects of
Highland and island economy, and the problems of a

1814 fast-moving world. No trait is more notable in Scott than his constant interest in economic and social questions, how human beings made a livelihood, how social change was to be combined with social persistence. In Orkney he observed the crofting system with a sagacious eye ; large farms were, he decided, the only economic solution, but he could not face the dispossession of the small folk. " Were I an Orcadian laird I feel I should shuffle on with the old useless creatures against my better judgment." In the Reay country he noted the growth of the big sheep farms, which were opening up a new source of profit for Highland landowners. But they meant the eviction of hundreds of families who had been there for generations and had provided stalwart soldiers for the British Army. Europe was not yet at peace ; was the economic to be preferred to the human factor ? " Wealth is no doubt strength in a country, while all is quiet and governed by law, but on any altercation or internal commotion it ceases to be strength, and is only a means of tempting the strong to plunder the possessors."

He crossed to Ulster, and at Portrush had news which clouded the remainder of his journey—the death of Harriet, Duchess of Buccleuch, to whom he was attached by every bond of clan loyalty and personal affection. He left the yacht at Greenock and made his first steamer journey to Glasgow, where he wrote to the Duke. But the Duke had anticipated him, and had already written a letter to tell him how the kind and gracious lady had made her farewell to the world. In his sorrow the bereaved husband desired to draw his friends closer around him. " I shall love them more and more because I know that they loved her." There are few things in the long literature of consolation to surpass the tenderness and fortitude of this interchange of letters.

Scott reached Edinburgh to find that Constable had sold three thousand copies of *Waverley*, and was eager to treat for a third edition.[1] The novelist was fairly

---

[1] There is a vivid account of Edinburgh's reception of *Waverley*, in Cockburn *Mem.*, 280-1.

embarked on his career, and we may pause to consider 1814 the auspices under which he entered upon it.

II

This is not the place to trace at length the progress of English fiction from its lowly beginnings to the high estate to which it was brought by the eighteenth-century masters. Scott entered upon a field already largely cultivated, though under divergent principles of husbandry. First for these principles. Defoe's had been the method of minute, conscientious realism. His technique was that of the detached reporter, giving fictitious events the air of a plain statement of fact, the art, as Sir Walter Raleigh has put it, of " grave, imperturbable lying." With Richardson we have the same elaborate pretence at factual accuracy ; his device of a narrative in letters had the same purpose as Defoe's minute particulars, to give the imaginative stuff the illusion of a chronicle of fact. With both the personality of the writer is withdrawn. In Fielding we find a radical change. He had the boldness to present fiction as fiction, and to propound a doctrine of the writer's part which since his day has been generally accepted. Verisimilitude is to be attained by the inherent logic of the characters and their doings ; the illusion he seeks is not that of history but of art. The author is no longer the impersonal chronicler ; he is the spectator who assumes omniscience, and therefore he is entitled to comment and philosophize as he pleases. In the fantastic impressionism of Sterne the freedom of the author was further enlarged. He could now cut capers on his own account, and, in revealing his characters, reveal every cranny of himself.

Fielding's achievement freed the hands of his successors. Simultaneously with the development of the methods of husbandry had come an enlargement of the arable land. Richardson had invented the novel of sensibility, which was the early form of the novel of personality—the record of events of which the chief interest lay in the reactions of the human soul. Smollett

1814 brought in the rough background of the streets and the
taverns, and the coarse sea-salt of life ; he was the first
to exult in the grosser oddities of human nature. With
Fielding, too, the domain of the novel was indefinitely
extended ; the new elasticity of his method made its
sphere co-extensive with all aspects of society. When
Scott began to write, the novel of manners was firmly
established, embracing the drawing-rooms of Richardson
and Miss Burney, the bar-parlours and streets and
highroads of Smollett and Fielding, and the impish
world of Sterne. Its aim, in Coleridge's phrase, was no
longer to copy but to imitate reality, and to interpret it.

But the great era of production seemed to have closed
with the publication of *Humphry Clinker* in the year of
Scott's birth. Jane Austen was indeed carrying one
branch of the novel of manners to its final perfection and
had published three of her masterpieces before 1814, but
they had not caught the public taste. That taste was
avid for fiction, and it was being fed on coarse fare.
The Minerva Press was sending out a stream of foolish
romances, which wallowed in sentimentality or horror,
partly translated from the French, partly imitations of
Matt Lewis and Mrs Radcliffe. The consequence was
that the novel had acquired an ill repute among serious
readers. But the underworld in which it lived was
populous ; of a forgotten work in six volumes, *Vicissitudes*, two thousand copies at thirty-six shillings were
sold on the day of publication. Such a vogue pointed
to a demand for something which the ordinary novel of
manners did not meet. Miss Edgeworth's Irish tales
had shown that there were untilled patches within the
confines of the British islands from which good harvests
could be reaped ; the success of Miss Jane Porter's
unhistorical melodramas revealed a popular craving for
the pageantry of past history ; and the crudities of the
Minerva Press proved that the fairy-tale, even in its
most vulgar form, had not lost its ancient glamour. The
time was ripe for a further extension of the domain of
the novel, the artistic value of which in one sphere the
eighteenth century had signally proved ; inside the

splendid mechanism which had been devised must be 1814
drawn the discredited romance.

An acute eighteenth-century critic thus summed up
the effect of Pope and his school : " What we have
gotten by this revolution, you will say, is a great deal of
good sense. What we have lost is a world of fine fabling."[1]
But all through the century the fabling had gone on, in
nursery rhymes and children's tales, in broadsheets and
chap-books and ballads, in the bombast of the popular
presses. The public appetite for the stranger and more
coloured aspects of life, the subjects which we call " romantic," had never ceased, but it had been satisfied with
indifferent fare, so that, when Scott began to write,
romance had got an evil name, being associated with
the feebly fantastic. The thoughtful fought shy of its
crude manifestations, so that Dr Johnson, in spite of
his taste for the old romancers, could nevertheless in his
Dictionary mark the word " chivalrous " as obsolete.
There was a sceptical spirit of counter-romance among the
cultivated : we find it in *Northanger Abbey*, we have
traces of it in Peacock's *Maid Marian*. What was
needed was a writer who could unite both strains, for
in the mediæval world the two had been inseparable,
the mystery and the fact, credulity and incredulity, the
love of the marvellous and the descent into jovial common
sense ; who could make credible beauty and terror in
their strangest forms by showing them as the natural
outcome of the clash of human character ; who could
satisfy a secular popular craving with fare in which the
most delicate palate could also delight.

In particular, the historical romance clamoured to be
rescued from the dingy *coulisses* of the Minerva Press.
It had a long ancestry and a continuing vogue, but,
except in a piece of brilliant mimicry like Defoe's
Memoirs of a Cavalier, it too had only a nodding acquaintance with the serious art of letters. As Sir Walter Raleigh
has written, " the historical novelists who preceded Scott
chose a century as they might have chosen a partner for
a dance, gaily and confidently, without qualification or

[1] Hurd, *Letters on Chivalry and Romance* (1762).

1814 equipment beyond a few outworn verbal archaisms."
Hitherto all the great novels had been studies of contemporary life ; the historical tale was a lifeless thing,
smothered in tinsel conventions, something beneath the
dignity of literature. Yet the exclusion of the past
gravely narrowed the area of fiction, and if the novel
was to take all the world for its province it could not
confine the world to the mutable present.

An historical novel is simply a novel which attempts
to reconstruct the life, and recapture the atmosphere,
of an age other than that of the writer. The age may be
distant a couple of generations or a thousand years ;
the novel may find its drama in swift external incident,
or in some conflict of the spirit ; it may be picaresque or
domestic, a story of manners, or of action, or of the
heart ; its technique may be any one of the twenty
different ways in which tribal lays and other things are
constructed. The point of difference is that in every
case the writer has to construct for himself, imaginatively,
not only the drama, but an atmosphere and modes of
life and thought with which he cannot be personally
familiar. So, it may be said, has the novelist of contemporary life, whenever he strays outside the narrow
orbit of his experience. But there is a difference. The
man who deals with contemporary life has the key
nearer to his hand. He is concerned with things which
are roughly within his world of experience ; the details
may be strange, but access to them is simple. The
historical novelist has to think himself into an alien
world before he can expound its humanity.

Such a type is capable of the highest flights. In the
hands of a master it permits that isolation of essentials
from accidentals, and that critical detachment which is
of the essence of the novelist's art, and which is hard to
attain when he is clogged with a " turbid mixture of con-
temporaneousness." But it is perhaps the most difficult,
and requires the most scrupulous gift of selection ; it is
so apt to be overloaded with accurate but irrelevant
bric-à-brac. Also it needs an austere conscience. It is
easy to play tricks, and to startle with false colour and

meretricious invention. The reader cannot check the 1814
result by his own experience ; he is in the novelist's
hands, and a point of honour is involved ; consciously
to pervert the past is a more heinous sin than to pervert
the present, for the crime is harder to detect. Above
all it demands a strong independent imagination. It is
fatally simple to project the mind of one's own age back
into the past and produce what is no more than a fancy-
dress party. Past modes of thought are harder to realize
than past ways of living. But the difficulties of the
form have been an incentive to bold minds. Since Scott
released the past for fiction, it is notable how many of
the masterpieces have belonged to that school. *War and
Peace* is an historical novel ; *Vanity Fair*, likewise, for
Thackeray wrote a generation or two after Waterloo :
most of Victor Hugo's and some of the best work of
Flaubert and Anatole France.

Scott in *Waverley* chose wisely to treat of history which
was just outside his own recollection, but within that of
many people with whom he had talked. He was a
child of two when Dr Johnson visited Edinburgh,
and since that year Scotland had moved into a new
world. But fragments of the old world remained, and
he had a pious desire to fix on canvas the fading colours
before they vanished for ever. He put into his first
novel a large part of the harvest of his youthful wanderings. The period—sixty years back—lived for him like
a personal reminiscence, so vividly had he been impressed
by what he had seen and heard and read. His prodigious
memory [1] enabled him to escape the toil of the ordinary
chronicler ; no need for him to hunt in books for the
correct details, since they were all clear in his head. He
wove into the tale traits of many real places and people.
The house of Tully-Veolan was drawn from Grandtully
in Perthshire and Traquair in Tweeddale. Davie Gellatley may have had his original in Daft Jock Gray, once a

---

[1] Hogg (*Dom. Manners*, 67-8) tells how he once went fishing at night with
Scott and Skene. He was asked to sing the ballad of " Gilmanscleuch " which
he had once sung to Scott, but stuck at the ninth verse, whereupon Scott
repeated the whole eighty-eight stanzas without a mistake.

1814 famous figure on the Border, and Fergus MacIvor may have been partly studied from his friend, Alexander Macdonell of Glengarry. The Baron of Bradwardine has hints of Stewart of Invernahyle, whom Scott visited in his youth ; of Erskine's neighbour, the old laird of Gask ; and—in his love of the classics and uncompromising loyalty—of the last Lord Pitsligo.[1] But all the portraits are composite, for Scott was no " barren rascal " to stick slavishly to one model.

The theme of the novel is the contrast of two civilizations—the impact upon the mind of an average educated Englishman of the alien world of the Scots Lowlands and the lingering mediævalism of the Highlands. To get the contrast in the highest relief he selects a tense historical moment, and the tragedy of a lost cause. With the evolution of the narrative inside the main theme he has obviously taken pains, for the actual plot of *Waverley*, as Stevenson noted, is better wrought than that of any of the other novels. The hero under the influence of love and chivalry drifts unconsciously away from the loyalties of his race and the service to which he belongs, and finds himself launched upon an equivocal line of conduct which only just stops short of disaster. The lost cause must issue in tragedy, but for the others the end must be peace, and in order to compass this happy conclusion the fate of the Baron of Bradwardine and his estate is most skilfully managed—with complete fidelity, be it noted, to the intricate Scots law of entail. Nor, when the prefaces and introductions are omitted—excellent things in themselves but with no part in the artistry of the tale—does the narrative ever drag. The action begins properly with Chapter VII, and I cannot feel that it ever loses its grip ; the pace at first is slow and leisurely, but soon we feel the rush of the true epic spirit.

In order to set the different modes of life in strong contrast it was necessary to present in detail the character of the hero, for, if one antithesis is Highland and Low-

---

[1] This subject he has fully treated in W. S. Crockett's *The Scott Originals* (1912).

land, the other is normal good sense set against im-
practicable chivalry and poetry. " The hero," Scott
wrote to Morritt, " is a sneaking piece of imbecility ;
and if he had married Flora, she would have set him up
upon the chimney-piece, as the Polish Dwarf's wife used
to do with him. I am a bad hand at depicting a hero
properly so called, and have an unfortunate propensity
for the dubious characters of Borderers, buccaneers,
Highland robbers and all others of a Robin Hood
description." One may take leave to differ. Edward
Waverley is the most carefully studied of Scott's younger
heroes ; he is indeed an elaborate portrait of one side of
Scott himself. Too little attention has been paid to the
curious merit of the first six chapters, which Erskine
and James Ballantyne found prosy. In reality they are
a careful, and often subtle, study of high-spirited and
imaginative youth, in which the author drew straight
from his own memories. Edward Waverley has Scott's
strong good sense combined with his poetic susceptibi-
lity ; above all he has Scott's habit of being abstracted
into a secret world. " Had he been asked to choose
between any punishment short of ignomimy and the
necessity of giving a cold and composed account of
the ideal world in which he lived the better part of
his days, I think he would not have hesitated to prefer
the former infliction." The sentence is self-revealing.
So, too, with the solid element of prose in Edward.
When Flora is for ever beyond his reach, he turns his
affections contentedly to Rose. Scott himself had done
the same.

The fullness with which the hero is realized and expounded provides the reader with a basis of judgment,
a standpoint from which to view the whimsicalities and
the heroics of the other characters. Such a norm is
needed, for the portraits are mainly of the abnormal.
The book is a comedy of manners, interwoven with a
tragedy, and the manners are those of people who are
mostly " characters "—survivals, grotesques, eccentrics,
persons with some inherited or induced strain of extravagance. Such figures as Cosmo Comyn Bradwardine,

1814 Davie Gellatley, Duncan MacWheeble, Balmawhapple, the Gifted Gilfillan, Callum Beg, Donald Bean Lean, Jock Jinker, are real enough in the sense that they have the vigour of life, but they are comedy figures, who live a little apart from the main road of humanity. They all have certain traits developed in an excessive degree, and out of the clash of these with normal existence comes humour. No novel of Scott's is more richly humorous, or even, in the narrow sense, wittier. Some have found the Baron's pedantry and MacWheeble's legalism dull, but the more they are studied the more subtly relevant their discourse must appear. The delicacies can perhaps be fully appreciated only by a reader with some knowledge of Scots law, for the humour is often professional. MacWheeble's talk, as Davie Gellatley said, is like " a charge of horning," and the manoeuvres by which Inch-grabbit is ousted from the lairdship of Tully-Veolan are highly technical.[1] But the great comedy scenes can be understood by all—the supper at Luckie Macleary's tavern, the halt at Cairnvreckan, the escape of Waverley from Gilfillan (one of the best in literature) and a dozen other unforgettable glimpses. When the pedlar whistles his dog and with the butt-end of a musket lays out the westland Whig in the midst of his soliloquies on cattle and Covenants, the comic spirit comes happily to her own.

As a background to this riot of fun and eccentricity there are the normal people like Waverley and Major Melville, and the full and sagacious pictures of social and economic conditions. Eccentricity, Walter Bagehot has written, " becomes a topic of literary art only when its identity with the ordinary principles of human nature is exhibited in the midst of, or as it were by means of, the superficial unlikeness. Such a skill, however, requires an easy, careless familiarity with normal human life and common human conduct. . . . It is this consistent acquaintance with regular life which makes the irregular characters of Scott so happy a contrast to the uneasy

---

[1] There is an interesting study of the Scots law in *Waverley* in the *Scottish Law Review*, Oct.-Dec., 1930.

distortion of less sagacious novelists."[1] As for the other 1814 normal element, the love-story, it is admittedly a half-hearted and tenuous thing, with no passion in it—an exchange of high sentiment with Flora and a comfortable down-sitting with Rose, though there is much that is graceful in the latter's courtship. Scott had James Ballantyne's "love of wedding cake," and liked to shepherd his lovers to church. But such climaxes are usually outside the real tale ; that tale, in *Waverley*, was concluded on its tragic side at Haribee, and on its comic side with the entranced MacWheeble, when he hears of Rose's fortune, preparing to make a " sma' minute to prevent parties frae resiling."

The tragedy is the clash of ancient loyalties in the persons of Flora and Fergus MacIvor with an unsympathetic world. Scott, as is his custom, shows a profound comprehension of the merits of the different points of view, however fiercely they may conflict in action, for there was much in him of the philosophic historian. The two MacIvors are drawn on the grand scale, with something of the high heels and brocade which were thought fitting for tragic actors ; they live only intermittently, for now and then they seem to fade into disembodied qualities of heart and mind. But what never ceases to live is the Highland world, as seen in the irruption of its denizens upon the Lowland towns and battlefields. Scott exulted in such a contrast, and the pageant of Prince Charlie at Holyrood is made the more real by the attendant pictures of chiefs and caterans in the unfamiliar streets. If it be complained that the Highlanders are drawn from the outside, the answer is that such is the plan of the book. It is not the inner life of the Celt that Scott is concerned with, but his external habits and manners, as they appeared when fate brought him into the glare of national history.

And at the end they rise to that supreme reality which is concerned only with the fundamentals of human life —the reality of the doomed Hector and the blinded Samson and the dying Lear—the ultimate truth of

[1] *Literary Studies*, II. 100.

1814 tragedy. The closing scenes at Carlisle have not often
been equalled for moving simplicity—the trial, when
Evan Dhu Maccombich first pleads with, and then defies,
the court, or the last farewell when Fergus passes under
the castle archway. With the supernatural in its crude
form, like the Bodach Glas, Scott is never happy, but in
great moments such as these he can trouble the mind
as with a whisper from another world. But characteris-
tically he does not leave us on the heights, for he must
always conclude with his feet in the valley ; like Samuel
Butler he preferred the Holy Family to be painted with
clothes drying in the background ; the last word is with
Waverley's servant, the pragmatic Lowlander, Alick
Polwarth, who is chiefly interested in the disposition of
the bodies. " They're no there. . . . The heads are ower
the Scotch yate, as they ca' it. It's a great pity of Evan
Dhu, who was a very weel-meaning, good-natured man
to be a Hielandman ; and indeed so was the Laird of
Glennaquoich too, for that matter, when he wasna in
one of his tirrivies." This anti-climax is cunning art,
for it prepares the mind for the mellow comfort of the
close and the homely pedantries of Macwheeble.

In *Waverley* Scott's capacity for prose begins to reveal
itself. Hitherto his style had been a workmanlike thing
on the whole, but without any shining qualities and with
many blemishes. The blemishes are still there. He has
now and then the vice of grandiloquence, as when he
calls an eagle " the superb monarch of the feathered
tribes " ; of pedantic stiffness—" Having thus touched
upon the leading principle of Flora's character, I may
dismiss the rest more slightly "—or when Fergus orates,
" You do not know the severity of a Government
harassed by just apprehensions and a consciousness of
their own illegality and insecurity " ; of a sensibility
which seems almost to parody itself :—

> " Incomparable Flora ! " said Edward, taking her hand.
> " How much do I need such a monitor ! "
> " A better one by far," said Flora, gently withdrawing her
> hand, " Mr Waverley will always find in his own bosom, when
> he will give its small still voice leisure to be heard."

There is a good deal of loose and ungrammatical writing 1814 and much that is dead and savourless. But the staple is sound, the sounder because it does not obtrude itself. It is easy, urbane, perspicacious, and, in the words of Adolphus, " imparts knowledge in the frank, unassuming and courteous manner of a friend communicating with a friend." Above all it is notably free from the restless self-consciousness of most contemporary Scottish writers, who were in terror of falling into northern solecisms. But its supreme merit is in the dialogues. We see in the talk of the Prince the beginning of that happy discovery of a conventional style of speech for great people at once simple and dignified, a new thing in fiction. The vernacular of the Lowland characters is perfectly rendered, but so is the broken speech of the Highland rank-and-file. For here was another new thing in fiction ; the poor man at a great moment was allowed to become a poet, to use in his simplicity a far subtler and more beautiful rhythm than could be found in the swelling periods of his betters. Take Evan Mac-combich at Carlisle. First the plea :—

" If the Saxon gentlemen are laughing because a poor man, such as me, thinks my life, or the life of six of my degree, is worth that of Vich Ian Vohr, it's like enough they may be very right ; but if they laugh because they think I would not keep my word, and come back to redeem him, I can tell them they ken neither the heart of a Hielander, nor the honour of a gentleman."

And then the defiance :—

" Grace me no grace. Since you are to shed Vich Ian Vohr's blood, the only favour I would accept from you is to bid them loose my hands and gie me my claymore, and bide you just a minute sitting where ye are ! "

Small wonder that the world first rubbed its eyes in astonishment, and then clamoured for more of this novelty, which was also truth. When Goethe in his old age re-read *Waverley*, he was constrained to place it " alongside the best things that have ever been written in the world."

1815   During the autumn of 1814 Scott finished *The Lord of the Isles* at a pace which surpassed any of his earlier feats in the making of verse. He corrected the proofs before setting out for Abbotsford on Christmas Day. The poem was published on January 18th of the following year ; the reviewers praised it but with many reserves ; the public bought fewer copies of it than even of *Rokeby*, and far fewer than of Byron's contemporary romances. The general impression, as James Ballantyne confessed, was one of disappointment. Byron, Scott told him, " hits the mark where I don't even pretend to fledge my arrow." He accepted the popular decision with cheerful resignation and turned to his new novel.

This had been begun late in the previous November, and two volumes had been completed in something less than two months. A Galloway exciseman, Joseph Train, for whom the Ballantynes had published a volume of poems, told him a story of an astrologer who had predicted the future of a child born in a house which he was visiting, a story which Scott had heard from other sources in his youth. That was in the first week of November, and Scott must have begun at once to make a novel out of it. The book was finished in six weeks, when the author professed to be taking a holiday to " refresh the machine," and was published under the title of *Guy Mannering* on February 24, 1815. Train's story, an indifferent Durham ballad, and the celebrated Dormont case, decided in the Court of Session two years before, supplied the groundwork. The Galloway scene was remembered from Scott's early circuit tours, and the Liddesdale landscape was never out of his mind. For the chief characters he drew from many sources. In Colonel Mannering there are hints of himself, and in Julia something of his wife. The piety of commentators has found prototypes for Tod Gabbie in Tod Willie, who hunted the hills above Loch Skene, and for Tib Mumps in Margaret Teasdale of Gilsland. Traits of Dandie Dinmont may have been borrowed from James Davidson of Hyndlee—at any rate the famous terriers came from the Hyndlee kennel. Dominie Sampson seems to have

been drawn from George Thomson, the son of the parish
minister of Melrose, with features added from one Sanson
of Leadhills. Pleydell was admittedly based on Adam
Rolland for demeanour and learning, while the " high-
jinks " side of him was suggested by Andrew Crosbie,
one of the heroes of the old Crochallan Fencibles. But
in Scott's case the search for authentic models is idle.
He picked a trait here and a feature there, and blended
them as he pleased.

The book is both a novel of character and a comedy
of contemporary manners. The theme is one of the
oldest in literature, that stuff of a thousand folk-tales,
the " missing heir." Scott's first intention was to make
it a psychological study, with the astrological prediction
the central fact—the story of a man conscious of a
predestined fate and bracing himself to meet it ; but he
wisely decided that such a subject was not for him. It
required, he said modestly, " not only more talent than
the author could be conscious of possessing, but also
involved doctrines and discussions of a nature too serious
for his purpose and for the character of the narration."[1]
He could not cumber himself with psychology when he
had a host of vivid mortals in his mind waiting to dance
at his bidding. Written as it was in six weeks, after a
laborious year, it is notably more careless than *Waverley*,
which had been simmering in his head for a decade.
The hero is stockish to the last degree, the most wooden
thing he ever glued together. Many of the minor
episodes, such as the Indian incidents, are crudely
conceived and casually told. The love-making is never
more than perfunctory, and Julia Mannering, though
she lives in a sense, is largely a borrowing from the
conventional fiction of the day : her letters are in the
worst tradition, and her vivacity leaves the reader
unmoved. Scott was not often happy in his younger
gentlewomen. There is much coy and cumbrous writing
of this sort :—" We omit here various execrations with
which these honest gentlemen garnished their discourse,
retaining only such of their expletives as are least offen-

[1] Introduction to *Guy Mannering*.

1815 sive "; and Bertram's reflections in the jail in Chapter
XLVIII are in the worst vein of prose-poetry. There
are pieces of clumsy artifice, as when Pleydell in Chapter
XLIX is made to praise the good looks of the Dutch
in order to drag in the hero by the heels. Lastly there
is a fault of which the beginnings were to be seen in
Bradwardine and MacWheeble and which was to grow
upon Scott—the trick of exaggerating and repeating a
single odd trait of a character. Dominie Sampson's
" Prodigious ! ! " tends to become the mechanical squeak-
ing of a doll.

But these are small things. Lovers of Scott will
always dispute which is his best novel, but all will put
Guy Mannering among the first three. He wrote of a
land which he knew intimately and of people whom he
understood and loved, and he devised an appropriate
tale for their revelation. In sheer narrative skill the
book is among the best. It begins with tremendous
events happening in a tense atmosphere of excitement
and mystery ; the interest is never allowed to flag, but
rises to a climax still more tense and exciting. And yet
there is no hint of melodrama. The wild doings follow
naturally from the characters of the protagonists.

Save for the hero and the heroine, Scott never for an instant loses his grasp upon his people. Colonel Mannering,
the pivot of the tale, is a careful and credible portrait,
drawn even more closely than Edward Waverley from
the writer himself, and revealing the stiff, imperious
element in Scott which underlay his habitual good-nature.
Admirable, too, is Godfrey Bertram, the slack-lipped,
degenerating laird, whose weakness is cunningly accen-
tuated by his proud genealogy. The lesser figures, such
as Macmorlan, Mrs MacCandlish and Jock Jabos, are
perfectly etched in ; Scott reveals the same power of
describing the confused popular mind, in his account of
the gossip of Kippletringan, as he was later to show in
" Wandering Willie's Tale " ; and it would be hard to
find a more masterly picture of manners than the funeral
ceremonies of Mrs Margaret Bertram. The villains,
Gilbert Glossin and Dirk Hatteraick, are what villains

should be, formidable but conceivable, not weary in ill- 1815
doing, and Glossin's terrors in Chapter xxxiii are as
subtly depicted as they are dramatically right.

There are two centres of gravity in the book, two oases
of peace in a disturbed country, which bring back the
tale to normality, and rest and balance the reader's
mind. One is Pleydell, and the other is Dandie Dinmont.
Pleydell is a lawyer after Scott's heart, a lover at once
of mirth and law, human nature and humane letters.
" A lawyer," he declares, " without history or literature
is a mechanic, a mere working mason ; if he possesses
some knowledge of these he may venture to call himself
an architect." He is the pick of the city as Dinmont is
the pick of the countryside. As for Dandie he remains
one of the most complete, four-square, three-dimensioned and vital figures in literature. We know him
better than we know our daily companions. Wherever
he appears he humanizes the scene, for he is triumphant
humanity. As has been well said, he is " wise like a
wise dog, with a limit to his intelligence but none to his
fidelity." [1] Like a fairy-tale hero we believe him immortal
and unconquerable ; when he appears we feel a sense of
security ; we are no longer anxious about young Bertram
in the jail at Portanferry when we hear Dandie's step
on the stair. The scenes at Charlieshope, skilfully led
up to by the adventure on Bewcastle Waste, belong to
an ancient happy world of pastoral, and wherever Dandie
goes he takes with him that charméd atmosphere of
essential sagacity, kindness and courage. He is like a
hill-wind that cleanses and vitalizes the world, and, like
all the major heroes in literature, he is kin both to
poetry and to reality.

Such a tale as *Guy Mannering* depends for its drama
upon the Aristotelian "reversal of fortune" and "recognition." Therefore it must include an element of tragedy,
something which troubles and solemnizes the mind. This
is given by Meg Merrilies, the greatest figure that Scott
has drawn from the back-world and the underworld
of Scotland. Half-crazy, wild as a hawk, savage yet

[1] Stephen Gwynn, *Life of Sir Walter Scott*, 227.

1815 with nobility in her savagery, when she appears the eery light of romance falls on the scene. Wherever we meet her—like some wise-woman of the Sagas by the ruins of Derncleugh laying her curse upon the house of Ellangowan, or speaking riddles in Tib Mumps's hostelry, or in the wonderful scene with Dominie Sampson at the Kaim of Derncleugh, or in the sea-cave when Dirk Hatteraick's bullet finds her breast—she is the fate that presides over the action, an embodied destiny working her secret purpose, a reminder in the midst of comedy of the mystery of life. Her speech is that of a great tragic heroine, descending now to an idiomatic homeliness, now rising to the heights of poetry, but always rhythmical and compelling and exquisitely faithful.

> " Do you see that blackit and broken end of a sheeling ? There my kettle boiled for forty years—there I bore twelve buirdly sons and daughters. Where are they now ?—Where are the leaves that were on that auld ash-tree at Martinmas ?— the west wind has made it bare, and I'm stripped too. Do you see that saugh tree ? It's but a blackened rotten stump now— I've sat under it mony a bonnie summer afternoon, when it hung its gay garlands ower the poppling water. I've sat there and . . . I've held you on my knee, Henry Bertram, and sung ye sangs of the auld barons and their bloody wars.—— It will ne'er be green again, and Meg Merrilies will never sing sangs mair, be they blithe or sad. But ye'll no forget her, and ye'll gar big up the auld wa's for her sake ? And let somebody live there that's ower gude to fear them of another world. For if ever the dead came back among the living, I'll be seen in this glen mony a night after these crazed banes are in the mould."

With a sure instinct, though Meg is the instrument of the "reversal of fortune," Scott does not make her the chief agent in the accompanying "recognition," since the latter belongs to comedy and the former to tragedy. It is the bleaching-girl's song about the woods of Warrick Head which awakens the hero's memory of the place, and the preposterous Dominie who recalls to him his true name.

The epithet " delightful " was used by contemporary writers of the book, and the delightfulness of *Guy Mannering* is the quality by which it lives. It does not

take us into the sounding arena of great deeds, or plumb 1815
—save at odd moments—the deeper wells of life. It is
concerned with plain country people in a remote corner
of Scotland, and the malefactors are humble folk—a
swindling local attorney and a homicidal smuggler. Nor
is there any serious love-interest. But nevertheless it is
true romance, for it both stirs and calms, both excites
and satisfies; it is what Bagehot calls a " union of life
with measure, of spirit with reasonableness." The
strange and the romantic are made to flower from the
normal, and thereby their effect is heightened, while the
normal is portrayed with a sober geniality which makes
it in itself romantic. In no other of his novels is there
quite the same happy spirit, the same delight in plain
human goodness, the same conviction of the cheerfulness
of the race of men. Nor do we find in any other novel
quite the same gusto of creation—a marvel when we
remember the circumstances of its production. The
explanation, I think, is twofold. *Waverley* had been
long on the stocks, and it was a reshaping of an historic
scene with which Scott's studies from boyhood had been
closely concerned. But in *Guy Mannering* he was
entering upon a new field and using material which he
had never before attempted. To find that it grew so
readily under his hand gave him that highest of pleasures,
the discovery of a new kind of creative power. Again,
more than any other of the novels, it explored the inner
life of his own Borderland. He was drawing upon the
happy days when he had scoured Liddesdale for ballads,
he was describing the land and the people most intimately
linked with his lost youth. Was it to be wondered at
that something of that young freshness of spirit should
have returned to inspire his mature experience ?

III

The year 1815, having opened laboriously, was to be
relieved by holidaying. When the courts rose in March
Scott set off by sea for London, accompanied by his
wife and his elder daughter Sophia, who was now a child

1815 of twelve. The parents stayed with the Doumerges in
Piccadilly, and Sophia was deposited with Joanna
Baillie in her little house at Hampstead. Scott was in
the best of spirits, for *Guy Mannering* was a success
beyond his dreams, and the terms he had got for it
included a certain lightening of the dead stock of the
Ballantynes' publishing business ; another novel—he
had many themes in his head—and that weariful concern
would be a thing of the past. Moreover it was a great
moment in the national history. The Corsican had been
vanquished and was now safe in the island prison of
Elba, a Bourbon sat again on the throne of France, and
a twenty-years' load of anxiety had been lifted from
honest hearts.

He found London in holiday mood, and, if his welcome
had been cordial six years before, now it was roses
everywhere. His poems had revealed Scotland to the
south and brought northward troops of visitors, and
there was a universal curiosity to see the magician
himself. Moreover, there were the two new novels,
which lay on every table, novels which opened up a
richer wonderland. Scott's, beyond doubt, was the
general verdict, but a glamour of mystery hung about
them, and mystery is always attractive. " Make up
your mind," Joanna Baillie wrote to him, " to be stared
at only a little less than the Czar of Muscovy and old
Blücher."

He met all the literary and political celebrities whom
he had known before, and made a new friend in Sir
Humphry Davy. But the two men chiefly associated
with this visit were the Prince Regent and Byron. The
Prince had long admired Scott's poetry and had com-
mended his behaviour over the Laureateship, so his
friend Adam, afterwards Chief Commissioner of the new
jury court in Scotland, was ordered to invite him to a
little dinner at Carlton House. Croker was of the party,
and Lord Melville, the Duke of York, Lord Huntly,
Lord Fife, and that formidable nobleman, Lord Hert-
ford, who was to figure variously in literature as Lord
Steyne and Lord Monmouth. It was a merry occasion ;

the Prince and Scott, both noted raconteurs, capped 1815 each other's tales ; and at midnight the host, looking towards his guest, asked for a bumper to the author of *Waverley*. Scott, an adept at this game, promised to convey the compliment to the real Simon Pure, and the Prince countered with the health of the author of *Marmion*. The Prince called him by his Christian name from their first introduction, gave another little dinner for him, at which he sang his favourite songs, and sent him a gold snuff-box set in brilliants with a medallion of the royal head on the lid. Scott was naturally pleased ; he had an old-fashioned reverence for royalty, and it was much for one of his prepossessions to be treated as an intimate by the heir-apparent. As his later correspondence shows, he had no illusions about George the Fourth, and condemned as strongly as any radical the grossness and folly of much of his career ; but it was given him to see that odd being at his best, to come under the spell of manners which could be most gracious and winning, and to get a glimpse of the genuine talents of one who was far more than the half-witted debauchee of the caricaturists. Scott had a singular gift of eliciting what was worthiest in a man, and the Prince Regent's relations with him are among the few creditable things in a dubious record.

It was the same with Byron. Scott met him first at John Murray's house, and the stately compliments of the previous letters were replaced by a friendly intimacy not without affection. The truth is that it was an attraction of opposites ; each was slightly mystified by the other, which is no bad basis for friendship. They agreed in contemning the man who was a writer and nothing else, but their aspirations towards the completer life took different roads. Byron was impressed by Scott's gusto and security and broad humanity ; Scott by Byron's exotic beauty and the glamour of one who lived romance. He told a friend afterwards that no portrait did him justice. " The lustre is there, but it is not lighted up. Byron's countenance is a thing to dream of." [1]

[1] Lockhart, IV. 147.

1815 He found that they agreed uncommonly well on most topics except religion and politics, and he decided that on these Byron had no very fixed opinions. He told him that he would probably end by joining the Roman church, and Byron seemed to assent. Byron's radicalism he could not take seriously : it seemed to him to be partly due to a love of paradox, and partly to disgust with certain Ministers. The two met nearly every day during the London visit, and like the heroes of Homer they exchanged gifts. These were in the best romantic fashion—Scott's to Byron a gold-mounted dagger which had belonged to Elfi Bey, and Byron's a sepulchral vase of silver from the Long Walls of Athens containing the bones of ancient Greeks. Their last meeting was in the early autumn when Scott was on his way home from France. On this occasion he found Byron cold towards his tales of Waterloo heroism, though he was to use them in the second part of *Childe Harold*. They were not fated to meet again, but in all the difficult later years Scott remained Byron's champion, and Byron cherished one of his few esteems for a man whose humanity had sweetened his bitterness and warmed a corner of his bleak house of life. Seven years later he wrote that he owed to Scott " far more than the usual obligation for the courtesies of literature and common friendship. . . . You disclaim ' jealousies.' But I would ask, as Boswell did of Johnson, ' of whom could you be jealous ? ' Of none of the living certainly, and (taking all and all into consideration) of which of the dead ? " [1]

The Scotts returned to Edinburgh in May, after the Hundred Days had begun and the gaze of the world was fixed upon Napoleon's last desperate bid for power. For a little men held their breath, till Waterloo let them draw it again. Then followed a riot of patriotic exultation, for was it not Wellington who had shaken down the spoiler ? An Edinburgh surgeon, Sir Charles Bell, had gone out to assist the medical staff after the battle, and a letter of his set Scott on fire. He had longed to visit the Peninsula during the campaign ; he

[1] *P.L.B.*,189 : Byron, *Letters and Journal* (Ed. Prothero), VI. 4.

could at any rate now visit Flanders and see the foot-prints **1815**
of war, and hear the British bugles sounded beside the
walls of Paris. He collected two young country neighbours, Scott of Gala and Pringle of Whytbank, and an
advocate friend, and on the 30th of August took ship
from Harwich. But first he provided for the expenses
of the trip by arranging for regular letters to be printed
by Ballantyne and published jointly by Constable,
Murray and Longman, letters which would first be
passed round among his family and friends.

Paul's Letters to his Kinsfolk deserves to be read, for
it is is a revealing piece of autobiography. It contains
no fine writing, for the scenes which Scott visited and
the company in which he moved seemed to him to be
too august for sentiment and to demand a faithful and
sober chronicle. It is journalism, no doubt, but journalism at its best. He describes the little ancient cities
of Flanders ; the field of Waterloo, and the battle which
he did not perfectly understand, since, like most of his
British contemporaries, he does scant justice to Blücher.
Then comes Paris, where his demi-god Wellington
received him kindly, and he hob-nobbed with monarchs
and field-marshals, and attended a review of the Russian
troops on a Ukraine charger, and was kissed in public
on both cheeks by Platoff the Cossack Hetman. Never
had a man of letters had such an experience, and Scott
felt that at last he was being given a taste of the life
of action. But more remarkable than the vivid narrative
of travel is the moderation and good sense of the book,
qualities which appear also in his poem *The Field of
Waterloo*, produced, like *Don Roderick*, in aid of war
charities. Napoleon for twenty years had ridden Scott's
imagination. When Abbotsford was beginning he used
to entertain French prisoners from Selkirk in its little
dining-room and eagerly cross-examine them about the
looks and sayings and doings of their Emperor.[1] He
recognized his surpassing greatness, and concerning him
there is none of the conventional railing of his contemporaries, only the romancer's regret that he did not

[1] See Sir Charles Oman in *Blackwood's Magazine*, Jan. 1929.

1815 choose to die with his Guard on his last battle-field. Nor is there any bitterness against the French people ; on the contrary, though Blücher had made much of him, there is a stern criticism of Prussian brutality. But even here he is reasonable ; he realizes how many scores Prussia and all Europe had to pay off ; he understands, though he does not approve, the feeling of Lord Dudley when he wrote : " I own I have a pleasure in seeing this confounded people, that have tormented all mankind ever since I can remember anything, and made us pay ten per cent. upon our incomes, to say nothing of other taxes, plundered and insulted by a parcel of square-faced barbarians from the Wolga." Staunch royalist, too, though he was, he saw the weakness of the restored Bourbons, and forecast the reaction which would bring them down.

He came home by way of London, where young Gala was enthralled by Byron's pale beauty, and by Sheffield, where a workman in a cutler's shop offered his master a week's free work for Scott's autograph. He had presents in his portmanteau for everybody at Abbotsford, family, servants and the estate workers. He returned to find his friend Skene of Rubislaw there, and the little drawing-room equipped with new chintzes, which he was blind enough not to notice. The house was growing piece-meal round the core of the old farm with the irregularity of the British Constitution, the young plantations were coming on, and the young Walter, now fourteen years of age, had killed his first blackcock. But his old charger Daisy, a white thoroughbred, had taken a sudden aversion to her master and would not suffer him to mount her ; Scott took it for a sign that he had reached middle age and must henceforth content himself with a homely cob. That autumn he acquired what he had long been in treaty for, the lands of Kaeside which ran south to the wild sheet of water called Cauldshiels loch, the legendary home of a water-bull. The original hundred and thirty acres of his estate were now nearer a thousand.

IV

Scott had found on his return another guest at Abbots- 1816
ford besides the laird of Rubislaw—James Ballantyne
with a load of bills, confused accounts, apologies and
supplications. The new novel which was to clear his
feet must not be delayed, so, while *Paul's Letters* was in
the press, and Terry was preparing a dramatic version of
Guy Mannering for the London stage, *The Antiquary*
was begun and finished within four months. It was
published by Constable early in May 1816, about the
time of the death of the author's eldest brother, John,
whose modest bequests did something to relieve the
embarrassment of the remaining brother, Thomas.

The Antiquary, though James Ballantyne shook his
head over it, was at once successful, and, according to
Lockhart, it was Scott's favourite among his works.
" It wants the romance of *Waverley* and the adventure
of *Guy Mannering*," Scott wrote to Terry, " and yet
there is some salvation about it, for if a man will paint
from nature, he will be likely to amuse those who are
daily looking at it." It was a novel of contemporary
life, a story of familiar characters, a picture of his own
early associations, and in some degree a portrait of
himself. He had his prototype for Edie Ochiltree in a
famous bedesman, Andrew Gemmels, who had fought
at Fontenoy and in Scott's youth had been a notable
figure on the Border, dying in 1793 at the age of 106.
Jonathan Oldbuck is drawn from the antiquary George
Constable, who had first awakened his boyish interest
in the past, and there are elements in him, perhaps, of
John Ramsay of Ochtertyre.

The plot is elaborate, artificial, and unimportant,
once again of the " missing heir " school ; Lovel, the
young hero, is colourless, and it is hard to be interested
in his love affair with Isabella Wardour. The construction is careless—the sun is made to set in the
east and there are two Tuesdays in one week ; and the
writing in its uninspired moments is apt to be pompous
and Grandisonian. Just before the great scene when

1816 the Wardours and Edie are cut off by the sea, there are leaden descriptions of scenery and weather, and Isabella on one occasion addresses her lover thus : " I am much embarrassed, Mr Lovel, by your—I would not willingly use a strong word—romantic and hopeless pertinacity. It is for yourself I plead, that you would consider the calls your country has on your talents, that you will not waste, in an idle and fanciful indulgence of an ill-placed predilection, time, which, well redeemed by active exertion, should lay the foundation of future distinction." " It is enough, Miss Wardour," Lovel replies, and it is certainly enough.

Having said this much, I decline to allow the devil's advocate a further word. There is little violent action in the book, but the interest never for one moment flags. It is primarily a comedy of Scottish country life, and the main characters, though carefully and truthfully drawn, are all given their " humours "—fantastic traits several degrees above reality—Oldbuck's pedantry, his sister's notableness, Sir Arthur's pride of race, Hector MacIntyre's inflammable conceit. The comedy key is perfectly maintained ; the only villain is Dousterswivel, who is no more than a pantomime rogue. To match the gentry we have peasants in the same vein—Jenny Rintherout, Mrs Heukbane and Mrs Mailsetter, Coxon the barber, Davie the post-boy—all faithful transcripts, but inspired with the comic spirit. Let me instance three episodes which seem to me comedy triumphant— Grizel Oldbuck's story of Rob Tull, the scene in which Mrs Mailsetter and her cronies gossip in the post-office, and that in which Oldbuck, at the alarm of invasion, girds on his old sword.

The dramatic contrast to this staple of homely humours and oddities is to be found partly in the dark stateliness of the Glenallans (which skirts, but does not stumble into, melodrama), and the two or three humble figures who are invested with an heroic or tragic grandeur. Of the latter Edie Ochiltree stands first, the most Shakespearean figure, it has been well said, outside Shakespeare. He is drawn with minute realism—his beggar's gaiety,

his vagabond's philosophy, his tincture of radicalism,
his resourcefulness like that of Odysseus. But at high
moments he is allowed to attain a homespun magnificence,
and to speak words which, though wholly in character,
are yet parts of the world's poetry. Take the scene of
the storm :—

> " Good man," said Sir Arthur, " can you think of nothing—
> of no help.—— I'll make you rich—I'll give you a farm—
> I'll——"
>
> " Our riches will soon be equal," said the beggar, looking out
> upon the strife of the waters—" they are sae already ; for
> I hae nae land, and you would give your fair bounds and barony
> for a square yard of rock that would be dry for twal hours."

Or take his classic profession of patriotism :—

> " *Me* no muckle to fight for ! Isna there the country to fight
> for, and the burnsides that I gang daundering beside, and the
> hearths o' the gudewives that gie me my bit bread, and the
> bits o' weans that come toddling to play wi' me when I come
> about a landward toun ?—Deil ! " he continued, grasping his
> pikestaff with great emphasis, " an' I had as gude pith as I
> hae gude will and a gude cause, I should gie some o' them
> a day's kemping."

Next there is Saunders Mucklebackit, the fisherman,
who, at his son's death, masters his grief till the coffin
has left the house, and then breaks down in a passion
of tearless sobbing, but next day is found mending the
" auld black bitch of a boat " which had drowned his
boy. He, too, is made through strong emotion to rise
to an epic dignity.

> " What would you have me do," he asks, " unless I wanted
> to see four children starve because ane is drooned ? It's weel
> wi' you gentles, that can sit in the house wi' handkerchers to
> your een when ye lose a friend ; but the likes o' us maun to
> our wark again if our hearts were beating as hard as my
> hammer. . . . Yet what needs ane to be angry at her, that
> has neither soul nor sense ?—though I am no that muckle
> better mysell. She's but a rickle o' auld rotten deals nailed
> thegither, and warped wi' the wind and the sea—and I am
> a dour carle battered by winds and foul weather at sea and
> land till I am maist as senseless as hersell. She maun be
> mended though again' the morning tide—that's a thing o'
> necessity."

1816   Saunders Mucklebackit is the east-coast fisherman
with Norse blood in him, and he has something of the
austere dignity of the Sagas.   But his mother, Elspeth
of the Craigburnfoot, is like some witch-wife out of the
Elder Edda.   She sits by her fireside, oblivious of the
deaths of her kin, with her crazy mind on unhappy
things that befell long ago in a world of pride and
pageantry far distant from a fisherman's hovel.   In her
madness she recites the best ballad Scott ever wrote,
the ballad of the Red Harlaw, and she expounds it in
the old manner of high romance.

> " Ye maun ken, hinnie, that this Roland Cheyne, for as poor
> and auld as I sit in the chimmey-neuk, was my forbear, and
> an awfu' man he was that day in the fight, but specially after
> the Earl had fa'en ; for he blamed himsell for the counsel he
> gave, to fight before Mar came up wi' Mearns and Aberdeen
> and Angus."

And when death comes to this great tragic figure, a
survival from another world, Scott, after his fashion,
artfully slackens the tension and brings the tale back to
the homely fisher life.

> " Your honour," said Ailison Breck, who was next in age
> to the deceased, " suld send doun something to us for keeping
> up our hearts at the lyke-wake, for a' Saunder's gin, puir man,
> was drucken out at the burial o' Steenie, and we'll no get
> mony to sit dry-lipped with the corpse."

The book is richer perhaps than any of the others in
cunning detail, for Scott wrote of a world which he knew
intimately—Monkbarn's antiquities, Sir Arthur's genea-
logical whimsies, the life of the burghs and the farm-
towns and the fishing-huts, the back-world of the peasant
mind.   And it is inspired throughout by the spirit of a
large and sympathetic understanding.   The stiff lairds
become human in the presence of sorrow.   The Tory
Sir Arthur is less tenderly dealt with than the Whig
Oldbuck.   Coxon the barber speaks his mind on " the
democraws, as they ca' them, that are again' the king
and the law, and hair-powder and dressing o' gentleman's
wigs—a wheen blackguards," but Edie the blue-gown

and Saunders Mucklebackit the fisherman, sturdy demo-
crats both, are the true heroes of the tale.

V

From the heights of creation Scott had to descend to
the dismal business of his trading ventures. It is a
subject on which it is impossible at this time of day to
get at the exact truth. The papers dealing with the
downfall of 1826 are extant, and may be studied in the
National Library of Scotland, but the relations between
Scott and the Ballantynes must remain largely in the
realm of guesswork. The books were never properly
balanced, the existing financial statements are obscure,
and the student has nothing to go upon but *ex parte*
and often contradictory declarations. Many since that
date have tried to shed light on the darkness, but all
have failed. Three years before his death Lockhart
wrote, " The details of Scott's commercial perplexities
remain in great measure inexplicable," and, if one so
near the events themselves was puzzled, a later com-
mentator dare not be dogmatic.

The settlement of the two businesses arrived at through
Constable's help in the autumn of 1813 was not final.
The publishing firm of John Ballantyne and Company,
though no longer operating, was not fully wound up ;
it had still many bills out against it, and in October 1814
Scott's own sheriff-substitute, Charles Erskine, who had
made it an advance, was asking for the repayment of
his money. The natural way to clear its debts was to
dispose of its mountainous dead stock, but Constable
had already done all he intended in that matter. The
result was that *Guy Mannering* went to Murray and
Longman, who took over stock to the value of £500.
But a large quantity remained, and meantime Scott had
to pay the interest on the renewals of the bills. Constable published *The Antiquary* but took over no stock,
and began to show himself disinclined to put his printing
in the Ballantynes' way, through exasperation with
John's tortuous methods. John was now very comfort-

1816 able in his business as auctioneer, drove tandem about Edinburgh in a blue coat and white cords, was a great figure at local race-meetings, and gave gay, Frenchified little dinners in his villa at Trinity, which he called ' Harmony Hall.' He acted as Scott's agent, and a worse could not have been found, for he was tricky and disingenuous, and had no great desire to wind up the publishing concern, since its entanglements kept him closely in touch with Scott, the chief source of pride in his life. That business had never been solvent from the start, and its floating liabilities, which came wholly upon Scott, continued until its final liquidation in 1817, when the balance of indebtedness was still estimated at £10,000—a debt which at that date was transferred to the printing firm.

As for the printing business it is not easy to decide whether it, too, at this point, was not bankrupt. It need not have been, for, as we have seen, its commitments were necessarily limited. In the later high tide of Scott's productiveness it undoubtedly attained a certain degree of prosperity, owing to the large amount of safe printing orders which it received, but I am inclined to think that, at any time between its beginning in 1805 and the year 1816, an honest balance-sheet would have revealed it as insolvent. Scott does not appear to have drawn much from it, scarcely the interest on his invested capital, but James Ballantyne seems to have habitually anticipated what he believed to be the realizable profits, and this led to constant recourse to accommodation paper. When the publishing house was started the two concerns lent each other money, or rather backed each other's bills, and so the finances were further complicated. In August 1813 the printing firm was clearly losing money, for we find Scott writing to John Ballantyne : " I cannot observe hitherto that the printing-office is paying off, but rather adding to its embarrassments—and it cannot be thought that I have either means or inclination to support a losing concern at the rate of £200 a month." In October 1814 James Ballantyne writes : " I trust the printing will cease to

be the burden which hitherto it has been." The actual 1816
trading therefore seems to have been conducted at a
loss, and the annual deficit was allowed to accumulate,
since no member of the firm had any exact notion of
the firm's position. Scott had to intervene repeatedly
and pay out of his own pocket some of the more pressing
demands, but these payments never cleared his feet.
Moreover, through John's cleverness, the practice of
double bills was largely used, under which, say, Ballantyne
drew a bill on Constable which was accepted, and
Constable drew a bill for the same amount, which was
accepted by Ballantyne, and was held as cover in case
the first bill should not be met. When a bill was discharged the covering bill was cancelled, but when a
bill was renewed the cover was continued, and, in the
event of a crisis, the debtor might find himself liable
for the same sum twice over. In 1814 James Ballantyne
had experienced the result of this practice, having to
pay twice over a private bill for wine.[1]

The position in 1816, therefore, was that the publishing
business was suspended, but still burdened with bills
and dead stock, while the printing business was carrying
on, possibly at a profit in its actual trading, but at a
heavy loss if its past liabilities were taken into reckoning.
John Ballantyne was leading the life of a virtuoso and
man of fashion, acting as Scott's literary agent, for which
he was well paid, and doing his best to embroil him
with Constable. James, besides looking after the printing,
was Scott's amanuensis, private critic, and proof corrector,
also for a handsome consideration. Both the brothers
were expensive people and lived well ; John was a
provincial Lucullus, and at a later date we find James
spending £100 on wine in three months.[2]

---

[1] A. Constable, III. 44-46. The material for the relations between Scott
and the Ballantynes will be found in Lockhart, in the Ballantynes' Refutation
(1838), in Lockhart's reply The Ballantyne Humbug Handled (1839), and in
the Ballantynes' Reply (1839). It is not an edifying controversy, and Lockhart
at first undoubtedly overstated his case, but he seems to me on the whole
to prove his main points. There is a judicious examination of the dispute in
Lang, II. 126-172.

[2] As early as 1807 he was astonishing the London publishers by the white
hermitage supplied at a luncheon which he gave to celebrate the enlargement
of his printing works. Memoirs of John Murray, I. 86.

In October 1815 James thought of taking to himself a wife. The lady was a Miss Hogarth, whose brother, knowing the earlier embarrassments of the firm, was not prepared to accept James as a suitor for his sister's hand unless his position was made secure and he was freed from indefinite liabilities. Accordingly Scott agreed to become sole partner in the firm of James Ballantyne and Company, retaining James as his salaried servant at £400 a year. The debts of the publishing business were taken over by the printing-house, though a certain number of the accommodation bills due by it were left afloat in John's name. James remained personally indebted to Scott in the sum of £3000, and the future printing profits which in view of the new novels might be considerable, were to be applied, after a fair remuneration to Scott for his advances, to the clearing off the old Ballantyne debts. The lady's brother assented, and early in 1816 James was married.

The centre figure in Scott's affairs is henceforth Constable. The latter had saved the Ballantynes from bankruptcy and had many claims upon Scott's gratitude, and, though I cannot believe that there could ever have been any warm friendship between the two, yet the relations might have been of the pleasantest but for John, who was always trying to frighten Constable into taking more dead stock by threatening that a new novel—or even a new edition of an old novel—would be carried elsewhere. On more than one occasion Scott lost his temper with his agent, but John was incorrigible. There is no prouder man than your rising Scots merchant with a lairdship in prospect, and it went against the grain with Constable to do business with the raffish John, whom he could not regard as his social equal. Hence there was no free and frank discussion with Scott himself, which might have led to the latter's affairs being taken in hand by a man of real business acumen. Constable beyond doubt was treated at this time with scant consideration, and he was not in a position to protest. For *Waverley* had opened his eyes to Scott's capacities, and it wrung his soul to think of

losing this wonder-worker to a rival publisher. So he **1816**
was compelled to submit to· John's exactions, and to
be very complaisant over the Ballantyne bills. He was
a self-made man, and had not amassed any great capital
reserves. What he had was a host of friends and ample
credit ; the banks would discount his bills to any
reasonable extent ; but he had already strained this
credit by his multitudinous undertakings. In self-
justification he talked grandly about the new novels—
the huge sums he had paid for them and the huge sums
they earned ; the world, even the banking world,
believed him, and the credit of publisher and author
rose so high that only very cool heads could have escaped
a certain *folie des grandeurs.*

Such a head neither possessed. Constable was shrewd,
but he was also adventurous and optimistic. Scott's
spirits, sunk low by reverses in a business which he did
not properly comprehend, would soar at the first hint
of better times. He had inherited some £12,000, and his
wife had a few hundreds a year ; he had an official.
income of £1600 ; he had received at least £10,000
for his poems, and he had made by his first two novels
probably double that sum. By 1816 he had spent on
land between £9000 and £10,000, and a good many
thousands on buildings and furniture. Cadell estimated
his total losses in the Ballantyne firms as £20,000, and
if we take as large a figure as £15,000 as·representing
the loss accrued up to that date, his balance-sheet in
1816 was not too unwholesome. Much of the capital
had indeed gone for good, but some was represented by
solid assets like land, books and copyrights. Had Scott
then cut himself loose from business, and continued his
expenditure on the comparatively modest scale of the
past, he would have been a wealthy man, even though
he had only written a novel once every three years.
Even as it was, the taking over of the printing firm
seemed to be a wise step, for now he could learn for
himself the exact position of the business, and could
limit any future commitments.

It was to prove on the contrary a long stride towards

1816 his undoing. He never made any serious inquisition into the affairs of the printing house, and James Ballantyne was as easy-going as a salaried servant as he had been when a partner. Moreover, Scott had got a business which he could treat as his banker. When he wanted money for the purchase of land or anything else he used the name of the company by obtaining bills on Constable and granting acceptances in return. Constable, eager to retain his good will, made no demur. These bills were, of course, met or reduced from time to time by his large literary earnings, but he got into the habit of invariably forestalling such receipts. His expenditure in one year would be greater than his income, but there was the certainty of that year's deficit being paid for by the next year's earnings. Yet at any one moment he was always in arrears, and if a sudden crisis came and a balance had to be struck it might be heavily on the wrong side. In such a crisis Constable could not help him, for Constable too would be caught, his adventurous business methods being much the same. In this perpetual forestalling, through the medium of a company which obscured in his eyes its real improvidence, seems to me to lie the main secret of Scott's disasters.

Meanwhile John Ballantyne was busy. *The Antiquary* had not cleared Scott's feet, but its author had an idea in his head which would. He had a scheme for a series of " Tales of my Landlord," collected and reported by one Jedediah Cleishbotham, schoolmaster of the parish of Gandercleuch. Constable would not take any back stock, so they should go elsewhere, but, in order to save Constable's face, the title-page would not bear the words " By the Author of *Waverley*." John approached Murray, and Murray's Edinburgh agent, Blackwood, an antiquarian bookseller in the Old Town, who readily accepted Scott's terms and agreed also to take over £500 of back stock. John, indeed, made rather a mess of the bargaining, for he almost sold the copyright outright. Blackwood, a plain-spoken man, was allowed to criticize the plot of one of the tales, *The Black Dwarf*, and Scott, who would accept rebuke cheerfully from his 1816 equals, but from James Ballantyne alone of his inferiors, replied : " God damn his soul ! Tell him and his coadjutor that I belong to the Black Hussars of Litera- ture, who neither give nor receive criticism. I'll be cursed if this is not the most impudent proposal that ever was made." The quarrel was patched up, the first two tales were completed during the spring and summer of 1816, together with Scott's narrative of the year 1814 for the *Edinburgh Annual Register,* and on the first day of December appeared in four volumes *The Black Dwarf* and *Old Mortality.*

VI

The *Black Dwarf* was an admitted failure, admitted by Scott himself, who felt his impetus slacken and huddled it to a close in a single volume. The Dwarf, Elshie, is a piece of Gothick extravagance, Matt Lewis crossed with Byron, and his speech a language which was never yet on sea or land. Cleishbotham in his introduction is at his clumsiest. Hobbie Elliot, the young Borderer, is a good portrait of the Dinmont school ; Westburnflat and Mareschal will pass muster ; but, well or ill drawn, the characters have no scope to exhibit themselves within the narrow melodrama of the plot. The Scots dialogue is always a delight, and sets in high relief the Dwarf's ponderous soliloquies. This could scarcely be bettered as an example of the warm, compassionate, whimsical Border speech.

" Wi' the young leddie's leave, I wad fain take doun Elshie's skeps o' bees, and set them in Grace's bit flower yard at the Heughfoot—they shall ne'er be smeekit by ony o' huz. And the puir goat, she would be negleckit about a great toun like this ; and she could feed bonnily on our lily lee by the burn side, an' the hounds wad ken her in a day's time and never fash her, and Grace wad milk her ilka morning wi' her ain hand, for Elshie's sake ; for though he was thrawn and cankered in his converse, he likeit dumb creatures weel."

1816 There are one or two good scenes, like the gathering of
the Jacobite gentlemen at Ellieslaw, and there are many
lame and impotent ones. Scott had met the original of
the Dwarf in Manor valley when he visited Adam
Ferguson at Hallyards and walked with Skene over the
hills from Megget, and felt bound to make a tale of him,
but the inspiration lagged behind the duty. It is an
instance of his occasional blunders in leaning too much
upon fact.

The failure was amply atoned for by *Old Mortality*.
Lockhart thought it "the *Marmion* of the novels," and its
only rival for the first place, it seems to me, is *The
Heart of Midlothian*. In it Scott attempted the historical
romance in its most difficult form, a reconstruction of a
period of history far outside living experience but
furiously alive in popular memory. The Covenanters
had become to the majority of the people of Scotland
a race of demigods and saints, and their story had been
written, even by sophisticated Edinburgh lawyers, in a
vein of hagiography. This perplexed epoch Scott set
forth through the eyes of a sober, reasonable, if plati-
tudinous hero, with the same detached fairness with
which he had described the French nation in *Paul's
Letters*. He does not blink the ugly side of Covenanter
or Cavalier, nor is he blind to their rival nobilities. His
is the moderate, central mind, like that of Montrose or
Robert Leighton; he has the true historical sense,
which was needed also for true dramatic effect, since it
alone could present the moving contrasts. His history
was violently attacked at the time by the biographer
of Knox, the "learned and unreadable McCrie," and
Scott replied in a review of his own novel in the
Quarterly, in which the literary criticism was provided
by Erskine. The historian of to-day cannot be in
doubt as to the side to which truth leaned in the
controversy. Scott for the first time brought a legend
into the searching light of day, and set in honest
perspective what had been hitherto seen through a
magnifying and distorting mist. If I may speak as
one whose studies have lain much in that period, I

think that he does ample justice to the best in the 1816 Covenant and does not exaggerate the worst; if he errs at all in fairness it is in his portrait of Claverhouse. Scott had read himself deeply into the literature of the time, and from books and the conversation of his old tutor he had mastered at least the forms of Calvinistic divinity.

The story has a fitting prologue, the beautiful tale of that real Old Mortality whose chisel clinked on the martyrs' headstones up and down Scotland. Of the greater novels it is one of the best constructed and its movement is the most swift and even. There is none of the delightfulness of *Guy Mannering* or the romantic sunset charm of *Waverley*; it is on the whole a grim tale, moving among ungenial folk on the highroad of national destiny, and rarely does it pause to rest and sport in the shade. It is indeed a very stern and conscientious piece of realism. There is little of Scott's customary trait-portraiture; only Lady Margaret Bellenden, with her stories of his " sacred Majesty's disjune," has her " humours "; the rest of the people are firmly drawn in the round. There is no weak scene, except the love-making between hero and heroine. There are no weak characters except Edith Bellenden and Henry Morton, though the latter is perhaps flat rather than weak, since his mental processes are most adequately portrayed. And the book rises to scenes of tragic intensity which Scott never excelled, and contains figures of the most masterful vitality. Curiously objective figures they are, for we feel that none of them strongly excites the author's sympathy; in no other novel do his characters live a life so independent of their creator.

It opens with a brilliant comedy scene in Niel Blane's tavern after the Wapinschaw, when the host and his daughter discuss the economics of innkeeping in troubled times. Then there enters the Archbishop's murderer, the red-headed man who " skellied fearfully with one eye," and when he and Morton go out into the night romance takes the road with them. Henceforth the

1816 moderate is linked with the fanatic and drawn unwillingly into a wild drama, always protesting, always holding fast to his own reasonable faith, and thereby providing a touchstone for the reader by which he can judge the aberrations of the rest. Morton is one such *punctum indifferens*, an oasis of common sense, and Niel Blane, with his canny indifference to all heroics, is another.

> "Let Bauldy drive the pease and bear meal to the camp at Drumclog—he's a Whig, and was the auld gudewife's pleughman—the mashlum bannocks will suit their muirland stamacks weel. He maun say it's the last unce o' meal in the house, or, if he scruples to tell a lie (an it's no likely he will when it's for the gude o' the house) he may wait till Duncan Glen, the auld drucken trooper, drives up the aitmeal to Tillietudlem, wi' my dutifu' services to my Leddy and the Major, and I haena as muckle left as will mak my parritch."

With such a reminder of the prosaic world in the background, Scott sweeps us into strange, grim, but always credible drama—the tortured meditations of Burley, the battle-scene of Drumclog, Morton's deadly peril in the moorland cottage, Bothwell Brig, Morton's return and his " recognition," and the great final encounter with Burley in the cave. At the proper moment the narrative rises to the appropriate intensity in some culminating incident, such as the death of Sergeant Bothwell at Drumclog, or Morton's escape from Burley by his leap across the chasm, and such incidents are told with an economy and a speed which Scott never surpassed. Take the scene in the cottage when the swords are out for Morton's death—

> " Hist ! " he said, " I hear a distant noise."
> " It is the rushing of the brook over the pebbles," said one.
> " It is the sough of the wind among the bracken," said another.
> " It is the galloping of horse," said Morton to himself. . . .
> " God grant they may come as my deliverers ! "

This fierce activity is supported by characters none of whom fall below the dignity of great drama. Of the

royalists, Claverhouse, Bothwell, Cornet Grahame, Lord 1816
Evandale, and old Major Bellenden are all in different
ways adequately realized and vigorously presented. But
it is with the Covenanters that Scott reaches the height
of his power. Balfour of Burley is the eternal fanatic,
inspired by a wild logic of his own, tortured and terrible
but never base. The ministers—Poundtext the trimmer,
the madman Habakkuk Mucklewrath, common clay like
Gabriel Kettledrummle, pure perverted spirit like Macbriar—are excellently done ; their wildest extravagances
are not caricature, as anyone will admit who remembers
Naphthali and Shields and Patrick Walker. Macbriar's
sermon in Chapter xviii is both superb prose and
historically true. It is hard to see how Scott can be
accused of maligning the Covenanters when in Macbriar's
defiance of the Privy Council he has shown to what
heights of courage they could attain, and in his picture
of Bessie Maclure has revealed tenderly and subtly the
beauty of holiness in the most humble. He has divined
the essence of what Lockhart calls their " stern and
solemn enthusiasm " far more truly than their conventional apologists.

The relief from the stress is found in the marvellous
chorus of plain folk which accompanies the action and
brings the mind back to the variety and comedy of the
ordinary world. They are always there at the right
moment to humanize the tale. Niel Blane and his
daughter provide the contrast for the advent of Burley ;
Gudyill the butler and Guse Gibbie leaven the cavalier
heroics, and Jenny Dennison's homely good sense is a
corrective to Edith Bellenden's conventional nobility.
Above all Mause Headrig, torn between piety and
maternal cares, is the element needed to relax the
tension of the grim hill-folk, and her son Cuddie is a
foil both to the hill-folk and to his mother. Scott shows
the greatness of his art in the skill with which he blends
the tragic and the comic, and portrays religious ecstasy
and madness always against the prosaic background of
life. He never raises the tale to a false key, and when
Morton returns and meets old Ailie Wilson, his uncle's

1816 housekeeper, the emotion of recognition is preceded by an account of the death of the miser, true to type to the last. "And sae he fell out o' ae dwaum into anither, and ne'er spoke a word mair, unless it were something we couldna mak out, about a dipped candle being gude eneugh to see to dee wi'."

The Scots speech is beyond praise, so exquisitely apt it is, so full of pregnant simplicities and vivid idioms and subtle humours. It is cunningly varied, too, to suit the characters, for the waiting-maid does not talk like the housekeeper or the ploughman like the butler. A forgotten Scotland lives again when Cuddie declares of Kettledrummle, "He routed like a cow in a fremd loaning," and Alison Wilson says of the Duke, "That was him that lost his head at London—folk said it wasna a very gude ane, but it was aye a sair loss to him, puir gentleman." The height is reached in the discourses of Cuddie and his mother. Mause has all the Scriptures in her head and makes noble use of them—farcical often, but never wholly farcical, and sometimes rising to a confused magnificence, while the Laodicean Cuddie is always at hand to pull her down to earth. Take the scene with Cuddie before he confronts the Privy Council—

> At that moment his shoulder was seized by old Mause, who had contrived to thrust herself forward into the lobby of the apartment.
>
> "O hinny, hinny!" said she to Cuddie, hanging upon his neck, "glad and proud and sorry and humbled am I, a' in ane and the same instant, to see my bairn ganging to testify for the truth gloriously with his mouth in council, as he did with his weapon in the field."
>
> "Whisht, whisht, mither!" cried Cuddie impatiently. "Odds, ye daft wife, is this a time to speak o' thae things? I tell ye I'll testify naething either ae gate or anither. I hae spoken to Mr Poundtext, and I'll tak the Declaration, or whate'er they ca' it, and we're a' to win free off if we do that—he's gotten life for himsell and a' his folk, and that's a minister for my siller; I like nane o' your sermons that end in a psalm at the Grassmarket."
>
> "O, Cuddie, man, laith wad I be they suld hurt ye," said old Mause, divided grievously between the safety of her son's

soul and that of his body, " but mind, my bonny bairn, ye 1816
hae battled for the faith, and dinna let the dread o' losing
creature comforts withdraw ye frae the gude fight."

" Hout, tout, mither," replied Cuddie, " I hae fought e'en
ower muckle already, and, to speak plain, I'm wearied o' the
trade. I hae swaggered wi' a' thae arms, and muskets and
pistols, buff-coats and bandoliers lang eneugh, and I like the
plough-paidle a hantle better. I ken naething suld gar a man
fight (that's to say, when he's no angry) by and out-taken the
dread o' being hanged or killed if he turns back."

" But, my dear Cuddie," continued the persevering Mause,
" your bridal garment ! Oh, hinny, dinna sully the marriage
garment."

" Awa, awa, mither," replied Cuddie, " dinna ye see the
folk waiting for me—— Never fear me—— I ken how to
turn this far better than ye do—for ye're bleezing awa about
marriage, and the job is how we are to win by hanging."

There is little fault to be found with the prose of the
narrative. Morton's conscientious troubles are told
simply and lucidly, the landscape is vividly described,
and in general there is an absence of the turgidity to
which Scott was prone. The explanation seems to be
that throughout the book the inspiration never flags ;
he escapes *longueurs* because he is caught up by a wholly
impersonal purpose ; his imagination is so absorbed by
the task of historical re-creation that he has no time
to turn back upon himself. Indeed, in the famous
outburst of Claverhouse, he reaches the high-water mark
of his English style.

" But in truth, Mr Morton, why should we care so much for
death, light upon us or around us whenever it may ? Men
die daily—not a bell tolls the hour but it is the death-note of
someone or other ; and why hesitate to shorten the span of
others, or take over-anxious care to prolong our own ? It is
all a lottery—when the hour of midnight came you were to
die—it has struck, you are alive and safe, and the lot has
fallen on those fellows who were to murder you. It is not the
expiring pang that is worth thinking of in an event that must
happen one day, and may befall us on any given moment—
it is the memory which the soldier leaves behind him, like the
long train of light which follows the sunken sun—that is all
which is worth caring for, which distinguishes the death of
the brave or the ignoble. When I think of death, Mr Morton,
as a thing worth thinking of, it is in the hope of pressing one

1816   day some well-fought and hard-won field of battle, and dying
with the shout of victory in my ear—*that* would be worth
dying for, and more, it would be worth having lived for!"

It would be easy to be critical of some of the details
of this passage, but it has the movement and elevation
of great prose.

Chapter VII

THE BROKEN YEARS

(1817–1819)

I

THE lawyer in Scott was fast disappearing into the background, and the forecast of Kerr of Abbotrule that a Lord President Scott might write poetry in the vacations as a Lord President Montesquieu had written philosophy was now outside the realm of the practicable. But in the winter of 1816–17 he had a sudden hankering after a legal office more dignified than his seat at the Clerks' table. Like Jeffrey he craved for what Jeffrey called the "dignified ease of a Baron of Exchequer." He was now the most famous living Scotsman, he was a sound enough lawyer to warrant a seat on the Bench, and his political friends were in power. "There is a difference in the rank," he wrote to the Duke of Buccleuch, "and also in the leisure of a Baron's situation ; and a man may, without condemnation, endeavour at any period of life to obtain as much honour and ease as he may handsomely come by." But the Duke had certain differences at the moment with the Government, and he was ailing ; when a year later he was in a position to press Scott's claims, Scott withdrew on the characteristic ground that he had a friend who had a better title to any vacant judgeship.

The desire for greater ease was based on something more than ambition. For the first time Scott began to feel his strength flagging. He was now to enter on that testing period of middle life when a man has to make terms with his body. For three broken years he had to struggle against serious ill-health, and when he

1817 emerged from the contest he had dropped permanently to a lower plane of physical well-being.

Since his youth he had borne too hardly on " his brother the ass." He had played his part in the high-jinks of the Covenant Close and in those Edinburgh dinner-parties where " drinking square " was a gentle-man's duty. Ever since then he had kept his powers of mind and body at full stretch. One half of his life was sedentary, with its long hours in court or at his desk : the other was crowded with violent physical exertion. It is an old mistake to believe that the two forms of toil counteract the mischiefs of each other. Scott, with his heavy frame and immense breadth of shoulder, needed much fresh air and exercise to keep him in health, and for six months in the year he did not get it. He was compelled to live in extremes. His only safety lay in a careful régime like his father's, but he was not the man to submit to such a discipline unless compelled. He had a hearty appetite for food, and he indulged it. His breakfast was like Dandie Dinmont's ; and this not only at Abbotsford, when he had a day on the hills before him, but in Edinburgh where he must sit cramped for hours in a stuffy court. He ate moder-ately in the evening, but Edinburgh dinners began early and finished late, and carried a full complement of wine and whisky-punch. He was careless in other ways. The amount of sleep he took was insufficient for such a life, for he would go to bed at midnight and rise at six, and spend an hour or so before he got up planning his day's work. In the country he was often soaked to the skin and would remain for half a day in his wet clothes. His one concession to what we should call hygiene was his morning's cold sponging of throat, chest and shoulders.

Before the end of 1816 he had had attacks of intestinal pain, which he had combated by drinking hot water. Suddenly, on March 5, 1817, the long-suffering body rebelled. He was giving a dinner-party in Castle Street, when he was seized with violent cramp in the stomach, which sent him to bed " roaring like a bull-calf." " All sorts of remedies were applied," he wrote to Morritt, 1817 " as in the case of Gil Blas' pretended colic, but such was the pain of the real disorder that it outdeviled the doctor hollow. Even heated salt, which was applied in such a state that it burned my shirt to rags, I hardly felt when clapped to my stomach. At length the symptoms became inflammatory, and dangerously so, the seat being the diaphragm. They only gave way to very profuse bleeding and blistering, which, under higher assistance, saved my life. My recovery was slow and tedious from the state of exhaustion. I could neither stir for weakness and giddiness, nor read for dazzling in my eyes, nor listen for a whizzing sound in my ears, nor even think for lack of the power of arranging my ideas. So I had a comfortless time of it for about a week." [1]

He had a comfortless time for more than three years. The malady was due to gall-stones, and his doctors, who left him "neither skin nor blood," did not touch the root of the mischief. Their one useful act was to put him on a diet, reduce his breakfast to porridge, and limit strictly his allowance of wine. He protested against the tyranny, but he obeyed, and this dieting, with frequent hot baths, and opium for the bouts of pain, became his rule of life. He rose from his bed to go back to his duties, scaring his friends by his drawn face and wan colour.[2] Many believed that he had got his death-blow, including James Ballantyne, who was nearly felled by James Hogg for giving voice to his fears. All the summer and autumn he struggled against languor, and found every exertion a burden, so that a cry of weariness was forced at last from one who had never

---

[1] Lockhart: IV. 58.

[2] Here is a picture of Scott during the summer of that year: " He was worn almost to a skeleton, sat slanting on his horse, as if unable to hold himself upright; his dress was threadbare and disordered; and his countenance, instead of its usual healthy colour, was of an olive-brown—I might almost say, black tinge. . . . 'The physicians tell me,' said he, 'that mere pain cannot kill; but I am very sure that no man would, for other three months, encounter the same pain that I have suffered, and live. However, I have resolved to take thankfully whatever drugs they prescribe, and follow their advice as long as I can. Set a stout heart to a stey brae, is a grand rule in this world.' " Gillies, 237-8.

¹⁸¹⁷ before complained. Viewing the familiar scene from the
hill above Cauldshiels loch, part of his latest purchase,
he found its beauties dimmed to his sick eyes.

> " The quiet lake, the balmy air,
>   The hill, the stream, the tower, the tree—
> Are they still such as once they were,
>   Or is the dreary change in me ?
>
> Alas, the warp'd and broken board,
>   How can it bear the painter's dye !
> The harp of strain'd and tuneless chord,
>   How to the minstrel's stroke reply !
>
> To aching eyes each landscape lowers,
>   To feverish pulse each gale blows chill ;
> And Araby's or Eden's bowers
>   Were barren as this moorland hill."

It was his only word of complaint. To his friends
he made light of his troubles, and he tightened instead
of slackening his habits of toil. The reaction of a man
to the ebbing of bodily strength in middle age is a
certain proof of character, and Scott revealed that tough
stoicism which can laugh even when the mouth is wry
with pain. He must labour if he would keep the place
he had won, and he forced himself to it though every
sense and nerve rebelled. In one thing he was fortunate :
he found a perfect helper. His friend of seventeen
years, William Laidlaw, formerly the tenant of Blackhouse, had been unlucky in his sheep-farming, so Scott
proposed that he should occupy the house of Kaeside
and act as the Abbotsford factor. Innocent, sentimental
and Whiggishly inclined, Laidlaw had little in common
with Scott except his love of the Border, but the affection
between the two was deep and abiding. He had a
slender literary talent and so was able in emergencies
to do the work of secretary. But in his presence, even
more than in his usefulness, lay his comfort to his
master. To listen to his perpetual " What for no ? " [1]
was for Scott to be convinced that the homely simplicities
were not gone from the world.

---

[1] Scott borrowed the phrase for Meg Dods in *St Ronan's Well*.

The agony of that first bout in March had scarcely 1817
abated before Scott was at work on an indifferent play,
ultimately known as *The Doom of Devorgoil*. In May
he contracted with Constable for a new novel, *Rob Roy*
—the title was suggested by the publisher—and on the
green at Abbotsford, though he had had an attack of
pain the day before, he talked in the highest spirits of
the hit he would make with " a Glasgow weaver whom
he would ravel up with Rob," and extemporized some
of their conversations. It was a bleak summer, and by
the 8th of June there was not an ash tree in leaf, so
Scott was the less tempted to leave his desk. He
finished the novel in the middle of December, most of
it having been hard collar-work done in the intervals
of pain and lassitude. One day James Ballantyne found
him sitting with a blank sheet before him. " Ay, ay,
Jemmy," said Scott, " 'tis easy for you to bid me get
on, but how the deuce can I make Rob Roy's wife speak
with such a curmurring in my guts ? "[1]
Meantime at Abbotsford he had enlarged his bounds
by the purchase for £10,000 of the estate of Toftfield,
which made him master of all the haunts of Thomas
the Rhymer. The house he re-christened Huntly Burn,
and he settled there his old friend Adam Ferguson, now
retired from the army. Abbotsford—the first plan of it
—was approaching completion, a queer jumble of
masonry new and old. Even in his sickness Scott was
filling the house with curious mementoes of the past—
painted glass representing the Scottish kings copied
from a ceiling in Stirling Castle, the old fountain from
the Cross of Edinburgh, plaster models of the Melrose
Abbey gargoyles—and buying freely books, armour,
pictures and " gabions." He was full of plans for
turning the steading of one of his farms into a model
hamlet of labourers, to be called Abbotstown. Guests
were plentiful, among them Washington Irving, who has
left a delightful account of his visit,[2] and Wilkie the

---

[1] " A countra laird had taen the batts,
  Or some curmurring in his guts."
                    BURNS, *Death and Doctor Hornbook.*
[2] Lockhart, IV. 88-95.

1818 artist, and that tragic lady, Byron's forsaken wife.
Scott found that autumn that he must give up shooting,
since he could not keep pace with the dogs, but in the
intervals of his cramps he could potter about his lands
for six hours at a time. Whenever the pain lifted and
the giddiness produced by narcotics passed off, his
spirits revived, and when God sent a cheerful hour he
did not refrain. Take this letter to Jeffrey, written in
the same month as the melancholy lines quoted above :

> Can you not borrow from your briefs and criticisms a couple
> of days to look about you here ? I dare not ask Mrs Jeffrey
> till next year, when my hand will be out of the mortar-tub ;
> and at present my only spare bed was, till of late, but accessible
> by the feudal accommodation of a drawbridge made of two
> deals ; and still requires the clue of Ariadne. Still, however,
> there it is, and there is an obliging stage-coach called the
> Blucher, which sets down my guests within a mile of my
> mansion (at Melrose bridge-end) three times a week, and
> restores them to their families in like manner after five hours'
> travelling. I am like one of Miss Edgeworth's heroines, master
> of all things in miniature—a little hill and a little glen, and
> a little horse-pond of a loch, and a little river, I was going to
> call it—the Tweed, but I remember the minister was mobbed
> by his parishioners for terming it, in his statistical report, an
> inconsiderable stream. So pray do come and see me. [1]

II

Rob Roy was published by Constable in the beginning
of 1818, the first edition, which was exhausted in a
fortnight, reaching the large figure of 10,000 copies.
In the previous November an agreement had been
signed for a new series of " Tales of my Landlord."
Owing to the dexterity of John Ballantyne and Constable's fear of the books going to Blackwood, whose
new magazine was now bearding his own *Edinburgh
Review*, the terms were very high, including the taking
over of the remaining unsaleable stock in Hanover
Street.[2] With the advance he received Scott was able

---

[1] Cockburn, *Life of Lord Jeffrey*, I. 418.
[2] According to Cockburn, Constable lost two-thirds of the £5270 which he
paid for the stock. But see Cadell's letter in *A. Constable*, III. 98.

to cancel his bond of £4000 to the Duke of Buccleuch. 1818 He had now discharged all his debts to personal friends, but at the cost of mortgaging far ahead his creative powers.

In February he was cheered by the fulfilment of an old hope. He had raised with the Prince Regent the question of disinterring the ancient regalia of Scotland from the lumber of the Crown Room in Edinburgh Castle ; a commission of inquiry had been appointed, and oi 4th February the question was settled which had long disquieted the country, whether the regalia, which by the Act of Union were never to be removed from Scottish soil, had not in fact been sent to London. The great dusty chest was opened, and therein were found, in perfect order, the Crown and the Sceptre fashioned in the reign of James V, and the noble Sword of State presented to James IV by Pope Julian II, as well as the silver mace of the Treasurer of Scotland.[1] To Scott the ceremony was of a sacramental gravity, and his feeling was shared by his daughter Sophia, who all but fainted when the chest was opened. One of the commissioners proposed to put the Crown on the head of one of the young ladies present, but was deterred by Scott's passionate cry of " By God, No ! " That day Edinburgh learned that its genteel antiquarianism was a very different thing from Scott's burning reverence for the past. So far did he carry it that he was willing to domesticate as family chaplain an uncle of Laidlaw, an aged Cameronian minister, merely because Richard Cameron had been chaplain to one of his own ancestors —a project which fortunately failed. He wrote to Laidlaw—" If, as the King of Prussia said to Rousseau, ' a little persecution is necessary to make his home entirely to his mind,' he shall have it ; and, what persecutors seldom promise, I will stop whenever he is tired of it. I have a pair of thumbikins also much at his service, if he requires their assistance to glorify

[1] Scott wrote a memorandum, describing the chequered history of the Regalia. *Misc. Prose Works*, VII. 298-357. At one time he contemplated a novel on the subject. *A. Constable*, III. 108.

1818 God and the Covenant. Seriously I like enthusiasm of
every kind so well, especially when united with worth
of character, that I shall be delighted with this old
gentleman." [1]

Meantime he was busy on the new "Tales of my Landlord." At first he had intended to include two stories
in the new series, but the first, *The Heart of Midlothian*,
so grew under his hand that it was published alone in
June in four volumes. It was received both in England
and Scotland with a universal approbation not accorded
to any of the other novels, for it pleased both the critical
and the uncritical. "I am in a house," Lady Louisa
Stuart wrote from Sheffield Place, "where everybody
is tearing it out of each other's hands, and talking of
nothing else. So much for its success—the more flattering
because it overcomes a prejudice. People were beginning
to say the author would wear himself out ; it was going
on too long in the same key, and no striking notes could
possibly be produced. On the contrary, I think the
interest is stronger here than in any of the former ones
(always excepting my first love, *Waverley*), and one
may congratulate you upon having effected what many
have tried to do and nobody yet succeeded in—making
a perfectly good character the most interesting." [2] This,
from his best critic, was good news for one who sorely
needed heartening.

In the summer of that year at an Edinburgh dinner-
party Scott met a young man, who entertained him
with an account of a recent visit to Goethe at Weimar,
and was promptly bidden to Abbotsford. The young
man was one John Gibson Lockhart, a briefless advocate
who dabbled in literature. Scott invited him to do some
work on the *Edinburgh Annual Register*, and during the
rest of the summer session had many talks with him.
Lockhart was then approaching his twenty-fourth birthday, an uncommonly handsome youth, with a pale,
clean-cut face, a shapely head, and wonderful dark eyes.
His manner, like his appearance, had a touch of the
hidalgo in it ; his slight deafness made him self-contained,

[1] Lockhart, IV. 131.   [2] *Fam. Letters*, II. 19.

though his shyness disappeared in congenial society; he had a biting wit, did not gladly suffer fools, and was apt to have the air of being superior to his company. His father was a Lanarkshire minister and his mother a minister's daughter; it must not be forgotten that Lockhart had in his blood that Calvinistic tincture which does not make for humility. He had other strains, for paternally he counted kin with the high race of the Lockharts of the Lee, one of whom had ridden with Douglas in the pilgrimage of the Heart of Bruce. He had been educated at Glasgow University, and had then proceeded to Balliol with a Snell exhibition. At Oxford he had done well, had become a good classical scholar, and had read widely in foreign literatures; had a fellowship been possible for a Scots Presbyterian, he might have remained there happily for the rest of his days. As it was, he returned to Glasgow, which he found uncongenial, and in 1816 was called to the Scottish Bar.

In Edinburgh he fell into the company of John Wilson, who had been a gentleman-commoner at Magdalen, and the two, having no practice, were engaged by William Blackwood to write in his new magazine. Blackwood, an astute, rough-grained man, decided that the elegant acerbity of the *Edinburgh Review* must be fought with stronger and coarser acids, and the first years of " ma Maaga," as he called his journal, were notorious for its offences against literary decency. The magazine was high Tory in politics, orthodox in religion, and intolerant of all things that did not conform to its strait canons. The Lake School and the Cockney School of poets were attacked—not by Lockhart—with blustering malevolence. In the " Chaldee Manuscript," a clumsy Biblical parody in which Lockhart had a considerable share, it presented contemporary figures in a mood of ferocious banter. Lockhart was never the typical *Blackwood* man; that part was better filled by John Wilson and by Hogg in his cups; but something frustrate and irritable in his soul made him consent to its extravagances. He was always a little at odds with his environment and his generation.

1818 At first sight there would seem to have been nothing in common between the superfine Oxford scholar, with a sneer on his handsome lips, and one who looked upon all men as his brothers. Scott, who disliked *Blackwood* and had no special love for its proprietor, cannot have been predisposed in favour of the young man who on that May evening took wine with him at Mr Home Drummond's table. But his reading of his fellows was rarely mistaken. Lockhart lived up to the badge of his family, the " heart within the fetterlock," and hid the depth and fineness of his humanity under a hard protective sheath. Scott's insight penetrated to the man beneath, and he detected a spirit too rare for rowdy Edinburgh journalism, while Lockhart's chilly soul was warmed by the sympathy of the one man who ever commanded his full reverence. Scott thought that he saw in this well-equipped stripling a successor to whom he might hand on the torch of his own loyalties, and in those weary days he was thinking much of his latter end. The result was the beginning of one of the sincerest friendships in the history of letters, through which the older man was to elicit what was best in the younger, and the younger was to give to the world an immortal picture of his master.[1]

The intimacy thus begun ripened fast. That autumn Lockhart, returning with John Wilson from the English lakes, paid his first visit to Abbotsford, and was given a glimpse of its feudal retinue and its feudal hospitality. It was a melancholy autumn for Scott, for the Duke of Buccleuch was dying, and his letter to Lord Montagu shows the depth of his anxiety.[2] The offer of a baronetcy in November was only accepted when he got the news that his wife's brother, Charles Carpenter, had bequeathed the residue of his fortune to his sister's family. The cost of Abbotsford and his enlarged estate and his desire to equip his eldest son for the cavalry made him

---

[1] Lockhart was not loved by his fellow-writers, except by Carlyle, and Miss Martineau, who never knew him, has poured vitriol on him in her *Biographical Sketches*. The real man has been adequately portrayed by Andrew Lang in his *Life of Lockhart* (1897).

[2] Lockhart, IV. 206-8.

agree to sell all his copyrights to Constable for the sum 1819
of £12,000 ; in 1826 the price had not been fully paid.

With the opening of 1819 the shadows again descended.
The baronetcy had pleased him more than he cared to
admit. He was glad that his ancient Border name
should be given a handle which it had often had in
history ; he anticipated the obvious quotation from
Henry V, " I like not such grinning honour as Sir
Walter hath," and he hoped to go to London in the
Easter vacation to receive the accolade. But now the
spasms of cramp returned with increased violence and
the remedies used to relieve them brought on jaundice.
His attacks of pain would last sometimes for ten hours,
to be followed by deadly sickness. " I have been ill—
very—very ill," he told the Duke of Buccleuch, and to
Southey he wrote :—

> If I had not the strength of a team of horses I could never
> have fought through it, and through the heavy fire of medicinal
> artillery, scarce less exhausting—for bleeding, blistering,
> calomel and ipecacuanha have gone on without intermission—
> while, during the agony of the spasms, laudanum became
> necessary in the most liberal doses, though inconsistent with
> the general treatment. I did not lose my senses, because I
> resolved to keep them, but I thought once or twice they would
> have gone overboard, top and top-gallants. I should be a great
> fool, and a most ungrateful wretch to complain of such afflictions
> as these. My life has been, in all its private and public relations,
> as fortunate perhaps as was ever lived, up to this period ; and
> whether pain or misfortune may lie behind the dark curtain
> of futurity, I am already a sufficient debtor to the bounty of
> Providence to be resigned to it. Fear is an evil that has never
> mixed with my nature, nor has even unwonted good fortune
> rendered my love of life tenacious.[1]

In May the Duke of Buccleuch died, and at that time
Scott must have believed that he would not long survive
his friend. Between the bouts of pain he was so weak
that the shortest letter fatigued him. " When I crawl
out on Sybil Grey," he wrote, " I am the very image
of Death on the pale horse, lanthorn-jawed, decayed in
flesh, stooping as if I meant to eat the poney's ears,

[1] Lockhart, IV. 239.

1819 and unable to go above a foot-pace." When Lockhart
went to Abbotsford at the end of the spring vacation
he found a shrunken figure, with a yellow face and
snow-white hair; but he found, too, fire in Scott's eye
and a most resolute will to live. " He sat at table while
we dined, but partook only of some rice pudding; and
after the cloth was drawn, while sipping his toast and
water, pushed round the bottles in his old style, and
talked with easy cheerfulness of the stout battle he had
fought and which he now seemed to consider as won."
That night Scott was in agony, but next morning he
took his visitor for a trot up Yarrow vale and did some
political canvassing among the farmers. When he returned to Edinburgh he found that for weeks at a time
he could not take his seat at the Clerks' table. He
had attacks which seemed to his friends to presage
death, and Lord Buchan, the master-bore of his generation, tried to comfort him by a promise that he himself
would take charge of the funeral ceremonies at Dryburgh.
One night in June it appeared that the end had come.
Lockhart has told the tale on his wife's evidence.

> He then called his children about his bed, and took leave of
> them with solemn tenderness. After giving them one by one
> such advice as suited their years and characters, he added :
> " For myself, my dears, I am unconscious of ever having
> done any man an injury, or omitting any fair opportunity of
> doing any man a benefit. I well know that no human life can
> appear otherwise than weak and filthy in the eyes of God, but
> I rely on the merits and intercession of our Redeemer." He
> then laid his hands on their heads and said, " God bless you !
> Live so that you may all hope to meet each other in a better
> place hereafter. And now leave me that I may turn my face
> to the wall." [1]

But it was not the end, it was rather the crisis of the
malady, for he fell into a sleep, and from that night his
slow convalescence began.

Yet those months of weakness and pain were also
months of intense literary activity. All spring he was
busy on *The Bride of Lammermoor*, dictating it either to

[1] IV. 278.

the swift and alert James Ballantyne or to the innocent 1819
Will Laidlaw, who was apt to interrupt with " Gude
keep us a' ! " and " Eh, sirs ! Eh, sirs ! " Scott refused
to pause during his spasms of pain. " Nay, Willie,"
he told Laidlaw, " only see that the doors are fast.
I would fain keep all the cry as well as all the wool to
ourselves ; but as to giving over work, that can only
be done when I am in woollen." He did the same with
The Legend of Montrose, and the two were published
by Constable in June in the third series of " Tales of
my Landlord "—four volumes full of misprints, since
the author was too ill to correct the proofs. The tales
would have been received with indulgence by those
who knew the circumstances of their composition, but
to his friends' amazement no indulgence was required,
for the old afflatus was there in ample measure. James
Ballantyne tells how, when the printed volumes of *The
Bride of Lammermoor* were put into his hand, Scott
read them anxiously, for " he did not recollect one
single incident, character or conversation." He had
dictated the book in a half-conscious world of suffering
upon which memory had closed the door.

There were other proofs of his miraculous vitality.
After he left Edinburgh that summer he had begun a
novel, *Ivanhoe*, which broke wholly new ground, for,
fearing lest his public might grow weary of Scottish life,
he marched horse and foot into England and occupied
one of the classic lists of English romance. Moreover,
he was engaged in all kinds of miscellaneous duties—
political articles for James Ballantyne's *Edinburgh Weekly
Journal*, fitting out his son Walter for his cornetcy in
the 18th Hussars, entertaining at Abbotsford the prince
who was afterwards to be King of the Belgians, recruiting
—to keep the peace which he believed to be threatened
by the new Radicals—a corps of Buccleuch Foresters,
and pushing the interests of the youth among his own
villagers, by whom he was known as the " Duke of
Darnick." He was also casting a proprietary eye over
Nicol Milne's estate of Faldonside, and contemplating
its purchase for £30,000 ; he believed that he could put

£10,000 down, and pay off the rest in a few years by
his literary earnings. From this rash project he was
not deterred by what had happened to his friend, Sir
John Riddell of Riddell, who had become bankrupt
from spending too much on farming. " Here they have
been," he moralizes, " for a thousand years ; and now
all the inheritance is to pass away, merely because one
good worthy gentleman could not be content to enjoy
his horses, his hounds, and his bottle of claret, like
thirty or forty predecessors, but must needs turn scientific
agriculturist, take almost all his fair estate into his own
hand, superintend for himself perhaps a hundred ploughs,
and try every new nostrum that has been tabled by the
quackish improvers of the time. And what makes the
thing ten times more wonderful is that he kept his
day-book and ledger and all the rest of it as accurately
as if he had been a cheesemonger in the Grassmarket."
Scott himself kept minute accounts, and he too was
spending capital which he hoped to realize out of future
profits, but he did not see that Sir John Riddell's course
was paralleled by his own.

With 1819 the broken years came to an end. By
Christmas his health was virtually restored, though he
had lost for good one-half of his physical strength.
Now at the age of forty-eight he was an elderly man.
It had been a year of bereavement as well as of bodily
pain, for in the bitter December weather he lost in a
single week his mother, his uncle Dr Rutherford, and
his aunt Christian Rutherford, one of the best loved
of his relatives. Spiritually he emerged from the valley
of the shadow a stronger and riper man, for he had
looked calmly in the face of death. His eyes were
graver, as of one who had been keeping watch over
man's mortality. His cheerful creed, that the good
were the happy, and, in the main, the successful, had
been better adjusted to reality. The fate of Rebecca in
Ivanhoe is a proof of this new philosophy. " A character
of a highly virtuous and lofty stamp," he wrote in this
connexion, " is degraded rather than exalted by an
attempt to reward virtue with temporal prosperity.

Such is not the recompense that Providence has deemed
worthy of suffering merit. . . . A glance on the great
picture of life will show that the virtue of self-denial,
and the sacrifice of passion to principle, are seldom thus
remunerated ; and that the internal consciousness of
their high-minded discharge of duty produces on their
own reflections a more adequate recompense, in the
form of that peace which the world cannot give or
take away."[1]

III

The five novels conceived and written during the
broken years, represent the peak of Scott's creative
power. They were the work of something less than
thirty months, a fecundity for which in literary history
there is scarcely a parallel. They were produced during,
and in the intervals of, deadly sickness ; but, with one
exception, the shadow of pain does not fall on them,
for they present the normal world of his imagination in
all its sunlit spaciousness.

In *Rob Roy* especially there is no hint of the shadows,
for the quality of delightfulness which was conspicuous in
Guy Mannering has made it for many good judges—Lord
Rosebery was one and Stevenson another—the favourite
among the novels. In Rob Roy himself, Scott had a figure
which had long filled his imagination—a Highlander with
Lowland affiliations, who continued the old banditry of
the Highland Line almost into modern days. The Northumbrian scene he knew from his many journeys across
the Cheviots ; he had been often in Glasgow on circuit,
and had an affection for its people not commonly felt
by " pridefu' Edinburgh folk." In 1817 with Adam
Ferguson he had explored the Lennox and the Macgregor
country, renewing his impressions of a quarter of a
century before when, as a lawyer's apprentice, he had
set forth to do legal execution upon the Maclarens.
He had recollections of his father to help him in his
portrait of the elder Osbaldistone, and in the adorable

---

[1] Gen. Introduction to *Ivanhoe*.

1818 Diana Vernon there are fleeting memories of his first
love.

In construction the novel is one of his worst. The
plot is in essence picaresque, the main interest being
movement in space, but the purpose of such movement
is casually conceived. The preliminaries are out of all
decent proportion, and many a reader has stuck fast in
them and never crossed the Border. The hero is only a
name, Edward Waverley many degrees further removed
from reality. The whole business of the missing bills
and Rashleigh's villainy is obscure, and there are other
signs of carelessness ; some of the journeys, for example,
take an unconscionable time, and Scott seems never to
have made up his mind at what season of the year the
events befell. The book is for the first third a somewhat
languid chronicle of manners, and for the rest a headlong
adventure. Yet the lengthy introduction has merits of
its own. There is a careful study of the elder Osbaldistone,
who, " as a man of business, looked upon the labours of
poets with contempt ; and, as a religious man and of
the dissenting persuasion, considered all such pursuits as
equally trivial and profane." The romance of commerce
is sympathetically presented, through the mouths both
of Owen and of the Bailie. Indeed Scott never wrote
brisker and better economics than in his account in
Chapter xxvi of the basis of Glasgow's prosperity and
of the condition of the neighbouring Highlands.[1] Nor
did he often write sounder political history. Take the
Bailie on the Union :—

"Whisht, sir !—whisht ! It's ill-scraped tongues like yours
that makes mischief between neighbourhoods and nations.
There's naething sae gude on this side o' time but it might
have been better, and that may be said o' the Union. Nane
were keener against it than the Glasgow folk, wi' their rabblings
and their risings, and their mobs, as they ca' them nowadays.
But it's an ill wind that blaws naebody gude—let ilka ane
roose the ford as they find it.—— I say, let Glasgow flourish !

---

[1] This should have revealed the authorship of the novel to the observant.
For Scott took it straight from a manuscript of Graham of Gartmore, which
he sent to Jamieson, who printed it in his edition of *Burt's Letters from the
North*, giving the name of the sender.

whilk is judiciously and elegantly putten round the town's 1818 arms by way of byword. Now, since St Mungo catched herrings in the Clyde, what was ever like to gar us flourish like the sugar and tobacco trade ? Will anybody tell me that, and grumble at a treaty that opened us a road west-awa' yonder ? "

In his picture, too, of Osbaldistone Hall Scott showed for the first time his power of presenting a scene and a mode of life outside his own experience and tradition.

The drama begins slackly, but our expectations are early roused, when the deep voice of the " Scotch sort of a gentleman," the drover Campbell, is heard in the Darlington inn. These preparatory hints are cunningly scattered throughout the Northumbrian chapters, as when Diana from the hill-top shows Frank the far-off speck of whitish rock and tells him how in two hours his horse will carry him into Scotland. Very good is the scene with Mr Justice Inglewood, and Jobson the attorney is one of Scott's best legal comic figures, but the tale only finds its true key when Frank, with Andrew Fairservice as his Sancho Panza, rides off in the darkness for the north. Thereafter we are in the grip of epic narrative. The midnight scene in the Glasgow prison, the journey to Aberfoyle, the night in the clachan alehouse, the fight on the lake shore, the Bailie's encounter with Helen Macgregor, Rob Roy's escape from Ewan of Brigglands at the ford, the meeting with Diana on the darkening heath—all are conceived in the highest vein of romantic invention. " Drama," Stevenson has told us, " is the poetry of conduct, romance the poetry of circumstance," and in the scene at the Aberfoyle inn the two are most artfully joined. Out of the night come the travellers from a prosaic world ; around them are the shadowy mountains where death lurks, and by the inn fire are men of a wild world ; at the threat of danger the prosaic is transformed into the heroic, and with a red-hot plough coulter snatched from the hearth the Bailie makes the Stuart's plaid " smell like a singit sheep's head." Every detail of that wonderful scene, which Scott never bettered, is at the same high pitch—

1818 not least when the half-drunken Garschattachin airs his Jacobitism—

> " The banes of a loyal and a gallant Grahame hae lang rattled in their coffin for vengeance on thae Dukes of Guile and Lords for Lorn. There ne'er was treason in Scotland but a Cawmil was at the bottom o't ; and now that the wrang side's uppermost, wha but the Cawmils for keeping doun the right ? But this warld winna last lang, and it will be time to sharp the maiden for shearing o' craigs and thrapples. I hope to see the auld rusty lass linking at a bluidy harst again."

Into the parochial affairs of merchants and blackmailers comes the high baronial note of an elder Scotland.

Of the characters it may be said fairly that none are weak except the young hero. Rob Roy is a brilliant study of two different worlds marred in the joining ; his wife, though she verges on melodrama, is not without a tragic verisimilitude ; and every Highlander that crosses the stage is vigorously presented. But three figures by common consent stand out as among Scott's masterpieces. In Diana Vernon he produced his one wholly satisfactory portrait of a young gentlewoman. Not only is the reader vividly conscious of her charm of person and manner and her fineness of spirit, but he is aware of a notable intelligence ; for she is the ancestress of another Diana, her of the Crossways. Her speech, indeed, sometimes belies her, for she can talk like a governess from Miss Pinkerton's academy. " We are still allies," she can say, " bound, like other confederate powers, by circumstances of mutual interest, but I am afraid, as will happen in other cases, the treaty of alliance has survived the amicable disposition in which it had its origin." Worse still, she can address Rashleigh thus : " Dismiss from your company the false archimage, Dissimulation, and it will better ensure your free access to our classical consultations." But these are only specks on the sun. At other times her talk can be gay, vivacious and gallant, and she has a wild subtlety of her own. Whatever she says or does, we are her devout henchmen, believing fiercely in her beauty, her goodness and her brains. We learn from her the kind of woman

that Scott most admired, for no other of his own class 1818
is so lovingly drawn. He had little liking for foolish
sylphs.

Andrew Fairservice is one of the great serving-men in
literature, and he is one of Scott's foremost creations,
for, just as Falstaff seems to have got out of Shakespeare's
hand and attained an independent life of his own, so
Andrew is now and then too much for his creator. He
is a real but a low type of Scot, cunning, avaricious,
indifferently loyal, venturesome in his own interest but
a craven in the face of bodily peril, an incorrigible liar
and braggart, and never more impudent than when his
bluff is called. But vitality has nothing to do with
ethics, and Andrew lives for us as vividly as Falstaff or
Sairey Gamp. Scott has a half-ashamed liking for the
rogue, but no admiration, and he delights to exhibit
him in the ugliest light. But Andrew refuses to be
degraded as successfully as Falstaff when he is renounced
by Prince Hal; whenever he appears he takes the
centre of the stage, and obscures the Bailie and Rob
Roy himself.

Scott put into him all the baser traits of his countrymen, but he added their quick interest in life, their
speculative boldness, their sentiment, their vivid consciousness of the past. Andrew comments freely and
fearlessly on any topic, and he is always shrewd and
humorous. He is a lamp to light the reader through
the undergrowth of Scots prejudices and idiosyncrasies.
He reveals for Frank's benefit the trade of the Scots
packman; the life of the Scots burghs " yoked on end
to end like ropes of ingans "; the downfall of local
government with the loss of the Scots Parliament—
" If ae kail-wife pou'd aff her neighbour's mutch, they
wad hae the twasome o' them into the Parliament
House o' Lunnon "; his contempt for episcopacy—
" clouts o' cauld parritch . . . mair like a penny wedding
than a sermon "; his smattering of law—" bonny
writer words . . . a' that Andrew got for a lang law
plea, and four ankers o' as gude brandy as was e'er
coupit ower craig; " the tale of the cleansing of Glasgow's

1818 cathedral at the Reformation from the " rags o' the muckle hure that sitteth on seven hills, as if ane wasna braid eneugh for her auld hinder end ; " his taste in letters—" He aince telled me (puir blinded creature) that the Psalms of David were excellent poetry ! as if the holy Psalmist thought o' rattling rhymes in a blether like his ain silly clinkum-clankum things that he ca's verse. Gude help him ! twa lines o' Davie Lindsay wad ding a' he ever clerkit ! " He never opens his disgraceful mouth but there flows from it a beautiful rhythmical Scots. Take this :—

> " I have been flitting every term these four-and-twenty years ; but when the time comes, there's aye something to saw that I would like to see sawn—or something to maw that I would like to see mawn—or something to ripe that I would like to see ripen—and sae I e'en daiker on wi' the family frae year's end to year's end. . . . But if your honour wad wush me to ony place where I wad hear pure doctrine, and hae a free cow's grass, and a cot, and a yard, and mair than ten punds of annual fee, and where there's nae leddy about the town to count the apples, I'se hold mysell muckle indebted t' ye."

Bailie Nicol Jarvie was regarded by Scott from the first as one of the twin pillars of the tale. He is the foil to Frank Osbaldistone—the shrewd middle-aged man of business set against the young dreamer ; the foil to Rob—the pragmatic and progressive Lowlander against the champion of a lost world : the foil to Andrew Fairservice, since his idiomatic pawkiness is based on courage and lit by generosity. His Whiggism is always coloured by honest sentiment, his carefulness by a large kindliness, and he has his own homespun poetry. Alone of all the characters he is perfectly at ease in the world and perfectly sure of his road. He is a conscientious man and must always be moralizing ; when he compounds a bowl of brandy-punch he tells the company that he had the receipt from one Captain Coffinkey—" a decent man when I kent him, only he used to swear awfully. But he's dead, and gaen to his account, and I trust he's accepted—I trust he's accepted." He has his ambitions, and dreams not only of the provostship, but of letting his lights burn before the Duke of Argyll—"for wherefore should they be hidden under a bushel?" He is for the plain man and his rights, since his father the deacon had carried his sword to Bothwell Brig, but he has also a deep respect for gentle blood. Into his counting-house came wafts from a different world, and he sighs as he shuts the door on them.

> "It's a queer thing o' me, gentlemen, that am a man of peace mysell, and a peacefu' man's son, for the deacon my father quarrelled wi' nane out o' the town-council—it's a queer thing, I say, but I think the Hieland blude o' me warms at thae daft tales, and whiles I like better to hear them than a word o' profit, gude forgie me !—— But they are vanities—sinfu' vanities—and, moreover, again the statute law—again the statute and gospel law."

There is steel in him as well as fire, for he can not only fight at a pinch, but, with his honest knees knocking together, can outface Rob Roy's terrible wife. In a word he is the triumphant bourgeois, the type which endures when aristocracies and proletariats crumble, but the Scots type of that potent class. His portrait is painted with a thousand subtle touches and every word he utters adds something to our understanding. I sometimes fear that the knowledge of the older Scots world, which is needed to make the Bailie wholly comprehensible, is fast passing away ; but, when I re-read him I seem to find behind the idioms something universal, which lifts him out of any narrow orbit of space and time, and sets him with the creatures of Molière and Shakespeare.

The Heart of Midlothian had for its basis the tradition of a remoter Edinburgh than that of the 'Forty-five, the jealous burgher life whose smouldering resentment at the Union of 1707 was fanned to a flame by the misdeeds of Captain Porteous. Scott welcomed the chance of recounting a vivid episode in the history of his own romantic city, and for the plot itself he had a true tale to work on—that of Helen Walker of Irongray, the "puirest o' a' puir bodies," who, like Jeanie Deans,

1818 walked to London to save her sister's life. Around
these centres he gathered a motley crowd of burgesses,
tacksmen, bonnet-lairds, smugglers and ne'er-do-wells ;
he carried his tale to the Court of London and into the
dens of the underworld ; and he made the network of
that underworld cover both Scotland and England, for
he knew that crime and misery overleap national boundaries. In no other novel is his canvas so large, or the
figures so many and so varied.

Critics as diverse as Lady Louisa Stuart, Walter
Savage Landor and Edward Fitzgerald have given it
first place among his works ; and, though in Scott's
case the scale of precedence is hard to fix, I think the
judgment is right, for every merit which the others
possess is shown here in a high degree. The first five-
sixths of the book are almost perfect narrative. The
start, after his fashion, is a little laboured, while he is
sketching in the historical background ; but when the
action once begins there is no slackening, and the public
and private dramas are deftly interwoven. The last
chapters have been generally condemned as weak and
careless, a picking up of loose ends and tying them into
a clumsy knot ; and indeed there is no defence to be
made for the death of Sir George Staunton at the hands
of his own son. There was a story there of the Greek
tragedy type, but it demanded a different kind of telling ;
as it stands, the reader is not awed by dramatic justice
but staggered by inconsequent melodrama. Yet, apart
from this blemish, I feel that the conception of the
Roseneath chapters is right. Scott was always social
historian as well as novelist, and he wanted to show
Scottish life passing into a mellower phase in which old
unhappy things were forgotten. Artistically, too, the
instinct was sound. The figures, who have danced so
wildly at the bidding of fate, should find reward in a
gentle, bright, leisurely old age. Even so Tolstoy
rounded off his *War and Peace.*

The other novels, even the best of them, resemble a
flat and sometimes dull country, where the road occasionally climbs to the heights, but in *The Heart of Midlothian*

the path is all on a tableland, in tonic air and with 1818
wonderful prospects. One great scene follows close on
another, but there is no overstraining of the tension,
for the comic and the tragic, the solemn and the fantastic,
are most artfully mingled. Interpolated in the horrors
of the Porteous Mob is the gossip of the Saddletrees· and
Mrs Howden, Peter Plumdamas and Miss Grizel Damahoy;
David Deans and his rigid decencies are set off by the
pagan death of old Dumbiedykes and the capers of his
son ; the suspense of Effie's trial is relieved by the
legal absurdities of Bartoline Saddletree ; Madge Wild-
fire with her songs flits among the midnight shadows of
Muschat's Cairn ; Jeanie's journey begins with the
comedy of Dumbiedykes, passes through the terrors
of Gunnerby Hill, and ends, as romance should, in
the courts of princes. There is no fault to be found
with this brilliant panorama ; but since each episode
depends with perfect logic and naturalness upon the
characters of the protagonists, so that it seems to
happen inevitably and to owe nothing to invention,
it is the characters that constitute the glory of the
book.

Of these Jeanie Deans is the chief. She dominates
the book because she alone is perfectly secure ; she has
a philosophy of life which withstands the fieriest trials,
and which makes the most foursquare of the others—
her father, Reuben Butler, the Duke—seem by contrast
like saplings to an oak. She is such a figure as is not
found elsewhere to my .knowledge in literature ; the
puritan in whom there is neither sourness nor fanaticism,
whose sane, rational instincts are wholly impregnable,
whose severity is for herself alone and not for others.
Scott gives her a homely person and few feminine
graces, but he makes her adorable from her invincible
goodness. She is no milk-and-water heroine, no type
of passive, suffering virtue, for her courage is that
of a man-at-arms, and is blown by the storms to a
stronger flame. " ' I fearna for his life—I ken how
strong-hearted he is—I ken it,' laying her hand on her
bosom, ' by my ain heart at this minute.' " She is a

1818 careful, practical soul, and her letters to her father and
to Butler during her journey mention a cure for the
muir-ill which she has heard of, and are full of house-
wifely details and shrewd observations about the strange
land she is exploring. She is quick-witted and sternly
logical ; she confounds the English rector by her theology,
and gives the Duke sage advice as to how to deal with
the Queen, and can even argue her father out of his
pedantries. She has an intense pride, the deeper because
it is free from vanity :—" I can only say, that not for
all the land that lies between the twa ends of the rainbow
wad I be the woman that should wed your son." She
has an eye, too, for the whimsicalities of life, as when
she contemplates the retreating figure of her suitor,
Dumbiedykes, borne off by Highland Rory.—" He's a
gude creature, and a kind—it's a pity he has sae willyard
a powny."

This most human and companionable of women is
involved in a crisis from which there seems no outlet
but tragedy. Scott never wrote anything more profound
psychologically than the scene between Jeanie and her
father, when he learns that on her word depends Effie's
life, and that between the two sisters in prison. Jeanie
stands firm—she could not do otherwise—but she directs
the same unyielding courage to the task of rescue.
Like Jacob she wrestles with the dark angel and compels
him to bless her. The climax is triumph, when she wins
her sister's life from the Queen ; and at that great
moment she, whose speech has hitherto had the homeliness of a country girl, rises, like Edie Ochiltree, to a
grave eloquence :—

> " Alas ! it is not when we sleep soft and wake merrily our-
> selves, that we think of other people's sufferings. Our hearts
> are waxed light within us then, and we are for righting our ain
> wrongs and fighting our ain battles. But when the hour of
> trouble comes to the mind or to the body—and seldom may it
> visit your leddyship—and when the hour of death comes that
> comes to high and low—lang and late may it be yours—— Oh,
> my leddy, then it isna what we hae dune for oursells, but what
> we hae dune for ithers, that we think on maist pleasantly. And
> the thought that ye hae intervened to spare the puir thing's

life will be sweeter in that hour, come when it may, than if **1818**
a word of your mouth could hang the haill Porteous mob at
the tail of ae tow."

Of the other characters no one is feebly drawn except
Effie's Byronic lover. Effie herself is true woman, the
passionate spoiled beauty, with the good breeding which
in any class may accompany bodily loveliness. Dumbiedykes, Reuben Butler, the Edinburgh burgesses, the
inimitable Captain of Knockdunder are all carefully
studied, even in their extravagances, as are the *macabre*
figures from the underworld like Daddy Ratcliffe and
Meg Murdockson; while in Madge Wildfire Scott shows
that sure hand in portraying madness which belongs only
to the eminently sane. But, after Jeanie, the dominant
figure is her father. David Deans is the Covenanter
who has lived into peaceable times which have a little
mellowed his austerity. He cherishes the memory of his
stormy past, and has still something of the wild poetry of
the hill-folk. " It has been with me as with the worthy
John Semple, called Carspharn John, upon a like trial—
I have been this night on the banks of Ulai, plucking
an apple here and there." But if he has the leaven of
high devotion he carries also a gross weight of spiritual
pride. " How muckle better I hae thought mysell than
them that lay saft, fed sweet, and drank deep, when I
was in the moss-haggs and moors wi' precious Donald
Cameron, and worthy Mr Blackadder, called Guess-
again ! "—" I wish every man and woman in this land
had kept the true testimony, and the middle and straight
path, as it were on the ridge of the hill, where wind
and water shear, avoiding right-hand snares and extremes and left-hand way-slidings, as weel as Johnny
Dodds of Farthing's Acre, and ae man mair that shall
be nameless." To such a man his daughter's shame
is a cataclysm, and his agony of spirit is subtly and
tenderly portrayed. He is weaker than Jeanie because
there is vanity in his pride; he throws back upon
her the responsibility for decision ; but he is strong
enough not to plead with her for what he desires but his
principles condemn. " I wunna fret the tender con-

1819 science of one bairn—no, not to save the life of the other." The depth of the old man's suffering is beautifully shown by his greeting to Jeanie on her return.

> "Jeanie—my ain Jeanie—my best—my maist dutiful bairn—the Lord of Israel be thy father, for I am hardly worthy of thee ! Thou hast redeemed our captivity—brought back the honour of our house. Bless thee, my bairn, with mercies promised and purchased ! "

The *Legend of Montrose* is based upon one episode in the most miraculous of Scottish epics, the murder after the battle of Tippermuir of the young Lord Kilpont by James Stewart of Ardvoirlich. Wisely Scott did not attempt a full portrait of Montrose, for, if he had, he must have failed. For one thing that great figure was still little realized by the world ; for another Scott's genius did not lie in the understanding of the searching and introspective intellect and the character in whom pure reason becomes a flame fiercer than any romantic devotion. Nor could he have coped with the doubts and subtleties of Argyll. He chose an episode in which he could give rein to his fancy, and bring upon the stage as the central figure a Scottish mercenary drawn from his readings in Turner and Monro. Sir James Turner indeed provided him with the very words of the mercenary's creed. " I had swallowed without chewing in Germanie a very dangerous maxime, which military men there too much follow : which was, that so we serve our master honestlie, it is no matter what master we serve."[1]

The book is like much of Dumas, swift, competent, careless narrative. It lives by virtue of a single character, the immortal Rittmaster. Dugald Dalgetty, compounded of Fluellen and Bobadil and Lesmahagow, and crossed with the divinity student of Marischal College, is one of those creations which, as Scott confessed, sat on the feather of his pen and led it away from its purpose.[2] He has his own way with the tale, and, when he is on the

---

[1] Turner's *Memoirs* (1829), 14.
[2] Introd. to *The Fortunes of Nigel*.

stage, the Sons of the Mist and Annot Lyle and Montrose 1819
himself sink into the background. He is a delight
whenever he speaks, whether he is laying down the
maxims of conduct for a soldier, or planning the forti-
fication of the sconce of Drumsnab, or discussing sermons
with Argyll's chaplain, or ridiculing the methods of
Highland warfare. He will fight for any cause, confident
that he has " fought knee-deep in blood many a day
for one that was ten degrees worse than the worst of
them all." The scenes in the dungeon of Inveraray
when Dugald's sober sense is contrasted with the heroics
of Ronald, and when later he discomfits Argyll, are
among the happiest that Scott ever conceived. We
rejoice to know that Dugald lived to a good age, " very
deaf, and very full of interminable stories about the
immortal Gustavus Adolphus, the Lion of the North,"
and our hearts go with him, as with Falstaff, to Arthur's
bosom or wheresome'er he be.

In *The Bride of Lammermoor* we have the one novel
written during the broken years which is overcast by
their shadow. It was not the work of the ordinary
Scott, but of a " fey " man, living in a remote world
of pain ; as we have seen, he had no recollection of its
composition, and pronounced it, after his first anxious
reading, to be " monstrous, gross and grotesque." It was
the product of a drugged and abnormal condition, even
as Coleridge composed " Kubla Khan " in an opiate
dream, from which he was roused by an inopportune
" person from Porlock."

Yet there are no loose ends in the book. In one way
it is the most perfectly constructed of all the novels,
for the sense of marching fatality is unbroken by any
awkwardness of invention or languor of narration. It is
a ballad subject, based on the legendary devilries of
Lady Stair, with the apparatus and something of the
simplicity of a great ballad. The key of painful expectation is perfectly maintained, and the dark wings of fate
obscure the sun. The story begins with a funeral,
passes to the warning of the blind Alice, and so to the

staging of tragedy ; it continues in storms, and the brief comedy interlude only deepens the surrounding darkness ; and it rises to a crescendo of guile and cruelty and folly, ending for the lovers in madness and death. Snatches of verse are introduced which haunt the mind and attune it to a dark mood of foreboding— Lucy Ashton's song at the beginning on the vanity of human wishes, and Thomas the Rhymer's prophecy—

> When the last laird of Ravenswood to Ravenswood shall ride
> And woo a dead maiden to be his bride,
> He shall stable his steed in the Kelpie's flow,
> And his name shall be lost for evermoe !

The landscape is artfully managed, and becomes, like Egdon Heath in Mr Hardy's *The Return of the Native*, almost a protagonist in the tale. The eastern end of the Lammermoors, where they break down to the sea, is to most people a green, open and friendly land where salt and heather mingle, but Scott makes it secret, dark and ominous. He never wrote better descriptive prose than in his picture of Wolf's Crag in Chapter VII.

The story is swift and brief, a succession of masterly scenes, each of which makes a notable contribution to the drama's development. Bucklaw's short commons at Wolf's Crag are contrasted with the Lord Keeper's visit and Caleb's raid on the village, when for one moment we enter the sunshine of comedy. Scott's aim is clear—to set off the snugness of the homely burgher life against the poverty and pride of decayed nobility. The scene at the cooper's cottage is more than a Dutch picture, it is an acute piece of social philosophy. Then for a little we are beguiled into cheerfulness, but the dusk gathers with the talk of the witch-wives sitting by the dead Alice, and we pass to deeper and still deeper gloom—Lucy signing the marriage contract and shrieking at the arrival of her rejected lover, her madness and death, Ravenswood riding at dawn to his doom across the wet sands, the old serving-man picking up the sable feather that is all that is left of his master, and placing it in his bosom.

There is no fault to be found with the plot, but for 1819 a theme so tremendous the characters must be commensurate. On the whole it may be claimed that they do not fall below the true tragic stature. Ravenswood is no Byronic imitation. He is a fully realized type of the aristocrat upon whom the ends of the earth have fallen, impotent in his pride, unpractical in his nobility. He is the only one of Scott's heroes who never ceases to dominate the story : in the words of Adolphus, he is " the ultimate and paramount object of every passion— whether admiration, hatred, love, hope or fear—which vary and animate the successive scenes." Lady Ashton is a female of the same breed, whose pride has been hammered into a hard mercantile ambition—Lady Macbeth *à bon marché*. Bucklaw, the honest loutish country laird, is an admirable foil to the Master's dark goodbreeding, as is the led-captain Craigengelt to Bucklaw's essential decency. Lucy Ashton is a passive creature, a green-sick girl unfit to strive with destiny, but her weakness does not make her unreal, and there is poignancy in her sad submissiveness.

" Dinna shut the cabinet yet," said Henry, " for I must have some of your silver wire to fasten the balls to my hawk's jesses. And yet the new falcon's not worth them neither. . . . She just wets her singles in the blood of the partridge, and then breaks away and lets her fly ; and what good can the poor bird do after that, you know, except pine and die in the first heather cow or whin-bush she can crawl into ? "

" Right, Henry—right, very right," said Lucy mournfully, holding the boy fast by the hand after she had given him the wire he wanted ; " but there are more riflers in the world than your falcon, and more wounded birds that seek but to die in quiet, that can find neither brake nor whin-bush to hide their heads in."

The great figures are firmly drawn, but—except for Bucklaw—on general lines ; the lesser folk are more closely realized and more cunningly differentiated. Take such a one as the minister Bide-the-Bent, and the villagers, and the old crones ; Caleb Balderston's " humours " are perhaps a trifle overdone, but he is real enough ; and in Mortsheugh, the grave-digger, Scott

1819 has drawn a character at once true to history and to human nature. Mortsheugh has been at Bothwell Brig as a henchman of the Ravenswoods, but he has no sentiment of loyalty. He regards himself as half a minister, " now that I'm a bedral in an inhabited parish," but his solemn profession gives him no dignity. Under the shadow of tragedy he will have his prosaic grumble. From a tale conceived in the highest mood of romance Scott seems to set himself to strip off all that is conventionally romantic. The old women are consumed with hatred of rank and youth and beauty, and Mortsheugh has no pity for the decline of a family which had forgotten his class.

> " If Lord Ravenswood protected his people, my friend, while he had the means of doing so, I think they might spare his memory," replied the Master.
>
> " Ye are welcome to your ain opinion, sir," said the sexton ; " but you winna persuade me that he did his duty, either to himsell or to huz puir dependent creatures, in guiding us the gate he has done. He might have gi'en us liferent tacks of our bits o' houses and yards—and me, that's an auld man, living in yon miserable cabin that is fitter for the dead than the quick, and killed wi' rheumatise, and John Smith in my dainty bit mailing, and his window glazen, and a' because Ravenswood guided his gear like a' fule ! "

The book, Scott's single unrelieved tragedy, stands apart from the rest. It has none of his mellow philosophy or his confidence in the ultimate justice of things. The shades of the prison-house are around it. There are passages in it strained and overdrawn, something bitter and violent, as if the delirium of sickness had broken the seal upon old passionate memories. Hence, for all its magnificence, it is outside the succession of the greatest tragedies, for it wounds without healing, and perturbs without consoling. Its tragedy is a ballad tragedy, cruel and inexplicable, for the ballads have no philosophy. The doom which overtakes Lucy and the Master is a blind doom, not due to any fault of their own, unless it be the girl's passivity ; Ravenswood is proud, but it is not his pride that works his undoing.

The fates are permitted to snap illogical shears. The 1819
bar between the lovers is " an ancient house destroyed,
an affectionate father murdered ; " but such a bar is no
more than the family feud of Montague and Capulet ;
it is no gulf the overpassing of which need wake a
sleepless Nemesis. It is not with the Greeks that we
can compare him, but with the Shakespeare who wrote
Romeo and Juliet. The book lacks the clean noble lines
of classic tragedy ; rather it is of the fantastic Gothick
pattern, with sometimes a tinge of the savagery of the
lesser Elizabethans. In his sickness things came to
Scott out of primordial deeps.

But it has the quality of such defects in its mastery
over that half-world, which is neither of nature nor
outside nature, but is beyond our understanding. Nowhere else does Scott show such a power of awaking
suspense and disquieting the mind with murmurings from
another sphere. Take the scene where the old women
talk in the churchyard :—

" He's a frank man, and a free-handed man, the Master . . .
and a comely personage—broad in the shoulders and narrow
around the lungies—he wad make a bonny corpse—I wad like
to hae the streeking and winding o' him."

" It is written on his brow, Annie Winnie, that hand of
woman, or of man either, will never straught him—dead deal
will never be laid on his back ; make you your market of that,
for I hae it frae a sure hand."

" Will it be his lot to die on the battle-ground, then, Ailsie
Gourlay ? Will he die by the sword or the ball, as his forbears
hae dune before him, mony ane o' them ? "

" Ask nae mair questions about it—he'll no be graced sae
far," replied the sage.

" I ken ye are wiser than ither folk, Ailsie Gourlay—but
wha tell'd ye this ? "

" Fashna your thumb about that, Annie Winnie," answered
the sibyl ; " I hae it frae a hand sure enough."

" But ye said ye never saw the foul thief," reiterated her
inquisitive companion.

" I hae it frae as sure a hand," said Ailsie, " and frae them
that spaed his fortune before the sark gaed ower his head."

" Hark ! I hear his horse's feet riding off," said the other ;
" they dinna sound as if good luck was wi' them."

1819   " Make haste, sirs," cried the paralytic hag from the cottage,
" and let us do what is needfu', and say what is fitting ; for, if
the dead corpse binna straughted, it will girn and thraw, and
that will fear the best o' us."

Observe the art of the phrase " frae a sure hand " ;
observe the cumulative impression of the broken dialogue
with its ghoulish details ; observe, above all, the tremendous effect of the sound of the horse's feet breaking
in. It is a scene which for unearthly tension is not far
behind the knocking at the door in *Macbeth*.

In *Ivanhoe* Scott opened a new lode in the mine of
his fancy, a vein of poorer but most marketable ore.
He had read widely in the mediæval chroniclers, and
had in his head a mass of more or less accurate antiquarian
knowledge, of arms, heraldry, monastic institutions, and
the dress and habits of the Middle Ages. He chose the
reign of Richard I as his period, and tumbled into it a
collection of other things which had caught his fancy.
To the forests of the English midlands he would fit the
appropriate romance, and do for them what he had
already done for the Highlands and the Border of his
own land. He got the sounding name of Ivanhoe from
an old Buckinghamshire rhyme, and Front-de-Bœuf
from the Auchinleck MSS., and he had Chaucer and
Froissart and the ballads and a wealth of legendary lore
to draw upon. He was writing fiction, not history, so
his conscience was elastic. Freeman [1] and others have
pointed out the historical errors of the book. The
customs of three centuries have been confused ; Robin
Hood, if he ever lived, belonged to a century later ;
Cedric and Athelstane are impossible figures for that
time, and Edward the Confessor left no descendants ;
Ulrica is some hundreds of years out of date and her
gods were never known to any Saxon pantheon. But
such things matter little in romance, which is a revolt
against the despotism of facts.

The real blemish is that this romance is concerned
only with externals. Scott was not depicting a life in

[1] *Norman Conquest*, V. note W.

whose soul he shared, as he could share in the ancient 1819 world of the Border ballads, or imaginatively construct for himself the confusion of the Scottish seventeenth century. Mediæval England was to him primarily a costume play. He was not like William Morris who, through some kink or fold of Time, became himself of the Middle Ages, acquiring their languor, their uniformity, even their endless prolixity. Nor could Scott, like Stendhal, think himself consciously into the mediæval mind. The scene he shapes is wholly literary, a mosaic of details put together by a learned craftsman, not the subtler creation of the spirit. We never find ourselves, as in the greater novels, " lone sitting by the shores of old romance," but in a bright, bustling world, very modern except for the odd clothes and the quaint turns of speech. There is nothing of the peculiar mediæval charm and aroma. It is a tale of forests, but only of their green highways ; we are not disquieted by any strange rustlings in the thicket.

What Scott has given us is a pageant so far-flung and glittering that, in spite of its artificiality, it captivates the fancy. There are no less than one hundred and fifty-three clearly individualized characters at some time or another on the stage. With generous profusion he piles excitement upon excitement, weaving, like his favourite Ariosto, many different narratives into one pattern, and managing it all with such skill that there are no gaps in the web. It is a success—though on a far greater scale—of the same type as Byron's metrical romances. Improbabilities, impossibilities, coincidences are accepted because the reader's mind is beguiled out of scepticism. The scene is so novel, the figures so vivid that we bow to the convention and forbear to doubt.

The artificiality being admitted, the plot is excellently managed. With two such figures as Ivanhoe and Richard at large, and with the woods full of Locksley's merry men, he can put his characters into the direst straits and leave us assured that at the blast of a bugle they will be rescued. One stirring episode follows another :—

the feast in Cedric's hall; the fanfaronade of the Ashby
tournament, with its sonorous heraldry; the revels of
the Black Knight and Friar Tuck in the hermit's cell;
the siege of Torquilstone with its many episodes : the
death of Front-de-Bœuf; Rebecca's trial before the
court of the Templars; Richard's disclosure of himself
to Locksley : Ivanhoe's last contest with Bois-Guilbert;
the arrest of Albert de Malvoisin; Rebecca's farewell to
Rowena. The speed and spirit of the narrative stifle
criticism, and on two occasions only is the reader inclined
to question. One is when Athelstane is surprisingly
raised from the dead, a portent introduced to satisfy
James Ballantyne. The other is Bois-Guilbert's end,
" a victim to the violence of his own contending passions."
The fact that something of the kind had once happened
in the Edinburgh law-courts does not make this climax
artistically more convincing.

The characters, within their artificial sphere, are carefully drawn. Gurth and Wamba do not live like Andrew
Fairservice and Caleb Balderstone, or Cedric like the
Baron of Bradwardine, or Ulrica like Meg Merrilies.
There is none of the familiar humour—save in the
mention of a Norman called Jacques Fitzdotterel of
whom we would gladly have heard more—for Wamba's
jests are for the most part clowning out of the old play-
books. But all the figures are real when they are in
action, for the action is most concretely imagined, and
all are held true to their conventional types—Isaac of
York, Richard, Prince John, Ivanhoe, Locksley, Cedric,
even the ponderous Athelstane. Moreover, Scott hit
upon the right kind of speech for his people, always
colourful and dignified, not too archaic to be difficult
or too modern to break the illusion. But only two of
his characters seem to me to have an independent life
outside their parts in the tale. One is Friar Tuck, who
has the jolly freedom of the woods in him. The other
is Rebecca, in whom, as in Di Vernon, Scott revived
his old dream of romantic maidenhood. He pairs off
his hero according to his custom with the more marriage-
able heroine, but he leaves Ivanhoe, as he had been left

himself, with long memories of Green Mantle.   Thack- 1819
eray's skit, *Rebecca and Rowena*, is amply justified.

It is hard for us to-day to recapture the atmosphere
in which *Ivanhoe* won its resounding success.   To us
the " halidoms " and " gramercys " are so much idle
" tushery," but then they were fresh and captivating.
The world of the book has become too familiar to us
from many repetitions.   If we would understand what
Scott's age thought of it, we must cast back our memories
to boyhood and recall how avidly we followed the
fortunes of the Disinherited Knight and how anxiously
we listened for Locksley's horn.   That was the mood
in which Dumas read it, and became in that hour an
historical novelist—" Oh ! then, little by little the clouds
that had veiled my sight began to lift, and I saw open
before me ampler horizons."   It is secure in the immortality which follows upon the love of recurrent
generations of youth.   But it is work on a lower plane
than the great novels that preceded it, for only once in
it does Scott seem to me to rise to the rarer and truer
romance, and set the bells of Elfland ringing.   That is
when, at Ashby, Locksley shoots at the butts, and
craves permission " to plant such a mark as is used in
the North Country."

Chapter VIII

EDINBURGH AND ABBOTSFORD

(1820)

I

1820 At the opening of the year 1820 Scott had recovered much of his bodily vigour. *Ivanhoe*, just published, promised to be the most popular of all his works, and the success of this extra-territorial adventure opened to his pen the whole realm of recorded history. In February his elder daughter Sophia became engaged to Lockhart, and her marriage took place at Abbotsford on the evening of 29th April. In March Scott visited London, when he sat to Sir Thomas Lawrence for his portrait, commissioned by the King for the great gallery at Windsor, and to Chantrey for the famous bust. His baronetcy was gazetted on 30th March and he returned home full of grandiose plans for enlarging and beautifying Abbotsford. In May he was offered a doctor's degree by both Oxford and Cambridge. Meantime, in March, *The Monastery*, which he had begun before *Ivanhoe* was finished, had been published by Longman and Constable,[1] and had been coldly received; but Scott during the summer was busy with its successor *The Abbot*, which pleased him better and which duly appeared in September. In it he drew a picture of Mary of Scots, and he had promised Constable a companion picture of Elizabeth in his next novel, for which Constable suggested the title of " Kenilworth." The relations between publisher and author were for the moment harmonious, for now that Scott had embarked upon the broad seas of historical fiction the former's bibliographical learning became of

---

[1] The bibliographical details of the novels have been carefully set out in Mr Greville-Worthington's *Bibliography* (1930).

the utmost service ; suggestions were freely offered and
gratefully received, and Constable in his high moods
used to strut about the room and claim that he was all
but the author of the novels. Things were prosperous
with the new baronet. Young Walter was doing well
in his regiment, Charles was preparing for Oxford,
Sophia was happily married ; he had plans for a more
spacious Abbotsford which filled him with delight, for
this kind of creation fascinated him as much as any
other ; he had no pressing financial troubles, and he
saw years ahead of substantial earnings from the new
lode of which *Ivanhoe* had been the first sample. Above
all he had got his health back and could enjoy life again.

Scott, like Dr Johnson and unlike most men of letters,
does not live for us only in his books. We think of him
as we think of famous men of action—as a living and
breathing human being and not a dim shade from a
library. Fortunately we have ample material for his
life, apart from its reflection in his writings. A hundred
contemporaries besides Lockhart have recorded their
impressions, and from such evidence we can make a
picture of his full and varied days.

II

Edinburgh in 1820 had grown into a modern city,
but had not yet lost the amenities of the country burgh.
Up on its back-bone of hill the Old Town was fast
changing, but much still remained from the Middle
Ages. Those " black banditti " the City Guard, with
their red coats and Lochaber axes, had disappeared
three years before and had been replaced by ordinary
police ; water was being brought in pipes from the
neighbouring hills, and the water-caddies, bent double
under their barrels, were no longer seen ; there was a
perpetual tinkering going on around Parliament Close,
and the Krames, the toy-sellers' booths planted like
wasps' nests on the north side of St Giles', were no more
the delight of childhood ; but the narrow wynds and
the tall houses remained, and the old Canongate gardens,

1820 and the elms which lined the ridge above what was once the Nor' Loch. The Edinburgh of that day was a leafy place, for all Leith Walk and the Calton slopes and Lauriston were set with trees. In the New Town classic squares still abutted on meadows. Lord Moray's lands, north of Charlotte Square, were ancient pasture dropping down to the thickets along the Water of Leith. The citizen on his evening walk could look north to the Firth and the Highland hills over meadows as rustic as Tweeddale. " How can I forget," Lord Cockburn cries, " the glory of that scene on a still night in which, with Rutherfurd and Richardson and Jeffrey, I have stood in Queen Street, or the opening at the north-west corner of Charlotte Square, and listened to the ceaseless rural corn-craiks, nestling happily in the dewy grass ! " [1] And the west wind still brought from the Pentlands the scent of moorburn in March and of heather in August.

Castle Street, where Scott lived, ran across the ridge of the New Town, with the Firth on the north to show silver in the dawn, and to the south the great Castle rock to catch the last fires of evening. Scott's library lay behind the dining-room, a small, high, square apartment which looked out upon the bleaching-green. It was always in perfect order—the volumes in the cases well cared for, with a wooden slip marking the place of a book which had been borrowed ; the great table at which he wrote covered with papers neatly docketed ; a massive antique inkstand ; on the open space of wall above the fireplace a portrait of Claverhouse flanked by Highland targes and claymores. There Scott did his " day's darg " before breakfast or during the evenings he spent at home. The big deerhound Maida, given him by Glengarry, kept him company on the hearth-rug, and when he was absent on leave the cat, Hinse of Hinsfeldt, descended from the top of the library ladder and mounted guard on a footstool. Scott used to talk to the animals while he worked, and would leave off every now and then to pat Maida's head. Yet he wrote at high speed and with a profound concentration. When

[1] *Mem.*, 403.

the work was tedious or inspiration flagged he forced 1820
himself to complete it before rising. "There is only
one rule in such cases, not to let the ink dry in your pen
till the task is done. ' Gutta cavat lapidem non vi sed
sæpe cadendo,' says the school copy-book, and on this
principle a scribbler sometimes becomes agreeably surprised at the extent of tiresome and rugged road that
he has got over." He never planned out his task before-
hand with any elaboration, so sometimes he came to a
dead halt. "One page—or, I should say, one line—
suggests another, and on coming to a stand-still, as it
occasionally happens—for we are all liable to ebbs and
flows—I very coolly lay it aside and take to something
else, till, with the next change of the moon, there begins
a new tide of thought." Except in emergencies he
considered three hours of literary labour sufficient for a
day, but in Edinburgh he liked to be uninterrupted,
so he preferred the early morning when others were
asleep.[1]

His dress in town was sober black as became a court
official ; his gown was ancient and shabby, and his lame
foot had made a huge hole in the skirt. When breakfast
was over a coach arrived to take him to the Court, and
there he sat all day in a dim litigious light, dozing a
little, dreaming much, till he was roused by Lord
Balmuto's fierce grunt of " Where are your cautioners ? "
The actual court work was for the most part mechanical,
though it involved the reading of many papers over-
night, a task which Scott conscientiously performed.
He had always a great gift of absenting his mind. At
Abbotsford, while he was watching his foresters at work,
his fancy would be busy with the novel he had in hand ;
so in court, while an advocate was droning along, he
would be happy with his own dream. Sometimes, when
his imagination had mounted its high horse, he would
forget his environment altogether, and once, when on
his way to an evening party, he wandered to the out-
skirts of the city and came to his senses at the bottom
of a wet gravel-pit. The routine occupation he had

[1] Gillies, 151, 161, 216.

1820 found was perfect for his purpose, for it gave him long hours of silent meditation.

After court he sought fresh air and exercise, walking in fine weather, or driving in an open carriage with a friend or member of his family. His favourite rounds were the Blackford Hills ; or to Ravelston and home by Corstorphine ; or to the shore at Portobello, where his coachman was instructed to drive along the edge of the tide. Or he would explore the Old Town, and expound to a companion the tale of every crooked gable in the Cowgate or the Canongate. Then with a sharpened appetite he returned to his five o'clock dinner, for he had not eaten since nine. Scott was a heavy eater of plain food. When he dined at home he liked homely dishes, and from Abbotsford there came every week by the Melrose carrier a great hamper of butter, cheese, eggs, fowls, vegetables and cream, and, in their season, game and salmon. His palate was not delicate, and he had little sense of taste or smell : he never knew when venison was high, or wine was corked, and he could not tell sherry from madeira. Claret was his ordinary drink, and he regarded a pint of claret as each man's share when the cloth was drawn ; he liked champagne, which had come into fashion since the war ; port he thought an unpleasant kind of physic ; he was fond of small drams of whisky in a quaigh, and on the whole preferred whisky-toddy to any wine. He had smoked a good deal in his Ashestiel days, had given it up, but had resumed it under the influence of Lockhart and young Walter, and used to have a couple of cigars before going to bed.

He went often to the theatre, sometimes in summer he drove abroad after dinner, and during the winter he frequently dined out. The Edinburgh dinner-party at that time might be as late as six, and was apt to be a formidable business. On state occasions Scott would array himself in white silk stockings, a scarlet silk waistcoat, and the dress coat of the Forest Club. There was a great deal of toast-drinking and giving of sentiments, and a generous consumption of wine. Later in the evening the supper-tables would appear, and the 1820 guests sit down to roast fowls and Welsh rarebits and broiled bones and huge bowls of punch. Scott was a noted figure at these Edinburgh parties, but he was at his best in his own house, where every Sunday night he entertained a few people. Thither came Skene and Erskine and Clerk and all the familiars. Sunday was the night for entertainment even in the strictest circles— did not Sir Henry Moncrieff give on that day his famous supper-parties in Queen Street ?—but music was not permitted, so after the Sunday dinners there was no harp-playing or singing of Scots songs, but instead he used to read aloud to the company. Shakespeare and the Elizabethans, Wordsworth, Southey, Crabbe and Byron were his favourites, and in passages of deep emotion he would become like one inspired. The critical Lockhart confessed that Scott read aloud " high poetry with far greater simplicity, depth, and effect than any other man I have ever heard."

Good conversation was one of the things for which Edinburgh was famous, but its excellences were of a special kind. The talkers were the lawyers and the professors, and the talk was largely made up of brilliant disquisitions by individuals and ingenious arguments between celebrated gladiators, while the rest of the company sat still and admired.[1] This was not Scott's native air, and for long he was considered as a little slow and commonplace. He spoke broadly, using many Scots words, and he was not greatly interested in the niceties of dialectic. Moreover, the good talkers were the young Whigs, and Scott's Toryism made him apathetic towards speculations on the advancement of science and the march of reason. But by 1820 he had won a great repute for a kind of conversation peculiarly his own— a combination of rugged sagacity and humour which humanized and brightened the atmosphere. Into the play of academic and forensic wit he brought a kindlier

[1] Benjamin Franklin in his *Autobiography*, speaking of what he calls the " disputative turn," writes : " Persons of good sense, I have observed, rarely fall into it, except lawyers, university men, and men of all sorts that have been bred at Edinborough."

1820 fellowship. His Edinburgh table-talk was not that of Abbotsford, where he would let himself go in riotous mirth, but it had always a country flavour. He refused to be drawn into disputes, and he would check any controversy in which tempers were rising with some comic phrase or whimsical tale. In the presence of that wise, rugged, brooding face—as massive and as masculine as Tom Cribb's—petty cleverness fell to a discount. " The strongest, purest and least observed of all lights," Lockhart has written, " is daylight ; and his talk was commonplace, just as sunshine is, which gilds the most indifferent objects and adds brilliancy to the brightest. . . . I can never forget the pregnant expression of one of the ablest of that school and party (the Whigs)—Lord Cockburn—who when some glib youth chanced to echo in his hearing the consolatory tenet of local mediocrity, answered quietly—' I have the misfortune to ·think differently from you—in my humble opinion Walter Scott's sense is a still more wonderful thing than his genius.' "[1] Cockburn indeed placed Scott as a talker on the same plane as Jeffrey himself. " Scarcely ever in his moods was he more striking or delightful than in society ; when the halting limb, the bur in the throat, the heavy cheeks, the high Goldsmith-forehead, the unkempt locks, and general plainness of appearance, with the Scotch accent and stories and sayings, all graced by gaiety, simplicity and kindness, made a combination most worthy of being enjoyed." [2]

He mixed with every element in the capital except the divines, for he rarely went to church.[3] His sympathies were with Pleydell's " suffering and Episcopal Church of Scotland " ; he had a pew in St George's church in York Place ; and it was the English prayer-book that he read to his friends ; though his son Charles was baptized by Thomson of Duddingston, and he himself had become in 1806 an elder of that parish and had sat as such in presbytery, synod and General Assembly.[4]

---

[1] IV. 155-6.   [2] *Mem.*, 267-8.
[3] Gillies, 193 ; *Dom. Manners*, 125.   [4] *S.Q.*, 32.

Edinburgh had never seen a more varied and confident 1820 social life or so many celebrities on her pavements. Haydon, the painter, has described the winter scene. " Princes Street in a clear sunset, with the Castle and the Pentland Hills in radiant glory, and the crowd illumined by the setting sun. . . . First you would see limping Sir Walter, with Lord Meadowbank ; then tripped Jeffrey, keen, restless and fidgety ; you then met Wilson or Lockhart, or Allan, or Thomson, or Raeburn, as if all had agreed to make their appearance at once." It was a pleasant place for the well-to-do, the successful and the physically strong ; less pleasant for a dyspeptic youth like Thomas Carlyle, who was then living in Bristo Street and struggling to maintain himself by tutorships. Carlyle gives us the other side of the medal. When he trod the pavements in summer " hot as Nebuchadnezzar's furnace," and met Scott, he cared nothing for what he was afterwards to call that " fine Scotch face, with its shaggy honesty, sagacity and good- ness ; " he saw in him only the " literary restaurateur of Europe." Below the comely surface there were new forces working of which even the illuminate Whigs knew little ; but the surface was all cheerfulness, good fellowship and a modest pride.

The Napoleonic Wars, having closed the Continent to travel, had sent many scions of great English houses to Edinburgh to study at the university, and this had introduced an agreeable cosmopolitanism, which in 1820 had not wholly disappeared. But the scene was still idiomatically Scottish. Figures still survived from an older world, notably some of the famous race of Scots gentlewomen—" strong handed, warm hearted and high spirited ; the fire of their temper not always latent ; merry even in solitude ; very resolute ; indifferent about the modes and habits of the modern world ; and adhering to their own ways, so as to stand out, like primitive rocks, above ordinary society."[1] Many of the great academic figures had gone, but Dugald Stewart and John Playfair were alive ; there was a national school

[1] Cockburn, *Mem.*, 58.

1820 of science and philosophy as well as of letters, and there
were scholarly country gentlemen, like Clerk of Eldin
and Sir William Forbes, to make a bridge between
learning and society.   Edinburgh was a true capital, a
clearing-house for the world's culture and a jealous
repository of Scottish tradition.

Above all there were the Bar and the Bench to emphasize her individuality. Never had the profession of
the law flowered into so engaging a variety of character
and attainment.   There was Lord Newton, whose purple
visage looks down at us from Raeburn's canvas, whose
legal lore was as deep as his potations, and whose one fear
was that, as the times degenerated, he should be left the
only claret-drinker on the face of the earth ; there was
William Adam, the Chief Commissioner of the new jury
court, whose judgments according to Lord Glenlee were
like an act of Parliament, with all the appearance of precision and all the reality of confusion ; at the Bar there was
still John Clerk, the brother of Scott's friend, a prodigiously successful advocate, lame, dishevelled, always
in a fury of excitement, the joy of clients and the terror
of judges.   And one fantastic figure had only just left
the scene, Adam Rolland the consulting counsel, who
walked abroad in mulberry velvets and satins " like one
of the creatures come to life again in a collection of
dried butterflies," and whose waxen cheeks were rouged
like a doll's.

Scotland was only now emerging from the dark ages.
Up till 1799 the colliers and salters had been slaves ;
there was no popular voice in the Government and
neither a free press nor free speech ; every institution,
municipal, political and judicial, stood in need of drastic
reform.   But the long war, the terror of Napoleon, and
the hegemony of Henry Dundas had officially stilled the
voice of criticism, and in the reaction against foreign
extravagance change was identified with revolution.   It
needed courage to profess liberal opinions, since they
shut the avenues to success.   So the younger Whigs
were driven to form a coterie, which suffered a little
from the defect of coteries in cultivating spiritual pride.

The vast bulk of educated opinion was against them, 1820 but they included most of the ablest living Scotsmen— Jeffrey and his fellow reviewers, Henry Cockburn, Playfair, Scott's friends George Cranstoun and Thomas Thomson, almost every one, except Scott, who carried weight with the larger public. They made a pleasant warm-hearted group, deeply attached to each other as companions in adversity, and the incomparable charm and gentleness of Henry Erskine in the previous generation had left them with a tradition of good manners and social urbanity. With their straiter opponents they had no dealings, but they mixed generally in society, and Scott filled the part which Erskine had once played and acted as a *trait d'union*. For Jeffrey especially, in spite of many feuds, he had a sincere affection. He loved the spirit in the small body, the ardour and candour of the bright dark eyes, and he would have agreed with Carlyle's estimate—" not deep enough, pious or reverent enough, to have been great in literature, but a man intrinsically of veracity."[1] Six years later he wrote in his journal : " I do not know why it is that, when I am with a party of my Opposition friends, the day is often merrier than when with our own set. Is it because they are cleverer ? Jeffrey and Harry Cockburn are, to be sure, very extraordinary men, but it is not owing to that entirely. I believe both parties meet with the feeling of something like novelty. We have not worn out our jests in daily contact."[2] There could be friendship with political opponents, but not habitual intercourse.

True intimacy for Scott demanded his own way of political thinking, or no politics at all. Like many men with a vast acquaintanceship his innermost circle was small. When he escaped from the Parliament House and descended the Mound, it was generally in the company of Will Erskine, the frail figure with the hectic cheek and the soft brown eyes, or of Will Clerk, with his shabby clothes and shrewd glances from under his pent-house brows. Closer still, perhaps, was James

[1] *Reminiscences*, II. 64. [2] *Journal*, I. 320.

1820 Skene, the Aberdeenshire laird, who had been his frequent
guest since the first days at Ashestiel and who shared
all his tastes in sport and letters. Two others of the
inner circle were at first sight less obviously kindred
souls. George Cranstoun, with his deathly pallor and
finicking manners and minute legal pedantry, was endeared by long association, and Scott was one of the
few who could penetrate to the man behind the exquisite
formalist. There was a still stranger ally in Charles
Kirkpatrick Sharpe, connoisseur, antiquary, reactionary
and wit, who walked the streets in a fantastic wig, and
in a thin soprano voice poured scorn on a vulgar world
and on all in it that was not long-descended. But
Sharpe was a sound scholar in his way and had a heart
beneath his corsets, and in Scott's presence the acid
dandy became genial and human.

It was an age of dining clubs, where men could talk
their own talk and pass the bottle with no need to join
the ladies. Scott loved such entertainments, and it was
he who in 1803 first started the Friday Club. That
sodality was broadly based, for it included as many
Whigs as Tories; Playfair, Sydney Smith, Francis
Horner and Kennedy of Dunure were members as well
as Scott and Erskine and Henry Mackenzie, and Jeffrey
and his friends found it for forty years the pleasantest
thing in Edinburgh. There was another club which
met from Friday till Tuesday at Blairadam, the country
house of Chief Commissioner Adam, whom Lockhart
thought the only man who rivalled Scott " in uniform
graciousness of *bonhomie* and gentleness of humour."
This was a smaller fraternity, nine in number, which
included a Fife laird or two, Thomas Thomson, his
brother the minister of Duddingston, Adam Ferguson
and Will Clerk. The Saturdays and Mondays were
spent in visits to famous spots in Fife and Kinross and
ramblings over Benarty and the Cleish hills—the landscape of *The Abbot*—and the Sundays in church-going
and talk. Till his last illness Scott never missed a
meeting.

There were the booksellers, too, as part of his circle,

the men upon whom his fortunes were grounded. Scott 1820 would often step from the Parliament House to Constable's office in the High Street, where daily the great publisher arrived in his sober barouche and pair. But he went there on business only, for he was never quite at ease with the " Emperor," and too many of the *Edinburgh Review* set haunted the place. More often he would turn down the Canongate and thread Coull's Close to the old building called Paul's Work under the shadow of the Calton Hill, where James Ballantyne reigned among his machines. Whatever James's imperfections in finance, he was an excellent manager of a printing shop, and he had a staff as eager and competent as himself. In 1822, besides much other work, he issued 145,000 volumes from Scott's pen alone, no small achievement in those days of the old hand-presses. Sometimes Scott would be a guest at James's house in St John Street near-by, where on the eve of a new novel there would be a mighty feast—none of John's French kick-shaws, but turtle and venison and solid beef and mutton, and ample allowance of strong ale, iced punch and madeira. At such banquets James would sing his best songs, and with a voice sacramentally hushed would give the toast of " The Great Unknown." Later in the evening, when the toddy bowl had appeared, the host would produce the proof-sheets of the new novel and roll out some dramatic scene in his rich bass, while every muscle of his face twitched in sympathy.

Sometimes on his way home Scott would be taken by Lockhart to William Blackwood's fine new shop in Princes Street. There was always a certain constraint in these visits, for he was a little shy of the noisy " Maga " group, and he was not attracted by Blackwood's blunt manner and the steady grey eyes under the shaggy brows. Yet, had he been in Blackwood's hands rather than in Constable's, his fate might well have been different, for the former was the canniest mind in the book-trade, one who would never venture where he could not comfortably retreat. But if Scott did not altogether take to Lockhart's friends, Lockhart

1820 violently disapproved of one of Scott's. The son-in-law had no taste for raffish Bohemianism, and he winced when the great man was hailed in the street by a fantastic little figure in the loudest sporting garb, driving a bright blue curricle. He disliked accompanying Scott to John Ballantyne's auction-room in Hanover Street where that sprightly being sold bibelots with melting eloquence. Still less did he approve of John's exotic dinners at Harmony Hall, where the wandering planets of the stage and the opera congregated. Lockhart liked neither of the Ballantynes, he could not understand Scott's taste for them, and he does imperfect justice to their merits. For James was a true pioneer in fine printing and a skilful manager in his actual craft, while John was stuffed with whimsical romance. He bought Montrose's sword from Graham of Gartmore and piously presented it to Scott, and his buttons, which less piously he wore on his own shooting-jacket. He must have had gifts of drollery amounting almost to genius. One has only to read the tributes of Hogg and Wilson to realize that to many of his contemporaries the ultimate wells of fun seemed to be sealed at John's death.[1]

On Saturdays and on the happy days which closed the legal sessions Scott did not dress in his usual black, but under his gown wore a green jacket and corduroys. Peter Mathieson was waiting with the carriage in the Parliament Close, and before dinner the Sheriff was in his sheriffdom.

III

Scott was not now the man he had been ; in his own phrase he had reached " the other side of the hill." He moved more stiffly, and he had twinges of rheumatism from the constant wettings of the old days. Though he could still ride long distances on Sybil Grey and walk five or six miles at a stretch, he had no longer that abounding zest for action which at Ashestiel had made him daily scour the hills. He had become more of a

---

[1] *Noctes Ambrosianæ*, III. 93-95.

home-keeper, and he told Lord Montagu, as proof of 1820
advancing age, that he had taken a liking to cats, which
he had aforetime detested, and a fancy for gardening,
an art which he had hitherto despised. He liked to
potter about among his tenants, and to supervise his
new buildings, and to arrange and catalogue his collections. But this growing sedentary habit did not impair
the gusto of his mind. He had still the ardour and the
wide horizons of youth. " The years which have gone
by," he wrote to Southey as late as 1824, " have found
me . . . tossing my ball and driving my hoop, a grey-
headed schoolboy."

The main routine of his life was as fixed at Abbotsford
as at Ashestiel and in Edinburgh. The pillar of it was
the late breakfast between nine and ten. Before that
he had completed the whole or the greater part of his
day's work ; after it he could see to his property and
entertain his friends. His custom was to let his immediate task simmer in his mind for an hour before he
rose, which meant that he could work quickly when he
sat down to his desk. He wrote, as I have said, with
intense concentration, and was not in the least put out
by the interruption of dogs or human beings. Indeed
his even temper could be ruffled by two things only—
the meddling with his pen or the maltreatment of a book.
The labours of those morning hours were not only in
creative literature. He had a large post-bag and made
a point of answering every letter without delay. Many
of the communications he received were merely vexatious
—the manuscript novels and poems of budding authors
who sought his patronage, and requests for introductions
and prefaces and pecuniary help. But some were welcome grist to the mill. Antiquaries sent him curious
pieces of lore ; a Tweeddale shepherd wrote to him
about fairies ; readers up and down the land contributed anecdotes of odd incidents and characters, or
ghost stories, or fragments of Jacobite tradition.[1] And
there might be epistles from old friends, Skene or
Morritt, or Mrs Hughes of Uffington, or Lady Louisa

[1] P L. B., 319-347.

1820 Stuart, letters which were joyfully reserved for reading
aloud to the family.

The breakfast-room, like the library, was encumbered
with dogs—Maida the deerhound; Hamlet the black
greyhound; Finette, Lady Scott's spaniel; Ourisque,
a Highland terrier from Kintail; a motley of dandies
named after the cruet-stand—Pepper, Mustard, Ketchup
and so forth; as well as the cat Hinse of Hinsfeldt.
Scott's morning garb was the famous green shooting-
coat, grey corduroy breeches, stockings and heavy shoes.
He was in the habit of making a leisurely meal, while
he discussed the post and the plans for the day. He
ate porridge and cream from a cogie with a silver-
mounted horn spoon; then he would do good work on
salmon, fresh or kippered, and on a home-cured ham,
a pie, or a cold sheep's head, and he would finish with
oatcakes or slices of brown bread spread thick with
butter. It was his chief meal of the day, and he had
earned it, for he had three or four hours of hard labour
behind him.

The family was not often alone, for Abbotsford received
as many guests as any nobleman's house in the land.
Many came on pilgrimage to see the great man in his
home, and Scott in his modesty felt that their entertainment was part of the return which he owed to a
public which had treated him so handsomely. There
would be an occasional foreign prince or English grandee,
taking Abbotsford as one of their houses of call, an
intermediate stage between Alnwick and Dalkeith. There
would be brother writers welcomed in the freemasonry
of the craft; Edinburgh lawyers, notably the other
Clerks of Court; and school friends and faraway kinsfolk.
Generally there was a Tweeddale or Teviotdale laird, as
often as not with wife and family, who at first mixed
shyly with the London fashionables and the Edinburgh
wits. But the geniality of the host dissolved all awkwardness. Abbotsford, even in its earlier stages, was a
comfortable dwelling, and Scott, with unhappy memories
of other houses, took care that there should be ample
writing materials not only upon the library tables but

in every bedroom. His wife used to accuse him of over-
walking, overtalking and overfeeding his guests, and no
doubt some who were more used to Mayfair than to the
hills may have found their days too strenuous. But the
talk was what they came for, and Scott dispensed it
generously ; it was the talk, varied cunningly to suit
every taste, which, in Lockhart's phrase, made them all
" equally happy with him, with themselves, and with
each other."

Expeditions were the order of the day. The anglers
in the party, such as Sir Humphry Davy, would set
off under Charlie Purdie's guidance for Lord Somerville's
reach of the Tweed. The others, mounted on shelties,
would thread the green rides of the young plantations,
ascend the Eildons, and drop down on Melrose and
Dryburgh, or, turning westward, explore Ettrick and
Yarrow. Sometimes there would be a coursing of hares
on the uplands between Tweed and Yarrow, when the
unwary floundered in well-heads and peat-haggs. The
ladies used to drive in a sociable and join the rest in a
picnic luncheon at some famous spot like the birchen
bower of Newark. Now and then a day was given up
to the river, when the party would feast by the waterside
on fresh-caught salmon, boiled in their *broo*, and at
night there would be a " burning of the water," when
Scott, though he could no longer wield a spear, took the
helm of a boat or held a torch. When he walked in the
neighbourhood of Abbotsford he was generally bareheaded, but on an expedition the old white hat would
appear, exchanged in rough weather for a sealskin cap.
One unfailing companion was a massive stick, called
Major Weir after the warlock, because of its necromantic
powers of disappearance.

There were certain high days and holy days observed
at Abbotsford—the football match on the Carter Haugh,
the " kirn " or harvest-home, when the neighbourhood
danced to John of Skye's bagpipes, and above all the
Abbotsford Hunt. This last was held usually on 28th
October, the young Walter's birthday. It meant a day's
coursing on the moors around Cauldshiels loch, or on

1820 the Gala hills, and all the yeomen and gentry of the
countryside attended. There followed a great dinner at
Abbotsford, with Scott in the chair, and victuals fit for
hungry men :—" a baron of beef, roasted, at the foot of
the table, a salted round at the head, while tureens of
hare soup, hotchpotch, and cockeyleekie extended down
the centre, and such light articles as geese, turkeys,
entire sucking pigs, a singed sheep's head, and the
unfailing haggis, were set forth by way of side dishes.
Blackcock and moorfowl, bushels of snipe, black puddings,
white puddings, and pyramids of pancakes formed the
second course. Ale was the favourite beverage during
dinner, but there was plenty of port and sherry for
those whose stomachs they suited. The quaighs of
Glenlivet were filled brimful, and tossed off as if they
held water." Thereafter toddy was made in huge bowls,
the Ettrick Shepherd being the chief compounder, and
the stories and the songs began and lasted till the
stirrup-cup far on in the small hours. " How they all
contrived to get home in safety," says Lockhart,
" Heaven only knows—but I never heard of any serious
accident except upon one occasion, when James Hogg
made a bet at starting that he would leap over his wall-
eyed pony as she stood, and broke his nose in this
experiment of ' o'ervaulting ambition.' One comely
goodwife, far off among the hills, amused Sir Walter by
telling him, the next time he passed her homestead
after one of these jolly doings, what her husband's
first words were when he alighted at his own door—
' Ailie, my woman, I'm ready for my bed—and oh,
lass (he gallantly added) I wish I could sleep for a
towmont, for there's only ae thing in this warld worth
living for, and that's the Abbotsford hunt ! " [1]

The dining-room was still a tiny place and John of
Skye had to pipe on the green outside. Scott was
generally in high spirits at dinner, though he ate little ;
he had no fixed seat at table, but would drop into
any place vacant. The company did not sit long when
the cloth was drawn, but joined the ladies in the library

[1] V. 17.

or the drawing-room, where about ten o'clock a light 1820
supper was served. Sometimes they danced reels, and
on most evenings there was music, when Adam Ferguson
would sing "Johnnie Cope" and Anne or Sophia
"Kenmure's on and awa'." Scott's talk at Abbotsford
was, by general agreement, better than his Edinburgh
performances, for he was in better health and could let
his fancy "run its ain rigg." Stories, reminiscences,
happy sayings were varied with discourses on books,
when, as he quoted some favourite passage, his voice
would swell and his face light up. Here are two pictures
of him in this mood. First Lockhart :—

> In the course of conversation he happened to quote a few
> lines from one of the old Border ballads, and, looking round,
> I was quite astonished with the changes which seemed to have
> passed over every feature in his countenance. His eyes seemed
> no longer to glance quick and grey from beneath his impending
> brows, but were fixed in their expanded eyelids with a sober,
> solemn lustre. His mouth (the muscles about which are at all
> times wonderfully expressive), instead of its usual language of
> mirth or benevolence or shrewdness, was filled with a sad and
> peculiar earnestness. The whole face was tinged with a glow
> which showed its lines in new energy and transparence, and
> the thin hair parting backward displayed in tenfold majesty
> his Shakespearian pile of forehead.[1]

Five years later we have Adolphus :—

> The hair upon his forehead was quite grey, but his face,
> which was healthy and sanguine, and the hair about it, which
> had still a strong reddish tinge, contrasted rather than har-
> monized with the sleek, silvery locks above, a contrast which
> might seem rather suited to a jovial and humorous than to
> a pathetic expression. But the features were equally capable
> of both. The form and hue of the eyes (for the benefit of
> minute physiogomists it should be noted that the pupils
> contained some small specks of brown) were wonderfully
> calculated for showing great varieties of emotion. Their
> mournful aspect was extremely earnest and affecting ; and,
> when he told some dismal and mysterious story, they had a
> doubtful, melancholy, exploring look, which appealed irresist-
> ibly to the hearer's imagination. Occasionally, when he spoke
> of something very audacious and eccentric, they would dilate

[1] *Peter's Letters*, II. 302.

1820   and light up with a tragi-comic, harebrained expression, quite
peculiar to himself ; one might see in it a whole chapter of
Cœur-de-Lion and the Clerk of Copmanhurst. Never, perhaps,
did a man go through all the gradations of laughter with such
complete enjoyment, or a countenanace so radiant. The
first dawn of a humorous thought would show itself sometimes,
as he sat silent, by an involuntary lengthening of the upper
lip, followed by a shy sidelong glance at his neighbours,
indescribably whimsical, and seeming to ask from their looks
whether the spark of drollery should be suppressed or allowed
to blaze out. In the full tide of mirth he did indeed " laugh
the heart's laugh," like Walpole, but it was not boisterous
and overpowering, nor did it check the course of his words ;
he could go on telling or descanting while his lungs did " crow
like chanticleer," his syllables, in the struggle, growing more
emphatic, his accent more strongly Scotch, and his voice
plaintive with excess of merriment.[1]

Apart from his writing and his entertaining Scott
had many duties to fill his time. He sat regularly in
the Selkirk sheriff-court, and had to have a legal section
in the Abbotsford library. He had his farms in his own
hand, but he cared more for his trees than for a good
field of oats ; he was always at work in his nurseries
and plantations, planting and thinning, waiting for the
day when a hoodie crow should build in an oak which
he himself had sown. He went much about among his
country neighbours, attended the dinners of the Forest
Club, and was now and then a guest at a burgh feast
in Selkirk, or at a banquet of the Galashiels weavers,
when John of Skye piped to them and he himself sang
" Tarry 'Oo."

Scott was by far the most popular figure on the
Border. " All who knew him intimately loved him,"
said James Hogg, who spoke for the hill glens, " nay,
many of them almost worshipped him. . . . He was the
only one I ever knew whom no man, either poor or rich,
held at ill-will." [2] And he has a story of his wife which
beautifully illustrates the spell which Scott laid on
simple hearts. Once when he had been dining with the
Hoggs at Mount Benger, he took up a little daughter,
kissed her, and, laying his hand on her head, said,

[1] Lockhart, V. 298-9.   [2] Dom. Manners, 112-4.

" God Almighty bless you, my dear child." Hogg found 1820 his wife in tears and asked what ailed her. " Oh," she cried, " I thought if he had just done the same to them all, I do not know what in the world I would not have given."

The servants, indoors and outdoors, were like members of one family, and if Scott knew one thing better than another it was the heart of the old-fashioned serving-man. He made their affairs his own, gave presents to their families, and, if one were overtaken by the wayside after a kirn, would himself wheel him to some shelter where he could sleep off his potations. Peter Mathieson, the coachman, was a Presbyterian of the old rock, and Scott's favourite after-dinner walk was to the bowling green, where he could hear Peter's evening psalmody. Dalgleish, the butler, was another stalwart ; and there was Robert Hogg, too, the head shepherd, who did not greatly admire his famous brother of Ettrick, and John of Skye, who was a hedger and ditcher when he was not piping, and the footman, John Nicholson, whose educa-tion Scott supervised, and a long string of foresters. But the true " laird's man " was Tom Purdie. Tom treated Scott and his fame as his own property. He was annoyed when Adam Ferguson was knighted, for he said, " it will take some of the shine out of us ; " when Scott once observed that it was going to be a fine spring for the trees, Tom added that it would be " a grand season for our buiks too." He used complete freedom with his master, and had often to be cajoled or argued into agreement with a plan. He was factotum out of doors and Scott's " Sunday poney " when he was fatigued : indoors he was librarian, and his horny hands treated the precious volumes with delicacy and reverence. Every Sunday evening he appeared after dinner to drink long life to the laird and the lady.

The brute creatures shared in the same intimacy. Scott had an extraordinary attraction for every kind of dog, as his Abbotsford following showed. Carlyle has a story of a small cocker spaniel in Edinburgh, which had a nose for insincerity in human beings and was

1820 never wrong. Whenever it saw Scott in the street the
proud little fellow would frisk round him and fawn at
his feet.[1] And there were other animals than dogs.
There was a hen that would not be separated from him,
and Sophia's donkeys, when they saw him, trotted to
the paling " to have a crack with the laird," and a little
black pig tried to attach itself to his retinue. [2]

There was nothing slack-lipped in Scott's geniality.
He exacted a full day's work from his servants and
willingly received it. His friendliness encouraged confidence but not presumption, for every man knew that
there was lightning slumbering behind the kindly grey
eyes. His hospitality had its limits and he could show
the door very fast to impertinent intruders ; there was
about him, says Lockhart " in perfection, when he
chose to exert it, the power of civil rejection." What he
possessed was a quick conscience towards his fellows,
especially towards the poor, and his letters show how
assiduously he reflected on the problems of poverty.
He discussed with Morritt the English poor law system,
rejoiced that Scotland was less infested with ale-houses,
and proposed a tax on manufacturers based on the
number of hands they employed, the proceeds of which
should go to the maintenance of the " manufacturing
poor." He believed in giving employment, not charity,
and in the winter of 1816 made tasks for thirty labourers
at Abbotsford on piece-work. He criticized acutely the
Edinburgh system of employment on public works, where
the wages paid were below the normal rate. Charity, he
held, should be reserved for emergencies, and then no
man gave more freely. In the snow-storm and floods of
the spring of 1820, he sent money to Will Laidlaw.
" Do not let the poor bodies want for a £5, and even a
£10, more or less." [3] He had the sound feudal notion
that property was a trust, involving more duties than
rights. The country children might go nutting in his
beloved woods, though they destroyed his hazels. Fire-

[1] *Critical and Miscellaneous Essays*, IV. 70.
[2] The same thing happened to Lord Gardenstone, one of the judges in the
Douglas case. *Letters of Sir W. Scott and C. K. Sharpe to R. Chambers*, 35.
[3] Lockhart, IV. 73, 85, 348.

wood he would not give away, but he sold it cheaply, 1820 and put the proceeds into a fund to provide free doctoring for the cottagers. Nothing could induce him to close a customary track though it came very near his lawn, and he would never permit a trespass warning to be set up. " Round the house," he told Basil Hall, " there is a set of walks set apart and kept private for the ladies— but over all the rest of my land any one may run as he likes. I please myself with the reflection that many people of taste may be indulging their fancies in these grounds, and I often recollect how much of Burns's inspiration was probably due to his having near him the woods of Ballochmyle to ramble through at his will when he was a ragged callant." [1]

Maria Edgeworth made a wise comment on the Abbotsford régime. " Dean Swift said he had written his books in order that people might learn to treat him like a great lord. Sir Walter Scott writes his that he may be able to treat his people as a great lord ought to do." [2] There lay the kernel of Scott's purpose, the heart of his dream. He realized his romance far less in the pepper-box turrets of Abbotsford and the plaster copies of the Melrose gargoyles than in his re-creation of a fragment of what seemed to him an older and happier world. He was living in his ancestral countryside as a little king, with all the felicities and some of the burdens of kingship. It rejoiced him to be the tap-root from which a modest covert drew the sap. He had restored, though only in a corner, the liberal and kindly customs of more spacious days, mellowed, indeed, and civilized, but preserving intact their freedom and manliness and courtesy. If the dream was baseless it was assuredly not ignoble

[1] Lockhart, V. 399.   [2] *Ibid*, VI. 61.

LIBRARY ST. MARY'S COLLEGE

Chapter IX

HIGH NOON

(1820–1825)

I

1820–25   *The Abbot*, published in the early autumn of 1820, retrieved much of the popularity which *The Monastery* had lost. It marked the beginning of a quinquennium which may be regarded as the high noon-tide of Scott's life. His greatest work was behind him, but he had now trained himself to the craft of the historical novelist, who can take any period of history and in some measure shape it for his readers. He had become a figure of national importance, not only a kind of consul-general for the republic of letters, but a man whose advice and help were sought on the most diverse public affairs. He was completing Abbotsford in the grand manner, and paying for it by overdrafts on his future labours, and, while it was growing into a Gothick fantasy, he was entertaining there a large part of the rank and intelligence of Britain. It was for Scott a time of ceaseless industry and of much varied enjoyment, enjoyment not only of the exercise of creative power but of its material rewards. His body had recovered a moderate vigour, and freedom from pain released his old sunshine of spirit. I do not think that there is a parallel in the whole history of letters to the position which Scott filled among his countrymen in the years between 1820 and 1825.

In Edinburgh he had become even more than Jeffrey the leader of cultivated society. Pitt dinners, meetings of the Royal Society of Edinburgh of which he was now President, the feasts of a certain Highland Club (where he seems to have worn the tartan and had John of Skye

224

in his tail) filled his evenings. In the beginning of 1821
after the publication of *Kenilworth*, he went to London
on Court of Session business, arranged for his eldest
son's transfer from the 18th to the 15th Hussars, and
had much to do with the establishment of the Royal
Society of Literature. On the 16th of June, when Scott
was busy on *The Pirate*, John Ballantyne died. He had
amused himself in his last year by turning some old
houses at Kelso into a fishing lodge which he called
Walton Hall, and in starting a Novelists' Library, unpleasing books in double columns for which Scott wrote
a number of lives. He died with the proof-sheets beside
his pillow, full to the last of new schemes, and, unaware
of the hopeless insolvency of his affairs, he bequeathed
£2000 for the fitting up of the new library at Abbotsford.
When Scott stood beside his grave in the Canongate
churchyard, the cloudy sky suddenly cleared ; he turned
to Lockhart and whispered : " I feel as if there would
be less sunshine for me from this day forth." It was a
fitting epithet for Rigdumfunnidos. He had gravely
embarrassed the life of his friend, but he had brightened
it with his jollity and affection.

In July Scott went to London for the coronation of
George IV. He proposed to take James Hogg with him
as a special reporter for the Scottish public, but Hogg
refused to absent himself from St Boswell's Fair. Scott
wrote a vivid account of the ceremony in the Abbey
for James Ballantyne's paper, since an historic pageant
was meat and drink to him, and he had a tribute paid
to his fame which gave him the sincerest pleasure.

Missing his carriage, he had to return home on foot from
Westminster after the banquet—that is to say, between two
and three o'clock in the morning—when he and a young
gentleman, his companion, found themselves locked in the
crowd, somewhere near Whitehall, and the bustle and tumult
were such that his friend was afraid some accident might happen
to the lame limb. A space for the dignitaries was kept clear
at that point by the Scots Greys. Sir Walter addressed a
serjeant of this celebrated regiment, begging to be allowed to
pass by him into the open ground in the middle of the street.
The man answered shortly that his orders were strict—that

1821 the thing was impossible. While he was endeavouring to persuade the serjeant to relent, some new wave of turbulence approached from behind, and his young companion exclaimed in a loud voice, " Take care, Sir Walter Scott, take care ! " The stalwart dragoon, on hearing the name, said, " What ! Sir Walter Scott ? He shall get through anyhow ! " He then addressed the soldiers near him. " Make room, men, for Sir Walter Scott, our illustrious countryman ! " The men answered " Sir Walter Scott ! God bless him ! "—and he was in a moment within the guarded line of safety.[1]

That autumn was a pleasant season. Scott brought back from London the plans for the completion of Abbotsford. The jasmine-covered porch of the old cottage had to go at last, and the main part of the present dwelling was begun—the new library and drawing-room, the courtyard and the lattice screen of stone between the house and the gardens. Sophia's first child had been born in the early spring, John Hugh, the " Hugh Littlejohn " of the *Tales of a Grandfather*, and in the autumn the Lockharts took up their country quarters at the little cottage of Chiefswood, beside the burn which flows from the Rhymer's Glen. There Scott could escape from his visitors, and, while Lockhart was correcting the proofs of his *Valerius*, he would be busy on *The Pirate* in an upstairs dressing-room, from which he would descend to labour in the tiny garden and train on the walls the creepers he had brought from Abbotsford. He was amusing himself with a *pastiche* in the shape of imaginary letters of the seventeenth century,[2] an enterprise out of which grew *The Fortunes of Nigel*, and before he returned to Edinburgh for the session he had contracted to sell to Constable the copyright of his last four novels for £5000. That meant that by these works, which had taken little more than a year to write, he had already earned £15,000. As he watched the masons beginning on the Abbotsford extension, and the whole place, as he said, " like a cried fair," he may have reflected with satisfaction that the money would easily be forthcoming for the bills.

[1] Lockhart, V. 98.
[2] One copy of this was printed and is now in the National Library of Scotland.

The three novels of the sixteenth century group themselves naturally together, for their inspiration is of a
different kind from that of the earlier masterpieces.
They are based in the main on book-work, on Scott's
wide miscellaneous reading. He is less concerned with
the human drama than with the pageantry of the times
and with the intricacies of court politics of which he had
an instinctive understanding. With none of his characters
do we feel that his affections are very seriously engaged,
nor, as in *Old Mortality*, is the public conflict one in which
he has a strong emotional interest. Consequently the
merit of the books is to be found mainly in their craft,
their conscious handiwork. At their best they are sound
pieces of historical reconstruction ; at their worst they
fall into melodramatic artifice, and what Professor Elton
has called " a kind of Elizabethan comic bluster and
hard animal spirits." As novels judged from the higher
standpoint they are notably inferior to his best, for they
rarely go deeper than the externals of life. He is on
unfamiliar ground, dealing with things of which he has
not secure possession, since they have not become part
of his blood and brain.

Yet in the weakest of the three, *The Monastery*, he is
in his own countryside, describing a landscape which
he could see from Abbotsford and people whose descendants were his neighbours. His purpose was to show the
crumbling of the old Church at the Reformation and
the downfall of a great religious house ; he had also
a notion of bringing in the heart of Bruce, which was
buried at Melrose, but forgot his intention and had to
make it the heart of the last abbot. But the subject
was not fortunately chosen. In the first place there was
no dramatic cataclysm in the Lowlands, since the old
Church was dead long before it fell. The true drama
came later when the people discovered the burdens of
the new religion. The early Reformation in Scotland
was too easy a business for tragedy. In the second
place Scott had little understanding of Catholicism.
This man, for whom when he was dying John Henry
Newman besought the prayers of the faithful, cherished

1820-21 a blunt Protestantism, to which he was never weary of testifying. He can describe vividly the secular aspects of Melrose, its routine, its polity and its humours, but, since he had no insight into its secret things, the mystic brotherhood of an ordered community set in the heart of darkness, he cannot move us by his tale of its fall. Boniface, Eustace, and even Edward Glendinning are only embodied humours and virtues. Scott understood perfectly the surface logic of the quarrel between the Church and the Reformers, and can state it with scrupulous fairness, but his heart was with neither side, and the preacher, Henry Warden, is as much a lay figure as the monks.

The story begins with a happy preface. Captain Clutterbuck, the Scots Fusilier, is for once entertaining, the portrait of the landlord of the George is excellent, and so is the introduction of the Benedictine—" a virtuoso, a clean virtuoso—a sad-coloured stand of claithes, and a wig like the curled back of a mug-ewe." But the tale belies the promise of the beginning. The plot is limping and confused, and the whole business of the lost Bible is clumsily conceived, as is that of Sir Piercie Shafton and the bodkin. The Euphuist, indeed, I do not find as tedious as most critics have found him, and a vast deal of curious learning has gone to the making of his absurdities, but nevertheless he has no business in the tale. For the White Lady of Avenel there can be no defence. She is neither credible nor awesome, her orations in indifferent verse are tedious, and repeatedly she carries the tale into the realm, not of fantasy, but of farce. Scott perversely turns a romance of deeds into a kind of parody of *Comus*. The conclusion, when Halbert Glendinning finds fortune and Julian Avenel gets his deserts, is hurried and unconvincing.

Yet there are many things in the book which it is hard to forget, for if Scott failed grievously in his main purpose he could not avoid incidental felicities. Nothing could be better than the spectacle of Moray's army as seen by Halbert and the pedlar advancing on the Glasgow road. The household in the tower of Glendinning is

vividly presented, and any peasant that shows his or 1820–21
her face is a foursquare being whose talk is a delight.
Tibb and old Martin, the Miller and his daughter, have
a vitality foreign to the churchmen and the gentlefolk;
Dame Glendinning is the homely Scots matron, whose
good sense rarely fails her; the Border pricker, Christie
of the Clint-hill, is true both to nature and to history,
and Halbert is the eternal boy, more real in his youth
than in his successful maturity.

> "I hate the monks, with their drawling nasal tones like so
> many frogs, and their long black petticoats like so many
> women, and their reverences, and their lordships, and their
> lazy vassals that do nothing but paddle in the mire with
> plough and harrow from Yule to Michaelmas. I will call none
> lord but him who wears a sword to make his title good; and
> I will call none man but he that bears himself manlike and
> masterful."

In that confession we have the spirit that was the
efficient cause of the Reformation.

The Abbot, the sequel to *The Monastery*, begins dole-
fully with lengthy speeches, an intolerable boy, and a
religious maniac. It is not till the eleventh chapter that
Catherine Seyton's sudden laughter wakes the reader to
attention. Thereafter the story marches strongly with
scarcely a halt, and with but one incongruity—the
impossible figure of Catherine's brother. Scott had that
romantic devotion to Mary of Scots which few of his
countrymen can escape, but he was wise enough not to
make her his heroine or to base his plot on a main
incident in her life, like Darnley's murder. She enters
from the wings, as an accessory in the love story of
Catherine and Roland Graeme. The book is full of
brilliant pictures: the election of the last Melrose abbot
and the irruption upon the solemnities of the Abbot of
Unreason—a scene not without its tragic irony; the
pageant of Marian Edinburgh and Roland's visit to the
mansion of the Seytons; the weary days at Lochleven,
and the escape. The only defect in the plot is that it
has no adequate conclusion, for the Queen has become
so much the dominant figure that it is to her fortunes

1820-21 rather than to those of Roland that the reader's interest
is pledged. Langside, which is not one of Scott's best
battle pieces, is clearly not the end ; that lay years
ahead in the intrigues and dolours of an English prison.
But it may fairly be said that the book fulfils the most
exacting standards of historical romance. It is perhaps
a little too full of antiquarian pedantries, which sometimes check the flow of narration ; but it atones for
them by many acute glimpses into the contemporary
mind. Take the scene between the Reforming Lords
and the Queen in Chapter XXII, when Ruthven sets
out a bitter indictment of Mary, and old Lindesay
subscribes to it with a generous hesitation. " Lady,"
he said, " thou art a noble creature, even though thou
hast abused God's choicest gifts. I pay that devotion
to thy manliness of spirit, which I would not have paid
to the power thou hast undeservedly wielded—I kneel
to Mary Stuart, not to the Queen." And later he tells
Ruthven, " I would I had as deep cause to be this lady's
friend as I have to be her enemy—thou shouldst see if I
spared life and limb in her quarrel."

Of the main characters the women excel the men.
Roland is drawn on conventional lines, Moray and
Morton are only sketches, and the rough-handed Lords
of the Congregation make too brief appearances. Some
of the lesser figures, like the quack doctor Luke Lundin
and the anabaptist Jasper Dryfesdale, have a fantastic
life of their own, and the English falconer Adam Wood-
cock is one of Scott's incomparable serving-men. Adam,
indeed, is something more, for he is the embodiment of
English good sense and good nature in contrast to the
dark enthusiasms of the North. His robust philosophy
makes a cool oasis in a feverish world, and it is he who
puts most eloquently the pathos of the Queen's downfall:—

> They may say what they will, many a true heart will be sad
> for Mary Stewart, e'en if all be true men say of her ; for look
> you, Master Roland, she was the loveliest creature to look upon
> that ever I saw with eye, and no lady in the land liked better
> the fair flight of a falcon. I was at the great match on Roslin
> Moor betwixt Bothwell—he was a black sight to her that

Bothwell—and the Baron of Roslin, who could judge a hawk's
flight as well as any man in Scotland. A butt of Rhenish and
a ring of gold was the wager, and it was flown as fairly for as
ever was red gold and bright wine. And to see her there on
her white palfrey, that flew as if it scorned to touch more
than the heather blossom ; and to hear her voice, as clear and
sweet as the mavis's whistle, mix among our jolly whooping
and whistling ; and to mark all the nobles dashing round her—
happiest he who got a word or a look—tearing through moss
and hagg, and venturing neck and limb to gain the praise of
a bold rider, and the blink of the bonny Queen's bright eye !—
She will see little hawking where she lies now. Ay, ay, pomp
and pleasure pass away as speedily as the wap of a falcon's wing !

Among the women Mary is the chief, though Lady
Lochleven is not far behind. Catherine Seyton is of the
school of Di Vernon but more hoydenish and artificial,
while Magdalen Graeme is not the most successful of
Scott's sibyls, a Romish Mause Headrigg without Mause's
humour. Mary is the best of Scott's pictures of famous
women in history, for we are made to realize her compelling power—not only her beauty of person and grace
of manner, but her brain and her flawless courage. We
are assured that nothing in heaven or earth could make
her afraid, and this assurance is increased by her sudden
storm of nerves when she cries for Bothwell.

Bid him come hither to our aid, and bring with them his
Lambs as he calls them—Bowton, Hay of Talla, Black Ormiston,
and his kinsman Hob. Fie ! how swart they are, and how they
smell of sulphur ! What ! Closeted with Morton ? Nay, if
the Douglas and the Hepburn hatch the complot together, the
bird, when it breaks the shell, will scare Scotland.

She is a queen in dignity and fortitude, and something
more than a queen in brains. It is this last which is
Scott's real triumph. In the wit of her talk, in her
subtle baiting of Lady Lochleven, he has portrayed a
brilliant allure of both mind and body.

The third novel, *Kenilworth* seems to me to be Scott's
masterpiece in sheer craftmanship as distinct from inspiration. He wrote it at Constable's request, wisely,
however, declining the publisher's suggestion to make
the Armada the central incident, for he realized the

necessity of the historical romancer keeping off the main roads. To the making of it he brought an immense stock of miscellaneous lore, acquired from ballads, chapbooks, chronicles, and especially from the Elizabethan plays. His learning was more voluminous than exact, and he took bold liberties with history. He makes Dudley's marriage to Amy a secret one, whereas it had been publicly celebrated in the reign of Edward VI; he postdates her death by many years so that he may compass a meeting between her and Elizabeth at Kenilworth; he traduces, contrary to the evidence, both Varney and Tony Foster. There are many minor inaccuracies; Kenilworth, for example, did not belong to Leicester in Amy's lifetime, and Shakespeare is made a familiar name at Court at a time when he was a small boy in Stratford. Such anachronisms matter nothing, and Scott handles his material with freedom and skill. The plot is one of his most intricate, but there are no gaps in it. He rarely wrote narrative which was better knit.

The book opens in the high romantic vein in the Black Bear at Cumnor with one of the best tavern scenes in the novels. The central interest depends upon two factors—the mystery of two houses, the crumbling manor of Cumnor which had caught Scott's boyish imagination in Mickle's verses, and the baronial magnificence of Kenilworth; and the character of Elizabeth the Queen. It is at Cumnor and Kenilworth that his touch is surest, for these places clamoured for the appropriate romance. To people them he has borrowed a motley of figures from history and the contemporary drama and local tradition—Leicester and Sussex and Walter Raleigh : Giles Gosling, Goldthread the mercer, Miles Lambourne the drunken mercenary, Wayland Smith and Flibbertigibbet. Among the episodes two seem to me to reach a high level of drama. One is the interview at Greenwich between Sussex and Leicester in the Queen's presence, when the reader holds his breath at the oscillations of fortune; the other is the famous meeting of Elizabeth, Amy Robsart and Leicester in the garden at Kenilworth, where for a moment the 1820–21 truth trembles on the brink of revelation. In the sheer craftsmanship of suspense Scott never bettered these scenes.

The character-drawing is ingenious, and sometimes subtle. Elizabeth is exhibited as as royal as Mary, though she lacks something of Mary's glamour. Leicester is not the historical Dudley, but his weakness is convincingly portrayed, and Sussex is admirable. Amy is the tragic ballad heroine, who is vivid because of the vividness of her sorrows. Most of the minor figures are good, especially Lambourne the adventurer. The two chief villains seem to have strayed from the cast of one of the darker Elizabethan plays. Varney is Scott's version of Iago, the Italianate bravo whose wickedness is without bounds ; but since Scott was never happy with pure evil, I prefer Tony Fire-the-Faggot, who is given some principles in his infamy.

It is a glittering piece of pageantry, wholly successful within its purpose, and if that purpose falls short of Scott's highest, the bow of Apollo cannot always be kept at stretch. He never set out his antiquarian bric-a-brac more skilfully, or revelled more joyously in the externals of life. But if his understanding was fully engaged in the business, his heart was a little aloof. There is nothing in *Kenilworth* from Scott's inmost world except perhaps such a comment as this upon Tressilian's moods, in which we may find an echo of his own experience :—

Nothing is perhaps more dangerous to the future happiness of men of deep thought and retired habits than the entertaining of a long, early and unfortunate attachment. It frequently sinks so deep into the mind that it becomes their dream by night and their vision by day—mixes itself in every source of interest and enjoyment, and when blighted and withered, it seems as if the springs of the heart were dried up along with it. The aching of the heart, this languishing after a shadow which has lost all the gaiety of its colouring, this dwelling on the remembrance of a dream from which we have been long roughly awakened, is the weakness of a generous heart.

II

1821　　*The Pirate* appeared before the close of 1821, and throughout the winter Scott was busy, apart from the editing of antiquarian reprints, on *The Fortunes of Nigel*. He had another matter in hand which gave him acute annoyance and which set him publicly in the posture which he liked least, that of apology and apparent timidity. The political partisanship of 1808, against which the Duke of Buccleuch warned him, had mellowed with the success of British arms, and after Waterloo had almost disappeared. In Edinburgh he lived on friendly terms with the older Whigs and with many of the younger ones. But the trial of Queen Caroline in 1820 stirred up some of the ancient antagonisms, and the distress and unrest in the land seriously alarmed Scott about the future of law and order. He had the fantastic idea that the miners of Northumberland might somehow join hands with the Glasgow weavers, and the Buccleuch legion, at whose recruitment he laboured, was designed to bar the road. Now he suddenly found himself involved in a shoddy newspaper scandal.

Scott had never any relish for journalistic savageries. He had protested vigorously against the excesses of *Blackwood*,[1] and had striven to wean Lockhart from his association with them. " Revere yourself," he told his son-in-law, " and think you were born to do your country better service than in this species of warfare." [2] Lockhart had taken the good advice, the more so as he had been shocked by the duel in February 1821 arising out of certain attacks on himself in the *London Magazine*, in which the editor had been killed by his friend Christie. Scott pressed upon Lockhart the necessity of breaking from the " mother of mischief," [3] and Lockhart was never again involved in the *Blackwood* quarrels. But the foundation of the *Scotsman* had restarted the newspaper war in Edinburgh, and in January 1821 a paper called the *Beacon* was launched, a group of Edinburgh

---

[1] See the undated letter of C. K. Sharpe in *A. Constable*, II. 348.
[2] Lang, I. 243.　　　　　　　　　　　　　　[3] *Fam. Letters*, II. 114.

Tories, including the Lord Advocate, guaranteed the 1822 capital, and Scott was persuaded against his better judgment to join in the bond for a small sum. The paper ran for less than eight months and was distinguished for what Lord Cockburn calls " political cannibalism " ; it was wretchedly and amateurishly edited, and when the outcry against it became formidable the guarantors cancelled their bond and the *Beacon* died.

But in its short life it did an infinity of mischief. Cockburn thought that Scott was deeply to blame : " the happiness of the city was disturbed, persons he had long professed and truly felt friendship for were vilified, and all this he could have prevented by a word or a look." Apart from the mistake of the initial guarantee, Scott was innocent, for he detested the paper and would not look at it, but he was as much aggrieved by the manner of its ending as by its conduct. To Erskine he wrote that he was " terribly malcontent." " I was dragged into the bond against all remonstrances I could make, and now they have allowed me no vote with regard to standing or flying. . . . Our friends went into the thing like fools and have come out very like cowards. I was never so sick of a transaction in my life." He was sad and sulky, he wrote to Constable, because he thought that " the seniors might have been mediators, not fugitives," and he added that he expected daily to hear that someone had been killed.[1] There was an excellent chance of this, for the lawyer Gibson (later Sir James Gibson-Craig of Riccarton) proposed to challenge Scott, enlisted Lord Lauderdale as his second, and only withdrew on being assured that Scott had no personal share in the libels. Tragedy came a few months later, when some articles in the *Sentinel*, the *Beacon's* Glasgow successor, led to the death in a duel of Scott's friend, Sir Alexander Boswell, at the hands of James Stuart of Dunearn.

In January 1822 Will Erskine went at last to the Bench as Lord Kinnedder, an appointment for which

[1] *A. Constable*, III. 162 : Cockburn, *Mem.*, 381-3.

1822 his friends had long schemed and pled. The late spring
of that year was another landmark in Scott's financial
history, for James Ballantyne was readmitted as a
partner in the printing business. In 1816, as we have
seen, he had been made a salaried official, and Scott
had taken the firm wholly on his shoulders. It was
burdened with a personal debt of James to the extent
of £3000, and a mass of floating bills, the debris of the
publishing business, which were partly in John Ballantyne's name, and which amounted to about £10,000.
During the five years between 1816 and 1821 the printing
shop, owing to Scott's novels, had been making reasonable
profits—about £2000 a year. When at Whitsuntide, 1821,
the partnership was reconstituted, Scott laid down, in
what was called a " missive letter," the terms of the new
arrangement. He made himself personally liable for all
bills then current, apart from James Ballantyne's special
debt, which was still in the neighbourhood of £3000 ;
the profits in future were to be equally divided between
the partners, but it was agreed that each should limit
his annual drawings to £500, the balance going to
discharge debt or increase stock.[1]

Now at this date the floating bills against the firm
amounted to nearly £27,000.[2] How had the increase
come about, when the actual printing business was
running at a profit ? Partly from the interest on and
the renewal of the old bills, partly no doubt from James's
slipshod financial methods, but mainly because Scott
had used the firm as the medium of raising advances
for his personal expenditure. During these years, apart
from capital sums received for copyrights, he had been
making from his novels an income of at least £10,000.
But none of this was used to reduce the printing house's
gross liabilities ; on the contrary these liabilities were
steadily increased by his drafts on the firm to meet the
cost of his princely hospitality, his purchases of land,
and his Abbotsford building. Scott considered that
most of his outlay was in the nature of a sound invest-
ment, that, since Abbotsford must one day be finished,

[1] *Ballantyne Humbug*, 66-69.   [2] *Refutation*, 28.

that outlay would cease, and that in a year or two by 1822 his pen he could clear his feet. He seems to have believed that, if necessary he could live on his professional and private income [1] and utilize his literary earnings for the rapid extinction of debt. It is a mistake to assume, I think, that he was in the dark about his financial position. The " missive letter " to James Ballantyne shows that he could be a careful man of business, and he kept a precise record of all the bills he drew. He was deliberately overspending, because he was assured that he had the power, when he chose, to put his affairs on an equilibrium. In the year 1821 he had, according to Lockhart, already spent £29,000 on the purchase of land,[2] he had an assured income of at least £2500, and he had earned £80,000 by his pen since 1811. On the other side there were the Ballantyne liabilities of £27,000, and overdrafts on Constable to an amount which cannot be ascertained.

He was living at a time when the machinery of credit was still in process of creation, and few, even among the bankers, had any clear conception of its true basis. There was great scarcity of coin, and there was an inadequate supply of cash even in the form of bank-notes ; value " floated ethereally in bills and promissory notes from man to man, calling at the banks for trans-mutation when and so long as that could be effected." Scottish banking had been built up largely on the basis of cash-credits, under which overdrafts were guaranteed by a man's friends, and in Scotland credit had become more of a communal business than elsewhere. Scott accepted the system as he found it and did not trouble to ask awkward questions. He drew bills on the Ballan-tyne firm which Constable backed ; he drew bills on Constable for work not yet done ; and always there were the counter-bills, whereby accommodation granted to one party was set off by a like accommodation granted to the other. The consequence was that the true meaning

[1] See letter to Constable in *A. Constable*, III. 282.
[2] In 1826 Gibson-Craig estimated that Scott had spent altogether on his estate £76,000. See article " Scott " in the *D. N. B.*

1822 of each transaction was obscured. When cash was received the temptation was to apply it for some purpose for which cash was obligatory, like the masons' accounts at Abbotsford, instead of paying off bills which could be easily renewed. So long as a man was able to work and in good repute there need be no hitch, but ill-health, death, or the disaster of a colleague might bring down the whole edifice in ruins. If Constable failed, the Ballantyne firm would follow, and with it Scott; if Scott fell sick or died, the Ballantyne house would go, and Constable, though he had heavily insured Scott's life, might not survive the loss of an author on whose work he had staked so heavily. All the fraternity had executed heavy mortgages on the future; they could pay the mortgage interest, and, if the fates were kind, might eventually redeem them, but any sudden calamity would send the fabric crashing.

In Scott's defence it should be said that he believed that in his land, houses, and personal possessions he had assets which would meet all his liabilities, while his brother-in-law's legacy had made provision for his family. Also he trusted implicitly in the soundness of Constable's firm. He sold him the copyrights of his novels in batches, and did not receive the full payment, which should have warned him that the great publisher had no greater command of ready money than himself. Various circumstances had combined to embarrass Constable. The retirement of one partner and the death of another had withdrawn from the business considerable capital sums, and the provident Mr Cadell had many hours of acute alarm. Constable's reach was apt to exceed his grasp, and he suffered the fate of all pioneers in having often to wait too long for his harvest. His pride would not allow him to reduce the printing orders of the *Edinburgh Review* and the *Encyclopædia Britannica*, even when the trade was glutted, with the result that he was often left with unsaleable remainders.[1] During the years 1821 and 1822 he had to spend most of his time for his health's sake in the south of England, and his

---

[1] Skene, 146.

letters to Cadell show the trouble that he had with the 1822
booksellers over dead stock.[1]

But he was like a drunken man, who can avoid a fall
only so long as he keeps running. Scott was his main
support, and it is probable that he consistently overpaid
him, for there was always the dread of a rival Murray
or Longman in the field.[2] Moreover, both he and Cadell
encouraged Scott to a more rapid output, not only of
novels but of poetry and miscellaneous work. They
gave him £1000 for *Halidon Hill*, which was the task of
two rainy mornings. Any loss on the swings would be
made up by the profits on some new roundabout. " I
would as soon stop a winning horse," wrote Cadell,
" as a successful author with the public in his favour." [3]
With such encouragement it was not unnatural for Scott
to take a roseate view of the future. The Ballantyne
debt was supported by Constable, and Constable, though
his bills were long-dated, seemed to be going from
strength to strength. His letters from the south—and
it was in the south of course that the main market lay
—had been full of confident forecasts ; they had repeatedly declared that an unsatiated public demanded
more and still more from the *Waverley* fields. Scott felt
his creative power as strong as ever ; he could therefore
complete Abbotsford with an easy conscience—perhaps
even buy Faldonside—and then straighten out his affairs ;
there was enough money in prospect for everything.

So it was with a new feeling of security that he turned
to the heavy duties of the summer. *The Fortunes of
Nigel* appeared in the end of May and was well received.
Constable predicted that it would be the most popular
of all, and Sydney Smith, who had become very critical
of the novels, admitted that it would sustain the reputation of the author and not " impair the very noble and
honourable estate which he has in his brains." The

---

[1] See *A. Constable*, III. *passim*.
[2] The terms for *Kenilworth* were adopted for all the later novels. Constable
printed 12,000 copies, for which he put up £1600 and the Ballantynes £400
each, the profits being divided proportionately. Scott received £4500 for the
edition and retained the copyright. The published price was £1, 10s. and the
trade bought at £1.
[3] *A. Constable*, III. 239.

1822 smack which carried the London orders reached the
Thames on a Sunday, the cargo was cleared at once,
and by half-past ten on Monday morning 7000 copies
were in the booksellers' hands.

That summer Scott was busy on *Peveril of the Peak*,
but July and August were useless for work, since
George IV had announced his intention of visiting
Edinburgh, the first reigning monarch to set foot on
Scottish soil since Charles I, and the only prince of the
house of Hanover since the ill-omened Cumberland.
Had Scott lived in another age he might have been a
great figure in statecraft, guiding a monarch through
difficult places by his own tact, sagacity and insight
into human nature. He had that talent for affairs
which is compounded of organizing power and the rare
gift of managing men. The visit seemed to him to be
an occasion of high public import. The last hope of
Jacobitism had died with the Cardinal of York, but
there was no popular sentiment for the reigning family
north of the Border. If that could be created, if the old
monarchical feeling of Scotland could be stirred and her
pride gratified by a sense of possession in her sovereign,
much might be done for the cause of both Scottish
nationalism and Scottish unity. To be sure, it was
something of a gamble. The trial of the Queen had
predisposed the rank and file of the people against
George, the notorious irregularities of his life had alienated
the serious classes, and politics, as we have seen, were at
the moment full of bitterness. To make certain of a
national welcome, the rivalries of grandees would have
to be harmonized, and the conflict of endless local
interests smoothed away. If the visit was in any sense
a fiasco, it would be nothing short of a public calamity.

The heavy end of the business fell upon Scott, since
he was the only man competent to arrange a national
pageant. All through July he laboured at the details
of the reception, setting the proper parts for Highland
chiefs and Lowland lairds and Edinburgh bailies—a
heavy task, for Lord Kinnedder was dying, killed
by a baseless slander which broke a too sensitive heart.

Every moment that Scott could spare he spent at 1822
his bedside, but on the very day of the King's coming
Erskine died. In the midst of the festivities Scott
attended his funeral at Queensferry, more dejected,
Lockhart tells us, than he had ever known him
before, and he had to play his part in the ensuing
pageant with a burdened mind. "If ever a pure
spirit," he wrote, "quitted this vale of tears, it was
William Erskine's. I must turn to and see what can be
done about getting some pension for his daughters."

The royal visit was an abounding success. Scott had
little admiration for the King, but he knew his abilities
and his gift of surface *bonhomie,* and he was determined
that the cause of monarchy should not suffer in its
representative. Nor did it, for George rose gallantly to
his part. This stout gentleman of sixty did his best to
fill the rôle of the Prince Charming who three-quarters
of a century before had danced in Holyroodhouse, and
he had the wisdom to lean heavily on Scott's knowledge
and good sense. The royal yacht, escorted by warships,
arrived at Leith on August 14th in a downpour of rain,
and Scott was received on board with enthusiasm. "Sir
Walter Scott!" the King cried, "The man in Scotland
I most wish to see!" and he pledged him in a bumper
of whisky. Scott begged the glass as a memento and
deposited it in his pocket. When he returned to Castle
Street he found that Crabbe the poet had arrived un-
expectedly; in the exuberance of his greeting he flung
himself into a chair beside him, there was an ominous
crackle, and fragments of the precious keepsake were
dug out of the pocket in his skirts. Crabbe's presence
at the festivities, like that of a sober parson at a war
dance of Indian braves, was one of the major comic
elements in the scene; another was the Rabelaisian
parody by a Glasgow weaver of Scott's song of welcome,
"Carle, now the King's come," which was popular among
the irreverent.

But the intricate programme passed off without a
hitch. Half Scotland flowed into Edinburgh to watch
the royal entry, when Scott, splendid in Campbell trews,

1822 was driven in a coach and four by Peter Mathieson, not less splendid in a cocked hat and a flaxen wig. Scott attended daily at the royal table at Dalkeith in his capacity as master of ceremonies. There were levees at Holyroodhouse, and a state procession to the Castle when Scott stood in the crowd with Sir Robert Peel; there were lengthy and splendid dinners; there was a command performance at the theatre, and a solemn service in St Giles's church. The King wore a kilt of Royal Stewart tartan, the laird of Garth being responsible for his toilet, but the most conspicuous figure in his entourage was not Glengarry or Macleod, but a London alderman, Sir William Curtis, who made a bigger, fatter and gaudier Highlandman than his Majesty. Not till the 29th of August did George embark for the south, after knighting Adam Ferguson and Raeburn the artist. It was to Scott that Sir Robert Peel wrote on the eve of the departure by the King's command, making him the channel to convey to the Highland chiefs the royal approbation and thanks.

So ended one of the most arduous chapters in Scott's life. The King's visit had amply fulfilled the purpose for which it had been planned and the monarchy had won a new popularity in Scotland. Scott had obtained a promise that that historic piece of ordnance, Mons Meg, would be sent back to Edinburgh Castle, and—what was still nearer his heart—that the peerages forfeited during the Jacobite rebellions should be restored. The visit completed the work which he himself had begun and brought the Highlands into a closer relation with Scottish life. It did more, for in the eyes of the outside world it gave certain Highland habits a national character which they have ever since retained. The kilt, the former garb of servants, was assumed to be the Scottish national dress, since it had been worn by the King. It was a golden age for the haberdashers. A bogus Celticism became the rage, and Scottish Lowland houses, whose ancestors would as readily have worn woad as the dress of their secular foes, were provided by imaginative tradesmen with family tartans.

The autumn of 1822 was spent quietly at Abbotsford, where the new buildings were now being roofed, and Scott was very busy corresponding with Terry about furniture. He had bought his land at high prices—it was a common saying in the countryside that a man " would wish for no ampler fortune than just the length and breadth of himself in land within half a mile of the Shirra's house "—but he showed wisdom in other matters, and had much of the ironwork and woodwork done by local craftsmen whose merits he had discovered. The plot of *Quentin Durward* had entered his head; it cheered him, for he was finding *Peveril* heavy going. Indeed, the loss of Erskine and the herculean labours of July and August had drained his vitality both of mind and body. In November in a letter to Terry we have the first hint of a graver malady than his now chronic rheumatism. " I have not been well—a whoreson thickness of blood, and a depression of spirits arising from the loss of friends . . . have annoyed me much ; and *Peveril* will, I fear, smell of the apoplexy."

The two novels of the preceding twelvemonth, *The Pirate* and *The Fortunes of Nigel*, have a connexion deeper than the chronological, for they show Scott as an artificer at his worst and his best. The first is a fine conception marred in the execution. His visit to the Orkneys and Shetlands in 1814 had left with him an abiding impression not only of a unique landscape but of a life widely different from that of the Scottish mainland. He found customs of a primordial simplicity, and a folk-lore in which still endured beliefs drawn from the heroic world of the Sagas. The sight of an American cruiser off the Hebrides had suggested to him how this remote Thule might be linked by sea with the greater world. In Bessie Millie at Stromness he had found a practising sibyl, and heard from her the true tale of John Gow the pirate who in the early eighteenth century had menaced the isles. What fitter subject for romance ? He would show the impact upon the frugal island life of adventurers from tropic seas, blood-stained, lustful,

1822 babbling of gold and gems. He would reveal that in the islands which was akin to this foreign colour, the wild Norse fatalism and hardihood. Above all he would show the spell which the exotic world could cast over beauty and youth. And as his setting he would have the wind-scourged ocean, the bare pastoral hills, and the shadowy northern sky. Stevenson has rightly interpreted Scott's purpose and the nature of his inspiration. " The figure of Cleveland—cast up by the sea on the resounding foreland of Dunrossness—moving, with the blood on his hands and the Spanish words on his tongue, among the simple islanders—singing the serenade under the windows of his Shetland mistress—is conceived in the very highest manner of romantic invention. The words of his song, ' Through groves of palm,' sung in such a scene and by such a lover, clinch, as in a nutshell, the emphatic contrast upon which the tale is built." [1]

Conceived ; but, alas, not realized. The figures which should have pointed the contrast and fulfilled the inspiration are as shadowy as a Shetland sky. Cleveland is no more than a buckram pirate—never one half so alive as his friend Jack Bunce—and his ultimate repentance leaves the reader not even incredulous, but only cold. According to Lockhart, he pleased the public because of his novelty, as did the Udaller's daughters, but later generations have not endorsed the verdict. Minna and Brenda are not less dim, and Minna's talk is strange and wonderful, being drawn half from a *Young Ladies' Companion* and half from a lexicon of northern antiquities. The whole of the exotic element is conceived in a bad theatrical vein ; there is melodrama even in the alliterative names, Mordaunt Mertoun and Clement Cleveland, and the plot is a tangle of crude coincidences. As for Norna of the Fitful Head she is Scott's supreme failure in the *genre* which had produced Meg Merrilies. As Sydney Smith noted, he was acquiring a habit of introducing a spae-wife and a pedant into all his tales ; in *The Pirate* we can accept the pedant, Triptolemus Yellowley, but the spae-wife is beyond us. Norna's

---

[1] *Memories and Portraits*, 270.

prose is as preposterous as her poetry, and her poetry is 1822 as turgid as the runes of the White Lady of Avenel. It is interesting to note how bad Scott's occasional verse becomes when his inspiration flags. Only twice in the book does it succeed in moving us ; once when Cleveland sings the " Groves of Palm " serenade, and there the charm lies in the contrast of sentiment and scene rather than in any poetic merit ; a second time when Mertoun is gravely wounded and Claud Halcro appears singing the wonderful lyric, " And ye shall deal the funeral dole." On these occasions, and on these alone, the romance of Scott's dream is given a local habitation.

He failed in his central purpose, since he could not bring out the full drama of the clash between the exotic and the insular because of his strained and ragged treatment of the former. But with the latter he amply succeeded. In none of the novels does he handle landscape with greater mastery. He reproduces for us the magic of the low benty hills, the tormented coasts, and the infinite chafing seas. The island life is described with gusto and humour, and in the sharpest detail. The plot, or what stands for a plot, soon fades from the reader's memory, but certain scenes remain in vivid recollection—the storm when Cleveland is washed ashore and the islanders scramble for the wreckage ; the feasting at Magnus Troil's home ; the whale hunt ; the visit of Magnus to Norna's dwelling ; the trivialities of the Kirkwall burghers. In all of these it is the homely characters that dominate the scene, and it is by the delineation of such characters that the book must stand.

Chief is the Udaller, Magnus Troil. He is the patriarchal landowner, but different in kind from anything in the preceding gallery of chiefs and lairds. He shows Scott's firm grasp of social conditions, for he is not only a vividly realized human being but the lawful product of his environment. He is an Homeric figure, like the son of Teuthras in the sixth book of the *Iliad*, who " built his dwelling by the roadside and entertained every wayfarer." Not less real are his neighbours. It was a happy thought to make old Haagen a survival of Montrose's last tragic expedition, who remembered nothing but its discomfort, and dashed Minna's sentiment by expounding the superior wisdom of running away.

> " And Montrose—what became of Montrose, and how looked he ? "
>
> " Like a lion with the hunters before him," answered the old gentleman ; " but I looked not twice his way, for my own lay right over the hills."
>
> " And so you left him ? " said Minna in a tone of the deepest contempt.
>
> " It was no fault of mine, Mistress Minna," answered the old man, somewhat out of countenance. " But I was there with no choice of my own ; and, besides, what good could I have done ?—all the rest were running like sheep, and why should I have stayed ? "
>
> " You might have died with him," said Minna.
>
> " And lived with him to all eternity in immortal verse ! " added Claud Halcro.
>
> " I thank ye, Mistress Minna," replied the plain-dealing Zetlander, " and I thank you, my old friend Claud ; but I would rather drink both your healths in this good bicker of ale, like a living man as I am, than you should be making songs in my honour for having died forty or fifty years agone."

There Scott attains perfectly the contrast at which he aimed.

The " humours " of Triptolemus Yellowley, like those of Claud Halcro, are perhaps too much elaborated ; but Triptolemus has a real comedy value, and his sister Baby's hard sense is at once a foil to his pedantry and the touchstone of the normal by which to test the aberrations of sensibility. Excellent, too, is the jagger, Bryce Snailsfoot, with his " green-glazen eyes," the unlovely combination of avarice and piety which Scott could handle so well.

> " Grace to ye to wear the garment," said the joyous pedlar, " and to me to guide the siller ; and protect us from earthly vanities and earthly covetousness ; and send you the white linen raiment, whilk is mair to be desired than the muslins and cambrics and lawns and silks of this world; and send me the talents which avail more than much fine Spanish gold, or Dutch dollars either."

"A marvel it is to think," the Ranzelman tells the old
housekeeper, "how few real judicious men are left in
this land. . . . I ken few of consequence hereabouts—
excepting always myself, and maybe you, Swertha—but
what may, in some sense or other, be called fules."
The prosaic aspect of life was rarely depicted with more
shrewdness and truth, and *The Pirate* would have been
a masterpiece had the romantic side of the balance
been as well weighted. It is the poetry which fails, not
the prose.

Nigel, on the contrary, succeeds largely because of its
craftsmanship. Scott's reach is not too ambitious and
his grasp never weakens. Its popularity was immediate,
and Constable saw people reading it in the London
streets. The critical Sydney Smith had no fault to find
except that the plot was "execrable."[1] Scott's purpose
was to provide a companion piece to *The Heart of
Midlothian*, and make George Heriot a masculine Jeanie
Deans, a hero "who laid no claim to high birth, romantic
sensibility, or any of the usual accomplishments of those
who strut through the pages of this sort of composition."
Just as the loveliest part of a country is where the
mountains break down into the lowlands, so he considered the most interesting age that in which barbarism
was passing into civilization, and on this principle he
chose his period. In the introductory epistle he sets
out frankly his view of the novelist's craft. He was
anxious to give the public what it wanted. "No man
shall find me rowing against the stream. I care not
who knows it—I write for general amusement." He
would not waste too much time on architecture. "I
should be chin-deep in the grave, man, before I had
done with my task, and, in the meanwhile, all the
quirks and quiddities which I might have devised for
my readers' amusement would lie rotting in my gizzard."
He claims the authority of Smollett and Le Sage, who
had been "satisfied if they amused the reader upon the
road, though the conclusion only arrived because the

[1] *A. Constable*, III. 218.

1822 tale must have an end—just as the traveller alights at the inn because it is evening." He defends, too, his rapidity of production. " A man should strike while the iron is hot, and hoist sail while the wind is fair. If a successful author keeps not the stage, another instantly takes his ground." A mercantile creed, maybe, but it was in all likelihood the creed of Shakespeare.

Nigel is brilliant book-work, a reconstruction based on wide and minute research ; but it differs from the other book-work novels in having various Scottish characters drawn from a rich first-hand experience. George Heriot is the Edinburgh burgher whom Scott had known, Richie Moniplies the familiar serving-man, and King James a compost of quiddities drawn from country lairds and Parliament House lawyers. The plot is negligible, the whole episode of the lost royal warrant and the wrongs of the Lady Hermoine is most clumsily conceived, and the marriage bells at the end ring perfunctorily. But the crude machinery does not interfere with the ripple and glitter of the narrative, which Dumas never bettered. The impression given of the colour and pageantry of life is as vivid as the middle chapters of *Monte Cristo*. The scene in Ramsay's shop, and the pictures of the brisk, bustling city are masterpieces of historical reconstruction, which nowhere smell of the lamp. Not less good are the Court chapters, for Scott was always at home in such an environment, and his eyes were not so dazzled by the tapestry on the walls as to miss the cobwebs in the corner. Alsatia, the enclave of blackguards in the midst of burgherdom, is brilliantly depicted, and the murder is an eery business. There are no scenes, perhaps, which rise to high drama, but that is because we cannot take Nigel and his troubles quite seriously, but there are many admirable comedy interludes. What, for example, could be better than the episode in the Greenwich inn and the talk of Kilderkin and Linklater, and the scene where Richie is hidden behind the arras and the King cries in the words of the old Scots children's game, " Todlowrie, come out o' your den ? "

The story lives by its colour and speed, and by the 1822
vigour of its characters. Some of these are poor enough,
for Nigel and Dalgarno are only embodied moralities.
But most of the lesser figures are competently drawn—
Huntinglen, Trapbois the miser and his daughter, the
Alsatian bullies, the prentice lads, and the sinister Dame
Suddlechop. On a higher plane stand George Heriot,
one of the most solidly realized merchants in fiction,
and Sir Mungo Malagrowther, the old, peevish, dilapidated
courtier. There must have been many Sir Mungos in
Whitehall in those days. Higher still stands Richie
Moniplies, whose humours and idioms are of the raciest,
and whose career, from the days when he slept out in
St Cuthbert's kirkyard to his attainment of wealth and
rank, escapes being farcical because the man himself is
so wholly credible. He is at once insolent and kindly,
sycophantic and independent, sordid and chivalrous,
greedy and unselfish—" though I was bred at a flesher's
stall, I have not through my life had a constant intimacy
with collops "—a perfect instance of one type of Scots
adventurer.

But the masterpiece is the King, a masterpiece both
of imaginative presentation and of historical truth.
Scott makes James ridiculous and also somehow impressive. His vanity has quality behind it, and he has
little gusts of tenderness and moods of melting sentiment. There is dignity even in his panics, and hi
buffoonery has a substratum of hard good sense—" O
Geordie, Jingling Geordie, it was grand to hear Baby
Charles laying down the guilt of dissimulation, and
Steenie lecturing on the turpitude of incontinence." He
is endeared to us because of his acute perception of the
whimsies of life, and the oddities of other people, though
he may be a little blind to his own. The portrait is one
of the subtlest and most carefully studied which Scott
has given us, and from first to last James is consistent
with himself. His speech is a delight, for it has the
idiom of one who is both Scot and scholar. It never
sinks below a high pitch of shrewd vivacity from the
moment in the palace ante-room where we first hear his

1823 broad accents—" Admit him instanter, Maxwell. Have ye hairboured sae lang at the Court, and not learned that gold and silver are ever welcome ? " His Scottish memories remind the reader of the homely world of the north from which he came, and thereby point the ironic contrast of the man and his office. " And John Anderson was Provost that year. The carle grat for joy ; and the Bailies and Councillors danced bareheaded in our presence like five-year-auld colts." Much of the success of his talk depends upon the sentences of Latinized jargon followed by pithy Scots translations. Appropriately the two main comedy figures are conjoined at the close.

> He took the drawn sword, and with averted eyes, for it was a sight he loved not to look on, endeavoured to lay it on Richie's shoulder, but nearly stuck it into his eye. Richie, starting back, attempted to rise, but was held down by Lowestoffe, while, Sir Mungo guiding the royal weapon, the honour-bestowing blow was given and received : " *Surge, carnifex.* Rise up, Sir Richard Moniplies of Castle Collop !—— And, my lords and lieges, let us all to our dinner, for the cock-a-leekie is cooling."

III

In January 1823 *Peveril of the Peak* was published, a lengthy novel of which Lockhart thought the plot " clumsy and perplexed," and which Sydney Smith considered a " good novel, but not good enough for such a writer," though he added that Scott's worst was better than other people's best. Meanwhile, with the help of a copy of Commines, a French gazeteer, a map of Touraine, and his recollections of his visit to France in 1815, he was making in *Quentin Durward* his first attempt at a romance of which the scene was laid outside Britain.

Though he was not a politician, he had largely inherited Henry Dundas's mantle as the " manager " of Scotland. In the first place he was the acknowledged leader in all literary and intellectual matters. David Hume had once held the position and Adam Smith had succeeded him. Henry Mackenzie had followed, but 1823 the " Man of Feeling " was now nearing his seventieth year, and Scott inherited the primacy. In the Edinburgh of that day social pre-eminence followed upon such leadership. He was the man to whom all well-accredited strangers brought introductions, the premier host and the public orator of Scotland. In the club life of the day, of which the fashion was spreading, he was a conspicuous figure. In 1818 he had been elected a member of The Club, Dr Johnson's famous foundation,[1] and he was Professor of Ancient History to the Royal Academy, the post created for Goldsmith. In Scotland he had the Friday Club, the Blairadam Club, the Highland Club, and, for decorous high-jinks, the Gowks, which met on All Fools' Day when every member contributed his best wine, and of which old Henry Mackenzie was the poet-laureate. In 1823 the " Author of *Waverley* " was chosen to fill a vacancy in the Roxburghe Club, and Scott was permitted to represent the Unknown. At the same time he was establishing in Edinburgh a Scottish counterpart of that classic fraternity—the Bannatyne Club, which was the first of several societies which have done excellent work in reprinting the older documents in Scottish history and literature. He was assiduous in his duties as president of the Royal Society of Edinburgh, and appeared in the forefront of every charitable enterprise.

Public business, too, engrossed much of his time, and the development of new inventions which appealed to his practical mind. He became chairman of a company to manufacture oil gas and introduced the contrivance at Abbotsford, where it turned out to be far more expensive than candles, and had a bad effect on his health. " Any foreign student of statistics who should have happened to peruse the files of an Edinburgh newspaper for the period to which I allude, would, I think, have concluded that there were at least two

---

[1] Not in 1823, as Lockhart seems to have thought. Scott attended one dinner in 1820, and three in 1821—his only appearances. *Annals of The Club* (1914.)

1823 Sir Walter Scotts in the place—one the miraculously
fertile author whose works occupied two-thirds of its
literary advertisements and critical columns—another
some retired magistrate or senator of easy fortune and
indefatigable philanthropy, who devoted the rather
oppressive leisure of an honoured old age to the pro-
motion of patriotic ameliorations, the watchful guardian-
ship of charities, and the ardent patronage of educational
institutions."[1]

In April he had news of the death in Canada of his
brother Thomas, the last of the old family circle. Miss
Edgeworth came to Scotland that summer and spent a
fortnight at Abbotsford—" a very nice lioness," Scott
wrote to Terry, " full of fun and spirits, a little slight
figure, very active in her motions, very good-humoured,
and full of enthusiasm." Meantime, in June, *Quentin
Durward* had appeared, and at first had been coldly
received, till the rapturous appreciation of Paris made
the home public reconsider its verdict. Hitherto Scott
had had little vogue on the Continent, except in Germany,
but now his reputation spread like wild-fire, and began
to threaten the pre-eminence of Byron. Constable,
who had been growing nervous about the future of that
popularity in which he had invested so heavily, was
more than comforted, and Scott was encouraged to
gamble a little with his reputation. One summer morning, while he rode with Lockhart and Laidlaw on the
Eildons, he spoke of laying the scene of his next tale
in Germany. Laidlaw dissented ; " No, no, sir—take my
word for it, you are always best, like Helen MacGregor,
when your foot is on your native heath ; and I have
often thought that if you were to write a novel, and lay
the scene here in the very year you were writing it, you
would exceed yourself." Scott liked the notion ; he had
not since *The Antiquary* written of contemporary Scotland, and he had a grim story in his mind which he had
come across in the course of his duties as Sheriff ; there
was the comedy, too, of a land advancing in wealth and
modishness at which he might try his hand. So during

[1] Lockhart, V. 264.

the autumn and early winter, while he was entertaining
Adolphus and inspecting with Lockhart the young
plantations of the Clydesdale lairds, and supervising the
decoration of the new Abbotsford, he was hard at work
upon *St Ronan's Well.*

The book was a bold experiment. The high manner
of romance was laid aside and Scott made himself the
chronicler of the small beer of a provincial watering-
place and a gentle satirist of the follies of fashion. Yet
the scene was laid in his own countryside, and he had as
a background the idiosyncrasies of his own people.
The English public was a little perplexed, but Scottish
readers recognized the pungent truth of the atmosphere
of a Tweedside burgh and of many of the portraits.
Unhappily the drama upon which the vitality of the
book depended, the tragedy of Clara Mowbray, was
fatally weakened by the prudishness of James Ballantyne,
who protested that, while a mock marriage might be
permitted, the seduction of a well-born girl would be
resented.[1] Scott had received from Laidlaw the inspiration of the tale, and he now accepted docilely Ballantyne's
remonstrance, and altered the crucial passage. James
was a valued proof-reader and a sound counsellor on
minor matters, but we may well regret that in this case
Scott did not treat his advice as he was to treat it three
years later.

> I had a letter from Jem Ballantyne—plague on him !—full
> of remonstrances, deep and solemn, upon the carelessness of
> ' Bonaparte.' The rogue is right, too. But as to correcting
> my style to the ' Jemmy jemmy linkum feedle ' tune of what
> is called fine writing, I'll be damned if I do.[2]

Peveril in truth " smells of the apoplexy." It was
written while Scott was much cumbered with the arrange-
ments for the visit of George IV, saddened by Erskine's
death, and depressed by the premonition of a new
disease. He chose a period of history in which he was
not perfectly at home, and had to lean upon hastily-

---

[1] In the same way Dickens, at Lytton's instance, gave a stock ending to
Great Expectations.
[2] *The Ballantyne Press and its Founders* (1909), 78.

1823 read documents. He was very conscious of the book's imperfections, and in the preparatory letter thought it right to apologize for other defects besides anachronisms. The opening is laboured and the narrative drags, the ravelled skein of the plot is never properly wound up, and the ending is huddled; the fatigue of its composition is reflected in the style, which sinks often to abysses of verbiage.[1] He handicapped himself unduly in making the action stretch over a period of twenty years, thereby condemning himself to *longueurs*. There is no craftsmanship in the story as a whole, and the good things are like comfortable inns scattered at long intervals through an unfeatured country.

The book is nearly half done before the action quickens with young Peveril's journey from the Isle of Man to London. Once on the road we are for a little in the old atmosphere of romance. The scene at the inn where Edward Christian and Chiffinch first appear, the storming of Martindale, Sir Geoffrey's farewell to his son—" God bless thee, my boy, and keep thee true to Church and King, whatever wind brings foul weather "—the attack on Moultrassie Hall, are episodes well conceived and vigorously told. So are many of the London scenes, such as the discussion between Buckingham and Jerningham, and especially the former's interview with Christian. But the pictures of the Court lack the verisimilitude of those in *Nigel*, and Scott never succeeds in reproducing the hideousness of the Popish Plot and of those responsible for it. All the later chapters are heavy, uninspired labour against the collar. The characters have the same patchiness. Lady Derby, till the moment when she confronts Charles at Whitehall, is only a sounding name. Sir Geoffrey and Bridgenorth are creditable pieces of book-work, conventional portraits of Cavalier and Puritan, but the King is the least successful of Scott's royal personages. He is happier when he gets into humble life, for Mrs Deborah and Lance and the jailers have a vitality denied to their betters. There

---

[1] For example, in Chapter xxxiii he describes a fat man as an " ominous specimen of pinguitude."

are some skilful essays in historical reconstruction—in 1823
Buckingham, Christian, Chiffinch and Colonel Blood—
and the dwarf, Sir Geoffrey Hudson, is done with humour
and insight. Fenella, upon whom the plot hinges, is the
most glaring failure. Scott avowedly borrowed her from
Mignon in *Wilhelm Meister* and marred her grievously
in the borrowing, for she is grotesque but not impressive.[1]

The tale lacks verve and speed as it lacks glamour,
for throughout the imaginative impulse flags. Yet there
are many passages on statecraft and the condition of the
country which show Scott's masculine understanding at
its best. Take one of Dumas' masterpieces ; compared
with its light and colour *Peveril* is like a muddy lagoon
contrasted with a mountain stream ; but there is never
in Dumas that background of broad and sane intelligence,
that lively interest in how life was conducted in past
ages, that insight into the social environment, which
redeem Scott's failures. The latter's characters may
stumble dully through their parts, but their platform is
a real world, while Dumas' figures dazzle and delight,
but they move on a wooden stage amid painted scenery.
Byron, said Goethe, is " great only as a creative poet ;
as soon as he reflects, he is a child." It is Scott's
reflective power which atones sometimes, as in *Peveril*,
for his defects in creation.

He was in the habit of consoling himself for a failure
by an immediate attempt at something new. " If it
isna well bobbit, we'll bob it again " was a phrase often
on his lips. There is no more remarkable proof of
Scott's mental resilience than that, after the dreary toil
of *Peveril*, he could produce a thing so vital and glancing
as *Quentin Durward*. The fifteenth century, when
chivalry and the feudal system were beginning to break
down, had always been with him a favourite epoch.
He did not know very much about France, but he had
an intuitive sense of its atmosphere and *décor*, as witness
the passage in the introduction about the terrace of the

---

[1] Goethe's comment was : " To go on making over again and expanding
the once finished thing, as for example Walter Scott has done with my Mignon,
whom, along with her other attributes, he makes into a deaf-mute—that kind
of alteration I cannot praise."

1823 Chateau of Sully, and France accepted the book as true to the spirit of her history. Not to the letter, perhaps, for there are many anachronisms, in addition to those which he acknowledged. Louis refers to Nostradamus, who was not born till twenty years after his death, and he has an amazing metaphor drawn from fly-fishing for salmon, a sport of which fifteenth-century France never dreamed.

Pedantic criticism would be absurd, for the book is a fairy tale, with all the merits of those airy legends which the folk-mind of Europe invented to give colour to drab lives. Crèvecoeur is right when he tells Quentin that he has had " a happy journey through Fairy-land—all full of heroic adventure, and high hope, and wild minstrel-like delusion, like the garden of Morgaine la Fée." Quentin, from the Glen of the Midges, is the eternal younger son who goes out to seek his fortune, as Louis is the treacherous step-mother. There are plenty of ogres and giants on the road—the Boar of the Ardennes, Tristan L'Hermite and Trois-Eschelles and Petit-André; there are good companions like Le Balafré and Dunois; the Bohemians are the malicious elves and Galeotti the warlock; the Lady Isabelle is the conventional fairy-tale princess; when Quentin, during the sack of Liège, leaves his pursuit of de la Marck to save Gertrude, he is behaving exactly as the fairy-tale hero behaves when he gives his cake to the old woman by the wayside; and Crèvecoeur's final comment is in the right tradition : " Fortune has declared herself on his side too plainly for me to struggle further with her humoursome ladyship—but it is strange, from lord to horse-boy, how wonderfully these Scots stick by each other." Nor is there wanting the douche of cold sense, to which the fairy tale is partial :—

" My lord of Crèvecoeur," said Quentin, " my family——"
" Nay, it was not utterly of family that I spoke," said the Count, " but of rank, fortune, high station, and so forth, which place a distance between various classes of persons. As for birth, all men are descended from Adam and Eve."
" My Lord Count," repeated Quentin, " my ancestors, the Durwards of Glen-houlakin——"

" Nay," said the Count, " if you claim a farther descent for 1823
them than from Adam, I have done ! Good even to you."

Quentin Durward is Scott's main achievement in the
vein in which Dumas excelled, and is therefore sure of
its market with youth. It is a better performance,
I think, than *Ivanhoe*, for it swings to its triumphant
close without a single hitch or extravagance. The
opening is provocative, and once inside the man-traps
and snares of Plessis-les-Tours the expectation is keyed
high. Nor is the expectation disappointed, for one
masterly scene follows another—the reception of the
Burgundian envoy, Quentin's vigil in the castle gallery,
the frustrated ambuscade by the Maes, the death of the
Bishop, Quentin's outfacing of de la Marck, Louis at
Péronne, the midnight interview between the necro-
mancer and the King, the assault on Liège, the whole
chain of breathless vicissitudes till the Wild Boar's
grisly head dangles from Le Balafré's gauntlet. It is all
Dumas at his highest, but Dumas with an undercurrent
of sound historical reflection. Quentin himself is the
best of Scott's young heroes, because he is content to
make him only young, chivalrous and heroic, and over-
weights him with no moralities. With the Archers of
the Guard he was of course on his own ground, and
Le Balafré is own brother to Dugald Dalgetty and
Corporal Raddlebanes and all the clan of stout men-at-
arms. As for the others, they live by their deeds and
at the worst are real enough for a fairy-tale. The
dominant figure is the King, who like a great spider
spins webs which entangle half a continent. We need
not ask if Scott has given us the true Louis XI ; modern
research has found more light and less shadow in that
strange career ; but at any rate he has given us a being
in whom we must needs believe, one who must rank
with King James in *Nigel* as the most careful and subtle
of his portraits of the great. We accept Louis' treachery
and superstition as we accept his iron courage, and so
masterful is his vitality that we forget his crooked morals
in admiration of his power.

IV

1824   The year 1824 produced only one novel, *Redgauntlet*,
which was published in June and indifferently received;
Scott had taken to heart the warning against " over-
cropping." He was at work on a new edition of his
Swift and on two tales of the Crusades, a subject which
he had long had in mind. For the rest he was very
busy with household concerns. His plantations were
sufficiently advanced to need thinning and he and Tom
Purdie made the woods ring. Tom had no liking for
the American axe with which his master had been
presented by an admirer, and which he declared was only
fit to pare cheese. In the autumn the Abbotsford fabric
was at last completed, and all that summer Scott's
mind was buried in upholstery. Terry in London was
his chief correspondent, and from him came cabinets,
tapestries, furniture, pictures, and cheap lots of carica-
tures to paper the lavatories. Gifts, too, flowed to the
new house from all over the land, every kind of " gabion,"
including a chair made from the beams of the house at
Robroyston where Wallace was betrayed, a hundred
volumes of the classics from the faithful Constable, and
a set of Montfaucon in scarlet morocco from the King.
One last addition had a melancholy interest—a " louping-
on stone " on which was carved the recumbent figure of
the dog Maida, whose long life ended in October, and
which bore an inscription by Scott in doubtful Latinity.

That autumn his second son Charles was entered at
Brasenose, having given up the nomination to the East
India service offered by Lord Bathurst, and Scott, with
this educational venture in mind, delivered himself of
his views on the training of youth at the opening of the
new Edinburgh Academy. They were eminently wise.
He pled for a comprehensive view of the subject which
would aim at a true discipline of the mind. He urged
the study of Greek, about which he had once been
contemptuous. It was not information that should be
sought, but education, the production not of smatterers
but of scholars. " The observation of Dr Johnson was

well known, that in learning Scotland resembled a
besieged city, where every man had a mouthful, but no
man a bellyful. It might be said in answer to this, that
it was better education should be divided into mouthfuls
than served up at the banquet of some favoured individual, while the great mass were left to starve. But,
sturdy Scotsman as he was, he was not more attached
to Scotland than to truth."

Christmas saw a great house-warming at Abbotsford,
to which came a clan of friends and relatives, including
his brother Thomas's widow and daughters. Basil Hall,
the sailor and explorer, who was the son of a Berwick-
shire laird, was a guest, and has described the elaborate
festivities. The party roamed the hills when the weather
was fine, and at night, under the blaze of oil gas, the
host read aloud from " Christabel " and the ballads, or
told them stories, and Adam Ferguson sang his songs,
and the New Year was ushered in with bumpers. Then
came a spate in Tweed and stormy skies, which promised
ill for the great ball on the 9th of January, the first and
last ball which Scott saw in Abbotsford. But the
weather cleared and the whole countryside flocked to
the carnival ; there were enough poor folk outside the
door, said Dalgleish the butler, to fill a decent-sized
parish kirk. The occasion was more than a house-
warming. Adam Ferguson had a niece, a Miss Jobson
of Lochore in Fife, a young woman with a pretty fortune
and a pleasing appearance. Her father was dead and
she was in the care of a somewhat difficult mother.
Sir Adam desired to make a match between her and
the young Walter, and Scott was not unwilling, for he
liked the girl, and her dowry of £60,000 would be a
useful buttress to the family which he had founded.
The Jobsons were at Gattonside during the summer of
1824, and the wooing progressed happily. At Christmas
the affair was settled, and at the Abbotsford ball Miss
Jobson was the guest of honour, though the engagement
was not formally announced.

It was the last unclouded Christmas and Hogmanay
in Scott's life, and to his guests he seemed to be in his

1824 sunniest mood. The miracle of miracles had happened,
and success so far from spoiling him had made him only
more modest and considerate. " He has been for many
years," Basil Hall wrote, " the object of most acute and
vigilant observation, and as far as my own opportunities
have gone, I must agree with the general report—
namely, that on no occasion has he ever betrayed the
smallest symptom of vanity or affectation, or insinuated
a thought bordering on presumption, or even a consciousness of his own superiority in any respect whatsoever. Some of his oldest and most intimate friends
assert that he has even of late years become more simple
and kindly than ever ; that this attention to those
about him, and absence of all apparent concern about
himself go on, if possible, increasing with his fame and
fortune. Surely if Sir Walter Scott be not a happy
man, which he seems truly to be, he deserves to be
so." . . . The trumpets still rang out bravely, but the
hour for the muffled drums was drawing near.

The completion of Abbotsford, his romance in stone
and lime, marked the end also of Scott's great era of
creation. In his last two books he had returned to his
native soil, and had not only shown the special qualities
of the early novels but had given promise of new and
unexpected powers, a promise which he was not fated
to fulfil. No student of Scott can pass hastily over
St Ronan's Well and *Redgauntlet.*

Had *St Ronan's Well* been the solitary book of a
writer otherwise unknown how should we have regarded
it ? It is necessary to ask this question, for its whole
temper and purpose are different from Scott's previous
work. To Lady Louisa Stuart it seemed that he was
trying to be as unlike himself as possible. His own
criticism was that the story was contorted and unnatural,
but we can agree with that verdict only so far as Clara's
tragedy is concerned. The main feature of the book is
its deliberate rejection of the romantic. He turned of
purpose to a petty by-road as a change from his old
glittering highway, turned a little nervously, for Miss

Edgeworth and Miss Austen had preceded him. It was 1824 a world of which he professed no special knowledge. "His habit of mind," he wrote, "had not led him much, of late years at least, into its general and bustling scenes, nor had he mingled often in the society which enables the observer to 'shoot folly as it flies.' The consequence, perhaps, was that the characters wanted that force and precision which can only be given by a writer who is familiarly acquainted with his subject." But this modesty is out of place. The romancer has become a realist, and the fribbles and bucks of the Well are drawn with a cruel fidelity. The key is kept low, and no glamour is allowed to veil the ugliness. Mowbray, for example, is painted without one touch of the romantic colour which Scott commonly permits himself in the case of the long-descended. Into this comedy of somewhat sordid manners enters tragedy, real tragedy, which is all the grimmer because it is played out against a background of "lions and lionesses with their several jackals, blue surtouts and bluer stockings, fiddlers and dancers, painters and amateurs." There is no longer any craving for wedding-cake and marriage bells, and goodness goes tragically unrewarded. We have left the world where the fates are the mechanical allies of virtue. Had we been compelled to judge the writer on this book alone, would we not have said that he was revealed as one with a notable gift of observation and satire, one who had no illusions about the frailty of mankind, a convinced anti-romantic? And we might have added that this writer, apart from one blemish, showed a gift of ruthless tragic presentation not paralleled among his contemporaries.

The keynote of the book is the irony of life, not its promise and splendour. Its obvious fault is that Scott weaves too intricate a web. Lord Etherington's intrigues, for example, and the dependence of his inheritance on marriage with a Mowbray are invented rather than imagined. Throughout there is too much minor theatrical business, like Etherington's theft of the letter from the post-office, and the sudden appearance of Hannah Irwin. It was as if Scott, having raided the country of the

1824 circulating-library novelists, felt bound to borrow some of their devices. These, however, are minor blemishes; the overmastering blunder is that which he made on James Ballantyne's demand, the explanation of Clara's warped and feverish mind. A mere trick like a mock-marriage could not have wrought such havoc, and it needed, too, a deeper wrong to justify Tyrrell's feelings towards his half-brother. As it stands, the reader is perplexed by the spectacle of unmotived passions.

Admitting such defects, the action is developed in a series of incidents adroitly conceived and most spiritedly recounted. The opening is admirable, where the homely decencies of the Cleikum Inn are made the foil to the absurdities of the Well. Scott never wrote dialogue which revealed more accurately the characters engaged, or was more germane to the development of the tale. Instances are Touchwood's encounter with the unwilling Jekyll, and Lady Penelope's visit to the cottage where Hannah Irwin is lying.

> " Have ye had no pennyworth for your charity ? " she said in spiteful scorn. " Ye buy the very life o' us wi' your shillings and sixpences, your groats and your boddles—ye hae gar'd the puir wretch speak till she swarfs, and now ye stand as if ye never saw a woman in a dwam before. Let me till her wi' the dram—mony words mickle drought, ye ken.—— Stand out o' my gate, my leddy, if sae be ye are a leddy ; there is little use of the like of you when there is death in the pot."

The great tragic scenes at the close—Mowbray's interview with his sister, Touchwood's visit to Shaws Castle, the flight and death of Clara—are done with a grim economy. Irony reaches its height when the gardener produces the weapon which came near to doing murder.

> " Master — St Ronans — Master — I have fund — I have fund——"
> " Have ye found my sister ? " exclaimed the brother with breathless anxiety.
> The old man did not answer till he came up and then, with his usual slowness of delivery, he replied to his master's repeated inquiries. " Na, I haena found Miss Clara, but I hae found something ye wad be wae to lose—your braw hunting knife."

The protagonists are drawn on general lines but with 1824 a sure hand. Tyrrell, Clara and Etherington are real within their limits, and Mowbray is a faithful portrait of the loutish squireen. Touchwood, too, lives, with his fussy wisdom and kindly vanity. The frequenters of the Well are mainly conventional comedy figures—Lady Penelope, Winterblossom, Sir Bingo Binks, Chatterly, MacTurk. Exceptions are the sullen beauty, Lady Binks, who is one of the rare successes among Scott's gentle-women, the excellent Mrs Blower, and—with something of farce added—Dr Quackleben. But it is with the Scots characters that Scott has the surest touch—the lawyers Meiklewham and Bindloose, the minister Josiah Cargill, and such lesser people as Trotting Nelly. Above all, in Meg Dods he has drawn one of the best hostesses in literature. Of her fierce vitality there is no question; from the moment when we first hear her voice uplifted against the sins of her maids she is victoriously alive, a being so foursquare that the others seem wisp-like by contrast. She testifies against the foolish Vanity Fair of the Well, but she has her own honest vanities, which are ennobled by her warm heart and her complete mastery of life. " My gude name !—if onybody touched my gude name, I would neither fash counsel nor com-missary—I wad be doun amang them like a jer-falcon among wild-geese." Meg talks perhaps the best Scots in the novels, with that rhythmical lilt which is the chief beauty of the vernacular speech. Take this of the Well—

Down cam the hail tribe of wild geese, and settled by the Well, to dine there out on the bare grund, like a wheen tinklers, and they had sangs and tunes and healths, nae doubt, in praise of the fountain, as they ca'd the Well, and of Lady Penelope Penfeather ; and, lastly, they behoved a' to take a solemn bumper of the Spring, which, as I'm tauld, made unco havoc amang them or they wan hame. . . . And sae the jig was begun after her leddyship's pipe, and mony a mad measure has been danced sin' syne ; for down cam masons and murgeon makers, and preachers and player-folk, and Episcopalians and Methodists, and fools and fiddlers, and Papists and pie-bakers, and doctors and drugsters, forby the shopfolk that sell trash and trumpery at three prices—and so up got the bonny new Well, and down fell the honest auld town of Saint Ronan's, where blithe decent folk had been heartsome eneugh for mony a day before ony o' them were born, or ony sic vapouring fancies kittled in their cracked brains.

Or this of the " ancient brethren of the angle " :—

They were up in the morning—had their parritch wi' maybe a thimbleful of brandy, and then awa up into the hills, eat their bit cauld meat on the heather, and came hame at e'en wi' the creel full of caller trouts, and had them to their dinner, and their quiet cogue of ale, and their drap punch, and were set singing their catches and glees, as they ca'd them, till ten o'clock, and then to bed, wi' God bless ye—and what for no ?

Redgauntlet stands to Scott's greatest novels much as *Antony and Cleopatra* stands to Shakespeare's four major tragedies. It is not quite one of them, but it contains things as marvellous as the best. In it he returned to his store of actual memories, and, according to Lockhart, it embodies more of his personal experience than all the other novels put together. He drew Saunders Fairford from his father, Darsie Latimer from Will Clerk, and Alan partly from himself : and he called upon his boyish recollections for the slow ebbing of the Jacobite wave whose high-water mark he had described in *Waverley*. In the portraits of the Quaker family he paid pious tribute to the Quaker strain in his own ancestry. His landscape is very much that of *Guy Mannering*, the ribbon of Solway which separated Scotland from England, Solway with its perilous racing tides, its wild shore-folk, and the smuggler craft that stole in in the darkness. In the book we have the sense of being always on a borderland—not only between two different races, but between comfort and savagery and between an old era and a new. A common criticism is that the use of letters impedes the narrative, and no doubt there is now and then a felt hiatus, when the reader's mind has to switch back awkwardly to a different sphere. This constitutes the main artistic defect ; the story is too much of a mosaic, a series of fragments of which the pattern is not immediately recognized. But the pattern is there, and the slow 1824 leisurely narrative of the early letters is a skilful preparation for the tumultuous speed of the later chapters. Throughout there is a sense, not of impending catastrophe as in *The Bride of Lammermoor*, but of the iron compulsion of fate. Redgauntlet himself lays down the book's philosophy. "The privilege of free action belongs to no mortal—we are tied down by the fetters of duty—our mortal path is limited by the regulations of honour—our most indifferent actions are but meshes of the web of destiny by which we are all surrounded."

The story has not a single irrelevant episode, and the plot itself is carefully framed to show in high relief the perversity as well as the tragic nobility of Jacobitism, that last relic of the Middle Ages. Against a background of misty seas and hidden glens the narrative logically unfolds itself. When Darsie meets the unknown horseman at the salmon-spearing our expectation is kindled and our imagination enchained. Back in Edinburgh comedy is rampant in the lawsuit of Peter Peebles, while high drama is a-foot on Solway sands, and presently the comic and tragic chains are interlinked. Scott never wrote a better comedy scene than Alan's *début* in the Parliament House, or his dinner in Dumfries with Provost Crosbie and Pate-in-Peril, or his visit on Saturday at e'en to the house of Mr Thomas Trumbull, or the interview of the Quaker with Peter Peebles ; or a scene more tremulous with romance than when Wandering Willie sings to Darsie in his prison. In all the novels there is no episode more pathetic than that of Nanty Ewart, or more charged with significant drama than the last great scene on the beach. It is high tragedy, when Redgauntlet watches the fall of the Cause which has been entwined with his decaying house, but the drama does not end there. It ends, as all great drama must end, in peace : in an anti-climax more moving than any climax, when a stranger—a Hanoverian and a Campbell—speaks over the dead Jacobitism a noble and chivalrous farewell, the epitaph of common sense.

1824   The character-drawing, though limited in range, is at as high a level of sustained excellence as in any of the novels except *Old Mortality*. The protagonists, Alan and Darsie, Redgauntlet and Green Mantle, bow now and then to false conventions, but they are well drawn in the main. The elder Fairford could not be bettered, with his tenderness and his fussiness, his legal acumen, and the dry humour exemplified in his tale of Luckie Simpson's cow, which drank up a browst of ale, but, since it drank it standing, was legally emptying a stirrup-cup, and so escaped liability. The Quaker, Joshua Geddes, is a subtle study in a rare type of courage; Crosbie and Summertrees, the rascally Trumbull, Nanty Ewart, are strong, three-dimensioned figures, Cristal Nixon is an adequate villain, and Wandering Willie is a happy incomer from the ancient vagabond Scotland. As for Peter Peebles he is the best of Scott's half-wits, a massive figure of realistic farce, not without hints of tragedy.

> It's very true that it is grandeur upon earth to hear ane's name thundered out along the long-arched roof of the Outer House — 'Poor Peter Peebles against Plainstanes, *et per contra* '; a' the best lawyers in the house fleeing like eagles to the prey . . . to see the reporters mending their pens to take down the debate—the Lords themselves pooin' in their chairs, like folk sitting down to a gude dinner, and crying on the clerks for parts and pendicles of the process, who, puir bodies, can do little mair than cry on their closet-keepers to help them. To see a' this . . . and to ken that naething will be said or dune amang a' thae grand folk for maybe the feck of three hours, saving what concerns you and your business—— Oh, man, nae wonder that ye judge this to be earthly glory ! And yet, neighbour, as I was saying, there be unco drawbacks. I whiles think of my bit house, where dinner and supper and breakfast used to come without the crying for, just as if the fairies had brought it—and the gude bed at e'en—and the needfu' penny in the pouch. And then to see a' ane's worldly substance capering in the air in a pair of weigh-bauks, now up, now down, as the breath of judge and counsel inclines it for pursuer or defender ! Truth, man, there are times I rue having ever begun this plea work—though, maybe, when ye consider the renown and credit I have by it, ye will hardly believe what I am saying.

The final scene of the book must rank among Scott's 1824
highest achievements, for it is the very soul of romance,
and yet it has an epic dignity, for it is the end of a
loyalty which had deeply moved men's hearts. One
other episode is universally admitted as a masterpiece,
the interpolated story told by the blind violer. It is
a piece which deserves careful study, for the proof-
sheets show that Scott took exceptional pains with it,
and it is a revelation of what he could do when he bent
his mind critically upon his work. It is told in Scots,
but the dialect is never exaggerated, and it is rather
English with a faint Scots colouring and many pithy
Scots phrases. The language is extraordinarily apt
and every detail is exactly appropriate. " Glen, nor
dargle, nor mountain, nor cave could hide the puir
hill-folk when Redgauntlet was out with bugle and
bloodhound after them, as if they had been sae mony
deer."—" Aye, as Sir Robert girned wi' pain, the jacka-
napes girned too, like a sheep's head between a pair of
tangs—an ill-faur'd, fearsome couple they were."—
" Are ye come light-handed, ye son of a toom whistle ? "
—" A tune my gudesire learned from a warlock."—
" It's ill-speaking between a fou man and a fasting."—
" There was a deep morning fog on grass and gravestone
around him and his horse was feeding quietly beside
the minister's twa cows."—And there is the famous
description of the company around the tavern-board
in Hell :—

There was the fierce Middleton and the dissolute Rothes,
and the crafty Lauderdale ; and Dalzell, with his bald head
and a beard to his girdle ; and Earlshall with Cameron's blude
on his hand ; and wild Bonshaw that tied blessed Mr Cargill's
limbs till the blude sprang ; and Dumbarton Douglas, the
twice-turned traitor baith to country and King. There was
the Bluidy Advocate MacKenzie, who, for his worldly wit and
wisdom, had been to the rest as a god. And there was Claverhouse, as beautiful as when he lived, with his long, dark curled
locks streaming down over his laced buff coat, and his left
hand always on his right spule-blade to hide the wound that
the silver bullet had made. He sat apart from them all, and
looked at them with a melancholy, haughty countenance ;
while the rest hallooed and sang, and laughed till the room

rang. But their smiles were fearfully contorted from time to time, and their laughter passed into such wild sounds as made my gudesire's very nails go blue, and chilled the marrow in his banes.

" Wandering Willie's Tale " is one of the greatest of the world's short stories by whatever test it be tried. Its verbal style is without a flaw, its structure is perfect, and it produces that intense impression of reality imaginatively transmuted which is the triumph of literary art. One point is worth noting, for it shows Scott's unfailing insight into human nature. The narrator, in telling of Steenie's interview with the old Sir Robert, allows time for the latter to write a receipt before death took him. " He (Steenie) ventured back into the parlour . . . He forgot baith siller and receipt, and down stairs he banged." But when Steenie meets Sir Robert's heir he tells a different story. " Nae sooner had I set down the siller, and just as his honour, Sir Robert that's gane, drew it till him to count it, and write me a receipt, he was ta'en wi' the pains that removed him." Now the supernatural explanation depends on the receipt being got from a dead man in the wood of Pitmurkie and signed that very night, which is consistent with the second story, whereas the first leaves room for the receipt being merely lost. Scott knew so profoundly the average man and his incapacity for exact evidence—compare the gossip in the ale-house of Kippletringan in *Guy Mannering*—that he makes Wandering Willie in telling the tale give two different versions of the crucial incident —one which is compatible with a prosaic explanation, and a second in flat contradiction and full of excited detail, which transports the whole affair into the realm of the occult. It is an astonishing achievement—to write a tale of *diablerie* which is overwhelming in its effect, and at the same time incidentally and most artfully to provide its refutation.

V

On the 3rd of February, 1825, the young Walter was 1825
married in Edinburgh. Scott settled Abbotsford upon
him that Border acres might match the Jobson money-
bags, and for £3500 purchased for him a captain's
commission in the Hussars. He was a most tender and
indulgent father-in-law, as his letters to the bride show,
and the marriage was all that he could desire. But it
had been an expensive affair, and for the moment he
felt, as he said, like his " namesake in the Crusades,
Walter the Penniless." He had begun a tale of these
same Crusades which was not going well, for the great
effort of *Redgauntlet* seems to have impoverished his
imagination. All that arid spring, when, because of the
drought, he found it difficult to let his grass parks, his
mind was much exercised by ways and means. " I must
look for some months," he wrote, " to be put to every
corner of my saddle." His friend Terry asked his help
in his proposed lease of a London theatre, and Scott
guaranteed him to the extent of £1250. But he wrote
him a sagacious letter, warning him against the danger
of embarking on an enterprise without a backing of
cash. He pointed out that, however much the venture
might succeed, receipts would lag behind expenditure.
" The best business is ruined when it becomes pinched
for money and gets into the circle of discounting bills,
and buying necessary articles at high prices and of
inferior quality for the sake of long credit. . . . Besides
the immense expense of renewals, that mode of raising
money is always liable to some sudden check which
throws you on your back at once." He therefore urged
him to get some monied man behind him with a substantial interest in the speculation.[1]

This advice must have been prompted by reflections
on his own position. He realized that the floating debt
of the Ballantyne firm was mounting rapidly, largely
owing to his own drawings. He was not happy about

[1] Lockhart, VI. 20-26.

1825 the whole business of accommodation bills, and in
St Ronan's Well had expressed his doubts.

> "There is maybe an accommodation bill discounted now
> and then, Mr Touchwood ; but men must have accommodation,
> or the world would stand still—accommodation is the grease
> that makes the wheels go."
>
> "Ay, makes them go down hill to the devil," answered
> Touchwood, "I left you bothered about one Air bank, but
> the whole country is an Air bank now, I think—and who is
> to pay the piper ? "

Constable, too, had his moments of disquiet. In August
1823 he pointed out to Scott that the accommodation
he had granted to the Ballantyne firm was as high as
£20,000 and asked that it should be reduced to a more
prudent figure, such as £8000. Scott agreed, but it
would appear that any reduction effected was only
temporary.[1] There had also been a proposal to get an
accountant to examine the whole state of affairs between
the two firms, but to this Scott seems to have objected.[2]
In the spring of 1825, when Scott reflected on his
situation, he must have been aware that it had its perils.
The Ballantyne debt was now in the neighbourhood of
£40,000 and he himself had also drawn direct on Constable for large advances. Abbotsford, to be sure, was
completed, and his expensive heir was finally settled in
life, but there were heavy arrears to be paid off before
he could clear his feet. In 1814 he had been in a position
of far less difficulty and had taken vigorous action ; why
in 1825 did he let matters drift—nay, was even toying
with the idea of purchasing Faldonside for a sum not
far short of the Ballantyne debt ? [3] The answer seems
to be that he felt that in two respects his status was
very different from that of eleven years before. In the
first place, he had won an immense public and could
earn at will immense sums. *The Betrothed* might be
labouring heavily, but he had other craft to launch. In
the second place he had behind him the monied backer
whom he had advised Terry to find, a man of infinite

---

[1] *A. Constable*, III. 275-288.   [2] *Ibid.*, 472-4.
[3] *Fam. Letters*, II. 260, 347.

resources who was deeply pledged to his interests. That 1825 man was Constable.

And Constable's behaviour was calculated to allay Scott's fears. The great publisher had returned from the south, not in better health but apparently in the best of spirits. For some time he had been fertile in his proposals to Scott—a book on popular superstitions, a collection of the English poets, an edition of Shakespeare —editorial schemes to fill up the novelist's leisure and prevent too frequent romances from glutting the market. But now he had ampler visions. He realized that the spread of the popular taste for reading must be accompanied by publications at a popular price. At Abbotsford in May he startled Scott and James Ballantyne by declaring in his impressive way that printing and bookselling were only in their infancy, and he had a mass of figures to prove his case. He proposed a new Miscellany, a volume every month, not in boards but in cloth, to be sold at some price like half a crown or three shillings. " If I live for half-a-dozen years," he said, " I'll make it as impossible that there should not be a good library in every decent house in Britain as that the shepherd's ingle-neuk should want the saut-poke ! Ay, and what's that ? Why should the ingle-neuk itself want a shelf for the novels ? . . . I have hitherto been thinking only of the wax lights, but before I'm a twelve-month older I shall have my hand on the tallow." Scott exclaimed that he was " the grand Napoleon of the realms of print." " If you outlive me," said Constable, " I bespeak that line for my tombstone."

It was a bold conception, and a sound, as Scott had the wit to see. He gladly consented to help this Buonaparte to fight his Marengo. The novels should take their place in the new Miscellany, but there must be other provender than fiction. Scott fired at the idea ; to turn his hand to popular history had long been in his mind, and he agreed that he would undertake a life of Napoleon.[1] So when *The Betrothed* was published in the following

[1] Lockhart (VI. 32) says that the proposal came from Scott, but there is evidence that the conception was Constable's. See *A. Constable*, III. 310-12.

1825 month there was an announcement in the introduction which prepared the world for the great venture. That introduction was a pleasant little account of a board meeting of the author of *Waverley* and some of his principal characters, done in the style of a company report. It concluded thus :—

> "The world and you, gentlemen, may think what you please," said the Chairman, elevating his voice, "but I intend to write the most wonderful book which the world ever read— a book in which every incident shall be incredible, yet strictly true—a work recalling recollections with which the ears of this generation once tingled, and which shall be read by our children with an admiration approaching to incredulity. Such shall be a Life of Napoleon Buonaparte by the Author of *Waverley*."

Scott flung himself joyfully into the study of the man who had enchained his imagination and dominated the world of his youth. He was not forgetful of the dangers of writing contemporary history, where, as Raleigh said, if a man follow truth too closely it may haply strike out his teeth, but his purpose was only a sketch on broad lines, to fill four of the duodecimo volumes of the proposed Miscellany. He wrote to his friends for letters and information and to foreign capitals for literature, and presently his little library in Castle Street became like an antiquarian book store. One item was no less than a hundred folio volumes of the *Moniteur*. This was work which did not require that he should wait for inspiration, and in which his tireless industry could have full play. The preliminary sketch of the French Revolution grew fast, and soon it became clear to Constable that it had outrun the scale which he had planned. It must be issued as a substantive work, and the Miscellany must wait.

Meantime the " Tales of the Crusaders " had been published, *The Betrothed* and *The Talisman*. Of the first Scott in the writing thought so ill—James Ballantyne heartily assenting—that he wanted to burn it. As it was, he turned to the second, and only completed *The Betrothed* because his advisers thought that *The*

Talisman would carry it off. It is an indubitable failure, 1825
and the reason is plain. The theme—the intricate
cross-currents in love made inevitable by the Crusades—
might have made a good novel, but the interest would
have lain chiefly in its psychology. Scott's strength did
not lie in reading the mind of the remote past but in
chronicling its deeds ; so he condemned himself to a
task outside his interest and beyond his powers. The
moral vicissitudes of Eveline and Damian are perfunctorily studied, and there is no swift tale of adventure
to atone for their flatness. There was a stirring romance
somewhere in the doings of Vidal, but he does not tell
it. The siege of the Garde Doloureux, the uncanniness
of the Red Finger, and the carrying-off of Eveline do
not move us, for the writer's heart is not in them. The
best scene is where the old Constable tests Damian's
honour in the dungeon, but that is spoiled by a hasty
and most impotent conclusion. Damian is too much the
chronic invalid to be a satisfactory lover, and the
villains are too shadowy to convince. Only the Fleming,
Wilkin Flammock, has the semblance of life, for he is the
type of homespun hero with whom Scott never failed.

It is otherwise with *The Talisman*. That novel is all
book-work, for Scott knew nothing of the East, and not
very much of the inner soul of the Crusades. But his
imagination fired at the thought of honest English and
Scots warriors in the unfamiliar desert, and especially
at the tradition of high chivalry attached to the figures
of Richard and Saladin. There is much in the tale that
is theatrical. The landscape, for example, is so much
pasteboard scenery, the secret chapel at Engaddi smacks
of the *Mysteries of Udolpho*, the two dwarfs are no
better than Fenella, and the hermit Theodorick is a
Gothick monstrosity. But he had devised an excellent
plot, a romantic love affair with a background of high
politics, and in the latter he showed his old power of
giving public matters the interest of tense drama. There
is nothing subtle in the delineation of Richard or Saladin
or Sir Kenneth of Scotland or the jealous crusading
chiefs, but each portrait is adequate for this kind of

1825 tale. The best figure is De Vaux, for Tom of the Gills, that " commodity of old iron and Cumberland flint," was a Borderer, and with him Scott was on his native soil. The book opens brilliantly with the fight beside the desert well, and a dozen scenes stick in the memory —the strife about the banner on St George's Mount. Kenneth's vigil and temptation, above all the attempt on Richard's life by the Assassin of Lebanon, which is a masterpiece of taut, economical narrative. The story " goes twangingly " to its close, and the full-throated speech of the characters is in the right manner. Sir Kenneth defies Richard :—" Now, by the Cross, on which I place my hopes, her name shall be the last word in my mouth, her image the last thought in my mind. Try thy boasted strength on this bare brow, and see if thou canst prevent my purpose." Richard's speech to the wavering princes is eloquence of the true heroic brand. The brave stir of the book and its sustained note of ringing gallantry make it more than a mere skilfully constructed pageant, and give it something of the reality of poetry.

Napoleon being firmly on the stocks, Scott permitted himself a holiday. In July, accompanied by Lockhart and his daughter Anne, he crossed to Ireland to see his elder son, who was stationed at Dublin. There he was entertained by all the celebrities, saw all the sights, and had the pleasure of visiting Maria Edgeworth at her home. He returned by Holyhead, called on the ladies of Llangollen, at Windermere met Canning (who had promised to visit Abbotsford that year but found that he could not find time to cross the Border) and was entertained to a regatta on the lake, saw Wordsworth at Mount Rydal, and spent two days at Lowther Castle. He reached home in the beginning of September, refreshed by his two months of idleness, and encouraged by the warm popular reception which he had met with everywhere on his travels.

That autumn at Abbotsford he sat tight at his desk. *Napoleon* proved to be a herculean labour, for the materials were voluminous, and Scott could not enjoy,

as he had enjoyed in the case of the novels, the task 1825
of swift and easy creation. He was as much a slave
of the pen now as he had been when he copied legal
documents in his father's office. Lockhart has described
him thus caught in the toils :—

> He read and noted and indexed with the pertinacity of some
> pale compiler in the British Museum ; but rose from such
> employment, not radiant and buoyant, as after he had been
> feasting himself among the teeming harvests of Fancy, but
> with an aching brow, and eyes in which the dimness of years
> had begun to plant some specks before they were subjected
> again to that straining over small print and difficult manuscript
> which had, no doubt, been familiar to them in the early time
> when (in Shortreed's phrase) " he was making himself." . . .
> It now often made me sorry to catch a glimpse of him, stooping
> and poring with his spectacles amidst piles of authorities, a
> little note-book ready in his left hand, that had always used
> to be at liberty for patting Maida.[1]

One or two visitors relieved the monotony of his work—
Tom Moore, whose warbling amused him, and who in
turn was deeply impressed by Scott's happy relations
with his neighbours, and that formidable lady, who had
been Harriet Mellon the actress, was now the widow of
Mr Coutts the banker, and was about to become Duchess
of St Albans. Mrs Coutts was a sort of Mrs Blower
in excelsis, a kind-hearted preposterous woman, and
Scott exerted himself to see that her feelings were not
hurt by his more fastidious guests.

It was a somewhat shadowed autumn. Scott felt the
burden of his new historical venture, and he confessed
to Moore that he found his imagination in his novels
beginning to flag. The pleasant Abbotsford circle was
about to break up, for the Lockharts were leaving
Scotland. Lockhart, after having failed to become
Sheriff of Sutherland, had accepted Murray's offer to be
editor of the *Quarterly* and adviser in connexion with a
projected newspaper, on behalf of which young Mr
Disraeli made a visit to Scott that autumn.[2] One reason
for his acceptance was the health of Hugh Littlejohn,
who, it seemed, could not survive another northern

---

[1] V. 88-9.   [2] *Life of Disraeli*, I. 62-71 : Lang, I. chap. xii.

1825 winter. It was a heavy blow to Scott. He agreed that Lockhart should go to London, though he was not altogether happy about his future there, fearing that he might " drop into the gown and slipper garb of life." But he hated change, he hated to think that now there would be a cold hearth at Chiefswood, and that he would no longer see daily the frail little grandson who was the joy and anxiety of his life.

Many " auld sangs " seemed to be coming to an end, and that year was the last for Scott of the Abbotsford Hunt. He tried to jump the prehistoric trench called the Catrail, but Sibyl Grey came down with him and spoiled for good his nerve for horsemanship. Twenty-one years before he had ridden with Mungo Park, who was on the eve of setting out on the African journey from which he never returned. Park's horse stumbled, and when Scott observed that it was a bad omen he got the answer : " Freits [1] follow them that fear them." As he returned to Edinburgh that autumn, a little burdened and saddened, he may have remembered that day on the Yarrow hills, and reflected that there were some omens which could not be averted by courage.

[1] Omens.

Chapter X

THE DARK DAYS

(1825–1826)

On his return to Edinburgh in November 1825 Scott 1825 began to keep a journal. He had often regretted his negligence in this respect, as he felt his memory growing weaker, and the sight of some volumes of Byron's notes suggested that it was not too late to begin a memorandum-book " by throwing aside all pretence to regularity and order, and marking down events just as they occurred to recollection." After a fortnight's trial he found that the thing worked well, for it gave him, when he grew sick of a task, a change of work which quieted his conscience. " Never a being, from my infancy up, hated task-work as I hate it. . . . Propose to me to do one thing, and it is inconceivable the desire I have to do something else. . . . Now, if I expend such concentric movements on this journal, it will be turning this wretched propensity to some account." Clearly he intended that no contemporary eye should see it, but he must have contemplated its ultimate publication, for he was a stout believer in keeping records. There may have been another reason for the experiment. In Erskine he had lost his closest friend, and a journal would be an alternative to such a confidant, enabling him to clarify his thoughts and relieve his moods in times which promised a heavy crop of perplexities.

It is fortunate that we possess such a document for the most difficult years of Scott's life. Its biographical worth is inestimable, and not less high is its quality as literature. For one thing it is one of the most complete expressions of a human soul that we possess, as complete

1825 as Swift's *Journal to Stella*, but without its self-consciousness. There is no reticence and no posturing, because he is speaking to his own soul ; he gives us that very thing in which Hazlitt declared him lacking, " what the heart whispers to itself in secret." The greatest figure he ever drew is in the *Journal*, and it is the man Walter Scott. His style, too, is purged of all dross. It is English of no school and of no period, a speech as universal as that of St John's Gospel. " Whatever else of Scott's may lose its colour with time," Professor Elton has written, " the *Journal* cannot do so, with its accurate, unexaggerated language of pain." Here are qualities which are found only at long intervals in the romances ; a tenderness which keeps watch over man's mortality and neither quails nor complains, a strange wistfulness, as if a strong and self-contained soul had at last found utterance.

I

In November, before he left Abbotsford, life had been growing anxious. With his keen interest in public affairs he could not be blind to the perilous state of the money-market. Earlier in the year there had been an orgy of speculation, and the new-formed companies, many of them bubble, showed a subscribed capital of some two hundred million pounds. The tide had turned before midsummer, when prices began to fall, and the amount of gold in the Bank of England was reduced by export to a third of what it had been in January. The stock-jobbing mania had extended to the book trade, and eminent publishers had been gambling in South American mining shares, and railways, and gas companies, while Constable's London correspondents, Hurst and Robinson, were said to have ventured one hundred thousand pounds in hops. Early in October Constable went to London, and found that firm in a troublesome temper. They had opposed the inclusion of the Waverley novels in the new Miscellany on the ground that they had still large quantities of the existing editions—indeed

they had been very critical of the whole scheme. Moreover, they had been drawing on him for accommodation
to an alarming degree. London was nervous and un-
settled. The bankers were restricting credit, and there
were rumours of many firms on the edge of bankruptcy.
Constable realized that at all costs Hurst and Robinson
must be supported, and he was a little comforted by
the fact that the actual sale of books was better than
ever. Both he and his partner Cadell were convinced
that their very existence depended on the London house,[1]
and every scrap of credit he could raise was put at their
disposal. He returned to Scotland early in November,
worn out with his labours and anxieties, and collapsed
into bed.

Meantime Lockhart, who was in London over the
business of the *Quarterly*, heard disquieting tales, some
of them connected with Hurst and Robinson, which he
transmitted to Scott. These tales meant more to Scott
than to his son-in-law, for he knew how deeply Constable
was committed to the London firm, and how deeply he
himself was committed to Constable. Lockhart was
back in Chiefswood at the end of October, and there he
had a letter from a London lawyer which mentioned a
report that Constable's bankers had closed his account—
" thrown up his book " as the phrase ran. After dinner
he rode over to Abbotsford to give the news to Scott,
who received it with equanimity. But next morning
Scott turned up to breakfast at Chiefswood, and explained that he had been so perturbed by the story that
he had driven by night to Polton to see Constable, and
had got from him an unqualified denial. This incident
first opened Lockhart's eyes to the fact that Constable's
downfall might involve his father-in-law in heavier losses
than the non-payment of some sums due on the novels.
Later Lockhart had further news to give him, gossip
about the precarious condition of Hurst and Robinson
and their speculation in hops, which he reported in all
innocence, not realizing its gravity in Scott's eyes. On
18th November Scott looked in on Cadell on his way to

[1] *A. Constable*, III. 387.

1825 the Court, and mentioned what he had heard. He seems, also, to have expressed surprise at Constable's dallying at Polton when things in London were so critical. Cadell tried to reassure him, and wrote at once to Constable, whose gout was not improved by the letter. That evening Cadell called in Castle Street with emphatic denials from Constable, and verified his suspicion that the informant was Lockhart.[1]

Four days later Scott's fears were again aroused. " Here is a matter for a May morning, but much fitter for a November one "—this is the first hint which the *Journal* gives of the approaching disaster. He comforted himself by reflecting that he had " enough to pay forty shillings in the pound, taking matters at their very worst," [2]—an optimism which may be explained by his ignorance of the ultimate cross-ranking of the accommodation bills. He had a meeting that day with Constable, who arrived " lame as a duck upon his legs, but his heart and courage as firm as a rock." Constable had been leading a harassed life and had had little sleep for days, for the embarrassments of Hurst and Robinson were now beyond question. But he was clear that they must be supported, and Scott agreed to join him in borrowing £5000 for the purpose. The latter was solemnized rather than alarmed, and resolved then and there to begin a course of rigid economies—no more building, no more purchase of land, books, or " gabions " for the present, and the clearing off of encumbrances with the proceeds of the year's labour. On 5th December he said good-bye to the Lockharts, and turned straightway to his description of " that worshipful triumvirate, Danton, Robespierre and Marat." His health was fairly good, apart from heart palpitations and fits of lassitude,

---

[1] Some doubts have been cast on Scott's midnight visit to Polton (Carswell, *op. cit.*, 126 *n.*) on the ground that Thomas Constable could find no account of it in his father's papers (*A Constable*, III. 378). But Lockhart's story (VI. 106) is too circumstantial to be disbelieved. It would appear that Scott twice took Lockhart's rumours to Constable—once from Abbotsford on the affair of the bank account some time before November 12th when he left for Edinburgh, and in Edinburgh on November 18th on the affairs of Hurst and Robinson. Constable was not likely to keep any record of the Polton interview.

[2] *Journal*, I. 9. Lockhart (VI. 130) has " twenty shillings," which misrepresents Scott's mood.

and, all things considered, his spirits were equable. He 1825
found that he could still enjoy a walk home from the
Court in wild weather. " No man that ever stepped on
heather has less dread than I of catch-cold ; and I seem
to regain in buffeting with the wind a little of the high
spirits with which, in younger days, I used to enjoy a
Tam-o'-Shanter ride through darkness, wind and rain."
A little ominously he counts his mercies :—

> I have much to comfort me in the present aspect of my
> family. My eldest son, independent in fortune, united to an
> affectionate wife—and of good hopes in his profession ; my
> second, with a good deal of talent, and in the way, I think, of
> cultivating it to good purpose ; Anne, an honest, downright
> good Scots lass, in whom I could only wish to correct a spirit
> of satire ; and Lockhart is Lockhart, to whom I can most
> willingly confide the happiness of the daughter who chose
> him. . . . My dear wife, the partner of my cares and successes,
> is, I fear, frail in health—though I trust and pray she may
> see me out. Indeed, if this troublesome complaint goes on,
> it bodes no long existence. . . . Good-night Sir Walter about
> sixty. I care not, if I leave my name unstained and my family
> properly settled. *Sat est vixisse.*[1]

As the year drew to its close the tidings from the
south grew worse. In mid-December a great private
bank stopped payment, and for a week panic reigned in
the city of London. On 14th December Scott notes that
he intended to borrow £10,000 on the security of Abbotsford, which his son's marriage settlement entitled him
to do. At the worst he thought that he would be left
with a clear fortune of nearly £50,000. . . . On the 18th
he heard from James Ballantyne that Hurst and Robinson
were down and that the end had come, and at last he
realized his true position. His first thoughts were for
those who had made their home under his shadow :—
" This news will make sad hearts at Darnick and in the
cottages of Abbotsford " ; for his dogs—" poor things,
I must get them kind masters ; " for Willie Laidlaw and
Tom Purdie and James Ballantyne. His children would
not suffer, since they were provided for. His wife, sick
and suffering, was a little impatient with his fortitude,

1825–26 and blamed him for his past improvidence, but Anne
was stoical. For himself " the feast of fancy " was over.
" I can no longer have the delight of waking in the
morning with bright ideas in my mind, hasten to commit
them to paper, and count them monthly as the means
of planting such groves and purchasing such wastes."
. . . But the alarm was premature. In the evening
came Cadell to say that Hurst and Robinson still stood,
and next morning Ballantyne and Constable confirmed
the glad tidings. " I love the virtues of rough and
round men," Scott wrote—a surprising tribute to the
politic Mr Cadell. He flung himself with a redoubled
energy on Napoleon, and scribbled " Bonnie Dundee "
one evening before dinner. " Can't say what made
me take a frisk so uncommon of late years as to
write verses of free-will. I suppose the same impulse
which makes birds sing when the storm seems blown
over."

But the sky was not clear, and that Christmas at
Abbotsford was a shadowed as well as a lonely one.
Scott had only Anne and his ailing wife for company in
the big new house. He executed the mortgage for
£10,000 and fretted because Constable remained obstin-
ately at Polton, though the news from London was
grave, and Hurst and Robinson were clearly still in
danger. His own health was bad, for the day after
Christmas he had an attack of kidney trouble, and
closed the year on a diet of calomel. A visit of the
Skenes did something to cheer him, and he forced himself
to get on with his novel *Woodstock*, in which his interest
had flagged. " I must take my own way, and write
myself into good humour with my task. It is only
when I dally with what I am about, look back and aside,
instead of keeping my eyes straight forward, that I feel
these cold sinkings of the heart." He had such a sinking
on 14th January, when he had a mysterious letter from
Constable saying that he had gone post to London,
where Scott believed him to have been for a fortnight.
" It strikes me to be that sort of letter which I have
seen men write when they are desirous that their dis-

agreeable intelligence should be rather apprehended than 1826 avowed."

On the 16th he returned to Edinburgh in a black frost. " Came through cold roads to as cold news," says the *Journal*. The news was that Hurst and Robinson had dishonoured a bill of Constable's, thereby making bankruptcy certain. It would appear that Scott at first did not grasp its full meaning. He dined with Skene, said nothing about the news, and seemed to be in good spirits. But next morning James Ballantyne made the situation clear to him, and when Skene arrived very early he was greeted with, " My friend, give me a shake of your hand—mine is that of a beggar."[1]

II

The details of the disaster will always be obscure, but the chief facts are plain. The sudden crack had come which split the whole complex fabric of credit. The banks had lent money in the fat years without any strict investigation, but they were in a privileged position, since they ranked before other creditors, and the crazy system of counter-bills doubled their security for each advance. There had been the same traffic in bills and counter-bills between Constable and Hurst and Robinson as between the former and James Ballantyne. When the London firm got into difficulties they discounted every scrap of Constable's paper, and he did the same with the Ballantyne bills. When Hurst and Robinson found themselves unable to meet their liabilities, their creditors had recourse to Constable, and Constable to Ballantyne, and so their fall brought down the whole connexion. The floating debt of the Ballantyne firm had increased to some £46,000—largely through accommodation to Scott, though part was no doubt due to James Ballantyne's own considerable drawings,[2] and to the fact that the accounts were carelessly kept and the books never balanced. Much of this sum was doubled

---

[1] Lockhart, VI. 213-14 ; Skene, 135-6.
[2] *Ballantyne Humbug*, 112, etc.

1826 by the granting to Constable of counter-bills. Constable owed Scott a large amount for recently purchased copyrights, and Scott in turn owed Constable for advances made on account of future literary work. The consequence was that the Ballantyne liability—which was Scott's—amounted to about £130,000, most of it due on bills held by the banks, though a few were in the hands of private traders and speculators. There was, of course, a large counter-claim on Constable—four years later it was estimated at £64,000[1]—but not much of this could be reckoned among the assets. Hurst and Robinson paid 1s. 3d. in the pound on their debts of £300,000; Constable 2s. 9d. on his total of £256,000; Ballantyne in the end paid every penny.

In that doleful January, Constable, gouty, dropsical and half-crazed with anxiety, made a desperate fight of it. He tried to get Lockhart to go with him to the Bank of England to raise anything up to £200,000 on his copyrights; he would have had Scott borrow £20,000 in Edinburgh and send it to him forthwith; his devices were many, and all of a bottomless futility. Thomas Constable was of opinion that his father might have been saved if these proposals had been listened to,[2] but it is hard to see how; any fresh loan would have gone into the pit which had already received the proceeds of the Abbotsford mortgage. It was these wild shifts, together with the futile Abbotsford borrowing, which broke Scott's trust in Constable. The gallant old gambler did not give up hope till the last. As late as 18th January he wrote to Cadell in a strain of high confidence.[3]

But for Scott the time for illusion was gone. He saw that, whatever Hurst and Robinson and Constable might ultimately pay, the Ballantyne firm was down and he himself insolvent. He was advised to make a trust of his property, and he was determined with his own hand to pay off every penny of debt. He turned straightway to work, and in that dark week he wrote a chapter of *Woodstock* every day. At the moment he had no hope of saving Abbotsford or anything else from the wreck.

[1] *Sederunt Book.*   [2] *A. Constable*, III. 430.   [3] *Ibid.*, III. 416.

" Naked we entered the world," he wrote in the *Journal*, 1826
" and naked we leave it—blessed be the name of the
Lord ! " But the very magnitude of the disaster tightened
his courage. Six days after he knew the worst he
wrote :—

> I feel neither dishonoured nor broken. . . . I have walked
> my last on the domains I have planted—sate my last in the
> halls I have built. But death would have taken them from
> me if misfortune had spared them. My poor people whom I
> loved so well ! There is just another die to turn up against me
> in this run of ill-luck ; *i.e.* if I should break my magic wand
> in the fall from this elephant, and lose my popularity with
> my fortune. Then *Woodstock* and *Bony* may both go to the
> paper-maker, and I may take to smoking cigars and drinking
> grog, or turn devotee, and intoxicate the brains another way.
> In prospect of absolute ruin, I wonder if they would let me
> leave the Court of Session. I would like, methinks, to go
> abroad,
>
> > " And lay my bones far from the Tweed."
>
> But I find my eyes moistening, and that will not do. I will
> not yield without a fight for it. It is odd, when I set myself
> to write *doggedly*, as Dr Johnson would say, I am exactly
> the same man that I ever was, neither low-spirited nor *distrait*.
> In prosperous times I have sometimes felt my fancy and power
> of language flag, but adversity is to me at least a tonic and
> bracer ; the fountain is awakened from its inward recesses, as
> if the spirit of affliction had troubled it in his passage.[1]

He slept badly these days, for he was little out of
doors. On 24th January he went back to the Court
for the first time since the tragedy, feeling " like the
man with the large nose," that everybody was talking
about him. Offers of help flowed in from the most
diverse quarters. Old friends like Sir William Forbes
proffered aid, and one unknown admirer was prepared to
put up £30,000 ; his servants desired to forgo their
wages, and an old music-master tendered his savings ;
his daughter-in-law wanted to sell out her holding in
the funds ;[2] the universal feeling was that which Lord
Dudley expressed to Morritt : " Good God, let every
man to whom he has given months of delight give him

1826 a sixpence, and he will rise to-morrow morning richer than Rothschild." There was even a proposal that the Government should do something. To all this spontaneous friendliness Scott had one answer. He was annoyed when the newspapers suggested a subscription, " calling upon men and gods to assist a popular author who, having choused the public of many thousands, had not the sense to keep wealth when he had it." He would have no charity, nor would he take the easy road of bankruptcy. The Ballantyne firm might have obtained a speedy discharge ; the creditors would have had a right to the life-rent and to the reversionary interest of Abbotsford, but the future printing profits and Scott's future literary earnings would have been his own. Such would have been the natural course for a business man to follow, but Scott viewed it differently, for he saw a principle involved. No man should lose by him if it lay in his power to prevent it ; otherwise in a court of honour he would deserve to lose his spurs. " No, if they permit me, I will be their vassal for life, and dig in the mine of my imagination to find diamonds (or what they sell for such) to make good my engagements, not to enrich myself. And this from no reluctance to allow myself to be called the Insolvent, which I probably am, but because I will not put out of the power of my creditors the resources, mental or literary, which yet remain to me."[1]

He soon recovered a measure of serenity. On 26th January he could write to Laidlaw : " For myself, I feel like the Eildon hills—quite firm, though a little cloudy. I do not dislike the path that lies before me. I have seen all that society can show, and enjoyed all that wealth can give me, and I am satisfied much is vanity, if not vexation of spirit."[2] More, he felt that old lift of the heart with which he had always faced a crisis. " It is not nature," he wrote to Miss Edgeworth, " to look upon what can't be helped with any anxious or bitter remembrances. . . . The fact is I belong to that set of philosophers who ought to be called Nymmites

---

[1] *Journal*, I. 94. [2] *Ibid.*, I. 97*n*.

after their good founder Corporal Nym, and the funda- 1826
mental maxim of whose school is 'Things must be as
they may.' "[1]   He was resolute in his magnanimity
and would blame no one but himself for his disaster.
For James Ballantyne he had only compassion. " I owe
it to him to say that his difficulties, as well as his advantages are owing to me." He had a grievance against
Constable, but he would not let Lockhart hint at it.
" While I live," he wrote, " I shall regret the downfall
of Constable's house, for never did there exist so intelli-
gent and so liberal an establishment. They went too
far when money was plenty, that is certain ; yet if
every author in Britain had taxed himself half a year's
income, he should have kept up the house which first
broke in upon the monopoly of the London trade, and
made letters what they now are." [2]

Nevertheless the breach with Constable could not be
healed. Scott could forgive him his old extravagant
optimism, but not his ultimate supineness, and the futile
Abbotsford mortgage rankled. He watched tenderly
over the Ballantyne interests ; James became manager
of the printing business under the Trust, and was soon
enabled to repurchase it for himself, while Scott insisted
that he should do all his printing. The Ballantynes had
been his retainers ; his galleon had towed their little
cockboat into prosperous seas ; he had given them a
merry life, and but for him they would have been
nothing but insolvent country tradesmen ; on that score
he had no reproaches. But Constable was different.
For Constable he had had admiration but no real
affection, and, however rash his own conduct had been,
Constable's had exceeded it. " He paid well and
promptly," he told Skene, " but, devil take him, it was
all spectral together. He sowed my field with one hand,
and as liberally scattered the tares with the other." [3]
Cadell broke with his partner, and Scott unhesitatingly
followed Cadell. There was a painful interview in Castle
Street, when Constable arrived, " puffing in like a steam-

[1] *Mod. Language Review*, XXIII. No. 3.
[2] Lockhart, VI. 217-18.   [3] Skene, 143.

1826 boat," and found Scott's manner unwontedly chilly. Of all his ventures he had now only the Miscellany left, and the success of this depended upon Scott's help. He pretended to be jocose, but his heartiness faltered, and he saw clearly that the end had come. With a final effort he tried to thaw the ice. " Come, come, Sir Walter," he said, " matters may come round, and I trust that you and I may yet crack a cheerful bottle of port together at Abbotsford." But Scott was adamant. " Mr Constable," he replied, " whether we ever meet again in these conditions must depend upon circumstances which yet remain to be cleared up." [1]

They rarely met again—certainly never on the old footing, though they exchanged letters of a reasonable friendliness. Here I find it difficult to acquit Scott of a defect in generosity. Constable was a suffering, indeed a dying, man, for next year he was in his grave. He had fallen from a giddy height, and now, cumbered with debt and disease, was struggling to climb a step or two out of the pit. He faced misfortune as gallantly as Scott himself, and with heavier handicaps. He had been lavish to a fault, had showered upon Scott gifts and kindnesses, and had laboured to provide him with material for the novels. He was perhaps the greatest publisher in the history of English letters. But the tribute which Scott readily paid to the bookseller he would not pay to the man. There had always been something about Constable's complacency, his bustling competence, which antagonized him, and he had never placed him, as he had placed the Ballantynes, in the circle of his friends. So he let the broken man hobble down the Castle Street stairs without a word of kindness.

" My own right hand shall pay my debt." Scott's decision was based on a clear-eyed survey of the past. He knew that he had been grievously to blame, for he had been perfectly aware of the slippery ground he had been treading. The sudden " check " had come of which he had warned Terry, and had thrown him on

[1] Skene, 145.

his back; the fates had not granted him the time on
which he had reckoned to clear his feet. He had suffered
from Constable's rashness and James Ballantyne's
slovenliness, but his main undoer had been himself.
He had gambled with his eyes open and had lost; it
remained for him with his eyes open to make restitution.
So at the age of fifty-five, already weary and in broken
health, he took upon himself a mountain of debt, and
thereby condemned himself to servitude for such years
as remained to him. It was a simple and faithful
following out of his creed, not quixotic or fantastic, but
a plain fidelity to his high standard of honour. He had
no sympathy, as he said, with the virtues " that escaped
in salt rheum, sal-volatile, and a white pocket-handker-
chief." He could not believe that rules of morality
which held in the case of the ordinary man, should be
slackened for the artist. Like his own James IV at
Flodden, he " saw the wreck his rashness wrought," and
offered his all in atonement.

Let it not be imagined that the decision was easy.
For such a man there could be no rougher ford to ride.
He had a proud spirit which loved to give and found
it hard to take; he had that fundamental trait of the
aristocrat that he was of the spending type, always
ready to hazard himself and his substance. Now he
had to submit to charity and pity and patronage. He,
who had been the first citizen of Scotland, was in the
same position as a bankrupt tradesman in the Lucken-
booths. But this downfall in worldly prestige was the
least part of his burden. The highroad of life, which
had been so crowded and coloured, was exchanged for
an alley which ran drab and monotonous to the grave.
Danger, excitement, action were the breath of his being,
but now there was for him only unfeatured drudgery.
Courage of the moss-trooping sort he had in plenty, but
this required a sterner fortitude.

There have been critics of the course he took. Thomas
Carlyle, for example, has a curious passage.—" It was a
hard trial. He met it proudly, bravely—like a brave,
proud man of the world. Perhaps there had been a

1826 prouder way still : to have owned honestly that he was
unsuccessful, then, all bankrupt, broken, in the world's
goods and repute ; and to have turned elsewhere for
some refuge. Refuge did lie elsewhere ; but it was not
Scott's course, or fashion of mind, to seek it there. To
say, Hitherto I have been all in the wrong, and this my
fame and pride, now broken, was an empty delusion and
spell of accursed witchcraft ! It was difficult to flesh
and blood ! He said, I will retrieve myself, and make
my point good yet, or die for it."[1] It is not easy to see
what the critic would be at. The pomps of the world
Scott did most whole-heartedly renounce in word and
deed ; they had never sat very near his heart. He had
no wish to restore the resplendent Abbotsford of 1825,
and asked only a shelter and a home. What he desired
was to retrieve his honour. Carlyle's passage is merely
loose rhetoric. If it means anything, it advocates some
kind of theatrical renunciation and retirement, which
would have meant that his creditors would not have
been paid, and that innocent people would have suffered
from the results of his folly. Such a course would have
been picturesque from the standpoint of the senti-
mentalist, but it would have been the shirking of a
plain duty, and repugnant to Scott's manly good sense.
He had made a blunder and it was his business to atone for
it. Had he robed himself in his literary mantle and retired
to a shieling among the hills to meditate on the transience
of human glory, there would have been no atonement.

Scott was aware of the path he had been walking and
its dangers, and therefore faced catastrophe with something of the calm of the man who has counted the risks.
He had played with fairy gold, but had not thereby lost
touch with reality. His fault was that of the gambler,
but he was ready to face the consequences. The secret
world to which he had so often had recourse had not filmed
his eyes, but it had helped perhaps to dull his conscience.
As Clarendon wrote of the Marquis of Newcastle, " the
articles of action were no sooner over, than he retired
to his delightfull Company, Musick." Scott's error cannot

---

[1] *Critical and Miscellaneous Essays,* IV. 84.

be excused on the ground of the artistic temperament 1826
which is at sea among facts ; he understood the situation
at least as well as Constable and far better than James
Ballantyne. Nevertheless there is something in Lockhart's plea that this gambling element in him, this
aversion to setting his affairs in order, was an inevitable
corollary of his genius, and, as a matter of sober history,
was largely responsible for his achievements.

Had not that adversity been preceded by the perpetual spur
of pecuniary demands, he, who began life with such quick
appetites for all its ordinary enjoyments, would never have
devoted himself to the rearing of that gigantic monument of
genius, labour and power, which his works now constitute.
The imagination, which has bequeathed so much to delight
and humanize mankind, would have developed few of its
miraculous resources except in the embellishment of his own
personal existence. The enchanted spring might have sunk
into earth with the rod which bade it gush, and left us no living
waters. We cannot understand, but we may nevertheless
respect even the strangest caprices of the marvellous combination of faculties to which our debt is so weighty. We
should try to picture to ourselves what the actual intellectual
life must have been of the author of such a series of romances.
We should ask ourselves whether, filling and discharging so
soberly and gracefully as he did the common functions of
social man, it was not, nevertheless, impossible but that he
must have passed most of his life in other worlds than ours ;
and we ought hardly to think it a grievous circumstance that
their bright visitors should have left a dazzle sometimes on
the eyes which he so gently reopened on our prosaic realities.
He had, on the whole, a command over the powers of his mind—
I mean that he could control and divert his thoughts and
reflections with a readiness, firmness and easy security of
sway—beyond what I find it possible to trace in any other
artist's recorded character and history ; but he could not
habitually fling them into the region of dreams throughout
a long series of years, and yet be expected to find a corresponding satisfaction in bending them to the less agreeable
considerations which the circumstances of any human being's
practical lot in this world must present in abundance. The
training to which he accustomed himself could not leave him
as he was when he began. He must pay the penalty, as well
as reap the glory, of this lifelong abstraction of reverie, this
self-abandonment of Fairyland.[1]

[1] VI. 120-1

III

A meeting of his creditors was held on 20th January, and his old friend Sir William Forbes was made chairman. Scott's lawyer, Mr John Gibson, put forward a scheme for a Trust deed, announcing that it was his client's " earnest desire to use every exertion in his power on behalf of his creditors, and by a diligent employment of his talents and the adoption of a strictly economical mode of life to secure as speedily as possible full payment to all concerned." The liabilities were stated at the time as £104,081 and the estate available for realization as £48,494. Among Scott's assets were included his Edinburgh house, his library and furniture, and the value of the life-rent of Abbotsford.[1] The proposal was unanimously accepted. Scott's spirits rose. He refused the suggestion of certain legal friends that an effort should be made to secure for him a seat on the Bench, on the ground that he had other duties to think of. " I am convinced," he wrote in the *Journal*, " that in three years I could do more than in the last ten, but for the mine being, I fear, exhausted. Give me my popularity—an awful postulate !—and all my present difficulties shall be a joke in five years ; and it is not lost yet, at least."

For three weeks there was a hitch. The Bank of Scotland, the second principal creditor, not only laid claim to the unfinished *Woodstock* and *Napoleon* on behalf of Constable's estate, but—what was more serious —insisted that the trustees should take proceedings to reduce the settlement of Abbotsford.[2] To this Scott would in no wise assent, for he considered that his offer to work for his creditors more than compensated for the withdrawal from them of Abbotsford.[3] In the end the Bank of Scotland withdrew its opposition ; Scott was given the house and lands of Abbotsford rent-free,

[1] *Sederunt Book.*
[2] The best legal opinion seems to have been that such an action would have failed.
[3] *Journal*, I. 123-4 ; Lockhart, VI. 224.

and allowed to retain his official incomes as Sheriff and 1826
Clerk of Court ; a Trust deed was duly signed, with as
trustees Mr Gibson, Mr James Jollie and Mr Alexander
Monypenny. The deed is in the usual form, except for
the absence of a discharge clause, since Scott asked for
no discharge ; instead it provided that after the payment of all the debts and expenses the Trustees should
reconvey to him the residue of the estate. Their first
step was to insure his life, so they bought Constable's
policy, continued the two held by the Ballantyne firm,
and took out a new one. After that they had to devote
themselves to the conduct of the printing business, for
it was a year before they got rid of it.[1]

The banks had on the whole behaved handsomely,
and Scott felt that he owed them some return. The
recent financial crisis had convinced the Government
that the whole banking system needed a drastic revision,
so it was proposed to limit the Bank of England to the
issue of notes of a value of £5 and upwards, and to take
away altogether from the private banks the privilege of
a note circulation. This latter proposal would be a
serious matter for Scotland, where coin was still very
scarce, and a disaster for the Scottish banks. On the
economic question there was much to be said for the
Scottish view, for, though the banking system was
gravely in need of reform, the weak point was not the
note-issue, which had hitherto worked well.[2] The real
motive of the Government was to introduce uniformity
in the currency of the three kingdoms, and this roused
the sleepless nationalism of the North. The national
rather than the economic significance of the proposed
change was what moved Scott, and his *Letters of Malachi
Malagrowther*, published in James Ballantyne's *Edinburgh
Weekly Journal* and issued as a pamphlet by Blackwood,
were devoted as much to the patriotic plea of the need
for preserving Scotland's individuality as to the practical
utility of the note-issue. " If you unscotch us," he told
Croker, " you will find us damned mischievous English-
men." The pamphlet, modelled to some extent on

---

[1] *Sederunt Book.*   [2] Kerr, *Hist. of Banking in Scotland,* 177, etc.

1826 Swift's *Drapier's Letters*, is written with immense gusto and is not only one of the most "literary" pieces of economic writing before Bagehot, but reveals a clear understanding of the commercial world. It created a great stir, and led to the withdrawal of the scheme so far as the Scottish banks were concerned. Scott was acutely aware of the irony of the situation. "Whimsical enough that when I was trying to animate Scotland against the currency bill, John Gibson brought me the Deed of Trust, assigning my whole estate, to be subscribed by me ; so that I am turning patriot, and taking charge of the affairs of the country, on the very day I was proclaiming myself incapable of managing my own."[1]

Malachi made trouble with Scott's political allies. Lord Melville, who was in charge of Scottish affairs, was furious ; Canning attacked him in the House of Commons ; Croker was set up by the Government to reply to the pamphlet, which he did with little effect. The Whigs were no better pleased, for they distrusted Scott's nationalism and objected to their pet topic of economics being handled so light-heartedly. "Poets," Cockburn wrote primly, "may be excused for being bad political economists. If a nice question of monetary or commercial policy could be settled by jokes, Malachi would be a better economist than Adam Smith. His lamentation over the loss of Scotch sinecures was very injudicious, and did neither him nor such of these things as remained any good. He was mentioned in Parliament by his own friends with less respect than one would ever wish to be shown him."[2] But for the criticism of friends or opponents Scott cared nothing. "I have, in my odd *sans souciance* character, a good handful of meal from the grist of the Jolly Miller." The knowledge that he could still make men listen to him and influence the course of affairs did much to restore his self-respect ; the bankrupt had not killed the citizen. "On the whole," he wrote, "I am glad of this brulzie, as far as I am concerned ; people will not dare talk of me as an

[1] *Journal*, I. 133.　　　　[2] *Mem.*, 433-4

object of pity—no more ' poor manning.' Who asks how 1826
many punds Scots the old champion has in his pocket when

> He set a bugle to his mouth,
> And blew sae loud and shrill,
> The trees in greenwood shook thereat,
> Sae loud rang ilka hill.[1]

IV

On 15th March Scott left Castle Street, which had
been his Edinburgh home for twenty-eight years, with
the words of Macrimmon's lament on his lips, " *Cha til
mi tulidh*—I return no more." At Abbotsford he found
a changed establishment. Willie Laidlaw was no more
at Kaeside ; Tom Purdie was no longer farm-bailiff
since there was nothing to farm, and had become personal
attendant ; one old labourer, Willie Straiton, had taken
to his bed at the news of his master's misfortunes, and
had never risen again. But there was a tumult of dogs
to welcome him, and, as he made his familiar rounds
amid the March snow-showers, he hugged to his heart
the thought that his home was still his own. He had
won peace of mind, whatever the burden of the future,
for he knew the worst. There was even a pleasure in
economizing—in keeping to his official salary and paying
out of it to his wife her modest housekeeping allowance,
and in looking for butter for his bread to an occasional
magazine article. There was comfort, too, in the solitude
after the bustle in which he had lived, for he felt less
able for company. For long he had been constantly
tired and had got into the habit of drowsing in Court ;
he had been sleepless of nights, too, had been tormented
by rheumatism and indigestion, and had lately been
suffering from an alarming fluttering of the heart. He
could resume his old unflagging habits of work, but he
had little margin left for other things, so he courted
solitude.

The love of solitude was with me a passion of early youth ;
when in my teens I used to fly from company to indulge in

---

1 *Journal*, I. 141.

visions and airy castles of my own, the disposal of ideal wealth and the exercise of imaginary power. The feeling prevailed even till I was eighteen, when love and ambition awakening with other passions threw me more into society, from which I have, however, at times withdrawn myself, and have been always glad to do so. I have risen from the feast satisfied. . . . This is a feeling without the least tinge of misanthropy which I always consider as a kind of blasphemy of a shocking description. If God bears with the very worst of us we may surely endure each other. If thrown into society I always have, and always will endeavour to bring pleasure with me, at least to show willingness to please. But for all this I had rather live alone, and I wish my appointment, so convenient otherwise, did not require my going to Edinburgh. But this must be, and in my little lodging I will be lonely enough.[1]

His routine of life was much what it had always been. By seven he was at his desk, and, having finished *Woodstock*, he forthwith began the *Chronicles of the Canongate*. In the afternoon he walked with Tom Purdie and the wolf-hound puppy which Glengarry had given him in Maida's place, " chewing the cud of sweet and bitter fancy." It was mainly bitter, for to the downfall of his worldly fortunes there was added a gnawing anxiety about those he loved best. The news from London was bad, and the Lockharts' boy was visibly losing strength. The frail bright child had twined himself round Scott's heart more than any of his own more robust offspring, and, since he could no longer visit him at Chiefswood, he tortured himself with memories. " The poor dear love had so often a slow fever that, when it pressed its little lips to mine, I always foreboded to my own heart what all I fear are now aware of." In April Laidlaw lost an infant, and Scott watched its funeral with a quickened sense of man's mortality. The *Journal* contains reflections new to one who had hitherto bustled gallantly through the world.

I saw the poor child's funeral from a distance. Ah, that distance ! What a magician for conjuring up scenes of joy and sorrow, smoothing all asperities, reconciling all incongruities, veiling all abnormalities, softening every coarseness,

doubling every effect by the influence of the imagination. A 1826
Scottish wedding should be seen at a distance ; the gay band
of the dancers just distinguished amid the elderly group of
the spectators, the glass held high, and the distant cheers as
it is swallowed should be only a sketch, not a finished Dutch
picture, when it becomes brutal and boorish. Scotch psalmody,
too, should be heard at a distance. The grunt and the snuffle
and the whine and the scream should be all blended in the
deep and distant sound which, rising and falling like the
Eolian harp, may have some title to be called the praise of
our Maker. Even so the distant funeral, the few mourners on
horseback with their plaids wrapped around them—the father
heading the procession as they enter the river, and pointing
out the ford by which his darling is to be carried on the last
long road—not one of the subordinate figures in discord with
the general tone of the incident—seeming just accessories and
no more—this *is* affecting.[1]

But presently came death unsoftened by distance.
His wife had joined him at Abbotsford, with Anne a
pale ghost from long nursing. She was suffering from
asthma and dropsy, and the Edinburgh doctors gave
little hope. Scott left Abbotsford on 11th May to resume
his Court work, and she was too ill to say good-bye.
He took up his quarters in shabby, bug-infested lodgings
in North St David Street, observing with Touchstone,
" When I was at home I was in a better place." Four
days later he had news that his wife was dead. It was
his first great intimate bereavement, and for the moment
it had a shattering effect on a spirit worn down with
toils and cares. He could not sleep, and his children
found him weeping. If his wife had been a stranger
to his innermost world she had shared most loyally
in his normal life, had been his counsellor and the
repository of all his plans, had watched solicitously
over his health, and had been a brave, mirthful and
kindly companion. He had come during the years to
feel for her that close affection which springs from long
comradeship. All his happiest memories were linked
with her presence, and her very foibles were endeared
in the recollection. Small wonder that he felt himself
naked and stripped, for here he had lost more than

[1] I. 172-3.

1826 fortune.   He tells his *Journal* that his heart must break.

> I have seen her.   The figure I beheld is, and is not, my Charlotte—my thirty years' companion.   There is the same symmetry of form, though those limbs were rigid which were once so gracefully elastic—but that yellow masque, with pinched features, which seems to mock life rather than emulate it, can it be the face that was once so full of lively expression ? I will not look on it again. . . . If I write long in this way, I shall write down my resolution, which I should rather write up, if I could.   I wonder how I shall do with the larger portion of thoughts which were hers for thirty years.   I expect they will be hers yet for a long time at least. . . .
>
> Another day, and a bright one to the external world, again opens on us, the air soft, and the flowers smiling, and the leaves glittering.   They cannot refresh her to whom mild weather was a natural enjoyment.   Cerements of lead and of wood already hold her ; cold earth must have her soon.   But it is not my Charlotte, it is not the bride of my youth, the mother of my children, that will be laid away among the ruins of Dryburgh, which we have so often visited in gaiety and pastime.   No, no.   She is sentient and conscious of my emotions somewhere—somehow ;   where, we cannot tell ;   how, we cannot tell ;   yet would I not at this moment renounce the mysterious yet certain hope that I shall see her in a better world for all that this world can give me. . . .
>
> I have been to her room : there was no voice in it, no stirring ; the pressure of the coffin was visible on the bed, but it had been removed elsewhere ;   all was neat as she loved it, but all was calm—calm as death.   I remembered the last sight of her ; she raised herself in bed and tried to turn her eyes after me, and said, with a sort of smile, " You all have such melancholy faces."   They were the last words I ever heard her utter, and I hurried away, for she did not seem quite conscious of what she said.   When I returned, immediately before departure, she was in a deep sleep.   It is deeper now.   This was but seven days since.
>
> They are arranging the chamber of death ; that which was long the apartment of connubial happiness, and of whose arrangements (better than in richer houses) she was so proud. They are treading fast and thick.   For weeks you could have heard a footfall.   Oh, my God ! [1]

These are the secular laments for the dead, but they were confided only to the *Journal*.   Scott exerted himself

[1] *Journal*, I. 193-5.

to comfort his sons, who had arrived from Ireland and 1826
Oxford, and to tend the drooping Anne, and for the rest
he turned to his work.   His wife's death had made his
material losses shrink to their proper proportions, and
he could face the world again, to use his own metaphor,
like the Bass Rock, and not like the waves that broke
on it.   The " stalk of carle-hemp " was firm in him, and
he choked down all unavailing regrets.   " The melancholy
hours of yesterday must not return.   To encourage that
dreamy state of incapacity is to resign all authority
over the mind, and I have been wont to say—' My
mind to me a kingdom is.'   I am rightful monarch ;
and, God to aid, I will not be dethroned by any rebellious
passion that may rear its standard against me." [1]

But it was to be a lonely kingdom.

[1] *Journal*, II. 201-2.

Chapter XI

SERVITUDE

(1826–1831)

I

1826 ALL of *Woodstock* was written in a time of anxiety, and much of it after the blow had fallen, in Scott's first desperate effort to begin the work of restitution. Yet the book bears no mark of this sad preoccupation. A certain tenderness in the picture of the old cavalier squire whose world has been upturned, some traits of the dutiful daughter, may reflect his own case, and the opening words of the last chapter seem to be a cry wrung from the heart—" Years rush by us like the wind. We see not whence the eddy comes, nor whitherward it is tending, and we seem ourselves to witness their flight without a sense that we are changed ; and yet Time is beguiling man of his strength, as the winds rob the woods of their foliage." But for the rest the book is amazingly light-hearted, and the narrative, hammered out with a perplexed mind, is notably compact. *Woodstock* ranks high among the novels for the architecture of its plot ; we know that Scott several times came to a standstill in writing it, and saw no solution for the puzzle he had invented, but the brownies who worked at the back of his head were kind to him. A great successor paid him the compliment of borrowing most of his machinery, for James III in *Esmond* is Charles, and Beatrix is Alice Lee, and Lockwood is Joceline, and Frank Castlewood is Albert Lee, and Colonel Esmond is Markham Everard. Nassau Senior's criticism, that Scott errs in making his chief figures personages of the first historical importance, is not really relevant, for Cromwell and Charles II are

300

introduced in incidents outside the main march of their 1826
familiar history. Scott was fortunate too in the setting
of his tale. There is something in the wide woodlands
and the soft muffled hills of the Oxford country which
appeals strongly to the Borderer, as the present writer
can bear witness, and he has caught its secret magic.
Also in the background he had what he loved, a great,
old, ruinous house. *Woodstock* is almost the best written
of the novels, and—apart from the circumstances of its
composition, which make it an astonishing achievement
—it has the charm of a wise and mellow philosophy.
If it is not to be ranked with the greatest, that is
only because it rarely touches the deeper springs of
life.

The book is a swift succession of dramatic episodes.
It opens brilliantly, with Trusty Tompkins' discourse
from the pulpit of Woodstock church—no man could
make a better sermon than Scott in any vein. The scenes
when Cromwell at Windsor looks on the Vandyke portrait
of the dead king, when Everard and Charles face each
other with drawn blades, when Cromwell's heavy foot
is heard on the stair of Everard's lodging, when Wildrake's
sword breaks on the Lord Protector's hidden armour,
when Tompkins dies at the hands of Joceline, when
Albert Lee outfaces Cromwell with the text " Had Zimri
peace who slew his master ? "—all are in a high key
of romantic drama. In the comedy vein I need only
cite the rabbling of the Parliament commissioners by
the Woodstock ghost, and the fight between the tipsy
Wildrake and the parson Rochecliffe. And behind them,
as always with Scott, is a background of sagely conceived
history. The figures are no puppets drawn from fancy
but true products of their times, historically as well as
dramatically significant. To take one instance—nothing
could be better than the sketch of the elements which
made up Cromwell's following ; Desborough the middle-
class adventurer ; Bletson the superstitious agnostic—
" The devils, we are assured, believe and tremble ; but
on earth there are many who, in worse plight than even
the natural children of perdition, tremble without

believing, and fear even while they blaspheme ";
Harrison, who looked forward to commanding a reserve
of pikes at Armageddon ; and, among the commonalty, Pearson the ex-pirate, Corporal Humgudgeon, and
the merciful Zerubbabel Robins. How acute, too, is
the exposition of the politics of the moderates, like
Everard, who accepted Cromwell as the only alternative
to anarchy.

There is no slackness of drawing in the characters.
Sir Henry Lee is a familiar figure, but not the less vivid
on that account, Alice Lee is fantastic only to such as
disbelieve in the courage of the pure in heart, and Markham Everard is saved from priggishness by his occasional
fits of bad temper and his loyalty to Wildrake. Trusty
Tompkins is a subtle portrait of a type of rogue common
enough at the time, and in Holdenough Scott has drawn
the honest, pragmatic English Presbyterian with truth
and kindliness. Charles is one of his royal successes,
infinitely to be preferred to the stock figure of *Peveril*.
As for Cromwell, if he is not altogether the real man, he
is nearer historical truth than any picture of him before
Carlyle's. Scott recognized the strange elements in his
nature, his mysticism, his power of self-deception ; and
in his communings with Pearson and his final magnanimity, showed that he understood also the greatness of
that lonely spirit. But to my mind the best of the
characters is Roger Wildrake, " gentleman, of Squattlesea
Mere, in the moist county of Lincoln." He is the rake-
helly cavalier of all time, bibulous, blasphemous, heroic,
and endearing. Wherever he turns his bleared eye the
narrative marches and the dialogue briskens. Take this
as a specimen, when he is striving to shape his mouth to
the Puritan speech :—

> " Are there any more news from Worcester fight ? " asked
> Everard, in a tone so serious that it imposed on his companion,
> who replied in his genuine character—
> " Worse ! d——n me, worse an hundred times than reported
> —totally broken. Noll hath certainly sold himself to the
> devil, and his lease will have an end one day—that is all our
> present comfort."
> " What ! and would this be your answer to the first red-coat

who asked the question ? " said Everard. "Methinks you 1826
would find a speedy passport to the next *corps de garde*."

"Nay, nay," answered Wildrake, "I thought you asked me
in your own person. Lack-a-day ! a great mercy—a glorifying
mercy—a crowning mercy—a vouchsafing—an uplifting—I
profess the malignants are scattered from Dan to Beersheba—
smitten, hip and thigh, even until the going down of the sun."

"Heard you aught of Colonel Thornhaugh's wounds ? "

"He is dead," answered Wildrake ; "that's one comfort—
the roundheaded rascal ! Nay hold ! it was but a trip of the
tongue—I meant the sweet godly youth."

"And hear you aught of the young man, King of Scotland,
as they call him ? " said Everard.

"Nothing, but that he is hunted like a partridge on the
mountains. May God deliver him and confound his enemies !
Zoons, Mark Everard, I can fool it no longer."

II

The summer in Mrs Brown's lodging-house was a
comfortless business, though his old butler Dalgleish
insisted on attending him and looking after his needs.
These were modest enough—a ploughman's dinner of
broth and boiled beef, relieved by little luxuries like a
bit of Gruyère cheese, which he would buy for himself
on his way home. June and July were very hot, and
outside the gutters stank and drunken chairmen quarrelled. Scott slept badly, and was haunted by dreams
of his dead wife ; but neither the discomfort of his
environment nor his bodily frailty was allowed to
interfere with his work. In former days his evenings
had been given up to his family and friends or to light
reading in an armchair, but now he seemed to grudge
every minute not spent at his desk. Imaginative writing,
which had once been done " at large leisure in noble
mornings," was now the weary task of the small hours.
His only exercise was his daily walk to the Parliament
House, and his return through Princes Street Gardens,
for which he had a private key, and the only break
which he permitted himself in his task seems to have
been occasional meetings with old friends and acts of
charity. Yet the toil was not the martyrdom it sounds.

1826 He loved the act of composition, and in the midst of his
labours wrote copiously in his *Journal*; and he had the
satisfaction of seeing his pile of work mounting steadily
and of knowing that every page meant a lessening of his
burden.

In the middle of July he went gladly to Abbotsford,
a little surprised at the eagerness with which he faced
again that house of sad memories. " Nature has given
me a kind of buoyancy, I know not what to call it, that
mingled even with my deepest afflictions and most
gloomy hours. I have a secret pride—I fancy it will be
so most truly termed, which impels me to mix with my
distresses strange fragments of mirth, which have no
mirth in them." A visit from Walter and Jane cheered
him, and the whole family made a pilgrimage to Drumlanrig. He found healthy exercise in thinning his
plantations, though the work soon tired him. " One
sure thing is, that all wise men will soon contrive to lay
aside inclination when performance grows toilsome. I
have hobbled over many a rough heugh in my day—no
wonder if I must sing at last—

> Thus says the auld man to the aik tree
> Sair failed, hinny, since I kenn'd thee.

And he could still get entertainment from the foppery
of the world. Sir John Sinclair, who ranked with Lord
Buchan as the most preposterous of living Scotsmen—
Scott's name for him was the " Cavaliero Jackasso "—
wrote to him proposing to arrange a marriage with the
widowed Duchess of Roxburgh, though Lady Scott was
scarcely four months in her grave.[1]

In the late autumn he found it necessary to go to
London and Paris, in the interests of his *Napoleon*, so,
when he had assured himself that he was in no danger
of arrest from his English creditors, he set out with Anne
on October 12th. They visited the Morritts at Rokeby,
and Scott was delighted with the unchangingness of old

---

[1] *Journal*, I. 254-5. *P. L. B.*, 130. There were other proposals of the kind,
such as that in July 1830 when a young man announced that his sister was in
love with Scott. *Journal*, II. 348.

England; " one race of red-nosed innkeepers are gone,
and their widows, eldest sons and head-waiters exercise
hospitality in their room with the same bustle and
importance." In London he saw many of his friends,
gave sittings to painters and sculptors, pulled various
political strings on behalf of Lockhart and Charles, and
—a proof of the diversity of his interests—breakfasted
one day with George IV at the royal cottage in Windsor
Park, and supped·next night on oysters and broiled bones
with Terry above the Adelphi theatre.

On October 26th he set out for France. Calais stirred
unavailing regrets :—" Lost, as all know, by the bloody
papist bitch (one must be vernacular when on French
ground) Queen Mary, of red-hot memory. I would
rather she had burned a score more of bishops." His
fame had not declined in Paris. The fish-wives from the
Halles presented him with a bouquet like a maypole ;
at the Odéon he saw the opera based on *Ivanhoe*, and
found it strange to hear the words, which he had dictated
to Laidlaw in the agony of his cramp, recited in a foreign
tongue ; at the Tuileries Charles X, as he passed into
chapel, stopped to say " a few civil words," a civility
which Scott was to repay when that monarch was again in
exile in Holyrood.[1] He had talks with Marshal Macdonald,
and Marmont, and Fitz-James, the great-grandson
of James II. But Paris was too full of ghosts. At
the British Embassy he remembered Castlereagh and
departed glories. " I have seen in these rooms the
Emperor Alexander, Platoff, Schwarzenberg, old Blücher,
Fouché, and many a maréchal whose truncheon had
guided armies—all now at peace, without subjects,
without dominion, and where their past life, perhaps,
seems but the recollection of a feverish dream."

He was back in London on November 10th, and Anne
and he spent a busy fortnight. He arranged for Charles's
nomination to the Foreign Office, saw much of Samuel
Rogers, Theodore Hook and Allan Cunningham, met for
the first time Fanny Burney, had long conversations
with the Duke of Wellington anent his *Napoleon*, and

[1] Lockhart, VII. 224-7.

1826 was entertained by Croker and Peel at ministerial banquets. On his way north he breakfasted with Charles at Brasenose and found to his grief that the beauties of Oxford had lost their charm for him, and that he thought more about luncheon and the excellent ale of University College. " Remembering the ecstatic feelings with which I visited Oxford more than twenty-five years since, I was surprised at the comparative indifference with which I revisited the same scenes. Reginald Heber, then composing his Prize Poem, and imping his wings for a long flight of honourable distinction, is now dead in a foreign land—Hodgson and other able men all entombed. The towers and halls remain, but the voices which fill them are of modern days. Besides, the eye becomes satiated with sights, as the full soul loathes the honeycomb."

Edinburgh was reached on November 27th. He had secured better lodgings in a house in Walker Street, and he sat himself down to a winter of unremitting toil. The weather was bleak, and he found his fingers cramped with chilblains, he suffered grievously from rheumatism and bile, and camomile poultices alternated with pen and ink. He had no one to look after him but old Dalgleish, and he remembered sadly how he had once enjoyed little illnesses when his wife was there to nurse him. The note of mortality in the *Journal* becomes more clamant. " There is some new subject of complaint every moment ; your sicknesses come thicker and thicker ; your comforting or sympathizing friends fewer and fewer ; for why should they sorrow for the course of nature ? . . . The best is, the long halt will arrive at last and cure all."[1] He realized the shortness of the time permitted him and the steady ebbing of his strength.

O Lord, what are we—lords of nature ? Why, a tile drops from a housetop, which an elephant would not feel more than the fall of a sheet of pasteboard, and there lies his lordship. Or something of inconceivably minute origin, the pressure of a bone, or the inflammation of a particle of the brain takes place, and the emblem of the Deity destroys himself or someone

---

[1] *Journal*, I. 325.

else. We hold our health and our reason on terms slighter 1827
than one would desire were it in their choice to hold an
Irish cabin.[1]

During the Christmas holiday at Abbotsford he struggled
with pain and overwork, and December closed with
sombre thoughts.

> It must be allowed that the regular recurrence of annual
> festivals among the same individuals has, as life advances,
> something in it that is melancholy. We meet on such occasions
> like the survivors of some perilous expedition, wounded and
> weakened ourselves, and looking through the diminished ranks
> of those who remain, while we think of those who are no more.
> Or they are like the feasts of the Caribs, in which they held
> that the pale and speechless phantoms of the deceased appeared
> and mingled with the living.[2]

The year 1827 brought improved health and spirits.
For one thing he began to sleep better, and he got a
chamois-leather knee-cap which eased his rheumatism.[3]
He resumed dining out in moderation, and on February
23rd took the chair at the celebrated Theatrical Fund
dinner, where he first publicly admitted the authorship
of the Waverley Novels. This had long been an open
secret, and the formation of the Trust, which revealed
all his dealings with Constable, had finally established
it. But, since this was his first public dinner since his
disaster, Lord Meadowbank, who was to propose his
health, wished to make a definite announcement. Scott
agreed, only bidding him not say much about so old a
story. Meadowbank's speech was received with wild
applause, and Scott replied gracefully, admitting the
charge, and adding " The wand is now broken and
the book buried." The affair made a great sensation,
but Scott seems to have considered it of little importance.[4]

Meantime he was toiling prodigiously at *Napoleon* and
the first *Chronicles of the Canongate* for his creditors, and
at magazine articles to earn a little pocket-money for

---

[1] *Journal*, I. 316.   [2] *Ibid.*, I. 329-30.
[3] Scott was a most careless patient, for he was always getting caught in the
rain and returning home dripping, as he said, " like a water-kelpy."
[4] Lockhart, VII. 15-20. *P. L. B.*, 114.

1827 himself. He was now living on his small private income and his official salaries. He had got James Hogg's nephew Robert as an amanuensis, and on a day when he was free from Court would dictate from six in the morning till six in the evening, breakfast and luncheon being served to him as he worked. Politics had begun to interest him again, for in January Lord Liverpool had resigned, and in April Canning, after breaking with Peel and Wellington, became Prime Minister. Scott's sympathies were on the whole with Canning, though he differed reluctantly from his idol the Duke.

At long last he finished *Napoleon*, and the book was published in nine volumes in the middle of June. He had begun it two years before, but it was virtually the work of twelve months, and it contained as much matter as any five of the novels put together. Its first two editions produced no less than £18,000 for his creditors. It was well received by the public, and for the most part neglected by the critics—which was what he had foreseen, since it was not condemnatory enough to satisfy the Tories or rhapsodical enough for the Whigs, and the pedants of history looked askance at this romancer who had raided their preserves. For critics and pedants Scott cared not at all. " I see you have got a critic in the *Athenæum*," he once wrote to Lockhart, " Pray don't take the least notice of so trumpery a fellow. There is a custom among the South American Indians to choose their chief by the length of time during which he is able to sustain a temporary interment in an owl's nest. Literary respect and eminence is won by similar powers of endurance." As for the pedants he classed them with schoolmasters, of whom he wrote that " no schoolmaster whatsoever has existed without his having some private reserve of extreme absurdity." [1]

Napoleon being off the stocks, he promptly began *The Tales of a Grandfather*, the history of Scotland as told to Hugh Littlejohn. This was to be his own book and not the creditors', for he considered it a *parergon* outside his contract, and the Trust good-naturedly

[1] Lang, II. 23, 31.

agreed. Sophia and her children were at Portobello for 1827
the summer, and when vacation came he found to his
delight that the sick boy was strong enough to ride with
him in the Abbotsford grounds. Scott had acquired a
horse known as Douce Davie on which he ambled about
the countryside, a sedate beast whose one foible was
that, when drinking from a burn, he was apt to lie
down in the water. That autumn was enlivened by a
visit of Adolphus, and by an excursion to Durham to
meet the Duke of Wellington. He felt more vigour in
his bones, for two events occurred to jog him out of his
servitude.

The first was the rumour of a cartel on its way from
General Gourgaud, who had taken offence at some plain
speaking in *Napoleon*. Scott rose joyfully to the occasion
—to the scandal of some of his more lady-like biographers ;
the scribe had had too long the upper hand and here was
something for the rough-rider.

> It is clear to me that what is least forgiven in a man of any
> mark or likelihood is want of that article blackguardly called
> pluck. All the fine qualities of genius cannot make amends
> for it. We are told the genius of poets especially is irreconcilable
> with this species of grenadier accomplishment. If so, *quel chien
> de génie !*

He selected Will Clerk as his second, and saw that
Napoleon's pistols, which he possessed, were in order.
But the challenge never arrived. Scott sent to the press
a careful statement of the case, Gourgaud made a furious
rejoinder, and the matter dropped.

Upon the risk of a bullet followed the risk of im-
prisonment for debt. Two of the Ballantyne bills,
amounting to £1760, had come into the hands of a Jew
broker called Abud—let the unhallowed name be remembered !—who refused to accept the arrangement of
the Trust and proceeded to take out " letters of horning "
against the debtor. Scott had two courses open to him ;
he could let himself be sequestrated, thereby preventing
Abud from obtaining any preference, or he could seek
refuge in a debtor's sanctuary from Abud's diligence.
To protect his other creditors, he decided upon the latter,

1827 and made preparations for taking up his quarters in the precincts of Holyroodhouse. There was some reason to believe that Abud had acquired the bills in the course of an usurious transaction, and the Trustees moved for a bill of suspension in the Court of Session. They lost their case, but in the meantime the matter was settled by Sir William Forbes paying the claim, and ranking for the amount as an ordinary creditor—a fact which was only known after Sir William's death.[1] So Scott had not to pack his traps and move down the Canongate, and the young Walter, who arrived in haste from Ireland breathing slaughter against all Hebrews, had no occasion for his valour.

Gourgaud and Abud between them did Scott a world of good in rousing him from the mechanical stupor in which he wrought. He was in danger of becoming a mere writing automaton. The first series of the *Chronicles of the Canongate* appeared in the early winter and was not well received. In the second series, immediately begun, Scott proposed to include more short stories, but both Cadell and Ballantyne objected and he embarked instead on *The Fair Maid of Perth*. Meanwhile the *Tales of a Grandfather* were running smoothly from his pen. " This morning was damp, dripping and unpleasant ; so I even made a work of necessity, and set to the *Tales* like a dragon. I murdered Maclellan of Bomby at the Thrieve Castle ; stabbed the Black Douglas in the town of Stirling ; astonished King James before Roxburgh ; and stifled the Earl of Mar in his bath in the Canongate." In Edinburgh that winter he leased the house of Jane's mother, No. 6 Shandwick Place, and the Abbotsford footman, John Nicholson, replaced Dalgleish as his attendant. In December the *Tales* appeared and were more warmly received than any of the novels since *Ivanhoe*.

This eased his private finances, and he had also the comforting thought that he was doing well by his creditors. The Constable trustees proposed to put on the market the copyrights of the novels owned by that estate. Now it was essential that the copyrights should

---

[1] *Sederunt Book* ; Lockhart, VII. 83-87 ; *Journal*, II. 57, etc.

be in the hands of Scott's own Trust in view of future 1827 annotated editions. At the auction they were bought by Cadell for £8500, a joint purchase on behalf of Scott and himself. Two days before the Trust had paid its first dividend—six shillings in the pound. In two years Scott had won for it £40,000, which meant that he who had made about £10,000 a year when he wrought for himself, had been earning at the rate of £20,000 a year for his creditors. He began to see light far ahead in the fog, and his Christmas reflections in the *Journal* have a sober contentment.

> If I die in the harness, which is very likely, I shall die with honour ; if I achieve my task I shall have the thanks of all concerned . . . and the approbation of my own conscience . . . I am now perfectly well in constitution, and though I am still in troubled waters, yet I am rowing with the tide, and less than the continuation of my exertions of 1827 may, with God's blessing, carry me successfully through 1828, when we may gain a more open sea, if not exactly a safe port. . . . For all these great blessings it becomes me well to be thankful to God, who in His good time and good pleasure sends me good as well as evil.[1]

III

If *Napoleon* is judged in relation to the circumstances of its composition it must appear as one of Scott's most remarkable achievements. It was task-work, no doubt, but a prodigious feat of task-work. Most of it was written in haste, with a mind overwrought and a heart distracted by cares. The materials were not available for a full and accurate chronicle, even had Scott had the capacity and the desire to use them. It is avowedly history for the ordinary reader and not for the scholar, and in such work the qualities necessary are a just perspective of view, a well-proportioned narrative, and vigour and colour in the telling. The first the book possesses in a high degree, for it might have been written after the lapse of centuries instead of almost under the shadow of the terror which for twenty years overhung Europe. Scott

---

[1] *Journal*, II. 94, 98-99.

is dispassionate about Napoleon; he thinks him a bad man but a very great one, and he labours to do justice to that greatness. His comments are always dignified, judicious and detached. " The term of hostility," he wrote, " is ended when the battle has been won and the foe exists no longer." The architecture, too, of the book is good, amazingly good considering the manner of its production. The events of the life are in due proportion, and the expository matter is skilfully interwoven. It was this sanity of outlook and clarity of exposition which attracted Goethe. " What could now be more delightful to me," he wrote in his *Kunst und Alterthum,* " than leisurely and calmly to sit down and listen to the discourses of such a man, while clearly, truly, and with all the skill of a great artist he recalls to me the incidents on which through life I have meditated."

The weakness lies in the third of the qualities I have cited. No one, I think, can read the nine volumes in the " Miscellaneous Works " without a good deal of admiration and a good deal of boredom. The inspiration flags, as it might not have flagged had Scott kept to his first intention to write something on the scale of Southey's *Nelson*; the colours grow dim, the story limps, the end is reached many times before the last page. Scott, had the chance been given him, might have written a great piece of biographical history on some topic which warmly engaged his affections; but Napoleon was not a potent enough inspiration to keep his interest at stretch over so long a period. For such a task there was required the emotion of either worship or hate. What this lack meant can be seen if we turn to Hazlitt's *Life*, with which Scott's is properly compared. Both are productions of men of genius; both are on a vast scale; neither is the work of a careful scholar. In point of manners and equipoise Scott's is incomparably the better. Hazlitt is the perfervid Radical who is rapt into an ecstasy of adoration at Napoleon's name and is grossly unjust to his opponents. He can write such a sentence as this of Sir John Moore's death :—" He was buried on the ramparts and ' left alone with his glory '—such as it

was ! " But he has a creed which he holds with a 1827
passionate conviction, and a man to exemplify it who
commands all his loyalties. Hence, with all its ill-
breeding, false rhetoric and absurdity, it has a vitality
denied to Scott's mellower task-work.

Very different is the case with *The Tales of a Grandfather*. Here Scott is writing about what he knew and
liked best, the long pageant of Scottish history. Since
he is writing for his darling grandson he curbs his prejudices, and he admits a little, a very little instruction
to balance the heroics. " When you find anything a
little too hard for you to understand at this moment,"
he tells Hugh Littlejohn in the preface, " you must
consider that you will be better able to make out the
sense a year or two afterwards ; or perhaps you may
make a great exertion and get at its meaning, just as
you might contrive to reach something placed upon a
high shelf by standing on your tiptoes." The book is
never written down to children, but it is all within the
comprehension of a child's mind, for the narrative is easy
and natural with the sound of a living voice behind it,
and every paragraph has something to catch the youthful
fancy. When Scott wrote, the history of Scotland had
not been attempted on scientific lines, and he often
accepts traditions which later research has exposed.
Nevertheless he gives us truth, the truth of spirit, and
a noble impartiality. Hugh Littlejohn, like many a
child since, was properly excited by it all, and set out
to dirk his young brother with a pair of scissors. But
he could not away with the instructive matter. His
views were communicated through Mrs Hughes of
Uffington : " He very much dislikes the chapter on
Civilization, and it is his desire that you will never say
anything more about it, for he dislikes it extremely."

In *St Ronan's Well* Scott seemed to be on the verge
of acquiring a new manner and entering fields hitherto
regarded as foreign to his genius. In the third work
published during 1827 we are tantalized by the same
hint of unsuspected gifts, flowering too late in the autumn
of his days to come to fruit. The first series of *The*

LIBRARY ST. MARY'S COLLEGE

1827 *Chronicles of the Canongate*, a collection of three short
stories, is chiefly notable for the figure of the narrator.
" The Highland Widow " is a picture of the disruption
of the old Highland life after the 'Forty-five, and, if
Elspeth MacTavish is perhaps too reminiscent of Helen
MacGregor, there is tragedy in her stubborn savagery
and the son Hamish is drawn with sober faithfulness.
In " The Two Drovers " we have a glimpse into the
perverse but logical Highland ethics and an unforgettable
picture of the old world of the drove-roads. There is no
trace of falsetto in Robin Oig, and his tragic fate is made
as inevitable as the return of the seasons. In these
stories Scott brought to the study of the Highland
character a new psychological insight. " The Surgeon's
Daughter " contains an admirable portrait of a country
doctor, based on his old friend Dr Ebenezer Clarkson of
Selkirk. The charm of the piece lies in the contrast
between the homely world of Middlemas and the mysterious East, and, though Scott's knowledge of India
was wholly at second hand, he succeeds in creating a
sense of the exotic, and in the scene where Hyder Ali
reveals himself he achieves a stirring *coup de théâtre*.
But we have the feeling throughout that he does not
take his puppets quite seriously ; they are Croftangry's
creations, and with Croftangry he is mainly concerned.

It is the narrator of the tale, and the narrator's friends,
that give the book its virtue. Scott is writing from his
own shadowed retrospect. Croftangry is himself, and
Mrs Bethune Baliol has much of his own mother and of
his childhood's friend, Mrs Anne Murray Keith. Here
there is none of the trait-portraiture, the rejoicing
comedy " humours " of the earlier novels. The figures
of Croftangry's world are seen in a cold autumnal light
which has lost the riotous colours of summer. All of
them—Croftangry, Mrs Bethune Baliol, Christie Steele,
Fairscribe, Janet MacEvoy—are done with a sure touch
and with a delicate and humorous wistfulness. Croftangry himself is a convincing figure of regret and dis-
illusioned philosophy, and Scott never wrote anything
more moving than the scenes where the returning exile

LIBRARY ST. MARY'S COLLEGE

finds his old friend the lawyer a helpless paralytic, and **1828**
where his mother's housekeeper shivers his palace of
dreams. Here there is a new philosophy, a " Winter's
Tale " philosophy, and a new technique. He paints in
finer strokes and in quieter tints, but with an economy
and a certainty which recall some of the best work of
Tourgeniev. The ebbing of the currents of life seems to
have left him with clearer eyes.

IV

The year 1828 was for Scott a period of better health,
renewed vitality and a moderate cheerfulness. He was
busy now with *The Fair Maid of Perth* which was
published in April, with its successor *Anne of Geierstein*,
with more *Tales of a Grandfather* for which the public
appetite was insatiable, and with his prefaces and notes
for what he called his *Opus Magnum*, the complete
reprint of the novels which Cadell's purchase of the
copyrights had made possible. There were also various
magazine articles, and two sermons of irreproachable
orthodoxy issued by Colburn, the fashionable London
bookseller.[1] The tale of these last is curious. He had a
friend, Huntly Gordon, the son of a half-pay officer in
Brussels, who had entered the ministry, found that his
deafness prevented his getting a charge, and had been
doing hack-work for the Ballantynes. Gordon was
chronically impecunious, and, in order to clear a debt,
sought and obtained Scott's permission to publish two
sermons which the latter had written for him when he
was taking orders. In estimating Scott's labours we
must not forget the demands which his unfailing charity
made on his time and his purse. More than half his
correspondence was devoted to helping lame dogs, and
in his worst days he managed to scrape together a pound
or two for some of the ragged regiment of Parnassus.
Most of his protégés, like Gillies, were impossible people,

---

[1] *Religious Discourses by a Layman.* The preface is signed " W. S." and
dated from Abbotsford. Gordon got £250 for the book.

1828 doomed to fail in everything they undertook, but Scott never lost patience nor wearied in his well-doing.

This year his work went smoothly on the whole. His manuscript was as neat as ever, but his handwriting had become villainously cramped ; he found that it took him longer to read than to write a page, and even James Ballantyne deciphered it with difficulty. The flood of fancy, too, was liable to sudden ebbs, and there was nothing to be done but to wait till it returned. When he had begun a novel he had never known how it would end, but now he would come to a dead stop in the middle of a chapter. An extra glass of wine at dinner and a night's sleep often brought back his inspiration. " I had thought on the subject for several days with something like the despair which seized the fair princess, commanded by her ugly stepmother to assort a whole garret full of tangled silk-threads of every kind and colour, when in comes Prince Percinet with a wand, whisks it over the miscellaneous mass, and lo ! all the threads are as nicely arranged as in a seamstress's housewife." [1] His pre-occupation with wholesome external interests is shown by the fact that from the beginning of July till the end of the year there is no entry in the *Journal*. Cockburn visited him at Abbotsford in September, and found his talk as good as ever. " His simplicity and naturalness after all his fame are absolutely incredible." In his evening dress he was " like any other comfortably ill-dressed gentleman," but in the morning " with his large coarse jacket, great stick and leather cap, he was Dandy Dinmont or Dick Hattrick—a smuggler or poacher." [2]

That year, in the spring vacation, he made his last journey to London as a comparatively hale man. It was the saddest event of the year, for he found poor

[1] *Journal*, II. 31.
[2] *Mem.*, 454-5. Haydon in his *Autobiography* has a similar testimony to Scott's simplicity of manner. "Scott enters a room and sits at table with the coolness and self-possession of conscious fame ; Wordsworth with a mortified elevation of head, as if fearful he was not estimated as he desired. Scott is always cool and very amusing; Wordsworth often egotistical and overwhelming. Scott seems to appear less than he really is, while Wordsworth struggles to be thought at the moment greater than he is suspected to be. I think that Scott's success would have made Wordsworth insufferable, while Wordsworth's failure would not have rendered Scott a whit less delightful."

Hugh Littlejohn sadly changed from the boy who had 1828
ridden with him the summer before in the Abbotsford
woods. On his way south he visited Stratford-on-Avon,
admired the view from Edgehill, and was pleased to find
that the rich land in the vale of Aylesbury brought a
lower rent than that which he got for some of his acres
at Huntly Burn. He found Walter with his regiment at
Hampton Court and Charles at the Foreign Office ; and
was delighted with the Lockharts' new house in Sussex
Place with its enchanting outlook over the Regent's
Park ; he dined in the company of Coleridge, who
delivered a harangue on the Samothracian mysteries and
then attacked the unity of Homer—" Zounds ! I was
never so bethumped with words " ; he got a road bill
rectified which threatened the amenities of Abbotsford ;
he dined and slept at Holland House, and dined with
the Duchess of Kent, where he was presented to the
little Princess Victoria, whom he thought plain but
pleasing, and whose name he hoped would be changed
before she came to the throne. Besides Johnnie Lockhart's health he had Terry's affairs to distress him, for
that cheerful being had become a bankrupt. " It is
written," he wrote in his *Journal*, " that nothing shall
flourish under my shadow—the Ballantynes, Terry,
Nelson, Weber, all came to distress. Nature has written
on my brow : ' Your shade shall be broad, but there
shall be no protection derived from it to aught you
favour.' "[1] It is almost the only doleful entry of the
year.

The Fair Maid of Perth shows no weakening of power ;
indeed it must rank high among the novels which are
based on book-work rather than on personal experience
and a still living tradition. The scene was Scottish, and
even on what Mrs Bethune Baliol called the " wilder-
nesses in Scottish history " the writer's imagination
worked with ease and certainty. Though he wisely did
not try to make his characters speak dialect, the idiomatic
northern flavour is never absent. Partly the book is the

[1] *Journal*, II. 160.

1828 familiar mediæval picture—a court, a tournament, the smug urban life of comedy, the quarrels of citizens and nobles, a too-gallant prince, a lovely burgher maiden. But Scott had so clear an insight into the old burghal life and such a wealth of knowledge about it that he repeoples the streets of Perth with folk who are anything but stage creations. Moreover Perth was near the Highland Line, and no book that I know of shows so vividly the contrast, as well as the ties, between the compact municipal life and the savage outlands. There is no " tushery " in the tale ; he describes mediæval Perth as he would have described eighteenth century Peebles.

Catherine Glover till the later chapters is too conscientiously noble, and her pacifism becomes a burden, but her instructor, Father Clement, the Lollard, is drawn with historical insight. The villains like Ramorny and Bonthron and Henbane Dwining and the mosstroopers like Devil's Dick are satisfying rascals, and all the court figures—the foolish amiable king, Rothsay, Albany, Douglas, March—are careful studies. So are the citizens, Simon Glover, and Hal o' the Wynd, and the luckless Oliver Proudfute. But the character on whom Scott lavished most pains, his tribute to the *manes* of his own unhappy brother, is Conachar the young Highland chief, who " has drunk the milk of the white doe," and, for all his spirit, fails in the commoner kinds of courage. In his later work Scott, as we have seen, had come to a deeper understanding of the Highland temperament, and Conachar is his best portrait of a character frustrate and divided. The book abounds in memorable scenes, such as the trial by combat, the clan battle on the North Inch, and the murder of Rothsay, scenes which in mere narrative skill rank with the best in the earlier novels. But there is one episode which is proof of the new technique to which Scott was feeling his way, that ironic subtlety which he had already shown in his picture of Croftangry—the scene where Dwining the apothecary is forced to cure the child of the man whose death he had compassed.

The year 1829 opened a little ominously with a return to the *Journal*. *Anne of Geierstein*, which was finished by the end of April, was a tough job, which he came to loathe before its completion. " I muzzled on," he wrote, " I can call it little better. The materials are excellent, but the power of using them is failing." He took to falling asleep over his work, and turned gladly for a change to the notes and prefaces of the *Opus Magnum*. He was happier over his next task, a two-volume survey of Scottish history for Lardner's Cyclopædia, for which he received £1500. His chief comfort was the huge success which promised to attend the *Opus*. Eight volumes were issued before the end of the year, and the monthly sales reached 35,000. Over this he had a brief difference of opinion with Cadell, who was not inclined to let James Ballantyne have all the printing. James wrote a plaintive letter to Scott reminding him of his promise when the catastrophe came—" We are three mariners escaping from a common shipwreck, and as the plank is broad enough for all, I cannot think it right to push any off from it." Scott was as good as his word, and the printing went to the Canongate house.[1]

He continued to mingle a good deal in the social life of Edinburgh. The Blairadam Club saw him at all its meetings, and in March he attended the ceremony when " the auld murderess Mons Meg " was replaced in the Castle battery—a kind of Celtic saturnalia, presided over by Cluny Macpherson, and followed in the evening by a dinner of the Highland Club. Politics occupied some of his thoughts, for he was a strong supporter of catholic emancipation, and did his best to curb Lockhart and Southey, thereby earning unwonted praise from Sir James Mackintosh and the Whigs. He gave, as usual, most of his time to lame dogs, for he was never content with the easy way of casual doles. Here is a typical entry in the *Journal* :—

A poor young woman came here this morning, well dressed and well behaved, with a strong northern accent. She talked

---

[1] *P.L.B.*, 362-5.

1829 incoherently a long story of a brother and a lover both dead.
I would have kept her here till I wrote to her friends, particularly to Mr Sutherland (an Aberdeen bookseller), to inform
them where she is, but my daughter and her maidens were
frightened, as indeed there might be room for it, and so I sent
her in one of Davidson's chaises to the Castle at Jedburgh,
and wrote to Mr Shortreed to see she is humanely treated. I
have written also to her brother.[1]

That seems to me to be charity of the early Christian
pattern—or of Dr Johnson's. But this practiser of
Christianity was not happy among its official exponents.
He records a meeting with Edward Irving, where he
was deeply impressed with the dark beauty of the face
marred by the terrible squint of the eyes, but rebelled
against the unction of the talk. Scott did not like those
who were at ease in Zion.

As the year went on his health steadily worsened.
Apart from his chronic ailments like rheumatism, indigestion and palpitation, he was subject to fits of
giddiness, for which he was cupped, and to long spells
of painful lethargy. Though he did not know it, these
were the precursors of apoplexy. Also, though he had
moments of exhilaration when Cadell brought him the
figures of the sales of the *Opus*, and had even dreams
of buying Faldonside after all, he found melancholy
creeping over him. The friends of his youth and middle
life were fast slipping away—Shortreed, who had been
his companion in his first incursion into Liddesdale ;
Terry who had been his ally in the equipment of Abbotsford ; Lady Jane, the mother of Williamina ; Sir William
Forbes, Williamina's husband and his own most loyal
friend. Neighbours and political allies, like Sir Alexander
Don and the first Lord Melville, were gone, and
Canning had finished his brief, bright day ; Constable
would puff no more along the High Street, and Lord
Buchan had been gathered to those ancestors who were
the pride of his life. Some of the living, too, were
changed. James Ballantyne was no longer the jolly
companion he had been, for he had lost his wife, retired

[1] II. 278.

to the country, and taken to Whiggism and piety. But
the heaviest blow was the death of Tom Purdie, which
befell in October. " There is a heart cold," Scott wrote
to Laidlaw, " that loved me well." One by one the
supports were falling from his house of life.

Anne of Geierstein, his only book of the year, is the
last of the novels written under anything like normal conditions. It was the work, he tells us, of his scanty leisure
in Edinburgh, not of quiet mornings in the country, and,
no library being at hand, the history was taken from
memory. This story of the epoch of Quentin Durward
from the Burgundian side has never, I think, had its
merits fully recognized ; it has been too much used for
the instruction of youth to have been considered seriously
as a piece of literature. It is not one of the great novels,
but it is a vigorous and competent one. The first thing
to be said about it is that the history, like all Scott's
history, is excellent. The long discussion between Oxford
and Charles of Burgundy gives us the substantial truth
about the high politics of the age, and Scott rarely wrote
better battle-pieces than the descriptions of Granson
and Murten. The troubadour court, too, of old René
of Provence is a piece of sound historical reconstruction.
The second thing to be noted is that, deprived of books
of reference, he went back, as old men will, to the
influences of his youth. *Anne of Geierstein* is drawn
from deep wells of memory. One half of it is high-
coloured melodrama—Arthur and Anne facing each other
across the Alpine chasm, the dungeons and the secret
passages of Breisach, the black priest of St Paul, Anne's
necromantic ancestry, John Mengs's inn, the descending
bed, and the whole business of the Vehmic tribunal.
This was the machinery of the Gothick romance, which
had fascinated Scott in his early days, and now he
returned to it with a hand practised in more delicate
crafts. Also, as Lockhart notes, he recaptured from
recollection the standpoint of youth. Arthur and Anne
are among the most natural of his lovers, Annette and
Sigismund and the Swiss lads among his best portraits
of young men and women. There is no sadness in the

1830 book; its spirit is happy, for Scott was living over in it again his own happy springtide.

V

On the 15th of February 1830, the four years of incessant toil exacted their price. Scott returned from the Court early in the afternoon, staggered into the drawing-room, and fell fainting at Anne's feet. For ten minutes he lost the power of speech, but in the evening, after being bled and cupped, he recovered possession of his faculties. In a day or two he was about again as if nothing had happened, though his friends noticed an odd nervous twist of the mouth and an occasional stammer. He submitted to a most drastic régime, scarcely touched wine or spirits, and gave up his evening cigar. The doctors tactfully told him that it was " from the stomach," but he knew the symptoms of a malady which had carried off his father and elder brother, and was aware that he had shaken hands with death. " It looks woundy like palsy or apoplexy," he wrote. " Well, be it what it will, I can stand it."

One of the medical prescriptions he refused to accept— to slacken his habits of work. This he would not do, for madness lay the way of idleness. So in 1830 his pen covered as many sheets as in 1829. He was busy at a series of letters on demonology and witchcraft for Murray's Family Library (an enterprise the profits of which, being outside the Trust, went to his own pocket), at further *Tales of a Grandfather*, dealing with French history, at notes for the *Opus*, and at a new novel on a Byzantine subject, not to speak of magazine articles. The *Demonology* is in no way to be despised, for, though the style and arrangement are sometimes confused, it is a delightful compendium of eerie tales drawn from his capacious memory, and he analyses the evidence with all his lawyer's shrewdness. But over the others has fallen the shadow of dissolution. He was suffering now not only from disease but from decay.

That year was his last as a Clerk of Court, for it was

convenient both to the Government and to himself that 1830 he should resign. He was given a retiring allowance of £800, thereby losing £500 of income, but he refused (the Trust assenting) to permit the authorities to make up the loss by a pension. George IV died in June, but before his death he had tried to do honour to the retirement from official life of his old friend. Scott was nominated chairman of a commission to examine and edit the manuscript collections of the Cardinal of York, a scheme which unfortunately came to nothing, and he was offered and refused a privy councillorship. " When one is poor," he wrote, " one ought to avoid taking rank."

By the late autumn he was free to live all the year at Abbotsford, and was beginning to comfort himself with the thought that by 1832 his feet would be clear. In October the Trust paid a second dividend of three shillings in the pound, and, on the motion of Gibson-Craig, requested Scott to accept the library and the plenishing of Abbotsford, " as the best means the creditors have of expressing their very high sense of his most honourable conduct, and in grateful acknowledgment for the unparalleled and most successful exertions he has made, and continues to make for them." [1]

This was a pleasant god-speed for his retirement. But his recovered home was to give him neither health nor peace. He had virtually completed the task he had set himself, but there was not to be that quiet evening, that

> old age, serene and bright
> And lovely as a Lapland night,

which his strenuous life deserved. The Lockharts, who were at Chiefwood that summer, saw with pain the

---

[1] *Sederunt Book.* This was the last dividend paid in Scott's lifetime. At a meeting of the Trustees on 29th October 1832, it was reported that the funds raised since the commencement of the Trust amounted to £51,127, and that funds in hand or in sight, including insurances, amounted to £34,178. These latter moneys, with £20,000 to be provided by the Scott family, would enable every creditor to be paid a further 9s. in the £ (18s. in all). This was accepted by the creditors as a final settlement, the value of the Abbotsford library, etc., gifted to Scott, being taken as equal to the remaining 2s. Cadell ultimately settled with the Scott family and paid off the mortgage on Abbotsford on the basis of the assignment to him of the remaining rights in Scott's works and of the profits of Lockhart's *Life.*

1830 ebbing of his bodily strength. In the autumn there
were more visitors than ever, and the labour of entertaining them taxed his powers to the uttermost. John
Nicholson was now his butler, and endeavoured also to
take Tom Purdie's place, but beyond an occasional
amble on Douce Davie and a slow walk in the grounds
Scott was little out of doors. In November he had
another slight apoplectic seizure, and found his lameness
of thigh, knee and ankle sorely increased. To make
matters worse he was obsessed with a morbid passion
for work, and could not be persuaded to leave his desk.
Lockhart and Cadell tried to induce him to be content
with light tasks, such as the notes for his *Opus* and a
catalogue of his library, but he stuck grimly to his
Byzantine tale, *Count Robert of Paris*, which was going
as ill as possible. He had chosen an arid subject and
he could not give the dry bones life. Ballantyne criticized
the early chapters harshly and Cadell did not conceal
his disappointment.[1] Scott was plunged in gloom, but
mercifully Willie Laidlaw, who was again his secretary,
liked the tale, and his simple-minded " Keep us a' ! "
did something to console the weary man.

There was another painful business. The news from
London to Scott's sick ears seemed to be of red ruin
and the break-up of society. The Duke of Wellington
ceased to be Prime Minister in November, and was
succeeded by Lord Grey with a ministry pledged to
reform. There was unrest everywhere in the land, and
to his horror he found many of his old friends inclining
to the new policy. The time had come when he felt
that he must stand in the gate. He began a pamphlet
on the *Malachi* lines, which was to be a trumpet-call
to awaken the nation's conscience. Cadell and James
Ballantyne posted down to Abbotsford in dismay, for
they realized that political excitement might kill Scott,
and that the kind of pamphlet he proposed would
gravely damage his repute. An author is often in love
with his least deserving work, and though the Whig
Laidlaw seems to have been impressed with the eloquence

[1] See the letters in *P. L. B.*, 365-9.

of the new *Malachi*, Cadell and Ballantyne criticized it 1831
so trenchantly that Scott in high dudgeon flung it into
the fire. But he did not change his purpose. He was
determined, while life was left to him, to fight against
what old Henry Mackenzie had called " epidemic in-
sanity." To Lady Louisa Stuart he wrote :—

> Your acquaintance with Shakespeare is intimate, and you
> remember why, and where, it is said

> " He words me, girl, he words me."

> Our modern men of the day have done this to the country.
> They have devised a new phraseology to convert good into
> evil and evil into good, and the ass's ears of John Bull are
> gulled with it as if words alone made crime or virtue. Have
> they a mind to excuse the tyranny of Buonaparte ? Why, the
> Lord love you, he only squeezed into his government a grain
> too much of civilization. The fault of Robespierre was too
> active liberalism ; a noble error. Thus the most blood-thirsty
> anarchy is glossed over by opening an account in a new name.
> The varnish might be easily scraped off all this trumpery.

But he had not the strength for the task. *Count
Robert*, the later chapters of which satisfied his critics
no better than the earlier, was laid aside for the moment,
and he began a novel about Douglas castle and the
War of Independence. In April 1831 Parliament was
dissolved, and the sole issue at the election was parlia-
mentary reform. The result could not be in doubt ;
Scott decided that the old constitution had fallen,
" thrown away like a child's toy " ; but he was resolved
to strike a last blow for it. He electioneered up and
down the Border, and on the 21st of March addressed
a meeting at Jedburgh where he told the weavers that
Lord Grey and his colleagues were like a parcel of school-
boys taking to pieces a watch which they could not put
together again. He was howled down, and left the place
with the words " Moriturus vos saluto."

The use of the participle was just, for on Saturday,
April 16th, he had a severe paralytic stroke. He bore it,
as Dr Johnson bore the same affliction, with humility,
fortitude and thankfulness. Within a fortnight he was

1831 back at work struggling with *Count Robert* and notes for the *Opus*. He would not take Cadell's advice to keep out of politics. " They are not worth your while," wrote that wise man ; " the river is in flood at present, and no one man, not even the King himself, can stop it. Many will incite you, many will hurry you on, but the kicklers and clappers of hands will not consider that the gallant actor may hurt himself, and probably may come in for a kick from some cart nag with not a drop of breeding in his carcase." [1] The prophecy fell true, for the kick from the cart nag came on election day at Jedburgh. A band of weavers from Hawick paraded the streets, Scott's carriage was stoned, and he was smuggled out of the place pursued by cries of " Burke Sir Walter." " Much obliged to the brave lads of Jeddart," he wrote in his *Journal*. " *Troja fuit*."

The world had become grievously out of joint for him. *Count Robert* pleased nobody, so its publication was delayed, and he turned to *Castle Dangerous* without zest or hope. Yet work was his only tie to life, and this was clear to Cadell and Lockhart, so that they dared not dissuade him. Cadell has been blamed for flogging the weary steed, but his intention seems to have been of the kindliest, and he was even prepared, in order to comfort Scott, to publish a *Malachi* outpouring when the election was over. He was a pawky, timid being, a follower in other men's tracks, who succeeded where Constable the pioneer had failed, but the fact that he ultimately made a large fortune out of Scott's works is not to his discredit. It is no crime to be a successful tradesman. As Cadell entered more into Scott's affairs, James Ballantyne disappeared. He had become valetudinarian and devout, and an ardent reformer. In April he had written to Scott, a week after his stroke, advising him to become a total abstainer—a tactless prescription for a man who had for long been living on prison fare.[2] He came to Abbotsford in July on a last visit, and left on the Sunday morning without saying good-bye, on the ground that he needed stronger spiritual

[1] *P.L.B.*, 373.　　　　[2] *Ibid.*, 370.

nourishment than the reading of the church service.
The two ancient friends were not destined to meet again.

That summer Scott made his last expedition in his native land. For the purposes of *Castle Dangerous* he wished to visit Douglasdale, so he and Lockhart set out on July 18th. He had long realized that his days were numbered, and on this journey his son-in-law reached the sad conclusion that the powers of memory and brain were already weakening. It was a heavy lowering day when they visited St Bride's kirk and the ruins of the castle, and as they drove away over the Lesmahagow moors Scott repeated verses from the old poets, particularly from Dunbar's " Lament of the Makars." Then he turned to " Otterburn," and broke down in tears when he came to the verse

> My wound is deep—I fain would sleep—
> Take thou the vanguard of the three,
> And hide me beneath the bracken bush,
> That grows on yonder lily lea.

At Milton Lockhart that evening he seemed to recover something of his spirits, but next morning he heard that his friend, Mr Elliot Lockhart of Borthwickbrae, whom he had met at dinner, had had a stroke and was believed to be dying. He insisted on leaving at once. " I must home to work while it is called day ; for the night cometh when no man can work."

Of the two novels of the year, Scott's last publications, the critic can have little to say. They must be judged not by the canons of art, but as desperate deeds, the final blows struck by a failing man in the cause of honour. *Count Robert* is history rather than fiction, a compilation from Gibbon and the *Alexiad*, and as prolix as Anna Comnena herself. The court of Byzantium in the eleventh century was not a subject with which Scott had any natural affinities, and he was too languid to reproduce the drama of the clash of West and East in the first Crusade. There are moments of vigour, like the fight with the tiger in the dungeon, but everywhere

1831 lassitude weights his pen. In *Castle Dangerous* he had matter which in earlier days might have been wrought into a great novel, and he walked familiar ground. But the craftmanship is weak, though the style is good ; the account of the friction between De Valence and De Walton is too lengthily done and is not strictly relevant to the plot ; the adventures jar from their suddenness, and the final combat in St Bride's kirk does not stir us as it should. He was too fatigued to rise to the mood of that furious Palm Sunday in Douglasdale. The oppression of his spirits is curiously reflected in the weather of the tale, for all the events take place under grey skies, in creeping mists and driving rain.

Scott had yielded to his doctors' entreaties and consented to spend the coming winter out of England, and Lord Grey's Government had magnanimously put a frigate at his disposal. Moreover, young Walter was given leave from his regiment in order to accompany him. The last autumn at Abbotsford had its cheerful hours. Adolphus came on a visit, and Burns's soldier son, and Turner the artist, who had to be prevented from endowing all his Scots figures with the kilt. There were pilgrimages to Ettrick and Bemersyde, and dinners under the trees at Chiefswood. Scott mounted Douce Davie again, and looked on at the coursing at Cauldshiels loch, admiring the horsemanship of his elder son. He had convinced himself that his debts had been paid, and all conspired to foster the delusion ; he was looking forward to his travels, too, though he could not forget that Fielding and Smollett had been driven abroad by ill-health and had never returned. The true farewell was appropriately spoken by the other great living king of letters. Wordsworth came to Abbotsford with his daughter, and on the last day of his stay the two poets visited Newark. They forded Tweed on their return when the hills were purple in an eerie gloaming. Wordsworth, himself sick and blind, saw in the mysterious light the presage of death, and his heart stirred for the

old friend whom he widely differed from and deeply ¹⁸³¹
loved. That night he wrote this sonnet :—

A trouble, not of clouds, or weeping rain,
Nor of the setting sun's pathetic light
Engendered, hangs o'er Eildon's triple height ;
Spirits of power assembled there complain
For kindred power departing from their sight ;
While Tweed, best pleased in chanting a blithe strain,
Saddens his voice again, and yet again.
Lift up your hearts, ye mourners ! for the might
Of the whole world's good wishes with him goes ;
Blessings and prayers in nobler retinue
Than sceptred King or laurelled Conqueror knows
Follow this wondrous potentate. Be true,
Ye winds of ocean, and the Midland sea
Wafting your charge to soft Parthenope !

CHAPTER XII

RELEASE

(1831–1832)

1831 "I AM perhaps setting," Scott wrote in the *Journal* in
September. "Like a day that has been admired as a
fine one, the light of it sets down amid mists and storms.
I neither regret nor fear the approach of death if it is
coming. I would compound for a little pain instead of
this heartless muddiness of mind. . . . I have no fear
on pecuniary matters. The ruin which I fear involves
that of my King and country."[1] This was the mood in
which he set out on his travels. But the change of
scene revived his spirits. In London, though he could
not dine out, he met many of his old friends, and though
the air was full of tales of mob violence, he seems to
have got an easier mind about politics. After all, the
Duke of Wellington was still alive, and Ministers, Whigs
though they were, had been uncommonly kind to himself.[2]
The doctors had examined him and found traces of in-
cipient disease of the brain, but they were confident that,
if he would only give up work, the malady could be
averted.

The journey started ill, for the *Barham* could not sail
for a week, and the party had to kick their heels in a
Portsmouth hotel. They sailed eventually on October
29th, but on November 2nd they were still beating

---

[1] II. 412-13.
[2] A tribute should be paid to the generosity of Lord Grey's Government
towards so stout an opponent. Apart from lending a frigate, they were prepared to help Scott when it was rumoured that he was short of means on his
way home, they gave Anne a pension, and when it was necessary to pass a
short Act to appoint a new Sheriff, since he was too ill to resign, Jeffrey conducted
the matter with such good feeling that Peel and Croker crossed the House to
thank him.

off Land's End, a very sea-sick company. When they had crossed the Bay of Biscay the weather improved, and Scott was much on deck, hobbling about with his creaking leg, and talking briskly to the ship's officers. As they passed Cape St Vincent and Trafalgar and Gibraltar the traveller's interest was stirred, and the mild airs improved his health ; his *Journal* is full of jottings of what he saw ; and when on November 22nd he entered Malta harbour he felt some vigour returning to both body and mind. He stayed three weeks in the island, living at a hotel though various private houses were offered to him, and was well enough to attend a ball given in his honour. The place gave him an idea for a new novel to be called *The Siege of Malta,* and a short story *Il Bizarro,* at which he worked for the next few months ; both are still extant in manuscript, but it may be hoped that no literary resurrectionist will ever be guilty of the crime of giving them to the world.

At Naples, which was reached on December 17th, the party stayed for four months. Scott was not very ill and not very unhappy, but both his senses and his mind were a little blunted. He attended the Court in the uniform of a Scottish archer, and conversed with the king in his awkward French, and dined with the nonagenarian Archbishop of Tarentum. He saw all the sights, but he was no classic, and Pollio's villa and Paestum meant little to him, while at Pompeii he could only ingeminate " The city of the Dead." On January 16th 1832 news came of his grandson's death, but Scott, who had sorrowed so deeply in anticipating it, merely notes in his *Journal* : " Poor Johnny Lockhart ! The boy is gone whom we have made so much of. I could not have borne it better than I now do, and might have borne it much worse." . . . That evening he went to the opera.

It would appear that the decay of his brain had now begun in solemn earnest, and he moved in an interior world of his own. Sometimes the weight of his debts hung over him like a cloud ; but more often he believed them paid off, and wrote cheerfully to Lockhart about

1832 the approaching purchase of Faldonside. He finished
his Malta story and had great schemes of future literary
work, including a poem in the style of *The Lady of the
Lake* to be a postscript to the novels. The subject was
to be a tale of chivalry connected with Rhodes, and for
the purpose he meant to visit Sir Frederick Adam in
the Ionian Islands and get him to accompany him to
Greece. But the plan was only a sudden fancy, for his
deepest desire was to go home. He saw the landscape
of Italy in terms of his own land, and when he visited
Avernus, which is not unlike a Highland loch, he was
heard to murmur

> Up the craggy mountain
> And down the mossy glen,
> We daurna gang a-milking
> For Charlie and his men.

At Naples in March Scott had word of Goethe's death.
He had intended to visit him at Weimar on his return
journey, and the tidings seemed to be his own summons.
" He at least died at home," he cried; " let us to
Abbotsford," and the phrase commonest on his lips was
Politian's " Grata quies patriæ." Moreover, Sir Frederick
Adam had been recalled from the Ionian Islands, so the
Greek plan dropped. A travelling carriage was bought,
and in the middle of April the party turned their faces
northward. Walter had had to rejoin his regiment, and
Charles now took his place.

Three weeks were passed in Rome, but Scott, who in
earlier years would have found the days spent there all
too short, was sunk in listlessness. His thoughts, so far
as they were more than vacant dreams, were all on
Scotland. He was not ill or peevish—" As I am now
good for nothing else," he said, " I think it as well to be
good humoured "—he was simply at the end of life and
pleasure. The only sights which woke a response were
the Cardinal of York's villa with its Stuart portraits and
St Peter's with the Stuart tombs. On May 11th Rome
was left behind, and the glimpse of the pines and the
late snows on the Apennines pleased him, for they

recalled Scotland.   After that all was blank.   Venice, 1832
Tirol, Munich, Heidelberg said nothing to him ; there
was a flicker of interest when they embarked on the
Rhine, which he had recently described in *Anne of
Geierstein*, but it died when they landed at Cologne. . . .
Then on June 9th near Nimeguen the body followed
the mind, and he had a fourth paralytic seizure.   On
the 11th he was lifted from his carriage into the boat
at Rotterdam, and two days later was put to bed in a
Jermyn Street hotel.

The rest of the *via dolorosa* is soon traced.   More
fortunate than Leyden, he was to die at home.   He lay
for some three weeks in London, sunk for the most part
in a painless coma, but able to recognize his children.
The faithful Cadell arrived from Edinburgh, and the
Lockharts and Anne watched beside his bed, while
every newspaper chronicled the progress of his malady,
and the royal family made daily inquiries.   Outside in
Jermyn Street Allan Cunningham found a group of
working men, who asked him, " Do you know, sir, if
this is the street where he is lying ? "   There were many
besides Newman to pray for the Minstrel.   In his waking
moments he longed for home, and on July 7th he was
carried on board ship, while a great crowd lined the
pavements.   Two days later he reached Newhaven, and
on the 11th he began the journey to Tweeddale.   As the
carriage descended the glen of Gala water he woke to
consciousness and murmured familiar names, and when
it rounded the hill at Ladhope and the Eildons came into
view he exclaimed in delight.   Tweed being in spate he
had to go round by Melrose bridge, and could scarcely
be kept in the carriage.   At Abbotsford Laidlaw and his
dogs were waiting.   " Ha ! Willie Laidlaw ! " he cried.
" O man, how often have I thought of you ! "

For a few days there was a break in the clouds and a
brief clearness revisited his mind.   He was wheeled by
Lockhart and Laidlaw out of doors among the roses,
and up and down the hall and the library.   " I have
seen much," he repeated often, " but nothing like my

1832 ain house." He would sit peacefully at the library window looking on Tweed, or in a shady corner of the grounds, while Lockhart read aloud to him from Crabbe and the Gospel of St John. One day he revived so far that he desired to be set in his chair at his desk and given his pen. But the pen dropped from his hand, and he fell back weeping among his pillows. " No repose for Sir Walter but in the grave."

That was all but the last gleam of light. He retired into a melancholy half-consciousness while his great bodily strength slowly ebbed—talking to the dead Tom Purdie, repeating the Jedburgh mob's cry of " Burke Sir Walter," or in a happier mood reciting the *Stabat Mater*, and texts of Scripture, and verses of the Scottish psalms. On the morning of Monday, September 17th, Lockhart was called to his bedside and found him conscious again, but in the last extremity of weakness. " Lockhart," he said, " I may have but a minute to speak to you. My dear, be a good man—be virtuous— be religious—be a good man. Nothing else will give you any comfort when you come to lie here." Walter and Charles were summoned, and in the presence of all his family Scott died in the early afternoon of September 21st. His eldest son kissed his eyes and closed them, while through the open window in the bright autumn weather came the gentle murmur of Tweed.

He was buried, by right of his Haliburton blood, in the ruined abbey of Dryburgh. The day was sombre and cloudy with a high wind, and the whole countryside in the same dark livery followed the coffin to the grave. A century later another great Borderer was brought from Bemersyde to lie near him. For Walter Scott and Douglas Haig the line of Homer, which Lockhart quotes, is the fittest epitaph—

> There lay he, mighty and mightily fallen, having
> done with his chivalry.[1]

---

[1] κεῖτο μέγας μεγαλωστὶ λελασμένος ἱπποσυνάων. *Iliad*, XVI. 776.

Chapter XIII

THE WRITER[1]

THE appeal of Scott to his own age was immediate and universal, and his influence on his contemporaries and successors was as great as Byron's and more enduring. The literature of every civilized country bears witness to it. In France Alfred de Vigny, Mérimée, Dumas, Balzac and Victor Hugo drew from him their first inspiration ; in Germany and Italy he was the patron of a new school of romance, Manzoni was his disciple, and the reading of *Quentin Durward* made Ranke an historian ; he was the earliest master of the Russian Dostoevsky ; in Spain he had a host of imitators, and he was the acknowledged source of the eager romanticism out of which Catalan nationalism sprang ; in Scandinavia, Tegnér and Almquist and Runeberg were his followers, and so different a writer as Strindberg confessed that before he approached an historical subject he steeped himself in Scott. He has been translated into every tongue, and no English writer save Shakespeare is so continuously reprinted in so many lands.[2]

This wide popular acceptance as a classic has had a paralysing effect on the critical study of Scott. He has been too much taken for granted, as if he were a statue in a public place. He has had detractors such as Borrow and idolaters such as Ruskin, but he has been praised and blamed in a spirit of rhetoric rather than of science. The really penetrating criticism of Scott could be collected in a slim volume—his own and that of Lockhart, Lady

[1] In this chapter I have used some sentences from an essay previously published.

[2] See Maigron, *Le Roman Historique à l'Époque Romantique; Essai sur l'influence de Walter Scott;* Mielke-Homann, *Der deutsche Roman;* Montoliu, *Manual d'Història critica de la Litteratura catalana moderna* (Barcelona, 1922).

Louisa Stuart, Adolphus, Nassau Senior, Bagehot, and in our own day A. W. Verrall and Professor Elton. For the rest we have had to content ourselves with appreciations by writers who were too much in love with the man to look judicially upon his work, and with essays in belittlement by adherents of some minor coterie. Yet he is worth the attention of the well-equipped critic, for at his best he stands the test of the most searching examination and the austerest standards.

I offer in this chapter modestly and tentatively my own conclusions. In the study of a practitioner of an art so rapidly developing as that of fiction, it is idle to attempt to devise a calculus of merit or to fix his exact rank in a hierarchy. There is one glory of the sun and another glory of the moon. The novel is the world as seen through the temperament of the novelist, and his success depends upon the depth of his insight and the richness of his temperament, the twin powers of perception and interpretation. In assessing his value the points which concern us are his competence as a student of life ; the nature of the technique by which he presents his conclusions ; and in the last resort his power of transforming and sublimating his world, that " stellar and undiminishable something " which was Emerson's definition of greatness.

I

Let us begin with the lesser matters, and take first his prose style, which has found many critics. The complaint on this score needs to be exactly stated. Obviously we cannot expect to find in him anything esoteric in the use of words, any delicate exercises in verbal dry-point, any of what Professor Elton has called " those false associations of painful, choice and fastidious language that have gathered for half a century round the word *art*." [1] To Scott, as to Balzac and Tolstoy and Dostoevsky, writing was a natural process ; not, as to Tourgeniev and Flaubert, a ritual. There is a revealing confession

---

[1] *Survey of English Literature*, 1780-1830, I. 347.

in the *Journal.* " I am sensible that, if there be anything good about my poetry or my prose either, it is a hurried frankness of composition, which pleases soldiers, sailors, and young people of bold and active dispositions." [1] Had Scott indulged in any *finesse* of language he would have been guilty of a grave fault of craftsmanship, and the result would have been as preposterous as the insertion of point-lace in a buff coat. In the mere verbal dandyism of style the world will never seriously interest itself, for it does not understand how the manner of saying something can have merit independent of the thing said. The *mot juste,* it holds rightly, is futile unless it be the right word for the right thing. To the monotonous exquisiteness of Flaubert it prefers the irregular movement and the more varied rhythms of less self-conscious writers, because it believes that the latter is the better art.

The real charge is a more serious affair. It is that Scott, from carelessness and ineptitude in the use of words, spoiled the artistic effect of his narrative ; that his tools were so blunt that they often failed to do their work ; that his extreme facility kept him always on the edge, and sometimes led him over the edge, of banality : and that he attains his great moments by a kind of happy accident in defiance of his style. The charge has been made by Stevenson, an admirer and follower, and it has been made in uncompromising terms. " His characters . . . will be wading forward with an ungrammatical and undramatic rigmarole of words. . . . He could . . . often fob us off with languid, inarticulate twaddle. . . . He conjured up the romantic with delight, but he had hardly patience to describe it. . . . He was a great day-dreamer . . . but hardly a great artist ; hardly, in the manful sense, an artist at all." [2]

There is some truth in this solemn bill of attainder. Scott was a master but not a schoolmaster of language, and sometimes grammar and syntax go by the board. Like Shakespeare he wrote fast, and like Shakespeare he could write abominably. He could produce fustian

<hr />

[1] I. 212-13.　　　　[2] *Memories and Portraits*, 273-4.

and jargon and " polite English " and false rhetoric. His sentences can trip up each other's heels, and he can weaken his effects by an idle superabundance of words. In previous chapters I have given many instances of these blemishes. The truth is that any man, whose business it is to portray life in action and who is caught up in the white heat of his task, is certain at times to take the first phrase that comes into his head, and jar the ear and the taste of a fastidious reader.

On the other hand it seems to me that the staple of his writing, even when he is least inspired, is sound and workmanlike. He is a master of easy, swift, lucid narrative, and he invented a mode of speech for the figures of past ages which is at once romantic and natural. His style is far more varied than appears at first sight, and, just as in his lyrics he could pass from the trumpets of war to the pipes of faery, so in his prose he can sometimes attain a haunting simplicity and grace, as in the narrative of Chrystal Croftangry and in a hundred passages in the *Journal*. But the true defence looks not to the levels but to the heights. As Dryden said of Shakespeare, he is always great when some great occasion is presented to him. When the drama quickens and the stage darkens he attains to a style as perfect and unforgettable as Shakespeare's, and it is most cunningly compounded. It is never "precious," but it is often beyond price. On such occasions he gives us harmonies as subtle and moving as can be found in the whole range of English prose, where every cadence, every epithet, every object mentioned plays its due part in the total impression. I need only cite the speech of Meg Merrilies to the laird of Ellangowan, Claverhouse's speech to Morton, Habakkuk Mucklewrath's denunciation of Claverhouse, the last chapters of *The Bride of Lammermoor*, "Wandering Willie's Tale," and the closing scene of *Redgauntlet*. Such passages are worth the patient, imaginative analysis which we give to the choruses of Æschylus.[1]

---

[1] The first has been analysed by Dr Verrall (*Collected Literary Essays*, 247, etc.), the second by Prof. Elton (*op. cit.*, 353-4) and the third by Prof. Saintsbury (*History of English Prose Rhythm*, 296).

On one point there is no dispute, the complete rightness of the speech of his Scots characters. Scott used the dialect of the Lothians with a slight Border admixture—that is to say, metropolitan Scots, the classic language of Scottish gentlefolk and peasants. Twice he permitted himself an experiment in the Aberdeen version—with Francie Macraw in *The Antiquary* and with Davie Dingwall in *The Bride of Lammermoor*. He varied the vernacular to suit his characters. Sometimes it is standard English with a delicate northern colouring ; sometimes it broadens into robust idioms, though it is never permitted to become an unintelligible clot of dialect. At great moments, as with Meg Merrilies and Jeanie Deans and Steenie Steenson, it has the high simplicity of the universal. One point is worth noting. He understood the undercurrent of rhythm in the vernacular, and half his felicities come from this submerged music, these repetitive dactyls and trochees and anapaests, which have both the hammer-strokes of prose and the lilt of poetry.[1]

II

From verbal style we pass to structure. It is important to remember the conditions under which the novels were produced. Scott wrote them, as Shakespeare wrote his plays, in the intervals of a busy life, and the amount of time available for the actual work of scribing was strictly limited. But the theme was always in his head ; he has told us that he was never consciously inventing and never not inventing ; as he sat in court, or walked the Edinburgh streets, or rode about the Forest, he was

---

[1] This applies not only to the more emotional passages but to plain narrative. Take this speech of Cuddie Headrigg's, an illustration which I owe to Prof. Harrower of Aberdeen :

> A feckless loon o' a Straven weaver,
> that had left his loom and his bein house
> to sit skirling on a cauld hill-side,
> had catched twa dragoon naigs,
> and he could gar them neither hup nor wind,
> sae he took a gowd noble for them baith.—
> I suld hae tried him wi' half the siller,
> but it's an unco ill place to get change in.

perpetually slipping over the frontier of his secret world ; he would have agreed with Bagehot, who wrote " There is no time for quiet reflection like the intervals of the hunt." The hour before rising, too, he usually gave up to a forecast of the morning's work. Apart from details, he did not compose at his desk. The stories built themselves up half-unconsciously in his mind, while his fancy ran free. Hence his structure was not an artificial thing beaten out by laborious cogitation, but an organic development proceeding slowly and naturally like the growth of a tree. In none of the greater novels are we offended by any jerking of the wires.

This structure is sometimes defective, chiefly because Scott was in too great a hurry to get on with the story. Stevenson has noted an instance in the " recognition " scene in *Guy Mannering* when Harry Bertram lands at Ellangowan and hears the tune on the flageolet. There Scott has omitted to prepare the reader's mind for certain details, and he does it in haste with a sentence clumsily interpolated. Sometimes he brings an episode to a huddled conclusion, and now and then there is a grave lack of proportion. The novel, when he wrote, was still in process of changing from the rambling, inconsequent, picaresque tradition. But it may be said on the other hand that the main drama is nearly always well shaped, though that drama is not always coterminous with the whole story. The novels, it seems to me, do in a large measure achieve an artistic unity. Scott's purpose is always to present the manifold of experience winnowed and sifted and free of inessentials. He was not content, as many of the great Russians have been content, to produce a huge mass of the data of fiction, on which the shaping spirit of imagination only works at intervals. Can it be denied that much of Tolstoy and Dostoevsky has a scientific rather than an artistic interest ? There are moving " plays within the play," but the whole is formless because it is not wrought to the human scale. It is no justification to say that it is life; a novelist does not transcribe, he creates life; life is not art till it is moulded and clarified, it is only art's raw material. Unity of impression is essential for the whole and not merely for episodes. If the scale is too grandiose and the complexities too many, the result may be a contribution to knowledge, but it cannot make that single, undivided and intense impression which is the aim of the artist. Mere mass and intricacy are valueless unless transfused and transformed by the creative mind ; otherwise an interminable Alexandrian epic would transcend the *Iliad*, and a sprawling mediæval romaunt would be ranked above Chaucer.

A common charge against the structure of the novels is their *longueurs* and excessive padding, and up to a point the charge is just. Scott did not write with a narrow thesis, and therefore he is loath to discard what interests him, even if its relevance is not very clear. His affection was so pledged to his characters and their doings that he is apt to linger with them in side-walks. But the complaint may easily be overdone. Do Scott's irrelevancies ever reach the heights of tediousness which we find in some of the greatest of his successors—in *War and Peace*, for example, with its roods of amateur military discussion and its acres of turgid pamphleteering ? May not his *longueurs*, too, have an artistic value ? In his review of Jane Austen he wrote :—

> Let any one cut out from the *Iliad* or from Shakespeare's plays everything . . . which is absolutely devoid of importance or interest in itself ; and he will find that what is left will have lost more than half its charm. We are convinced that some writers have diminished the effect of their works by being scrupulous to admit nothing into them which had not some absolute, intrinsic, and independent merit. They have acted like those who strip off the leaves of a fruit-tree, as being of themselves good for nothing, with the view of securing more nourishment to the fruit, which in fact cannot attain its full maturity and flower without them. [1]

The metaphor is perhaps not exact, but there is justice in the point. Scott's padding, antiquarian and otherwise, provides relief, a rest for the mind, in the midst of exciting action.

Something of the same kind may be said in defence of

[1] *Misc. Prose Works*, XVIII. 229.

his stockish heroes and heroines, who should properly be considered as part of the structure of the tale, rather than studies in character. They are passive people for the most part, creatures of the average world, not majestic men and women of destiny. But they are not unreal, for the earth is full of them ; they are the more natural for being undistinguished. They seem to me to play on the whole a vital artistic part, for there is such a thing as too stimulating fare. They form a solid background, a kind of Greek chorus repeating all the accepted platitudes, and keeping the drama, which might otherwise become fantastic, within reach of our prosaic life.

The point is worth dwelling on, for it is bound up with the meaning of romance. It is one of Scott's characteristics that, though sympathizing in every fibre with the coloured side of life, with man's exaltations and agonies, he feels bound to let common sense put in its word now and then, to let the voice be heard of the normal pedestrian world. In a great painting, as has often been pointed out, there is always some prosaic object which provides a point of rest for the eye, and without which the whole value of the picture would be altered. This duty is performed in literature by the ordinary man, by Kent in *Lear*, by Horatio in *Hamlet*, by Banquo in *Macbeth* ; they are, so to speak, the " eye " of the storm which rages about them, and serve to measure the departure of the others from virtue, sanity, moderation, or merely normal conduct. Each is like the centre of a great wheel, which has little movement in itself but controls the furious revolutions of the circumference. This *punctum indifferens* is the peaceful anchorage of good sense from which we are able to watch with a balanced mind the storm outside. No great art is without it. Scott never loses his head, and the artistic value is as undeniable as the moral value. The fantastic, the supernatural and the quixotic are heightened in their effect by being shown against this quiet background ; moreover, they are made credible by being thus linked to our ordinary world. Behind all the extravagance we feel the Scots lawyer considering his case ; we hear a voice like Dr Johnson's reminding one that somewhere order reigns. If we compare Scott with Victor Hugo we shall understand the difference made by the lack of this quality. For the great Frenchman there is no slackening of the rein, no lowering of the top-note, till the steed faints from exhaustion and the strident voice ceases to impress our dulled ears.

A consequence of this gift of central steadfastness is Scott's skill in anti-climax, which, like the " falling close " in a lyric, does not weaken but increases the effect. Like the Gifted Gilfillan in *Waverley* he can pass easily and naturally from the New Jerusalem of the Saints to the price of beasts at Mauchline Fair. In previous chapters I have given instances of this breaking in upon romance of a voice from the common world, which does not weaken the heroic, but brings it home. Without some such salt of the pedestrian, romance becomes only a fairy-tale, and tragedy a high-heeled strutting. The kernel of romance is contrast, beauty and valour flowering in unlikely places, the heavenly rubbing shoulders with the earthly. The true romantic is never the posturing Byronic hero. All romance, all tragedy, must be within hailing distance of our humdrum lives, and anti-climax is a necessary adjunct to climax. We find it in the Ballads—this startling note of common sense, the sense of the commonalty, linking fact and dream. We find it in Shakespeare, who can make Cleopatra pass from banter with a peasant to the loftiest of human soliloquies.—" Hast thou the pretty worm of Nilus there ? . . . Those that do die of it do seldom or never recover. . . . I wish you joy o' the worm." And then :—

> Give me my robe, put on my crown ; I have
> Immortal longings in me.

We find it in Scott, whose broad sane vision saw that tragedy and comedy are sisters, and that, like Antæus, neither can live without the touch of her mother, the earth.

III

The staple of the novelist's task is the understanding
and presentation of human character. How does Scott
fare when judged by this test?

Badly, says Carlyle. " Your Shakespeare fashions his
characters from the heart outwards ; your Scott fashions
them from the skin inwards, never getting near the
heart of them." Bagehot after his fashion puts the
charge precisely, when he finds Scott weak in his treatment of two of the deepest human interests, love and
religion.

It is important to recognize frankly Scott's limitations.
" Everything worth while," said Nietzsche, " is accomplished *notwithstanding* " ; we cannot rightly measure a
man's powers till we know what he cannot do. Scott's
world was a very large and rich one, larger and richer
perhaps than that of any other novelist, but it had its
boundaries. We may put his heroes and heroines aside,
for they are not characters in the true sense of the
word ; as we have seen, they are rather part of the
staging and the scenery ; their fault is that, except in
a few cases like Croftangry, the drama is not seen
through their eyes, and they are far inferior in insight
and power to the imaginary narrator. For the rest,
Scott's world was one in which things worked out
normally by some law of averages, where goodness was
on the whole rewarded and evil punished, a friendly
universe not commonly at war with human aspirations.
It was a world not grievously perturbed by thought,
and there was little room in it for figures of profound
intellectual or moral subtlety. The struggles of the
twilight of the soul did not interest him. He could not
draw the Hamlet type as Shakespeare and Tourgeniev
could draw it, though in Conachar in the *Fair Maid of
Perth* he comes near it. Nor could he have given us,
even if he had wished to, any penetrating studies in the
religious consciousness. The saint in the narrower sense,
a figure like Dostoevsky's Alyosha or Prince Myshkin,
was outside his experience and his comprehension. Nor

was he capable of penetrating, like Proust, into the submarine jungle of the half-conscious.

Again, he is no great exponent of the female mind and temperament—in his own class, that is to say, for the criticism is certainly not true of his peasants. For women he had an old-fashioned reverence and regarded them very much as a toast to be drunk after king and constitution. With the *nuances* of feminine character he was little concerned, and towards high passion between gentlefolk he showed always a certain timidity and repugnance. He was incapable of delving in the psychology of sex, since he felt it ill-bred to pry into matters which a gentleman does not talk about in public ; an intimate study of the matter would have been impossible for him without a dereliction of standards. Even had he tried he would most certainly have failed, for he recognized that his " big bow-wow strain " was an impossible medium.[1] We may well agree with Bagehot's pontifical sentences. " The same blunt sagacity of imagination, which fitted him to excel in the rough description of obvious life, rather unfitted him for delineating the less substantial essence of the female character. The nice *minutiæ* of society, by means of which female novelists have been so successful in delineating their own sex, were rather too much for his robust and powerful mind." Woman — cultivated, gently-born woman—remained for him a toast.

What do these admissions amount to ? That his knowledge and imaginative understanding of life had its limits—which is true of every writer that ever lived, even of Shakespeare ; that with certain rare types of character, in which Shakespeare excelled, he must have failed ; that he regarded gentlewomen with too respectful an eye. Not, assuredly, that the interest of the novels depends only on costume, and that the characters are drawn from the skin inwards, and have no souls. Within the wide range of his understanding Scott drew character with a firmness, a subtlety, a propriety, which are not easy to match. He has given us a gallery of living

[1] *Journal*, I. 155.

three-dimensioned figures, who are as completely realized in their minds as they are vividly depicted in their bodies. Carlyle chose a bad test for his denigratory comparison, for Scott's method is pre-eminently the method of Shakespeare. Neither peeps and botanizes and flourishes the scalpel; they make their characters reveal themselves by their speech and deeds in the rough contacts of life.

The two are alike in another point—their attitude towards sex. They are not obsessed by it; no more than the other great writers of the world do they pretend that the relations of man and woman are the only things of first-class importance, and that the only real tragedy is a disastrous love affair. The solitary love tragedy in the *Iliad* is the story of Anteia and Bellerophon, and it occupies six lines out of fifteen thousand. They would have agreed with Dr Johnson that " poetry is not often worse employed than in dignifying the amorous fury of a raving girl." Few of Shakespeare's greatest plays deal with love in the ordinary sense, and the reason given by Johnson was that " love has no great influence on the sum of life." Scott might have qualified this dictum, but he would have urged that love was only one among the major influences, and that to pretend otherwise was to make a hothouse of a spacious garden.

The charge against Scott's character-drawing made by hasty critics may be due to his avoidance of two habits, which have given certain novelists a specious appearance of profundity. One is the trick of dissecting a character before the reader's eyes and filling pages with laboured analysis. No doubt a certain amount of analysis is required from the writer, but Scott held it his main business to make men and women reveal themselves by speech and action, to play the showman as little as possible, to present a finished product and not to print the jottings of his laboratory. In this he was undoubtedly right if we regard the central purpose of the novel. Much remarkable work has been produced on a different theory, but it seems to me to lie apart from the main

high road. The danger before the analyst who is not
content to expound his people through action is that
he is apt, like Proust and in a lesser degree Henry James,
to carry his analysis too far—to reduce his characters
to elements too minute for the business of life, and leave
them mere nebulæ of whirling atoms. Proust has given
us a marvellous world, like some green twilight at the
bottom of the ocean, but its dramas cannot move us
like the doings of the upper globe, for they lack the
larger influences of life. The atoms are too disintegrated
to combine. It is fantastic science rather than art.

The other trick which he shuns is the spurious drama
which is achieved by a frequent recourse to the pathological. Scott is honourably averse to getting effects by
the use of mere ugliness and abnormality. He was
perfectly aware of the half-world of the soul and glances
at it now and then to indicate its presence, but he held
that there were better things to do than to wallow in its
bogs. The truth is that the pathological is too easy.
Take the case of religious mania, which he sketches in a
figure like Ephraim MacBriar. James Hogg has treated
the same topic with power and subtlety in his *Private
Memoirs and Confessions of a Justified Sinner*, but Scott
has given us no such detailed study, since he did not
consider that such perversions were of much significance
in life.

It is the same with other forms of ugliness. He loves
freaks and oddities but he has a clean palate and avoids
the rancid. He reverences humanity too deeply to
emphasize the side which humanity shares with the
animal creation. He has no curiosity about sexual
aberrations—

> the simple vice of brutes
> That own no lust because they have no law.

His interest, like Shakespeare's, is in the " innocency of
love "; but he had not, like Shakespeare, been down
into the dark abysses, and he has no trace of that
repulsion towards the mere fact of sex which we find in
Lear, and *Timon*, and *Hamlet*, and *Measure for Measure*.

It is not prudishness, as Balzac thought, but moral sanity and a due sense of proportion.[1] There is a wonderful little scene in *The Antiquary*, when Mrs Mailsetter and her gossips meet, and Mrs Heukbane recalls the gallantries of her youth :—

> Ah! lasses, an ye had kend his brother as I did—mony a time he wad slip in to see me wi' a brace o' wild-deukes in his pouch, when my first gudeman was awa at the Falkirk tryst—weel, weel—we'se no speak o' that e'enow.

In that scene you have the essence of all the sordid amours of the small Scots village, and Scott just notes their existence, and then goes his way to better things. He was not inclined to make the kitchen-midden the family altar.

As compared with many of his successors, Scott develops his characters in a limited space. He has no such elaborate studies in personality, where the whole is built up cell by cell like a honeycomb, as Flaubert's Emma Bovary, or Tolstoy's Prince Andrew Bolkonsky and Levin, Anna Karenina and Natasha. He works with loins girt inside a narrower field. But he led the way in showing his figures in relation to their environment. No novelist has ever painted in more convincingly a social and historical background, for he anticipated Stendhal and Balzac in regarding each character as largely the product of certain material conditions. His Dinmonts and Nicol Jarvies and David Deanses and Croftangrys have as logical a relation to the world from which they spring as that marvellous company of Balzac's— Goriot, and Poiret, and Grandet, and Rubempré, Philippe Brideau and cousin Bette. He has not the gift of tracing every strand in the social web, which makes Balzac in some ways the greatest of novelists, but he has the same close consciousness of the interlocking of human lives. It is this constant sense of background which enables him to draw to perfection the ordinary man—people like Tolstoy's Vronsky, who in line and tint have a strict

---

[1] In contrast to his eighteenth-century predecessors and to certain moderns, he is always decorous in his language, but that is largely a matter of the current fashion, a question not of morals but of manners.

fidelity to life. Compared to these figures most of the characters in Thackeray and Dickens seem bookish. The background, too, which he draws, is as large as life itself, for it is limited to no one social grade, no enclave of space or time ; almost alone among English novelists he is at his ease both in the city and in the wilds.

IV

The novel at its greatest is subject to the tests by which all imaginative creation is ultimately tried. It must present life in the round, in the deeps, and on the heights. It must possess that " stellar and undiminishable something " which can

> tease us out of thought,
> As doth eternity.

It must have a high seriousness and a profound vision of life. If this is wanting in Scott, then he must be excluded from the inner circle of greatness and relegated to the populous borderland of mere skilful entertainers. Wordsworth found the lack in his poetry. " As a poet Scott cannot live, for he has never in verse written anything addressed to the immortal part of man." Others have found it in the novels. " We have mind, manners, animation," says Bagehot, " but it is the stir of this world. We miss the consecrating power." Carlyle is no less emphatic. " They do not found themselves on deep interests, but on comparatively trivial ones ; not on the perennial, perhaps not even on the lasting ; " and he shakes the disapproving head of a fellow Scot, who would fain revere but can only admire :—" Not profitable for doctrine, for reproof, for edification, for building up and elevating in any shape ! The sick heart will find no healing here, the darkly struggling heart no guidance ; the Heroic that is in all men no divine awakening voice."

Much of Carlyle's criticism is clearly beside the point. He hankered after something which we have no right to ask from an imaginative creator, something for which we must go to the professed philosophers and to certain poets—a definite, formulated creed of life. He was a very serious man, a Reformer born out of season, come of a serious stock and belonging to a perplexed generation. Dr Chalmers said of him after a conversation, " That young man prefers seriousness to truth." He wanted a message, a formula, but it is not easy to pin the greatest imaginative writers down to one moral, or even to a code of morals. What is the teaching of Homer ? What is the lesson of Shakespeare ? It would wrong their magnificence to force them into the bonds of any creed.

But Carlyle has still to be reckoned with. We are entitled to demand from the greatest not only a picture of the superficies of life, but an interpretation, something profitable for doctrine and edification. Bagehot's phrase is the best. There must be a " consecrating power."

It is because I find this in Scott in the highest degree —higher than in any other English novelist, higher than in Balzac, as high as in Tolstoy and Dostoevsky at their best—that I feel assured of his immortality. He has the largeness and rightness of the immortals. He makes our world more solemn by his sure instinct for the tragic, which is the failure of something not ignoble, through inherent weakness or through a change of circumstances to which it cannot adapt itself. Previous chapters contain many instances of such figures revealed in some great moment of drama. They are mirrors in which we can discern the futility of our dearest hopes. Always in his bustling world Scott is aware of the shadow of mortality. It is a gay world, but at the last it is a solemn world, and few can so cunningly darken the stage and make the figures seem no longer men and women, but puppets moving under the hand of the Eternal.

In such passages we can read Scott's purpose, which lay deep in his consciousness, to inculcate " reverence and godly fear." He has a very clear philosophy, of which the basis is the eternity and the wisdom of the divine ordering of things. His aim is that of Greek tragedy, to secure a valiant acquiescence in the course of

fate and in the dispensations of human life. To him
Zeus always governs ; Prometheus may be a fine fellow,
but Zeus is still king of gods and men. He believed
that in the world as it was created there was a soul of
goodness, and that, in spite of evil, the " inward frame
of things " was wiser than its critics. Throughout history
there have been rebels against this doctrine. The
passionate worship of the Virgin in the Middle Ages was
a symptom of the revolt against the austerities of the
Father and the Son. " Mary concentrated in herself the
whole rebellion of man against fate ; the whole protest
against divine law ; the whole contempt for human law
as its outcome ; the whole unutterable fury of human
nature beating itself against the walls of its prison-
house." [1] Scott's purpose is the classic reconciliation.
Like Meredith's Lucifer in starlight, he is always aware
of the " army of unalterable law." To him peace and
fortitude are to be found in a manly and reverent
submission. *In la sua volontade è nostra pace.*

But his reconciling power lies not only in submission
to law but in his joyous recognition of its soul of goodness. If he makes the world more solemn he also makes
it more sunlit. That is the moral consequence of comedy,
and of comedy in the widest sense Scott is an especial
master. He has Shakespeare's gift of charging our life
with new and happier values. His people do not, like
Tourgeniev's, fight a losing battle ; they are triumphant,
they must be triumphant, for there is that in them
which is in tune with the inner nature of things. The
novels enlarge our vision, light up dark corners, break
down foolish barriers, and make life brighter and more
spacious. If they do not preach any single maxim they,
in Shelley's words, " repeal large codes of fraud and woe."
They restore faith in humanity by revealing its forgotten
graces and depths.

We have noted, in considering the novels as they
appeared, the many cases where Scott in high tragic
moments performs the task which Aristotle attributed
to tragedy, of purifying the emotions by pity and fear.

[1] Henry Adams, *Mont-Saint-Mickel and Chartres,* 276.

Such moments dignify life for us and link it with the universal, they widen our terrestrial horizons and reveal the infinite heavens above us. This gift alone would rank him with the great creative forces in literature. But I find in him another and a rarer gift, in which tragedy and comedy seem to blend, and to which heart and brain subtly contribute—the power of looking at life with such clear and compassionate eyes that he can find in its ironies both mirth and pity. The result is not an intensifying but a calming of the emotions, for the discords are resolved in an ultimate harmony. Swinburne writes somewhere of finding " in love of loving-kindness, light," and in that word loving-kindness we have Scott's secret. It is the quality which we meet when, in Homer, the Elders of Troy see Helen on the battlements and because of her beauty forgive her all the woes she has brought upon them : when Odysseus comes upon his father digging alone in the vineyard in shabby gaiters, with his old hands protected by gauntlets against the thorns : when Don Quixote finds that there are no birds in last year's nest. We feel the pity of things, but also, strangely, their mercy.

Scott was wholly free from sensibility, the crying fault of his age. He could write its jargon in his careless moods, but when he came to serious business there is a noble austerity in his reading of character. But there is also the insight of the healer and the reconciler. He has the Greek quality of *sophrosyne*, which means literally the possession of " saving thoughts." He can penetrate to the greatness of the humble, the divine spark in the clod. No other writer has done quite the same thing for the poor. Many have expounded their pathos and their humours, and some few have made them lovable and significant, but Scott alone has lifted them to the sublime. Through their mouths he proclaims his evangel. It is not the kings and captains who most eloquently preach love of country, but Edie Ochiltree the beggar, who has no belongings but a blue gown and a wallet. It is not a queen or a great lady who lays down the profoundest laws of conduct, but Jeanie Deans, the peasant girl. It is Bessie Maclure, a lone widow among the hills, who in the Covenant strife has the vision of peace through a wider charity.

Scott has what Stevenson found in Dostoevsky, a " lovely goodness." He lacks the flaming intensity of the Russian ; his even balance of soul saves him from the spiritual melodrama to which the latter often descends. But like him he loves mankind without reservation, is incapable of hate, and finds nothing created altogether common or unclean. This Border laird, so happy in his worldly avocations that some would discard him as superficial, stands at the end securely among the prophets, for he gathers all things, however lowly and crooked and broken, within the love of God.

CHAPTER XIV

THE MAN

A WRITER lives by his books, and in our judgment of his art the man himself does not concern us. But since humanity is interested in itself, and will always look for the person behind the achievement, we are bound to speculate on the character of the author, and, if other evidence be wanting, to seek to deduce that character from his work. The blind Homer will be sought behind his epics, and the man Shakespeare behind the plays. Had we known nothing of Dr Johnson except his publications a great figure would be absent from our pantheon, and without Keats's letters we should have gone far astray in our verdict on the poet. With Scott the case is different. Out of the immense and varied mass of his work a picture of the worker emerges which is substantially the truth. Even without Lockhart and the *Journal* we should have had a full and true conception of Walter Scott. The man and his achievements were of a piece, and there was no schism between fact and dream.

It is not difficult to make a picture of one whose nature is all crude lights and shadows and sharp angles, for a character with anything of the fantastic or perverse in it lends itself to easy representation. But it is hard to draw on a little canvas the man whose nature is large and central and human, without cranks or oddities. The very simplicity and wholesomeness of such souls defy an easy summary, for they are as spacious in their effect and as generous in their essence as daylight or summer. In these days of emotional insecurity we are apt to confuse the normal with the mediocre, and to assume that largeness is also shallowness. We are a little afraid of the high road and find more attraction in the crooked by-ways. Such a mood is not conducive to a fair judgment of Scott, or even to an understanding of him at all. For he is the normal man raised to the highest power, eschewing both fantastic vices and freakish virtues.

He stood at the heart of life, and his interests embraced everything that interested his fellows. That is the keystone of his character and mind—they were central and universal. He was impatient of nothing that God had made ; and he did not merely tolerate, for he was eager to understand. His interest was as acute in the way a merchant managed his counting-house and a banker his credits as in the *provenance* of a ballad or some romantic genealogy. No lover of the past had ever his feet more firmly planted in the present. He was pre-eminently a social being, recognizing his duty to others and the close interconnexion of humanity. The problem of his character is, therefore, the way in which imaginative genius and practical sagacity ran in harness, how the spiritual detachment of the dreamer was combined with this lively sense of community.

I

The first question we ask is how he regarded the craft which gave him his fame and his livelihood. Of one thing there can be no doubt—he loved it and gave to it his deepest interest and the best powers of his mind. The instinct to express himself in words was at the root of his being ; he must always be writing, and if there was no more urgent task there was the *Journal*, and letters to friends, or scraps of verse in which he could give rein to his fancies. He felt himself a member of a great fraternity and cherished a masonic loyalty towards his colleagues. But he had no heroics about it and claimed for it no privileges. The rewards it brought were so utterly incommensurate with the pains that his attitude was always a little apologetic, as of one to whom the gods had given too generous gifts.

This point of view needs further analysis, for it was different in kind from Byron's aristocratic condescension. There were baser elements in it, no doubt, for in the Edinburgh of his day the business of letters, at least of the lighter letters, was not too well regarded. Scott would not have been his father's son if he had not felt an unwilling respect for the professions which carried with them social predominance, like politics, the services, and the law. But the true source lay deeper. In the first place he did not rank his own achievements very high. He would have been ready to give Shakespeare a place far above any prince or potentate, but he did not consider himself to be in the same world as Shakespeare. He thought quite seriously that many of his contemporaries wrote better than he did ; consequently he was as wholly free from literary jealousies as any man that ever lived. For Wordsworth and Coleridge and Jane Austen, who could do things outside his powers, he had a sincere reverence. He was eager to discern every scintilla of merit among his contemporaries, and to praise it generously. Apart from his own ragged regiment of Parnassus he was the friend and encourager of every man and woman who used the pen. He could appreciate writers who were at opposite poles from himself ; he went out of his way to praise Mrs Shelley's *Frankenstein* because he thought that Shelley had written it ; he took no part in the attack on the " Cockney School," though Leigh Hunt gave him ample provocation ; and he tried to induce Charles Lamb to visit him at Abbotsford. Such a spirit of catholic appreciation was possible only for a man who had no vanity. He had none of that peasant vice of jealous irritation into which at times Carlyle sank.

There was a graver element in his view of his craft. He was free from the social vulgarity which made even so wise a woman as Lady Louisa Stuart write of Maria Edgeworth that she " was as good a gentlewoman as any of us had she not drowned her gentility in her inkpot." But he had something of Byron's dislike of the " mere writer." He considered that the man who retired from

the bustle of the world to spin his fancies was something
of a deserter from the combatant ranks of humanity.
He had so many fighting strains in his ancestry that he
hungered always for action, for a completer life than
could be lived only in the mind.   Dr Johnson once
angrily withdrew Mansfield from the category of " mere
lawyers," and Scott had the same impatience of professional limitations.   It was this instinct which was
responsible for his commercial and political ventures
and—largely—for the *folie des grandeurs* of Abbotsford,
but it also gave him his insight into the heart and the
prepossessions of the ordinary man.   He never lost
himself in the stuffy parlours of self-conscious art.

In the main it was a sound instinct, for it was based
on his conviction of the overriding importance of character.   The plain fellow who shouldered a musket for
his country seemed to him to have a moral dignity to
which the belauded artist had no claim.   His deepest
respect was for the homespun virtues.   He told his
daughter that he thanked God that " nothing really
worth having or caring about in this world is uncommon."
" I fear," he once chid Lockhart, " you are too apt to
measure things by some reference to literature—to disbelieve that anybody can be worth much care who has
no knowledge of that sort of thing or taste for it.   God
help us !   What a poor world this would be if that was
the true doctrine !   I have read books enough, and
observed and conversed with enough of eminent and
splendidly cultivated minds, too, in my time ;   but I
assure you, I have heard higher sentiments from the lips
of poor uneducated men and women, when exerting the
spirit of severe yet gentle heroism under difficulties and
afflictions, or speaking their simple thoughts as to circumstances in the lot of friends and neighbours, than I
ever yet met with out of the pages of the Bible."[1]
When he was warmly greeted by Wellington he could
not believe that it was due to his literary fame—" What
would the Duke of Wellington think of a few bits of
novels ? "   Great deeds performed in a great spirit

[1] Lockhart, VI. 60-1.

seemed to him the only source of honour. In Lockhart's
words, " To have done things worthy to be written was
in his eye a dignity to which no man made any approach
who had only written things worthy to be read."[1] This
ethical bias may have been overweighted, but it was
the faith which moved him to the heroism of his last
years. Let it be remembered that it was shared also
by Keats, who in a famous letter dismissed the view
that " works of genius were the finest things in the
world," and set far above them the " probity and dis-
interestedness " of one of his friends.[2]

Such a man, with such a creed, will run two risks.
His world of fancy and thought, since he refuses to
parade it, may become a secret domain which, owing to
its very seclusion from outer realities, may insensibly
colour his whole attitude to life. Again, his robust
insistence upon the value of common standards may
induce a vein of worldliness, a false approbation of things
as they are. The first peril is abundantly manifested
in Scott's career. During the dark days of 1826 he
gave a list of his consolations to Lady Louisa Stuart,
and one of the chief was his " quiet thoughts." From
these thoughts came the immortal part of his work, but
also his disasters. " I have worn a wishing-cap, the
power of which has been to divert present griefs by a
turn of the wand of imagination, and gild over the
future prospect by prospects more fair than can ever be
realized."[3] If the task chimed in with his wishes, no
man could be more painstaking and sagacious in practical
affairs, but if not, he would take refuge in his waking
dreams, and become a visionary and a gambler. Of this
there were graver consequences than indolence in directing
his own affairs. His secret world made him a little
insensitive to the anomalies of the real one. It killed
in him, except at rare moments, the soul of the reformer.
It was a domain where the soul turned in upon itself,
and dreams did not result in action. Being mainly
concerned with the past it was a static thing, and bred

[1] III. 376.   [2] Colvin, *Letters of John Keats*, 54.
[3] *Journal*, I. 66.

few ideals for the future. The dweller in it could not be
one of those

> who rest not ; who think long
> Till they discern as from a hill
> At the sun's hour of morning song,
> Known of souls only, and those souls free,
> The sacred spaces of the sea.

More ; the man who issued from it had his eyes dazzled,
and the glamour of his dreams was apt to gild ugly
realities.

Scott's worldliness, which is Carlyle's main charge
against him, needs to be exactly stated. At its best,
it was an acute appreciation of the conventions by which
life is conducted ; at its worst, it was an overvaluing of
these conventions. It gave him the grasp of the mechanism of society which the novels reveal, but it shut out
from his ken one side of the spiritual world and one type
of human soul. It made him tolerant of public abuses
which he would have rooted up had they shown themselves in his private life. But he had no abiding relish
for the grosser material rewards and pomps of success ;
he might like the notion of them, but he was soon
satiated by a little of the substance. Abbotsford was
rather an aerial dream than a terrestrial pleasure house ;
it was endeared to him partly because it was a thing of
his own creation, but largely because of the human
relationships that grew up around it.

And there was nothing in it of what we call snobbery.[1]
Scott was too great a gentleman ever to feel insecure,
and insecurity is the mark of the snob. He liked to
live among long-descended and cultivated people, because
they talked his own language, but since he took no
liberties he permitted none. His relations with the
chiefs of his own sept, the Buccleuchs, are a model of
well-bred friendship. He had a romantic veneration
for the great Border house and a warm affection for its
successive heads, but when it came to shutting out the
Selkirk people from the grounds of Bowhill he could

[1] George Borrow's excited diatribe (*The Romany Rye.* App. VII.) is a
melancholy example of the error into which prejudice may lead an honest man.

speak his mind, so that Duke Charles wrote to him, " I have reason to thank God for many things, but especially for having given me friends who will tell me the truth." He bore himself in any company with an easy modesty, and a breeding which Lord Dudley contrasted most favourably with Byron's. In his parties at Abbotsford he singled out for special kindness the humbler guests. Could any man with a trace of the snob in his composition have tolerated for a moment the *gaucheries* of James Hogg ? His chivalry was manifested not only in his manner to high-born ladies but in his treatment of every woman he met, from the preposterous Mrs Coutts to his cotters' wives. Twice in his life he was guilty of a defect in generosity, once towards his brother and once towards Constable ; but I can find no instance where he failed in that respect towards anyone humbler than himself.

II

Scott was pre-eminently a social being, living his life in close contact with his fellows, and he could not hold himself aloof from the problems of society. The French Revolution left no one in Britain unaffected : one class of mind it stimulated to speculative ardour and bold schemes of change : another, not less honest, it drove into a stiff conservatism. In the eyes of the latter the first duty was to preserve the historic fabric now threatened, even at the cost of perpetuating blemishes. To mend your roof in a gale might mean the destruction of the whole house. Scott was not interested in the political game for its own sake.

In general I care very little about the matter, and from year's end to year's end have scarce a thought connected with them, except to laugh at the fools who think to make themselves great men out of little by swaggering in the rear of a party. But either actually important events, or such as seemed so by their close neighbourhood to me, have always hurried me off my feet, and made me, as I have sometimes afterwards regretted, more forward and more violent than those who had a regular jog-trot way of busying themselves in public matters.[1]

That is to say, he had the occasional intemperance of
the suddenly aroused layman ; he had a natural bias
against all change, and he hated wholeheartedly what he
regarded as the central doctrine of the French Revolution,
what Coleridge called that " science of cosmopolitanism
without country, of philanthropy without neighbourliness
or consanguinity, in short, of all the impostures of that
philosophy . . . which would sacrifice each to the shadowy
idol of all."

Unfortunately this view was more than a revolt against
those unstable progressives who were for ever itching to
tinker at the social machine. It was more than Falkland's
philosophical conservatism—" When it is not necessary
to change, it is necessary not to change ; " or Burke's
classic warning—" The old building stands well enough,
though part Gothic, part Grecian, and part Chinese,
until an attempt is made to square it into uniformity.
Then, indeed, it may come down upon our heads
altogether in much uniformity of ruin." Scott opposed
change even when the old building stood very ill. The
notorious instance is the matter of Scottish reforms.
Scotland in his day was, as Cockburn put it, no better
than a village at a great man's gate, the electoral system
was rotten to the core, and the best elements in the
land were unrepresented in public life. There were
only 2600 voters on the county rolls and 1300 town
councillors elected the burgh members. Of this farcical
situation Scott was fully aware ; yet he called men
scamps for desiring a juster system. The judicial edifice
was no more satisfactory than the political, but he
resisted every attempt to better it. In both cases the
reason was the same ; he feared that if reform once
began it would pull down the good with the bad,
and destroy that Scotland which he knew and loved.
Hazlitt's famous rhodomontade on the subject of his
politics is ludicrously unjust, with its declamation
against one who " stooped to the unworthy arts of
adulation and abetted the views of the great with the
pettifogging feelings of the meanest dependant on office
. . . who repaid the public liberality by striking a

secret and envenomed blow at every one who was not
the ready tool of power ; " [1] but impartial observers
might well have been perplexed by this relic-worship, so
inconsistent with Scott's practical good sense.

To his prepossession against change, a feeling born of
fear and love, must be added two other causes which
determined his political views. As we have seen, his
mind was wholly unspeculative. He had no theory of
the state, no philosophy of society, and the *pruritus
disputandi* of Edinburgh dinner-parties had sickened him
of the whole subject. Like Lady Louisa Stuart, he
hated " marches of ages and all that vile slang." [2] His
mind was eminently concrete, he had no interest in
what was valuable in the Whig speculative activity, and
he was acutely sensitive to what was bad. For in the
Whiggism of the time there was much that was shallow
and foppish. Scott had Burke's conviction that life
could not be conducted by abstract reasoning.

> The Whigs will live and die in the heresy that the world is
> ruled by little pamphlets and speeches, and that if you can
> sufficiently demonstrate that a line of conduct is most con-
> sistent with men's interest, you have therefore and thereby
> demonstrated that they will at length, after a few speeches on
> the subject, adopt it of course. [3]

He was not disposed to set much value on new theories
of society and morals, for he put all theory in the second
class of importance. If he was told that such and such
a thing was in accordance with the spirit of the age, he
replied that the spirit of the age might be a lying spirit
with no claim to infallibility. The rejoicing dialectic of
his Whig contemporaries left him cold and suspicious.
He admitted their enthusiasm and honesty, but the
truth they proclaimed he thought at the best a half-
truth. The deeper verities of the imagination and instinct
seemed to him to be eternally beyond their dapper
logic. " This will never do," Jeffrey had written of
Wordsworth, and the sentence was a flashlight to reveal
the whole arid world of Whiggism. If Scott was a little

---

[1] *The Spirit of the Age.*
[2] *Letters to Miss Louisa Clinton*, 60. [3] *Journal*, I. 16.

blind to the merits of the new school, he saw with acid clearness its limitations.

A second reason predisposed him against them. Their practice seemed to him to limp far behind their professions. They contented themselves with cultivating at high tension emotions towards humanity at large, but they had little themselves of the human touch. Scott knew the commonalty of Scotland better than any man of his day, and he was an assiduous practical philanthropist; he resented—as many have resented since his time—the claims of a little coterie of intellectuals to speak for a people of whom they knew nothing. Their creed was noble, their performance trivial. They were like Obadiah's bull in *Tristram Shandy*, " who, though he never certainly did produce a calf, nevertheless went about his business with so much gravity, that he commanded the respect of the whole parish." He felt about them as Lady Louisa Stuart felt about the Welsh hierarchy. She found one bishop who " was liberal, proposed to equalize the sees, argued against the wealth and power of the Church, and, being enraged against not getting the highest preferment himself, never dreamed of troubling his head about his paltry diocese. The illiberal prejudiced bishops come and reside." [1]

Yet, apart from certain Scottish questions, it would be an error to regard Scott as a Tory of the Eldon type. Like Burns in his great days, he was a Pittite, rather an anti-revolutionary than an anti-reformer. In the last months of his life he told a friend that he was no enemy to reform—" if the machine does not work well, it must be mended—but it should be by the best workmen you have." [2] This last phrase gives the key to his faith. He believed in persons rather than in policies. " Away," he would have exclaimed with Canning, " with the cant of ' measures not men,' the idle supposition that it is the harness, and not the horses, that draws the chariot along ! " He had deep in him the instinct to find a leader and cleave to him, and he found what he sought

---

[1] *Letters to Miss Louisa Clinton*, 2nd Series, 113.
[2] Lockhart, VII. 372.

in Wellington. Wellington might have led him very far
on the path of radical progress, but in the newer men,
the Greys and Russells, and in the talkative lawyers like
Brougham, he did not find the quality he could trust.

In many ways he misread the signs of the times, as
in his belief in the rising of the north-country colliers
and weavers which led him to organize the Buccleuch
legion, and in the tragic fears of his last illness. What
had happened in France haunted him like a spectre.
When Sir John Sinclair told Adam Smith that the
country would be ruined, the dying economist replied,
" My dear young man, there is a good deal of ruin in a
country." But if Scott is to be blamed for sometimes
losing faith in the soundness of heart of the nation, it
may well be argued that he was alive to a peril to which
too many of his contemporaries were blind. Looking
back to-day, it is clear that Britain in the two decades
after Waterloo was treading a far more perilous path
than she had trod in the war with Napoleon. Liverpool,
Eldon and the rest blundered many times, but those
stiff and prosaic gentlemen had in them something of the
heroic, and they brought the country out of the jaws of
destruction, for other and showier people to win the
credit. Scott saw the fires smouldering beneath the
crust, though he may have underestimated the crust's
strength, and he was impatient, rightly impatient, with
the sciolists and dreamers who believed that they walked
on impregnable rock. He was not prepared to see his
country ruined to make a belletristic holiday. " Fallait-il
laisser périr l'Angleterre pour plaire aux poètes ? "

The Whig creed was potent in its day, and it had
many beneficent consequences, but, since it was concerned chiefly with the form of things, with mechanism,
it has long since ceased to be a living force among us.
So far as it attempted to provide an organic philosophy
of politics, it signally failed. Let us turn to the positive
substance of Scott's faith, which was a deeper thing than
his antipathy to Whig merits and Whig defects. Its
first element was nationalism. He believed firmly in
the virtue of local patriotism and the idiomatic life of

the smaller social unit. Whenever Scotland was concerned he was prepared to break with his party, with his leaders, and with the whole nobility, gentry and intellectuality of Britain. " The Tories and Whigs may go be damned together, as names that have disturbed old Scotland, and torn asunder the most kindly feelings since the days they were invented."[1] This was no mere petulant parochialism, but a deep conviction that on the strength and individuality of the part depended the value of the whole. The second element was a sense of community, of society as an organic thing where every man's life was linked with that of his fellows. For this reason he disliked the intense preoccupation of a man with his own soul, which he thought had been the weakness of Scottish Calvinism, and which the imported evangelicalism from England was reviving north of the Tweed. For this reason, too, he detested the selfishness of the new industrialism.

This latter was the public question on which he felt most passionately. " God's justice is requiting, and will yet further requite, those who have blown up this country into a state of unsubstantial opulence, at the expense of the health and morals of the lower classes."[2] He agreed with Southey's terrible comparison of the submerged classes to the dogs of Constantinople, " a nuisance to the community while they live, and dying miserably at last." But he was fair on the matter, and did not attempt to set up a golden past against a dingy present. Take the discussion between Christie Steele and Croftangry—

" An older family, perhaps, and probably more remembered and regretted than later possessors ? " . . .

" Mair regretted—mair missed ? I liked ane of the auld family very weel, but I winna say that for them a'. How should they be mair missed than the Treddleses ? The cotton mill was such a thing for the country ! The mair bairns a cotter body had the better ; they would make their own keep frae the time they were five years auld, and a widow wi' three or four bairns was a wealthy woman in the time of the Treddleses."

---

[1] *Journal*, I. 87. [2] *Ibid.*, I. 313.

"But the health of those poor children, my good friend—their education and religious instruction——"

"For health," said Christie, looking gloomily at me, "ye maun ken little o' the world, sir, if ye dinna ken that the health of the poor man's body, as weel as his youth and his strength, are all at the command of the rich man's purse. There never was a trade so unhealthy yet but men would fight to get wark at it for twa pennies a day above the common wage. But the bairns were reasonably cared for in the way of air and exercise, and a very responsible youth heard them their Carritch, and gied them lessons in Readiemadeasy.[1] Now, what did they ever get before? Maybe on a winter day they would be called out to beat the wood for cock or siclike ; and then the starving weans would maybe get a bite of broken bread, and maybe no, just as the butler was in humour."[2]

It is Scott's own voice speaking ; he had no illusions about the eternal problem of the poor.

A friend of mine, a famous professor of economics, once proposed to write a book on the political economy of Scott, for he held that he had a stronger grasp of the subject than most of its professional exponents. It was the fashion in his day for the pundits of both parties to sneer at his romancer's economics, but the whirligig of time has avenged him. We have learned in recent years that so-called economic laws are in the main deductions from contemporary data and have no universal validity, and we have been compelled to look upon facts with shrewder eyes than the classic theorists. Just as Whig views of the mechanism of the state have now only an historic interest, so the economic dogmatism of the early nineteenth century is a speech strange to our ears. But Scott remains singularly up to date, for he had imagination, and was very close to the imperishable things in life. *Malachi Malagrowther* will well repay study, for, apart from its sane and honourable nationalism, it is full of acute economic thinking. He argues for the localization of the issue of credit, which involved the slight inflation that the circumstances of Scotland required, very much in the language of to-day. He feared the craze for uniformity, because he realized that it

---

[1] Reading made easy.
[2] *Chronicles of the Canongate*, 1st ser., Chap. IV.

rould bring to Scotland the disasters of the unreformed
English poor law, and he made merry with the extreme
aissez-faire dogma merely by stating it.

> Leave your kelp-rocks to the undisturbed possession of seals
> and mermaids, if there be any—you will buy *barilla* cheaper
> in South America. Send your Highland fishers to America
> and Botany Bay, where they will find plenty of food, and let
> them leave their present sterile residence in the utter and
> undisturbed solitude for which Nature designed it. Do not
> think you do any hardship in obeying the universal law of
> nature, which leads wants and supplies to draw to their just
> and proper level, and equalize each other ; which attracts gold
> to those spots, and those only, where it can be profitably
> employed, and induces man to transport himself from the
> realms of famine to those happier regions, where labour is
> light and subsistence plentiful.[1]

The same realism is seen in his attitude to the poor.
He had no belief in the wizardry of abstract political
rights ; his view was Coleridge's—" It is a mockery of
our fellow creatures' wrongs to call them equal in rights,
when by the bitter compulsion of their wants we make
them inferior to us in all that can soften the heart and
dignify the understanding ; " so he set himself within
his own orbit to make a better commonwealth. He
introduced at Abbotsford a system of health insurance,
and being always mindful of the moral issue, he refused
the easy path of charity, and in bad times arranged for
relief work at full wages. He was a foe to tippling
houses, and defended the Scottish reluctance to grant
licences as compared with England. He proposed a
scheme of unemployment insurance in factories, the
premiums to be paid wholly by the owners, on the
ground that it would retard unhealthy industrial expansion and compel manufacturers to rely less on casual
labour.[2] These are scarcely the notions of a crusted
Eldonite.

It may be admitted that Scott's sympathies with labour
and his knowledge of its problems were circumscribed.
To the pathetic early struggles of trade-unionism he was

---

[1] *Misc. Prose Works*, XXI. 382.
[2] Lockhart, IV. 73, 85-6. See p. 222 *supra*.

always hostile, for he scented conspiracy, and he was horrified to discover symptoms of it in Galashiels. He was above all things a countryman, who knew and honoured the peasant ; of the proletariat in the towns, and

> the fierce confederate storm
> Of sorrow barricadoed evermore
> Within the walls of cities,

he had Wordsworth's ignorance and restless fear. But for the poor man whom he understood, who was knit to him by a common domicile and ancestry, he had sympathy and understanding in the amplest measure. He proposed to show Washington Irving " some of our excellent plain Scotch people—not fine gentlemen and ladies, for such you can meet everywhere, and they are everywhere the same." They were the stock which he most honoured, for they were the most idiomatic and enduring thing in the nation. It was this love of plain folk which made Crabbe his favourite reading. They are the true heroes and heroines of his novels, and they were his best friends in life. He respected them far too much to sentimentalize over them ; indeed he had their own contempt for sensibility. When a perfervid young lady swooned on being presented to him and then kissed Henry Mackenzie's hand, Scott's comment was that of a Border peasant : " Did you ever hear the like of that English lass, to faint at the sight of a crippled clerk of session, and kiss the dry withered hand of an old tax-gatherer——! " He had the same tenderness, the same tough fescennine humour, the same rugged sense of decency. He never entered the " huts where poor men lie " with the condescension of a district visitor, for you cannot patronize that which is yourself. Of all great writers, perhaps, he was the one who lived closest to the poor. He was nearer to them than Shakespeare, who saw only their comedy and their vices ; far nearer than Shelley, to whom the poor were the " polluting multitude," though he might pity and defend them ; nearer even than Wordsworth, who did not know how to unbend. Of Wordsworth a country neigh-

bour said that he " was not a man as folks could crack
with nor not a man as could crack wi' folks," whereas
of Scott the report was that he talked to everyone as if
he were a blood-relation.

As an old man Wordsworth confessed that, while he
had never had any respect for the Whigs, he had always
had a great deal of the Chartist in him. Of Scott it may
be said that he had much of that practical socialism
which Toryism has never lacked. He envisaged life in
terms rather of duties than of rights ; he hated the
rootless and the mechanical ; he believed in property
but only as something held on a solemn trust ; his
social conscience was too quick to accept the calculating
inhumanity of the economists. To him, as to Newman,
it seemed that a worthy society must have both order
and warmth. If he had ever sought a formula for his
creed it might well have been Bagehot's famous phrase,
" Toryism is enjoyment".

III

Scott had not the metaphysical turn of his countrymen,
and he had no instinct to preach, but the whole of his
life and work was based on a reasoned philosophy of
conduct. Its corner-stones were humility and discipline.
The life of man was difficult, but not desperate, and to
live it worthily you must forget yourself and love others.
The failures were the egotists who were wrapped up in
self, the doctrinaires who were in chains to a dogma, the
Pharisees who despised their brethren. In him the
" common sense " of the eighteenth century was coloured
and lit by Christian charity. Happiness could only be
attained by the unselfregarding. He preaches this faith
through the mouth of Jeanie Deans—indeed it is the
basis of all his ethical portraiture, it crops up everywhere
in his letters and *Journal,* and in his review of Canto III
of *Childe Harold* in the *Quarterly* he expounds it to
Byron and labours to reconcile him with the world.
This paper should not be forgotten, for in it Scott
professes explicitly his moral code. Its axiom is that

there is no royal road to heart's ease, but that there is a path for the humble pilgrim. The precepts for such are—

> to narrow our wishes and desires within the scope of our present powers of attainment ; to consider our misfortunes as our inevitable share in the patrimony of Adam ; to bridle those irritable feelings which, ungoverned, are sure to become governors ; to shun that intensity of galling and self-wounding reflection which our poet has described in his own burning language ; to stoop, in short, to the realities of life, repent if we have offended, and pardon if we have been trespassed against ; to look on the world less as our foe than as a doubtful and capricious friend whose applause we ought as far as possible to deserve, but neither to court nor to condemn.

To this philosophy he added a stalwart trust in the Christian doctrines, a trust which was simple, unqualified and unquestioning. His was not a soul to be troubled by doubts or to be kindled to mystical fervour, though he was ready to admit the reality of the latter. There is a passage in the *Journal* where he defends the work of Methodism as " carrying religion into classes in society where it would scarce be found to penetrate, did it rely merely upon proof of its doctrines, upon calm reasoning, and upon rational argument."[1] But such excitements were not for him ; for his mind to seek them would have been like drug-taking, a renunciation of self-discipline. In the Scotland of his day this teaching was much in season. The old fires of Calvinism had burned too murkily, the light of the *Aufklärung* had been too thin and cold, but in Scott was a spirit which could both illumine and comfort his world. He gave it a code of ethics robuster because more rational, and he pointed the road to a humaner faith.

IV

The strong wine of genius too often cracks and flaws the containing vessel. The mind revolts against the body, the subconscious against the conscious, and there

[1] I. 102.

is an expense of spirit in a waste of fears and frustrations. But just as there was no strife or sedition in Scott's intellectual powers, so there were no fissures in his character. Carlyle spoke truth when he said that a sounder piece of British manhood was not put together in that eighteenth century of Time. He was a man of the centre, like his own Johnny Dodds of Farthing's Acre. There was a clearing-house in his soul where all impulses were ordered and adjusted, and this repose gave him happiness. That was the secret of his geniality, for throughout his crowded life he was at peace with himself, and had the gift of communicating his peace to the world. This balance did not chill, as it does with many, the emotional side of his nature, but it gave it depth and stability ; instead of sentiment he had pity and tenderness, and his perfect courage was never marred by bravado. The words which Sir Walter Raleigh has used of Shakespeare apply most fully to him ; he was a " man cast in the antique mould of humanity, equable, alert and gay."

Such a one makes a light and a warmth around him. Scott had no enemies, except a prejudiced few who had never met him. No class, no type escaped his glamour. To Byron, who did not praise readily, he seemed " as nearly a thorough good man as a man can be." [1] He was the centre round which for thirty years there clustered a whole community of most diverse men and women, and when the sun set the constellation was scattered. James Ballantyne died four months after his friend, James Hogg followed him after three troubled years, and those who survived him longer were to the last under his spell. To Lady Louisa Stuart, to Lockhart, to Morritt and Cranstoun, even to Jeffrey and Cockburn he remained the major influence in their lives. Skene, who wandered about the world for thirty years more, was found by his daughter just before his death sitting by the fire with a strange radiance in his face. " Scott has been here," he cried, " dear Scott ! He told me that he had come from a great distance to pay me a visit,

[1] *Letters and Journals*, V. 221.

and he has been sitting here with me talking of all our old happy days together. He said it was long since we had met, but he is not in the least changed ; his face was just as cheerful and pleasant as it used to be." [1]

Skene's dying vision is a parable of Scott's bequest to the world. He has left us not only the products of his fancy but almost his bodily presence, a personality which to his lovers is as real as if in the flesh he still moved among us. Alone of the great imaginative creators he draws us to an affectionate intimacy. It is the man rather than the writer that still haunts his own Border, like an emanation from its changeless hills and waters, so that on some forgotten drove-road in Ettrick one almost looks to see in an autumn gloaming his ruddy face and silvery hair, and to hear the kindly burr of his speech. It has been given to him to conquer the world, and yet remain the tutelary genius of his native glens.

He seems to me the greatest, because the most representative, of Scotsmen, since in his mind and character he sums up more fully than any other the idiomatic qualities of his countrymen and translates them into a universal tongue. John Knox gave his land the Reformation, an inestimable but a perilous gift, which led to high spiritual exaltations, but also to much blood and tears. By itself it was a forcing-house to produce monstrous growths, and it required to be freshened by the sun and winds of the common world. Burns, with a Greek freedom in his soul, gave Scotland her own French Revolution, burned up much folly with the fires of poetry, and reconciled in a common humanity ancient warring elements in the national life. Scott completed what the eighteenth-century philosophers had begun and gave her her own Renaissance. He is, with Burns, her great liberator and reconciler. He saved his land from the narrow rootless gentility and the barren utilitarianism of the illuminates ; he gave her confidence by reopening to her the past ; and he blended into one living tradition many things which the shallow had despised and the dull had forgotten. Gently he led her

[1] *Blackwood's Magazine*, June 1896.

back to nature and the old simplicities. His mission was that of Hosea the prophet :—" Behold, I will allure her, and bring her into the wilderness, and speak comfortably unto her. And I will give her vineyards from thence, and the valley of Achor for a door of hope ; and she shall sing there as in the days of her youth."

THE END

INDEX

INDEX

Charles Edward, Prince, 117, 125, 135
Chaucer, 113, 198, 341
Chiefswood, 226, 276, 279, 296, 323, 328
Child, Professor, 65
Childe Harold, 105, 106, 146, 369
Christabel, 69, 70, 259
Chronicles of the Canongate, 296, 307, 310, 313-315
Clarendon, Lord, 290
Claverhouse, John Graham of, 161, 165, 204, 338
Clerk, Sir John, of Eldin, 39, 210 ; John, 210 ; William, 39, 40, 46, 97, 207, 211, 212, 264, 309
Clubs :
Bannatyne, 251
Blairadam, 212, 251, 319
Forest, 206, 220
Friday, 87, 95, 202
Highland, 224, 251, 319
Roxburghe, 251
Speculative Society, 41
Teviotdale, 41
The Club (Edinburgh), 41
The Club (London), 251
The Gowks, 251
The Literary Society, 41
Cockburn, Henry, Lord, 34 n., 36, 45, 49, 204, 208, 211, 235, 294, 361, 371
Cockburn, Mrs (Alison Rutherford), 30, 32
Coleridge, S. T., 69, 71, 82, 115, 128, 193, 317, 356, 361, 367
Commines, Philippe de, 250
Constable, Archibald, 61 ; starts as bookseller, 73 ; founds *Edinburgh Review*, 73-74 ; 78, 80, 81 ; publishes *Marmion*, 84 ; quarrel with Scott, 94, 96, 98, 99 ; reconciliation, 107-108 ; 121, 123, 126, 147, 149, 153, 155 ; business methods, 156-158 ; 172, 179, 202, 203, 213, 226, 231, 235, 237, 238, 239, 247, 252, 258, 270 ; his scheme for a Miscellany, 271, 272 ; 278, 279, 280, 282 ; bankruptcy, 283, 284, 287, 289 ; 292, 293, 320, 326 ; George, 31, 149 ; Thomas, 280 n., 284
Corehouse, Lord, *see* Cranstoun, George
Cranstoun, George (Lord Corehouse), 40, 45, 47, 211, 212, 371 ; Jane Anne (Countess Purgstall), 47, 50
Corstorphine, 206
Count Robert of Paris, 324, 325, 326, 327
Coutts, Mrs (Harriet Mellon, Duchess of St Albans), 275, 360

Covenanters, the, 16, 134, 160, 161, 163, 174, 191, 353
Cowper, William, 71
Crabbe, George, 207, 241, 334, 368
Craighall, 49
Croker, J. W., 109, 144, 293, 294, 306, 330 n.
Cromwell, Oliver, 27,301, 302
Crosbie, Andrew, 139
Cumnor Hall, 42
Cunningham, Allan, 305, 333
Curtis, Sir William, 242

DALGLEISH, WILLIAM, 221, 259, 303, 306, 310
Dalkeith, Lady, *see* Buccleuch, Harriet, Duchess of ; Lord, *see* Buccleuch, Charles, Duke of
Dalzell, Professor Andrew, 37
Darnick, 179, 281
Davy, Sir Humphry, 144, 217
Defoe, Daniel, 127, 129
Demonology and Witchcraft, Letters on, 322
Dempster, George, 15
Dickens, Charles, 253 n., 349
Disraeli, Benjamin, 275
Dogs, 90, 204, 221-222 :
Camp, 90
Douglas, 90
Finette, 216
Hamlet, 216
Maida, 204, 216, 258
Ourisque, 216
Pepper, Mustard, etc., 216
Percy, 90
Don Quixote, 352
Don, Sir Alexander, 320
Doom of Devorgoil, The, 171
Dostoevsky, 335, 336, 340, 344, 350, 353
Douglas, Dr, 102 ; Frances, Lady, 60 85 ; Castle, 325
Douglasdale, 327-328
Doumergue, family of, 87, 144
Downshire, Arthur, second Marquis of, 55
Drapier's Letters, 294
Drumclog, 162
Drumlanrig, 106, 304
Dryburgh Abbey, 22, 88, 178, 217, 334
Dryden, John, 338 ; Scott's edition of, 79, 80, 81
Dudley, John William, first Earl of, 110, 148, 285, 360
Dumas, Alexandre, 201, 255, 335
Dunbar, William, 18, 327
Dundas, Henry, *see* Melville, first Lord